WERNER PEPELS

Marketing Communications

Marketing Communications

By

Werner Pepels

Duncker & Humblot · Berlin

Bibliographic information of the German national library

The German national library registers this publication in the German national bibliography; specified bibliographic data are retrievable on the Internet about http://dnb.d-nb.de

Cover: © saicle – Fotolia.com

All rights reserved.
© 2021 Duncker & Humblot GmbH, Berlin
Typesetting: TextFormArt, Daniela Weiland, Göttingen
Printing: buchbücher.de GmbH, Birkach
Printed in Germany

ISBN 978-3-428-18512-2 (Print)
ISBN 978-3-428-58512-0 (E-Book)

Printed on no aging resistant (non-acid) paper according to ISO 9706 ∞

Internet: http://www.duncker-humblot.de

Preface

When it comes to advertising, everyone in marketing and especially beyond likes to contribute and many are supposed to know a lot about it. Yet behind marketing communications stand complex and complicated issues which are rarely formulated with the necessary theoretical depth and practical relevance. This is certainly not the case in this book, which provides an in-depth and comprehensive overview of the most important facets of marketing communications. After all, lasting market success can only be achieved with deep knowledge of the underlying principles. Exactly this is the mission of this book.

Book concept:

The content is characterized by a clear composition and fair knowledge representation. The text design, numerous diagrams, and a deep structure contribute to this.

A special feature of this book is that in addition to all theoretical foundation, the transfer of application is always sought through practical examples. This succeeds here among other things because the author disposes of authentic vocational practical experiences over a dozen years in the advertising industry and more than two dozen years of teaching experience in the subject at state universities. This distinguishes this book from purely scientific works of theoreticians, but also from somehow more fictional works of practical experts.

Book overview:

"Marketing communications" in the German original version is one of the established introductory books in the domain. Due to the respectable success, an English edition was now considered necessary, which offers non-native speakers a meaningful insight into marketing communications. The book takes a German perspective.

The content of this book is a transfer of the contents from the current German version in its 3rd edition with some specific additions. The translation of a highly specialized technical text still poses a great challenge, translation programs still fail with elaborate technical texts. At least the author's training as a state-certified translator comes in handy. Nevertheless, despite careful review, there are certainly shortcomings that remain. The publisher is very interested in receiving feedback on this matter directed to D & H publishing house.

Target audience:

The book is aimed at

- Students in English-speaking bachelor and master programs in marketing or related fields at German and international universities of higher education or applied science,

- young professionals, working in industry, services, trade and export,
- career shifters from non-economic specializations,
- ascenders in the subject, especially at advertising/media agencies, management consultancies, special service providers or similar,
- professionals in marketing, sales and advertising who want a knowledge updating.

Acknowledgements:

The author would like to thank Duncker & Humblot-Verlag, Berlin, for the offer of the new edition and the valuable support during the realization, especially Dr. Andreas Beck, program planning, and his team around Heike Frank, head of production, and Anke Geidel, production editor.

The author wishes all readers every success possible in using the experiences presented here for their own advancement and the well-being of their organization.

Set-up of work:

The book consists of eight main chapters:

1. Basics of communication
2. Cornerstones for marketing communications
3. Advertising campaign formatting
4. Media of classical advertising
5. Online advertising
6. Non-classical advertising
7. Integrated marketing communications
8. Marketing communications controlling

Table of Contents

1. **Basics of communication** 19
   - 1.1 Principles of communication 19
     - 1.1.1 "One cannot not communicate!" 19
     - 1.1.2 "Not the reality is the reality in the market!" 20
     - 1.1.3 "The worm must taste to the fish and not to the fisher!" 20
     - 1.1.4 "Advertising does not sell, instead advertising helps to sell!" ... 21
   - 1.2 Communication process 22
     - 1.2.1 Constitutive elements 22
     - 1.2.2 Communication chain 22
     - 1.2.3 Disturbance sources 24
     - 1.2.4 Modified stage model 25
   - 1.3 Terms of communication 26
     - 1.3.1 Direction of communication 26
     - 1.3.2 Scope of communication 27
     - 1.3.3 Communication definition 29

2. **Cornerstones for marketing communications** 30
   - 2.1 Variety of forms 30
     - 2.1.1 Types of advertising 31
     - 2.1.2 Levels of perception 32
     - 2.1.3 Special form of collective advertising 33
   - 2.2 Advertising goals 35
     - 2.2.1 Economic marketing objectives 35
     - 2.2.2 Psychographic advertising objectives 37
   - 2.3 Advertising objects 39
   - 2.4 Advertising budget 41
     - 2.4.1 Experience-based, monovariable budgeting techniques 42

　　　　2.4.2　Experience-based, polyvariable budgeting techniques 44
　　　　2.4.3　Model-based, monovariable budgeting techniques 46
　　　　2.4.4　Model-based, polyvariable budgeting techniques 49
　　　　2.4.5　Critical review of budgeting techniques 51
　　　　2.4.6　Allocation of budget funds 53
　　2.5　Advertising period and timing 54
　　2.6　Advertising area and density 57
　　2.7　Meaning and representation of the brand 61
　　　　2.7.1　Brand content 61
　　　　2.7.2　Brand characteristics 62
　　　　2.7.3　Brand name development 64

3. Advertising campaign formatting 67
　　3.1　Determination of target groups 67
　　　　3.1.1　Business target groups 67
　　　　　　3.1.1.1　General market characteristics 67
　　　　　　3.1.1.2　Main market actors 68
　　　　　　3.1.1.3　Decision-making relations 70
　　　　3.1.2　Consumer target groups 74
　　　　　　3.1.2.1　Demographic demarcations 75
　　　　　　3.1.2.2　Actiographic demarcations 77
　　　　　　3.1.2.3　Psychographic demarcations 79
　　　　　　3.1.2.4　Sociographic demarcations 81
　　3.2　Benefit promise in advertising 83
　　3.3　Style components in advertising 87
　　3.4　Requirements for good practice advertising 89
　　　　3.4.1　Basic principles 89
　　　　3.4.2　Points of reference 93

4. Media of classical advertising 96
　　4.1　Advertising material adverts 96
　　　　4.1.1　Newspapers 96
　　　　4.1.2　Magazines 97
　　　　4.1.3　Other print titles 100

		4.1.4	Directory entries	101
		4.1.5	Special forms of print advertising	102
4.2	Advertising material spots			104
	4.2.1	Television		104
		4.2.1.1	TV-station landscape	105
		4.2.1.2	Channel graduation	108
		4.2.1.3	Special forms of TV advertising	109
	4.2.2	Radio		113
	4.2.3	Movie theater display		117
4.3	Advertising material posters			118
	4.3.1	Stationary outdoor advertising		119
	4.3.2	Mobile outdoor advertising		120
	4.3.3	Special forms of outdoor advertising		120
4.4	Classical media profiles			122
4.5	Requirements for media selection			127
	4.5.1	Quantitative criteria		127
	4.5.2	Contact quality		130
4.6	Media selection for classical advertising			131
	4.6.1	Market media analyses		132
	4.6.2	Validation		139
	4.6.3	Ranking		141
		4.6.3.1	Reach value	142
		4.6.3.2	Contact intensity	143
		4.6.3.3	Affinity score	143
		4.6.3.4	Cost-efficiency	144
	4.6.4	Mediaplan combinations		144
	4.6.5	Gross rating points		147
4.7	Optimization of media performance			149
4.8	Special features of business advertising			151
4.9	Media implementation			154
	4.9.1	Advertising inventory and placement		155
	4.9.2	Advertising intensity and flexibility		156

Table of Contents

  4.9.3 Work tools in media purchasing 158

  4.9.4 Calculation of media conditions 160

  4.9.5 Media processes and documents 163

5. Online advertising 166

 5.1 Non-web applications 167

  5.1.1 Electronic mail 167

   5.1.1.1 Design of acquisitional e-mails 167

   5.1.1.2 Newsletter management 168

  5.1.2 Other non-web internet services 170

 5.2 Web 1.0 applications 172

  5.2.1 Website presence 172

   5.2.2.1 Conceptual dimensions 172

   5.2.1.2 Usability of webpages 177

   5.2.1.3 Website as advertising medium 179

  5.2.2 Function of the search engines 181

   5.2.2.1 Types 181

   5.2.2.2 Search engine marketing 183

   5.2.2.3 Search engine optimization 183

   5.2.2.4 Search engine advertising 184

  5.2.3 Banner advertising 185

   5.2.3.1 Integrated banner ads 185

   5.2.3.2 New window ads 186

   5.2.3.3 Layer ads 187

  5.2.4 Special forms of web advertising 188

  5.2.5 Targeting 189

  5.2.6 Measuring success of web advertising 190

 5.3 Web 2.0 applications 191

  5.3.1 Social network 192

  5.3.2 Community 193

  5.3.3 Weblog 193

  5.3.4 Microblog 196

  5.3.5 Media sharing 196

  5.3.6 Wiki 197

		5.3.7 Social bookmarking	197
		5.3.8 Other web 2.0 services	198
	5.4	Mobile advertising	199
		5.4.1 Multimedia opportunities	199
		5.4.2 Advertising modes	201
		5.4.3 Service applications	202
6.	**Non-classical advertising**		**205**
	6.1	Public relations	205
		6.1.1 Traditional forms	207
		6.1.1.1 General market actor-PR	207
		6.1.1.2 Opinion leader-PR	209
		6.1.1.3 Internal PR	212
		6.1.2 Modern forms	213
		6.1.2.1 Placement	213
		6.1.2.2 Sponsoring	216
		6.1.2.3 Unconventional PR	220
		6.1.3 Cause-related marketing	222
		6.1.4 Olfactoric impact	223
		6.1.5 Customer clubs	223
	6.2	Live advertising	227
		6.2.1 Exhibition	228
		6.2.2 Point of sales presence	233
		6.2.3 Event	233
		6.2.4 Brandpark presentation	234
	6.3	Direct advertising	235
		6.3.1 Electronic offline direct advertising	236
		6.3.1.1 Direct response television	236
		6.3.1.2 Direct-response radio	237
		6.3.2 Phone advertising	237
		6.3.3 Printed direct advertising	239
		6.3.3.1 Direct-response advert	239
		6.3.3.2 Direct mailing	239
		6.3.4 Documentation	246

	6.3.4.1 Sales literature	246
	6.3.4.2 Pre-sales advertising material	249
6.4	Supporting activities	250
	6.4.1 Sales promotion	250
	6.4.2 Product features	254
	6.4.3 Brand licensing	255
	6.4.4 Personal communication	256
6.5	Intermediary comparison of non-classical advertising	259

7. Integrated marketing communications — 262

- 7.1 Integration substance — 262
- 7.2 Corporate identity — 264
- 7.3 Public perception of the advertiser — 266
- 7.4 International marketing communications — 269
  - 7.4.1 Hypotheses of global advertising — 269
  - 7.4.2 Focusing alternative — 271
  - 7.4.3 Generalising alternative — 271
- 7.5 Advertising agency integration — 274
  - 7.5.1 Servicer types — 274
  - 7.5.2 Selection criteria — 275
  - 7.5.3 Contact initiation — 276
    - 7.5.3.1 Framework — 277
    - 7.5.3.2 Evaluation — 278
    - 7.5.3.3 Briefing — 281
    - 7.5.3.4 Workflow — 282
- 7.6 Ethics in advertising — 285

8. Marketing communications controlling — 294

- 8.1 Measurement of advertising performance — 294
- 8.2 Advertising impact prognosis — 296
  - 8.2.1 Exploratory test methods — 297
  - 8.2.2 Actualgenetic test methods — 298
  - 8.2.3 Psychomotoric test methods — 299

	8.2.4	Mechanical test methods	300
	8.2.5	Projective-associative test methods	301
	8.2.6	Special communication tests	302
8.3	Advertising success prognosis		303
8.4	Advertising impact check		306
	8.4.1	Transport analyses	306
	8.4.2	Contact analyses	307
	8.4.3	Reception analyses	309
8.5	Advertising success check		309
8.6	Problems of advertising test methods		312
	8.6.1	Potential problems with pre-tests	312
	8.6.2	Potential problems with post-tests	314

References 316

Index 321

About the author 325

List of figures

Fig. 1:	Semiotic elements of communication	23
Fig. 2:	Communication phases and possible disturbance sources	24
Fig. 3:	Phases of purchase decision process	25
Fig. 4:	Design of communication channels	27
Fig. 5:	Alternative scopes of communication	28
Fig. 6:	Types of advertising	30
Fig. 7:	Forms of collective advertising	34
Fig. 8:	Economic marketing goals	35
Fig. 9:	Development of buyer classes	36
Fig. 10:	Possible communication objects	39
Fig. 11:	Advertising budgeting techniques	41
Fig. 12:	SoA – SoM relation	47
Fig. 13:	Options for advertising timing	55
Fig. 14:	Options for advertising coverage	58
Fig. 15:	Alternatives of international market penetration	60
Fig. 16:	Options for advertising density	60
Fig. 17:	Typologies of organizational buying behavior	69
Fig. 18:	Private target group demarcations	74
Fig. 19:	Optional endbenefits	83
Fig. 20:	Style components of advertising	87
Fig. 21:	Characteristics of print advertising	96
Fig. 22:	Categories of journals	98
Fig. 23:	Characteristics of electronic advertising	104
Fig. 24:	Types of TV broadcasting	108
Fig. 25:	Special forms of TV advertising	110
Fig. 26:	Structure of important electronic media	116
Fig. 27:	Characteristics of poster advertising	119

List of figures

Fig. 28:	Requirements for media selection	127
Fig. 29:	Intermediary comparison of classical advertising	129
Fig. 30:	Types of market media analyses	132
Fig. 31:	Steps for media planning	138
Fig. 32:	Media peformance identifiers	142
Fig. 33:	Advertising placements and materials	145
Fig. 34:	Steps of media implementation	154
Fig. 35:	Options of advertising intensities	157
Fig. 36:	Media processing documents	163
Fig. 37:	Forms of online media	166
Fig. 38:	Forms of non-classical advertising	205
Fig. 39:	Forms of public relations	206
Fig. 40:	Forms of live advertising	227
Fig. 41:	Forms of direct advertising (examples)	235
Fig. 42:	Forms of sales promotion	252
Fig. 43:	Layers of communication	257
Fig. 44:	Intermediary comparison of non-classical advertising	260
Fig. 45:	Requirements for integrated communication	262
Fig. 46:	Corporate identity elements	266
Fig. 47:	Advertising agency integration	274
Fig. 48:	Types of marketing communications controlling	295
Fig. 49:	Methods of advertising impact prognosis	296
Fig. 50:	Methods of advertising success prognosis	303
Fig. 51:	Methods of advertising impact check	306
Fig. 52:	Methods of advertising success check	310

List of abbreviations

AIDA	Attention – Interest – Desire – Action (Stage model of advertising)
AIO	Attitudes – Interests – Opinions
ARD	First German television
A-t-l	Above the line (Classical advertising)
B-t-b	Business to business
B-t-c	Business to consumer
B-t-l	Below the line (Non-classical advertising)
b/w	Black/white (Single-colored)
Captcha	Completely automated public Turing test to tell computers and humans apart
CD	Corporate design
CEO	Chief executive officer
CI	Corporate identity
CMYK	Cyan – Magenta – Yellow – Key (Color mode)
CRM	Customer relationship management-System
CSR	Corporate social responsibility
CUG	Closed user group
DIY	Do it yourself
DTP	Desk top publishing
e.g.	exempli gratia (for example)
ERP	Enterprise resource planning-System
ERPG	Ethnocentric – polycentric – regiocentric – geocentric (Perlmutter)
ESG	Environment – Social – Governance
GDP	Gross domestic product
GI	General interest
GRP	Gross rating point
HKS	Color scale
HTML	Hyper text mark up language
i.e.	id est (that is)
I-TV	Interactive television
IP	Internet protocol
IPO	Initial public offering
NGO	Non-govermental organization
OEM	Original equipment manufacturer
OMD	Online – Multimedia – Digital
OTC	Over the counter
OTS	Opportunity to see
POS	Point of sale
PR	Public relations
Pro7	German private television station
QR	Quick response
R	Radio

RAL	Color scale
RTL	German private television station
SAT	German private television station
SERP	Search engine result page
SoA	Share of advertising
SoM	Share of market
TV	Television
URL	Uniform resource locator
ZBB	Zero base budgeting
ZDF	Second German television

1. Basics of communication

As few people are aware, communication is one of the most complicated things in our lives and often enough leads straight to chaos. In many cases, conflicts in the business as well as in the private sphere are in substance only about peanuts, the actual escalation is rather based on communication problems about this matter. Because

- said means not heard,
- heard means not understood,
- understood means not agreed,
- agreed means not implemented,
- implemented means not proven.

In essence, communication management (according to Lasswell) is all about

- *Who* (= communicator) *says what* (= message) *to whom* (= target person) *via which path* (= channel) *with which effect* (= goal).

1.1 Principles of communication

There are few basic principles as to workable communication, but they have to be observed strictly. Their meaning is explained subsequently.

1.1.1 "One cannot not communicate!"

Communication is therefore not only vital, but also the cause of many evils. The big problem is that you cannot escape it, because you cannot not communicate (Watzlawick). Therefore, there is no choice between communication or non-communication, because non-communication also communicates, and to a much greater extent non-verbally. This is even more revealing, because in most cases it is difficult to consciously control it, whereas words can lie.

This means that the opinion, still widely held in companies and industries comparatively far removed from marketing, that advertising can be dispensed with, is no longer valid. Because the market forms its image of a seller anyway, only then without the seller being able to influence it. Since this image can be decisive for a purchase and thus promote the company's existence, investments in advertising make a lot of sense and are money well spent. But the questions remain, where to allocate the financial means, which creative implementation could be a smashing one and how to get a good idea about the efficacy of the invest.

1.1.2 "Not the reality is the reality in the market!"

Another key sentence for understanding communication is (based on B. Spiegel): "Reality is not the reality in the market, but the target persons' ideas about reality". This means that marketing communication takes place on an emotional meta level, which more or less overlaps the underlying real (factual) level. Both levels can now, even permanently, differ from each other.

One example of this was the tobacco industry. On a real level, cigarettes are nothing more than rolls of tobacco wrapped in white paper with a fiber attachment in front of it, which are filled into packages of 20 and successively burned by ignition. The smoke that escapes, which is also extremely harmful to health, is inhaled and differences between the various brands within a sort are difficult or impossible to discern, even by experts. On this real level, however, hardly anyone would be willing to spend € 6–7 for a pack of cigarettes. Only the superimposition of the meta-level of communication turns these profane products into objects of desire, whereby the individual cigarette brands are then no longer considered interchangeable. Instead of rolled up cut tobacco, communication took place via Rocky Mountains, wild jungle, world view and multicultural exchange. The fact that there is a permanent gap between the two levels not only does not impair the market success of these products, but is even a strict prerequisite for this.

This applies, although perhaps not so strongly, to practically all products, especially consumer goods. The reasons for this are clear. First, the reality of the vast majority of market offerings is as boring as that of cigarettes. It is therefore not even worthwhile to advertise them. Secondly, the offers of different market participants are usually objectively similar to each other, so that it is hardly possible to offer comparative competitive advantages on the real level. This is even true for many capital goods. And thirdly, even where they actually exist, differences are usually no longer easily comprehensible for buyers, so that a real offer of a reward easily overtaxes their assessment capacity. Therefore it is almost unavoidable to aim at the meta-level during communication if one wants to achieve success in the market.

1.1.3 "The worm must taste to the fish and not to the fisher!"

Also of immense importance for communication is the statement that the worm must taste to the fish and not to the fisher. It says that the value of a message is defined only from the point of view of the addressees. This means that not the sender's need to communicate what he wants to get rid of should be the focus of communication, but only the presumed needs of his addressees. This would not be tragic if both interests were not significantly different. For example, the sender wants to convince addressees to buy his product instead of or in addition to another one and to give up purchasing power in return to balance his business. But the addressees are quite indifferent to just this, they are rather interested in acquiring only such benefits, which they estimate higher than the money sacrifice, which they have to pay for it. If the sender now argues from his point of view, he does not hit the nerve with it, i.e. the attention and interest of his addressees, and the communication is in vain, though not for free. For a promising communication it is rather necessary to regress one's own needs in favour of the needs of others, namely the potential customers. So although communication costs one's own money, one must not use it to serve one's own interests, but rather the interests of others. Success can only be achieved to the extent that communication can offer benefits that potential customers find attractive because they meet their needs. Communication that primarily satisfies the needs of the sender, on the other hand, will inevitably fail. Often this failure is to be found precisely in industries where marketing thinking is not yet firmly anchored, such as in the advertising of capital goods, which all too often still reflects the pride of the producers about their, admittedly often really considerable, performance, instead of showing that it is possible to successfully put oneself in the users' shoes and offer tailor-made problem solutions.

1.1.4 "Advertising does not sell, instead advertising helps to sell!"

Finally, one last, very decisive hint belongs here. "Advertising does not sell, instead advertising helps to sell." Naturally the expectation of all advertisers is to receive concretely measurable sales results for their good money. This attitude is solely dictated by the commercial duty of care. Dubious advertising consultants are easily able to claim this for their advertising, because they know that the release of the budget depends on it. But nobody can really guarantee that X € advertising budget will generate at least €X + 1 profit. Realistic is only to promise to do everything professionally possible to reach this goal. Because advertising does not sell, but advertising is only one factor among countless others that lead to purchase or not purchase. This problem also prevents advertising success measurement, which is always welcome by advertisers. Because if advertising is only one factor among countless others, which is responsible for the economic success, an attribution of the share of advertising would only be feasible if it is possible to determine the performance contribution of all factors involved. But this is where practice has failed so far.

1.2 Communication process

The communication process is comparatively complicated. It includes basic elements, which are combined to a communication chain, which itself is exposed to several disturbance sources which can be tentatively formed into a stage model.

1.2.1 Constitutive elements

Various elements are needed to create communication. There is always an exchange of signals. Signals are perceptible stimuli (e.g. sound waves). Signals with meaning content are signs (e.g. words). Signals are examined by syntactics with respect to their structure as well as rules and their meaningful connection, at first without consideration of aspects related to meaning and effect. If these signs are combined in a meaningful way, they result in a message (e.g. text). After semantics, the signs are thus examined with respect to the coding of their meaning content. If this message is also of importance for the addressees by its novelty character, it becomes information (e.g. new product announcement). Pragmatics thus examine the effect of messages on recipients and the origin background at the sender. And sigmatics examine the relationship of the information to the real advertising object.

1.2.2 Communication chain

On closer inspection, the communication chain is therefore as follows (*see figure 1: Semiotic elements of communication*):

- First there is a sender, the advertiser, who wants to spread an intended message/ idea as *objective*. This can be, for example, the intention of announcing a new product.

- In order for the thoughts in his head to become communication, they must be encoded into signals. Because communication can only come about through perceptible stimuli. Such *encoding* takes place in words, pictures, texts, graphics, sounds, colors, shapes, etc. This is how the message first materializes.

- In order for it to be perceived by others, the recipients as the target persons, a *transmitter* is required which emits these signals to the outside. In humans, for example, this is their voice. Since this rarely reaches far enough in the market, however, media are used as a substitute in the form of adverts, spots and posters as a mouthpiece.

- For dissemination, a means of *transport* is still needed to bridge the space and time difference between the delivery and reception of a message. In the simplest case, these are sound waves, but in marketing they are mostly advertising

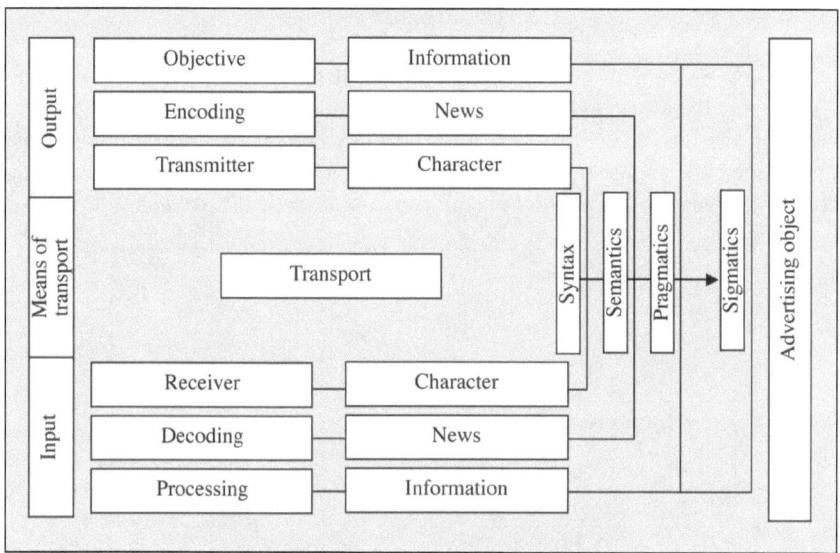

Fig. 1: Semiotic elements of communication

media in the form of magazines, newspapers, radio and television stations, cinema screens, outdoor advertising space, etc. This means that all the conditions for communication to take place are then fulfilled.

- On the recipient side, a *receiving device* is required which can pick up the transmitted signals. The five senses of sight, hearing, smell, touch and taste are available to the human being. However, the signals only arrive when these senses are switched to receive, i. e. not when looking away from or not hearing advertising.
- This is followed by perception as *decoding* of the received signals in order to arrive at an adequate understanding of the message. For this purpose, the signals are registered, interpreted and packed into consistent bundles by recipients.
- This is done by the recipient, who hopefully is also the target of the advertisement, since otherwise there is a false scattering. Above all, however, the message must be *processed* by him/her so that it can be reactivated in the decision situation and can assert its influence.

1.2.3 Disturbance sources

Communication can only be successful if all these stages run consecutively without any disturbance. Even inadequacies at an early stage lead to the process breaking off unsuccessfully due to intracommunicative or intercommunicative disturbances. There are numerous sources of error for communication within this chain (*see figure 2: Communication phases and possible disturbance sources*):

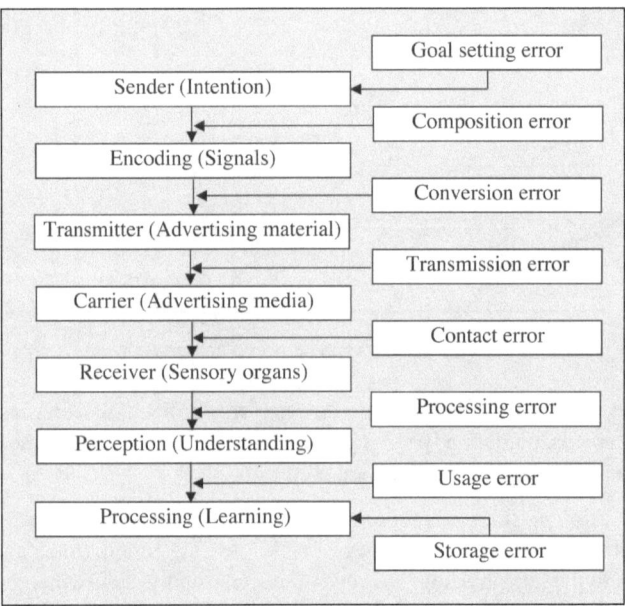

Fig. 2: Communication phases and possible disturbance sources

- Errors in *goal setting* occur when a given problem cannot be solved adequately by communication. In this case, advertising measures are doomed to failure from the outset.

- Errors in the *composition* mean that consciously or unconsciously relevant information in the message is withheld or falsified.

- Errors in *conversion* occur when messages are encrypted in such a way that the recipient does not understand them or only understands them differently than intended. Then the message content cannot arrive.

- *Transmission* errors occur if the selected communication channel is not suitable for the specific case.

- Errors in *contacting* as a result of unsuitable choice of advertising media prevent recipients from coming into contact with the message at all or at least sufficiently.

- Errors in *processing* are due to the fact that recipients decode the message incorrectly or do not receive it correctly at all. This may be due to objective or subjective shortcomings.
- Errors in *usage* mean that the information offered is not or only insufficiently used because its true meaning remains hidden.
- Errors in *storage* result from misunderstanding, incorrect storage or forgetting the information at all.

1.2.4 Modified stage model

Traditionally, the purchase decision process which can be influenced by advertising is represented according to the AIDA formula (Lewis) as acronym for attention, interest, desire, action. Although such stage models are not tenable according to today's knowledge of the advertising effect, they have a high degree of clarity. In modified form, the AIDA formula today instead would have to be AAICPPCR (which admittedly does not come that easily) (*see figure 3: Phases of purchase decision process*):

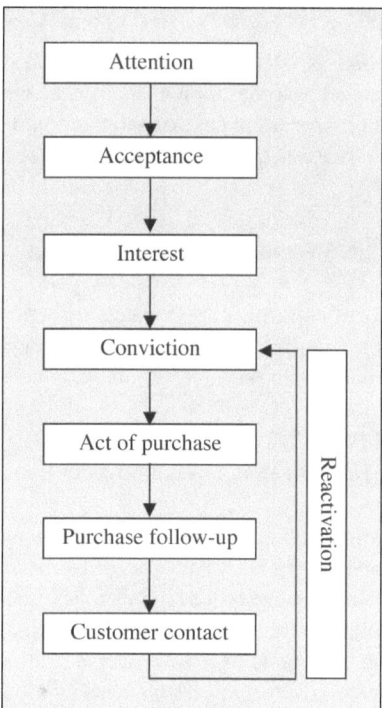

Fig. 3: Phases of purchase decision process

- A: First, the basic willingness to deal with the advertised offer must be awakened. This is done by setting stimulus signals to provoke *attention*.
- A: Only after repeated perception of the message brand-related, image-building effects may occur and thus *acceptance* of the provider and his brand core statement.
- I: Now it is necessary to arouse closer *interest* in order to make understandable what the offer wants, what claim it makes, how it positions itself in relation to the customers and the competition.
- C: In the case of success, this is followed by *conviction*, especially by presenting the benefits of the offer in an emotionally effective way and by plausibly securing the presented benefit derivation.
- P: Successful communication then leads to the triggering factor in the form of the act of *purchase*. However, this by no means marks the end of the process, but rather the beginning of a new cycle.
- P: The long neglected *post-purchase* activities of follow-up begin.
- C: Continuous *customer contact* should be maintained in order to keep the product range present.
- R: Finally, *reactivation* is, strictly speaking, already the first phase of the follow-up cycle. The need becomes topical again, the entrance takes place into a new, shortened decision process in case of satisfaction or in case of dissatisfaction in the extensive process sequence for the search for alternatives.

1.3 Terms of communication

Important parameters of communication are its directions and its scopes. This leads to a working definition of communication especially in the context of marketing.

1.3.1 Direction of communication

The communication process can be one-way or two-way (*see figure 4: Design of communication channels*). In the case of a *one-way* message flow (*simplex* channel), the sender of the message sends signals to addressees in the more or less justified hope that they will arrive, be perceived and processed. However, this hope becomes less and less in view of an excessive oversaturation with signals from all possible directions. Because the target persons react rigorously due to information overload, in that they are only willing or able to receive a small section of all the information actually intended for them; it is assumed that 97–99 % of information is lost (based on Kroeber-Riel). Although their ability and capacity to receive changes depending on situational influences such as replacement needs, living conditions, etc., they remain strictly limited overall. Only a *two-way* interpretation of communication can overcome this limitation. Thereby not only does a message flow from the sender to the addressees, but also a feedback from them about the receipt of the message and possibly already activities from it.

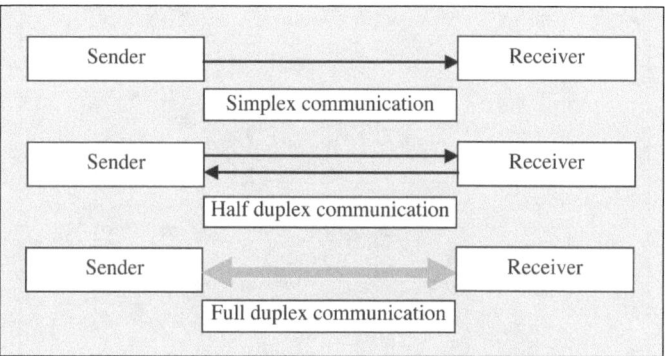

Fig. 4: Design of communication channels

This feedback can take place parallel to the incoming signals (full duplex channel) or alternately afterwards (half duplex channel). In case a message has not arrived correctly, the sender can correct it; in case it has not arrived at all, the sender can repeat the pledge. However, interactive media which can be used *full-duplex*, such as telephone, salesperson, e-mail, etc. have the major disadvantage that the higher communication security is burdened with considerably higher costs. Where this is not viable, an option for feedback through reactive media (*half-duplex*) can also be used, e. g. coupon display, direct mailing.

1.3.2 Scope of communication

Communication can still be addressed to individually addressable recipients or a large number of anonymous recipients. The former is called individual communication, the latter mass communication (*see figure 5: Alternative scopes of communication*). *Mass communication* as media advertising takes place publicly with the help of technical means of transmission, with spatial and/or temporal distance between communicator and recipient, directed to a not physically present audience and predominantly monologically interpreted.

The public is created by means of advertising media that transport the advertising material of the message sender. The necessity to bridge the time-space distance makes it necessary for communication logistics to be present with advertising

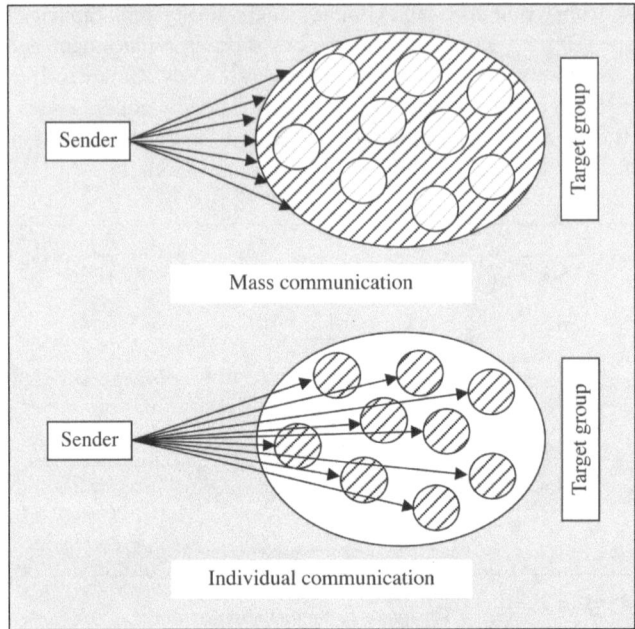

Fig. 5: Alternative scopes of communication

everywhere and at all times possible. This is like a "hail of shotgun shells" in the ever decreasing hope of at least getting the right target persons. This cannot be a reasonable basis for work in the long run.

In this respect, *individual communication* is gaining importance. It takes place personally, without technical means of transmission, with spatial and/or temporal unity between the communication partners, directed to a present audience and predominantly dialogically designed.

However, its potentially higher impact is offset by the inevitable higher investment. In this respect, it is necessary to weigh up on a case-by-case basis to what extent the higher chance of impact justifies the higher costs or not. In recent times, there has been a sustained shift in favor of individual advertising, although media advertising remains indispensable for achieving widespread awareness and familiarity. It is only on this basis that individual advertising can lead to a selective consolidation or acquisition of contacts.

Communication can be made with a variety of intentions. The intention of sales support is only one, which is covered by *advertising* (in this text the term is also used as an interchangeable term to *marketing communications*).

It must be distinguished from the intention to disseminate ideological, e. g. political or religious, messages, which is propaganda. Advertising, on the other hand, also has the intention of promoting sales, but it is superficial, blatant and unconvincing. In this respect, it is a pejorative term for advertising. Advertising is also distinct from public relations, which promotes public trust instead of concrete offers. The superordinate term is again marketing communication and covers beside sales support still procurement advertisement for operational funds, finances, personnel, etc., in this text however only the sales advertisement is regarded.

1.3.3 Communication definition

Marketing communication (resp. advertising) *is the deliberate influencing of market-effective opinions by means of instrumental use with the intention of aligning the reality of opinions in the market with one's own objectives.*

This definition contains several explanatory elements:

- *Conscious influencing* means a strategically intended influence, without regard to its effectiveness, as well as permanent, random influencing.

- *Market-effective opinions* concern an intellectual, free influence with regard to factors which are decisive for market effects, such as attitude, behavior, etc.

- *Instrumental use* refers to the instruments of the communication mix in marketing.

- The *intention* on the part of the sender is understood to be creative, political measures which intervene in a corrective and dynamic manner.

- In order to adapt the *reality of opinion* to one's own objectives, it is necessary to actively influence, instead of passively adopting market conditions, in order to assert one's own reality in the market environment.

2. Cornerstones for marketing communications

"For the skipper, who does not know his destination port, every wind is an unfavorable one." (de Saint-Exupéry) Likewise, any advertising whose target is not clearly defined can only be effective by pure chance. But it is certainly too expensive for that. That is why determining the communication goals is a core requirement of any professional approach. A major problem is that goals are often not defined clearly enough. This makes it impossible to monitor success properly. This is why it is necessary to structure the advertising objectives.

Objectives are generally desired states of the future. In order to be operational, they must obey requirements such as reality reference, order, consistency, topicality, completeness, enforceability, congruence, transparency and verifiability.

2.1 Variety of forms

The types of communicaton can be divided into the following criteria (*see figure 6: Types of advertising*).

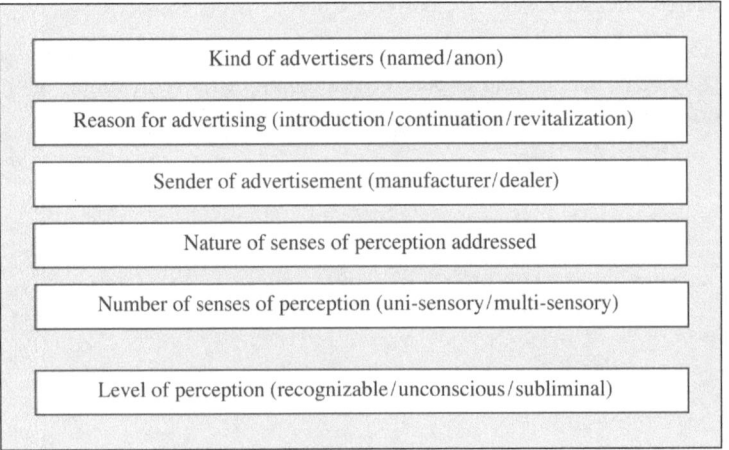

Fig. 6: Types of advertising

2.1.1 Types of advertising

In terms of the *kind of advertisers*, the vast majority is *named sole advertising*, i. e. a single advertiser acts alone. Again, this is mostly done by name, i. e. by stating the brand as name of the product and/or the company as name of the supplier. The anchoring of this is the very aim of the exercise. In exceptional cases, however, there is also *anonymous* sole advertising, e. g. the sign "P" for the nearest petrol station or "P" for a pharmacy.

According to the *reason for advertising*, a distinction is made between *introduction, continuation* and *revitalization advertising*. Introductory advertising has the task of the basic announcement and profiling the positioning of the offer. Continuation advertising serves to maintain the marketability and competitiveness of the offer by updating and penetrating it. Revitalization advertising starts when an offer has reached the zenith of its life cycle and is replaced by a similar successor (product variation) in order to initiate a new life cycle.

The *sender of the advertisement* can be a manufacturer or an intermediate. *Manufacturer advertising* can in turn be directed to the next economic level in the sales channel (wholesale or retail) as *push advertising* or to the last economic level of private or commercial end users as *pull advertising*. The content of professional advertising is acquisition messages to secure and improve the re-sale into the sales channel. The content of pull advertising is the conditioning of end users to a brand in order to monopolize it and make it a mandatory brand for the trade. In addition, the intermediates themselves also advertise to end customers (*dealer advertising*). Their content is the conditioning of the end customers to a real or virtual store, largely independent of the individual brands purchased there, as long as only the own store is frequented and not the competing store next door/click. Cross-level advertising therefore focuses on interbrand competition, while dealer advertising focuses on intrabrand competition. Incidentally, the two activities do not always complement each other, but are quite capable of provoking conflicts.

With regard to the type of *senses of perception addressed*, there is *visual*/optical advertising (e. g. display), *auditory*/acoustic advertising (e. g. radio spot), *olfactory*/scent advertising (e. g. odor additives), *gustative*/flavor advertising (e. g. tasting) or *haptic*/material advertising (e. g. demonstration). Each sense addressed has its advantages. According to the imagery thesis, however, a superior effect is claimed when seeing especially pictures, because they are perceived faster, learned better and retained longer than other signals. In contrast, the sound is said to be impossible to evade, because the hearing cannot be blocked deliberately. Smells are still rarely used in advertising, but they are very effective because they are transmitted unfiltered via receptors directly to the brain. The sense of taste has an extremely convincing effect on food products. And the sense of touch is capable of the most sustained memory performance through physical experience, which is crucial in advertising.

In terms of the *number of senses of perception* addressed, *uni-sensory* advertising means addressing only one sense of perception at a time (e. g. posters only optics, radio commercials only acoustics). *Multi-sensory* advertising, on the other hand, addresses more than one sense of perception at a time (e. g. as a TV commercial with optics and acoustics). It is assumed that the strength of the impression increases with the number of senses addressed simultaneously. In addition, this offers greater creative freedom for the implementation of statements.

2.1.2 Levels of perception

With regard to the level of perception, there is informative communication which strives for an objective, non-manipulative representation. However, its success seems doubtful, since every factual informative communication inseparably has several relationship aspects. Approaches can only be found outside of advertising (e. g. "Tagesschau" on 1st German TV-station ARD). Advertising, on the other hand, always belongs to suggestive communication. It wants to manipulate, whereby the negative smack already disappears if the term manipulation is replaced by seduction. And who doesn't like to be seduced or likes to seduce others? In this respect, morally insane accusations go wrong, at least as long as it is a *recognizable* suggestion, i. e. the manipulation is obvious for recipients and they can protect themselves from it or be protected by competition laws.

Problematic, on the other hand, is the case group of *unconscious* advertising, which is not separately identifiable as advertising. For this reason, advertisements in print media which are editorially presented in a confusing manner must bear the clear reference "advertisement". And in non-print media, a clear insertion of the word "advertisement" is required for long time commercials. However, this requirement is often disregarded, legitimized or tolerated, for example when placing products in television films or sponsoring sports, cultural or social events, even if they are unpaid.

Finally, clearly reprehensible is *subliminal* perception, which is neither recognizable as such nor identified as advertising and therefore leaves no chance of defense. Legendary are the alleged short-term insertions (The hidden pursuaders/ Packard) below the perception threshold of the eyes for popcorn ("Hungry? Eat popcorn!") and cola ("Thirsty? Drink Coca-Cola!") in 1957 in a cinema in Fort Lee, New Jersey, at five-second intervals, which are said to have lead to significantly increased sales of these products in the auditorium after the end of the screening in the cinema relative to a comparison group without these short popcorn and cola shots (+ 57.8 % for popcorn, + 18.1 % for cola). In the meantime, however, it has been sufficiently proven that such a form of perception is ineffective or at best knows how to arouse generic needs, and is therefore also not worthwhile in purely economic terms, regardless of all justified ethical concerns, which is probably the best protection of the audience from their use.

2.1.3 Special form of collective advertising

Collective advertising is more of an exception, i. e. several advertisers appear on the market together. The reason for this lies in the possibility of sharing the costs incurred, which often makes it possible to finance advertising media and equipment which each party involved could not afford on its own. Then the participants expect synergy effects from their collective presence, because each of the offers benefits from the attention and interest of all others, but must also share this with them. After all, collective advertising is often used to stabilize supplier-customer relationships, e. g. as joint dealer advertising in the automotive industry.

There are various forms of collective advertising:

- The advertised offers may or may not be related to each other. One example of collective advertising with unrelated offers was the "Schaufenster am Donnerstag" on 2nd German Television (ZDF), which merely created an institutional bracket for otherwise isolated offers. In the case of collective advertising with linked offers, these can be in a substitutive or complementary relationship to one another. *Substitutive* means that each partial offer is individually suited to cover a replacement need (advertising in the same sector), *complementary* means that the partial offers together can cover a supplementary need, e. g. advertising for special occasions such as Christmas, summer festivals, school enrolment. However, the partial offers can also be in a neutral relationship to each other, i. e. they are unconnected, but have a common origin, e. g. advertising for district centers, shopping arcades, shopping malls.

- The offer can be advertised *anonymously*, i. e. without mentioning the names of the individual advertisers, but instead with joint sender information, e. g. advertising by associations, or *identifiable* with the names of all participating advertisers.

- In this case, it may be *industry-wide* or *selective* collective advertising. The former takes into account all the providers represented in an industry, the latter only individual providers, usually the financially strongest, who generically advertise for their entire sub-market.

- Finally, there may be advertising in which all participants are active at the same economic level, i. e. only manufacturers or only dealers; this is referred to as *horizontal* collective advertising. If the joint advertisers operate at different economic levels, i. e. manufacturers and wholesalers, manufacturers and retailers or wholesalers and retailers, this is referred to as *vertical* collective advertising.

The criteria mentioned can occur in almost any combination of collective advertising (*see figure 7: Forms of collective advertising*):

- For example, *joint* advertising is advertising with substitutive offers, without naming the parties involved, industry-wide in the relevant market and horizontal (e. g. Better homes through new wallpapers).

	Joint advertising	Concerted advertising	Group advertising	Composite advertising I	Composite advertising II
substutive	X				
independent		X			
complementary			X	X	X
anonymous	X				
identifiable		X	X	X	X
industry-wide	X		X		
selective		X		X	X
horizontal	X	X	X	X	
vertical					X

Fig. 7: Forms of collective advertising

- *Concerted* advertising is advertising with unrelated offers, mentioning the names of the participants, with selective choice and horizontal relationship (e. g. Milka bar + Pelikan writing utensil at the school enrolment).
- *Group* advertising is advertising with complementary offers, with mentioning the parties by name, industry-wide in the relevant market on horizontal level (e. g. various kitchen appliance manufacturers) or vertical (e. g. car manufacturers and authorized dealers).
- *Composite* advertising is advertising with complementary offers, with mentioning the parties by name, selectively both on horizontal (e. g. Lufthansa + Avis) and on vertical level (e. g. Wempe + Rolex).

2.2 Advertising goals

Objectives may generally be of economic, i.e. quantitative, but indirect nature, or of psychographic, i.e. qualitative, direct nature. Both stand in a means-end relation, i.e. the latter are means to reach the former as end.

2.2.1 Economic marketing objectives

The economic goals can be divided into abstract and concrete ones. On a more abstract level, the following basic variables are possible, but can only be addressed very indirectly through communication (*for context see figure 8: Economic marketing objectives*):

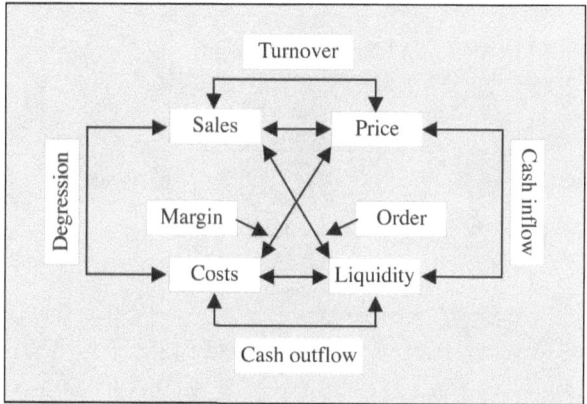

Fig. 8: Economic marketing goals (Source: own illustration)

- *Sales* as the company's quantitative output in the market,
- *price* as a value-based measurement of the individual output units,
- *costs* as evaluated consumption of goods to produce the output,
- *liquidity* as cash and cash equivalents in the company.

Further economic goals can be derived from these four cornerstones by combining them. These are:

- *Turnover* as the product of sales and price,
- *cash inflow* as monetary return (price/liquidity) of the company's performance on the market,
- *cash inflow* as a monetary expense (costs/liquidity) to bring an offer to market,
- *degression* as economies of scale (sales/costs) in the preparation of this offer,

- *order* (sales/liquidity) as a prerequisite for any market success,
- *margin* as the profitable difference between price and cost.

On a more concrete level, however, there are tangible communication targets. Here not company goals are set, but market goals, like this corresponds to the primacy of the customer in marketing. Different buyer classes can be distinguished (*for context see figure 9: Development of buyer classes*):

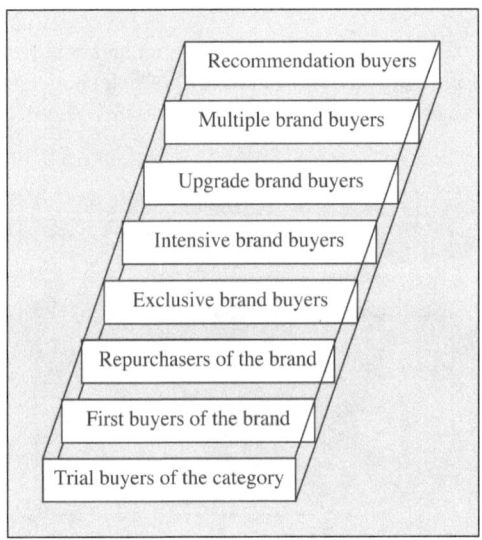

Fig. 9: Development of buyer classes (Source: own illustration)

- *Trials buyers* are persons, who are to be induced by communication to buy a new offer for the first time. This can be a market innovation, i.e. a product which was not previously available on the market, or a company innovation, i.e. a product which was not previously available in a company's program.
- *First buyers* are persons who are to be induced by communication to buy a brand offer for the first time. This can be a first-time purchase of the sort at all or an experimental change of brand within an already frequented genre.
- *Repurchasers* are persons who are to be induced by communication to repurchase an offer loyal to the brand. Depending on the rhythm of consideration of this brand, they may be regular buyers (predominant use) or swing buyers (partial use).
- *Exclusive buyers* are persons who are to be induced by communication to exclusively repurchase the offer of a brand. This requires a unique position in the buyers' perception of the offer.

- *Intensive buyers* are persons, who are to be induced by communication to buy an offer increased. This can involve both a shortening of the purchase distances, i. e. a higher purchase frequency, and/or an increase of the purchase quantity, i. e. a higher purchase volume.

- *Ugrade buyers* are persons to whom communication is intended to provide an incentive to embark on a product career loyal to the brand, i. e. to increase the value per purchase, whether through a value-enhanced basic offer or optional supplementary offers additional to a "normal" basic offer.

- *Multiple buyers* are persons who, within a brand or manufacturer offer, not only buy one product but perceive products from different product groups and thus enable sales-increasing cross-selling (e. g. shirt and tie, car purchase and financing, soccer and air pump, fitness equipment and iso-drink, coffee machine and bean coffee, TV set and warranty extension, kitchen equipment and dishwasher).

- *Recommendation buyers*, finally, are people who not only buy an offer themselves, but also act as multipliers within their social environment by buying for others or recommending the purchase.

2.2.2 Psychographic advertising objectives

Psychographic goals refer first of all to the knowledge and understanding of an advertised offer. Advertising here should primarily lead to an announcement on new markets or to an increase or maintenance of the level of awareness on existing markets. Awareness is, apart from rather rare exceptions such as spontaneous purchases, a necessary prerequisite for any purchase decision, since only the offers anchored in consciousness can be present at the time of decision and thus selectable at all.

Psychographic target values can also refer to the sympathy for an offer or provider. Here emotional elements should positively influence the attitude. Because with the objective similarities found in most markets and the increasing complexity of the offers, the "head" stops and the "gut" takes over the irrational evaluation often enough.

Finally, psychographic target values also affect the creation or strengthening of the intended effect of action. This requires a more or less intensive information gathering or deepening. This results in conditioning of the prospective customers on an offer and therewith a higher chance for the purchase conclusion with these.

The psychographic target values of cognition, affection and conation thus concern the qualitative advertising impact, economic target values concern the quantitative advertising success of purchase or non-purchase. Unfortunately, these two dimensions are usually not considered separately enough, so that misunderstandings about the later assessment of communication performance are virtually inevitable. This is because psychographic advertising objectives are not equal to economic advertising objectives, but rather are upstream of them, i. e. the achievement of economic advertising objectives more or less presupposes the achievement of psychographic advertising objectives.

While economic advertising goals remains hidden, why and how advertising works or does not work, only the quantifiable result counts. Thus, only the relation between the advertising signal as stimulus and the economic reaction as purchase is considered to be important. Whatever happens between the two variables is of no further interest or should not be analyzed further (so-called black box model). Accordingly, it is not possible to optimize advertising in accordance with economic advertising objectives, but only as a sequence of trial and error, in which measures producing better results displace others, without knowing whether there are yet other, even more suitable measures.

Psychographic advertising goals, on the other hand, are about achieving the effects that are a prerequisite for economic results, i. e. answering the questions of why and how. For this purpose, however, it is necessary to analyze those factors as intervening variables in the communication concept which lie between the advertising message in stimulus and the psychographic reaction in attitude, whereby this reaction cannot be used to reliably conclude on the actual purchase. The intention is thus an isolating optimization of those factors which are considered responsible for advertising impact and, consequently, their target-oriented design.

However, the decisive factor is that marketing communication, apart from exceptions such as certain forms of direct response advertising, can only actively address the dimension of psychographic advertising objectives as advertising impact, but target persons are also influenced by numerous other effects not related to advertising, e. g. word-of-mouth. In concrete terms, this means that sales advertising accounts for only one, more or less small part of market success. Even more serious, however, is the fact that even if the advertising impact can be considered achieved, there is no dependence of the advertising success on it. Because purchase decisions are made in the long run from various motives, only one of it is advertising impact, others are e. g. special offer, availability of goods, quality judgement.

In this respect it is questionable whether at all economic advertising goals are really given, if these are not operational to strive for anyway. Rather, they are marketing goals to whose achievement advertising makes a more or less large, generally rather uncertain contribution. Thus, only psychographic targets are operational in advertising, but advertisers regard their achievement as a means to achieve higher economic goals. The dilemma therefore lies in the fact that advertising can undoubtedly only contribute to market success, but does not yet constitute it.

2.3 Advertising objects

It is by no means always clear from the outset which offers are to be advertised within a company program and which are not. On the one hand, this has something to do with relevance, because of course only the best offers will be advertised, and on the other hand something to do with money, because just as naturally the existing advertising budget is not sufficient in the end to actually support all desired offers in the case of widespread multi-product companies. So there are several possible communication objects (*see figure 10: Possible communication objects*).

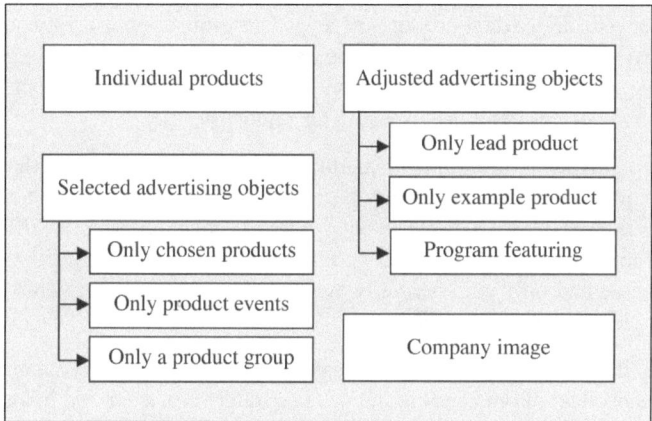

Fig. 10: Possible communication objects

Only as theoretical possibility therefore serves the advertising consideration of all *individual products/services* in the program range being evenly allocated. Because this leads to the fact that mostly even large budget volumes are split up in such a way that the presence of each individual product is too weak to sustainably assert itself against penetrating competitors. Almost all major branded companies work according to this principle, e.g. Procter & Gamble, Unilever, Nestlé, etc., mostly in order to be able to occupy markets several times over and thus exploit them more effectively by giving their various products a high profile in brand strategies. For small companies however this is not feasible.

Another possibility is the *selection* of advertising objects out of the program range. This means, that not all products can be supported. The choice of a *few products* raises the question of selection criteria. If one forms the priority in favor of the successful products in the program, then all remaining products, which would need a communicative support in the doubt more strongly, are neglected, and threaten to fall back into insignificance. If, on the other hand, the problem products are selected for advertising, this is just as careless, since the business pillars are not considered as successful products and therefore threaten to become less important.

Another form of selection is the restriction to the advertising of *product events*. This includes new product launches, product upgrades, relaunches, etc. On the occasion of these events, products can be appropriately advertised and profiled. Here, too, the question arises as to what will happen to those products for which no event is currently taking place and which, perhaps for this very reason, need to be updated much sooner. Since, in addition, there are always comparatively few product events in the program, this leads to more budget per advertising object, but also to a possibly negligent of the "normal" offer.

However, advertising a selected *product group* or range brand may yield better results. In this case a specific, relatively homogeneous program section of a supplier, i.e. several individual products of a product group, is uniformly advertised. This is also widely used by branded companies like Beiersdorf, KJS/Mondolez, Henkel, etc. This is because each individual product benefits from the positive thrust of the entire product group and in turn nourishes it.

One step further is the *adjustment of advertising*, which means that it is no longer the individual product which is the object of advertising, but rather the entirety of the services which these outstanding products represent. This is often found in the capital and production goods industry, where offers are individual, unmanageable and only commercially available like Siemens, etc. This results in several implementation alternatives.

First of all, the implementation as an advertising *lead product* is conceivable. In this case, a product of outstanding importance in terms of quantity, image, degree of novelty, etc. is selected from the entire range of products, which can be used to demonstrate the performance of the whole program. To this extent, a "flagship" is selected for advertising.

Another possibility are promotional *example products*, which are highlighted individually but alternately in order to demonstrate the performance of the entire program. For recognition, however, a formal "frame" (corporate design) is required as a connecting element.

The entire program can be advertised, i.e. jointly highlighted in the course of the *program* advertising, in order to demonstrate the spectrum of the program's capabilities. However, this usually involves design problems in the advertising implementation, as the individual products in program featuring compete with each other for the attention of the target persons.

The most far-reaching approach is to advertise only the provider instead of parts or the entire range of products, by focusing on the radiating effect of the *image* enhancement of the company on all products bearing this brand name. This is mainly used for services because of their intangibility. However, it is questionable whether this is not too indirect as an approach, i.e. whether the radiating effect is inferior to direct advertising. In addition, successful product advertising still produces the best provider profiling.

2.4 Advertising budget

A wide variety of techniques can be used for budgeting. Firstly, there are techniques which see the budget level as model-based and dependent on the achievement of the advertising objectives, and those which determine the budget level based on experience. Secondly, there are techniques which make the determination of the budget dependent on a single influencing factor or those which see it as dependent on more than one influencing factor (based on Meffert). Taking these two dimensions, each with two subdivisions, the result is as follows (*for context see figure 11: Advertising budgeting techniques*):

- Experience-based, monovariable budgeting techniques (2.4.1),
- experience-based, polyvariable budgeting techniques (2.4.2),
- model-based, monovariable budgeting techniques (2.4.3),
- model-based, polyvariable budgeting techniques (2.4.4).

	Experience-based	Model-based
Mono-variable	Share of profit Per unit Fixed amount Objective-task Competition comparison	Little model Koyck model Share of advertising/ Share of market Investment calculation
Poly-variable	Residual value Extrapolation Macro variable ADBUDG Kuehn approach	Vidale/Wolfe model Fischerkoesen model Dorfman/Steiner model Optimization

Fig. 11: Advertising budgeting techniques

2.4.1 Experience-based, monovariable budgeting techniques

With *share of profit*, a percentage of company success factors such as profit, ROI cash flow, etc. is spent on advertising. This results in a pro-cyclical trend which does not at all match the theoretically postulated anti-cyclical trend of the advertising budget, which has a stimulating effect on sales during a recession and a dampening effect on demand during a boom. However, this approach regularly fails in face of the reality, as during a recession there are not enough funds available to advertise intensively, and during a boom it is easy to provide sufficient advertising budgets. Advantages of this procedure lie in the simplicity of the calculation and in the fact that this corresponds to the principle of commercial caution. The disadvantage is undoubtedly the procyclical advertising effect. In addition the causality of input, the advertising budget, and output, the result, is turned upside down.

The choice of this reference value means the orientation on the sales quantity planned in the future or already realized in the past or on the amount *per unit* by apportioning the advertising budget to the sold quantity as percentage of sales. In reality, sometimes quite high amounts per unit for advertising are shown here. However, the mark-up calculation levels out the different cost-bearing capacity of products, and as the financial burden increases, these products reach the limits of demand's willingness to pay prices. The simple calculation is probably the only advantage. In terms of content, however, there is a causality reversal, i.e. the output figure sales determines the input figure advertising budget. Furthermore, there is still uncertainty about the appropriate amount of advertising per product unit.

In the automotive sector, advertising expenditures per new vehicle sold can reach significant levels. In the past, Mazda has spent more than € 500 per newly registered vehicle, Alfa Romeo and Peugeot more than € 600, Honda more than € 700, Toyota more than € 800 and Saab and Citroen more than € 900 on advertising.

With a *fixed amount* a defined sum of money is made available for advertising. This is usually done by discretionary reservation of a certain budget share for advertising within the overall budget. The main danger arises that if this amount is not questioned in time it cannot be changed once it has passed the relevant committees. This is therefore an unsatisfactory situation. The simplicity of the allocation is probably an advantage. However, the disadvantage is that there is no evidence-based connection between the advertising budget and the reference value. Furthermore, the necessary advertising budget fluctuates over time because of life cycle, competition, etc.

In the *objective-task scale*, the advertising budget is measured according to the advertising objectives. This usually fails already because the success effects of advertising measures are only hardly prognosticable. If however effect connections are missing, also no valid financial goal means reference can be made. However, this method is preferred by the theory. On the surface, there may be a plausible relationship. However, it is not possible to reliably quantify the funds required to achieve certain advertising objectives owing to lack of measurement of advertising success. In addition, the financial situation of the company is not adequately taken into account.

The *competition comparison* means that the own advertising budget is fixed in dependence on competitive advertising expenditures as share of advertising/SoA. This is by far the most frequently used method in the marketing practice of branded companies. Behind this hypothesis stands that one can buy market success quasi over advertising budget. Because appropriate diagrams suggest a valid interdependency between both sizes. But this is not the case. Because the other input instruments of marketing have the same effect on the output as advertising. In fact, this false fixation then leads to spiralling higher advertising expenditure, because each provider wants to exceed the competitive benchmark of the previous period and is in turn exceeded by the competition in the following period. This is one of the main reasons for the rapidly increasing industry-wide advertising expenses and is reflected in the reality of advertising, where quantity often seems to replace quality. However, there are also products which have grown up entirely without media advertising, e. g. Swatch, Fisherman's Friend, Zara, as well as those which have flopped despite massive media advertising, e. g. the print titles Ja, Super.

In any case, competitive advertising efforts can thus be neutralized. In addition, a productive use of resources is achieved by choosing a pragmatic reference base. However, data determination is often difficult despite Nielsen S & P advertising statistics or at least expensive.

The special technique of competition-dependent budgeting according to Weinberg is designed to clarify the question of how high an advertising investment "y" should be in order to achieve a market share increase of "x" percent. As antecedent conditions are mentioned that the advertising success depends on the extent and quality of one's own advertising efforts and those of the competition. The relative effectiveness of one's own advertising efforts is expressed by a coefficient. It is calculated by evaluating historical sales trends, advertising expenditures and shifts in market share over eight years as a logarithmic-linear regression function.

Weinberg's approach thus starts from the implicit goal of increasing market share. However, this is hardly a goal which can be generalized, because an excessive increase in market share may have to be bought by excessive advertising expenses with falling profits. For profit maximization, therefore, the point would have to be known up to which it is worthwhile to expand the market share through increased advertising. However, this is not made explicit. The effect of the other marketing instruments is neglected, i.e. it is assumed that past sales are solely attributable to advertising. The estimation of the sales and advertising expenditures of the competition is inevitably subject to great uncertainty. At least competitors are taken into account, but not temporal spillover effects of advertising. In this respect, it is a static model. Likewise, all general conditions other than the competition are not taken into account. The quality of the budget decision also depends on the estimation of the model variables. Above all, it is questionable whether empirical values from the past can be easily transferred to the future in a rapidly changing environment.

2.4.2 Experience-based, polyvariable budgeting techniques

The case of the *residual value* rules, that after all available financial resources have been budgeted, any remaining liquidity-related balance will be dedicated to advertising measures ("all you can afford"). This is a very unsatisfactory form of calculation. It is particularly common in companies which are not yet firmly anchored in marketing thinking and therefore do not appreciate the importance of communication. This is because it reflects a lesser importance of advertising compared to other investments in the company. In fact, the investment in customer acquisition and retention is considered to be the most valuable of all. However, the simplicity of the calculation represents a significant advantage. A disadvantage is the unmistakable element of arbitrariness, because there is no justifiable connection between the advertising objective and the use of financial resources.

Thus many companies complain about the cut-throat competition they face on the market and envy those who manage to remain stable by means of a strong brand. What is easily overlooked, however, is that these so enviable companies have at some point decided to invest instead of in fixed or current assets or at least additionally in their brand. This investment in preference building for customer acquisition and retention is the only one which does not lose value and has to be written down, but on the contrary becomes more and more valuable the more sustainable it is operated. However, it does not have the charm of the factual, but remains immaterial. Therefore, it seems more advantageous to invest in material production factors in the short term, but then one should not complain about the consequences of this.

Extrapolation means that the advertising budget of the previous period, anyhow it has come about, is continued. This is based on factors such as media price increases, projected company growth, etc. in order to maintain real purchasing power or budget significance. In reality, however, this is a fixed rule for inefficiency, which is called into question at the latest with overhead cost value analysis (OVA) or zero-base budgeting (ZBB). The most important advantage is certainly the simplicity through indexing. The disadvantage is that the calculation is not cause-related and cements existing budget relationships, regardless of whether they are currently still justified or not. Furthermore, there is no competitive orientation in budgeting.

With a *macro variable* for the first time, inter-company references such as industry growth index, inflation rate, gross national product change, etc. are established.

However, if a company holds above-average success positions, individual market opportunities are easily missed if the aggregated variables signal reluctance. And vice versa, funds are tied up in below-average success positions if the aggregated variables signal commitment. The advantage is that it is sufficiently easy to determine, while the disadvantage is that it is a question of past values/future estimates and does not take into account the individual company situation.

Computer-aided *ADBUDG* follows the decision calculus approach, which simulates changes in market share as a function of advertising expenditure. An S-shaped yield-law effect function is assumed. Four pieces of information are required as data input for the simulation:

- The market share for which the advertising expenditure in the period is assumed to be zero.
- The market share which represents the saturation quantity and is only reached with extremely high advertising expenditures.
- The advertising expenditure necessary to maintain the previous market share.
- The market share which can be achieved by a 50% increase in advertising expenditures.

These data must be qualified estimated subjectively, if not already available. Furthermore, carry over, time transfer effects can be taken into account by extending the approach, as well as a variation in the quality of the advertising material, the quality of the advertising message and the effect of marketing instruments other than advertising.

However, all results are ultimately based on subjective estimation, as it can be assumed that objective data are not available as input. In this respect, there is a considerable risk of bias. Furthermore, the market share in this model is assumed to be the sole advertising target, which is practically certainly too simple.

The model developed by Kuehn is based on a decision rule that maximizes the sum of all present and future discounted profits with respect to the current budget based on Markoff chains. The turnover of a period is then calculated by buyers of the previous period who are certain to buy their own brand again, and the share of all potential brand changers who decide to buy a brand by using the entire range of sales policy instruments of the industry. If the distribution and shelf space as well as the attractiveness and price of the own brand are competitive and if there is a constant and for all brands identical customer churn rate, the sales of a period consist of the brand loyal customers of the previous period, the attracted new customers by the marketing mix of the company and the interaction effects of all marketing mixes including advertising. Taking into account a market growth rate with profit maximization as a target function and an advertising cost function, the optimal advertising budget can be determined at least theoretically. It is c. p. the higher, the higher the advertising expenditures of the competitors is, the higher the profit margin before advertising of the enterprise, the total turnover of the industry, the portion of disloyal competitor brand buyers or loyal buyers of the own brand, the advertising effectiveness and the lower the advertising costs in relation to other investments are.

2.4.3 Model-based, monovariable budgeting techniques

Little tries to determine the advertising response function of a specific company in a specific market situation. It starts with an estimation of this function, preferably as a concave or S-shaped function. The resulting budget is invested in period t in a test market. On a first control market, less money is spent on advertising in low spending, on a second control market, more money is spent in high spending. The revenues generated in the sub-markets provide information on the advertising efficiency. For the next advertising period, the information improved by experience is now available. With continuous adjustment, the function renders the advertising efficiency more and more precisely, so that the budget is approaching optimum.

In the Little model, therefore, only past values are used and projected into the future. This fails if sudden changes in competitive activities or other exogenous market factors occur as discontinuities. Also changes in the own sales policy activities lead to variations which are not considered in the model. A yield-legal course of the reaction curve is assumed, which remains largely unproven, but which makes possible the marginal-analytical determination in the first place. Keeping other model parameters constant is a simplification which leads to errors. The practical feasibility of the experiments is probably only possible for large markets, since otherwise a sufficient delimitation of the effects is not possible. Moreover, the experimental design with test and control markets is very costly and the entire information acquisition is connected with high expenditure. Furthermore, it must be ensured that the underlying assumptions are complete and realistic, which requires a deterministic situation instead of real stochastic situations.

The Koyck model is used for dynamic advertising budgeting, taking into account a time lag of demand response to advertising activities. It therefore takes the time factor into account. A geometric sequence is assumed as a function of the effects of the use of earlier advertising expenditures on today's sales. At the same time, a basic sales volume is assumed, which occurs even if no advertising is used at all. In addition, a constant repurchase rate is taken into account. Analogous to the time lag, it is still possible to take into account a carry-over effect of advertising expenses of past periods on the current advertising period.

The *share of advertising/share of market relation* is most popular. Share of advertising (SoA) is the share of own advertising expenses in the total advertising expenses of all sellers in the relevant market (*for context see figure 12: SoA – SoM relation*). Share of market (SoM) is the market share of the own company in this relevant market. The SoA/SoM budgeting technique relates both figures to each other. The own market share as denominator of the quotient should be known from corresponding market research (Nielsen/GfK). The own advertising share as numerator of the quotient is also known from corresponding market research (Nielsen/S&P) or can be estimated sufficiently. In principle, there are two possibilities for the value of the quotient:

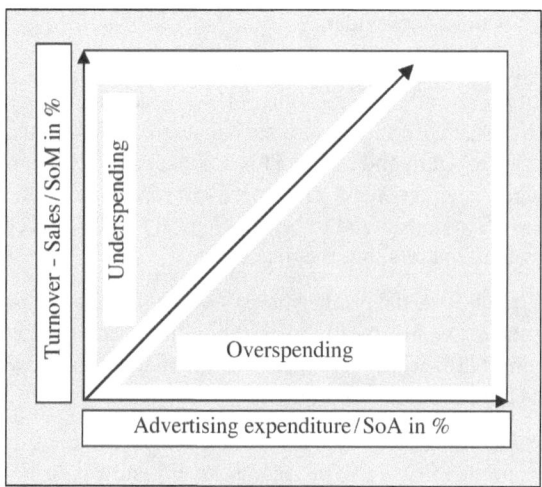

Fig. 12: SoA – SoM relation (Source: own illustration)

- SoA/SoM values > 1 means that advertising expenses are disproportionately high in relation to the share of sales achieved with it, i. e. advertising either seems to be comparatively inefficient or a higher market share is to be purchased.
- SoA/SoM values < 1 means that advertising expenses are disproportionately low in relation to the share of sales achieved. This indicates particularly efficient advertising or a voluntary or involuntary surrender of market share.

However, this ratio also depends on the market position. Long-established, large companies can very often afford relatively low advertising expenses because the reputation of their brand is in itself an acquisition factor. However, if this brand strength is not continuously recharged, there is a risk that the brand core will be emaciated. Furthermore, the SoA/SoM ratio depends on the life cycle phase of the advertised product. At the beginning, disproportionately high advertising expenditure is usually required in order for the product to gain a corresponding position in the market. Later, the relative media performance can be reduced.

From the SoA/SoM ratio it can be extrapolated how much advertising expenditure is considered a prerequisite for achieving a strived for market share. In practice, there are numerous distorting influencing factors, but a regression-analytical dependence can be calculated. This is because there is something like an advertising experience curve, i.e. a more or less fixed relation between advertising share and market share. Although this relation varies from industry to industry, graphically shown in different gradients/quotients, it is relatively rigid within an industry, even with changing budgets. Advertisers whose SoA/SoM ratio is better than the average quotient are compensated to the average by those whose SoA/SoM ratio is worse. The former are usually domestic and traditional providers, while the latter are importers or new providers.

This leads to the less pleasant realization that advertising success is determined less by the quality of the advertising content than by advertising penetration. This applies at least to low-involvement products which are widespread and have to buy their market presence again and again. This also helps to explain why companies are market leaders, e.g. Procter & Gamble, Ferrero, Henkel, whose advertising brand presence is often considered to be deficient. It is not so much the quality of the advertising which matters, but the quantity.

Instead of share of advertising, the share of voice (SoV) is often used as a provider's share of the gross advertising penetration in the competitive environment, or the share of mind (SoMi) as a provider's share of advertising awareness within the competitive environment, both are output-related.

The *investment calculation* is based on a long-term consideration, which correctly interprets advertising expenses as an investment to contribute to the generation of future sales. Consequently, the advertising budget can be fixed so as to maximize the difference between the cumulative advertising expenses of the past and the resulting cumulative revenues induced in the future. The net present value method can be used as the calculation method for this. For this purpose, past advertising expenses are discounted to the current decision date, while expected future advertising income is discounted to this common date. If the expenses and income of alternative advertising programs are determined and their effects dynamized, the program with the highest net present value as a target value is considered to be the best.

The main problem here is the allocation of future advertising income to past advertising expenses. It is also extremely difficult to forecast earnings data, although in this case it is probably not necessary to look too far into the future.

It is, however, of crucial importance to view advertising not as cost, but as investment. After all, advertising is an investment in future sales and thus in no more and no less than the company's existence. In business practice it is much more plausible to budget investment funds than cost items. The former are accepted as indispensable for survival, the latter, on the other hand, must be minimized. To speak of advertising investments and not of advertising costs therefore already contributes to the creation of awareness, and corresponds also to the facts.

2.4.4 Model-based, polyvariable budgeting techniques

Based on empirical analyses, Vidale/Wolfe attribute the relationship between advertising as model input and sales as model output to three constant parameters: the sales decline, the market saturation and the reaction:

- Sales decline is the value which results when advertising activities are discontinued or reduced, assumed in the model as a linear trend, a high value here means that sales without advertising decline sharply, and vice versa,
- the saturation limit of the market indicates the point at which no more sales increases can be recorded despite advertising efforts,
- the reaction constant as the ratio of the amount of turnover to the amount of advertising expenditure is defined as the increase in turnover achieved by an additional monetary unit of advertising expenditure with an initial turnover of zero.

The higher the reaction constant, the higher the unused sales potential, the higher the advertising expenditure and the lower the sales decay constant, the higher the change in sales. The most appropriate way to measure the parameters is by means of test advertising under controlled conditions. From this it is possible to determine the advertising expenditure which is necessary to maintain sales at a certain level or to guarantee a certain sales growth rate.

The advertising efficiency decreases with increasing sales volume. A constant, and therefore negligible, competitive behavior is assumed. The model is a dynamic one which takes into account the decline in advertising efficiency over time. It is difficult to determine the parameters reaction constant, saturation level and sales decrease. Most likely, the decrease in sales can be interpreted as a kind of forgetting constant that leads to a certain loss of previous buyers. For this to happen, however, a company would have to stop advertising. Furthermore, all three variables change due to changes in market conditions. Concentrating on maintaining turnover cannot be interpreted as a generally valid business objective. It is also problematic to address the potential buyers alone and to neglect the current buyers. It is assumed that all buyers are of equal importance, i. e. acquisition of equal product quantities, whereby the sales per buyer cannot be increased. In this respect, the model can only be assumed for market areas with constant consumption rates. The influence of competitive activities is not considered, although they are of central importance in marketing. The assumed direct relationship between advertising expenditure and achieved sales can hardly be proven in reality, since success and failure always depend on the use of all marketing instruments. Advertising success which only occurs after the planning period is not taken into account, but it would be necessary to discount it to the planning date.

The model by Fischerkoesen contains two influencing variables:

- Dissemination and resonance effect as the relative number of people who received an advertising stimulus or consciously incorporated it,

- Sales impact or efficiency as the relative number of people who become buyers of an item through the advertising campaign.

Efficiency and resonance are linked. If test persons are confronted with an advertising medium in an experiment, a certain efficiency results, i. e. the market share increases. The efficiency is maximum if all persons are reached by the advertising material used, it is minimum if no person is reached. The reality lies between these two extremes. In this respect there is a multiplicative connection between efficiency and resonance. Thus, an advertising impulse which reaches all target persons without achieving any sales effect there means that the previous market share remains unchanged. This also applies if no target person has been reached by advertising. Now, however, it is necessary to determine the parameters resonance and efficiency. The efficiency is measured by the marginal willingness to pay, the resonance by methods of experimental learning psychology.

But there are specific problems in this. It is extremely difficult to determine these values. Furthermore, different values result for each market. Finally, competitive reactions, which are typical for oligopoly markets, are not taken into account.

Dorfman/Steiner only include the advertising budget to the extent that it is about optimizing the marketing mix through marginal analytical calculations. The following premises apply: Single product enterprise, profit maximization as a goal, price and product quality as further parameters beside the advertisement, no effect compound of these instruments and existing information to proceeds and costs. The optimal marketing mix, and thus also the optimal advertising budget, is achieved when the price elasticity of demand, the marginal revenue of advertising and the demand elasticity as to quality changes multiplied by the quotient of price and average costs are exactly the same.

Thus the optimal advertising budget is derived in a formally exact way. A condition for this however is the continuity and repeated differentiability of the underlying effect functions, which is more doubtful in reality. In addition, no restrictions can be taken into account, so the specified optimum can lie outside the permissible solution range. The use of marketing instruments other than advertising is negated. Interdependencies between non-advertising parameters are therefore not considered. It must be possible to determine the influences of marginal changes in the advertising budget from the accounting system, which is unrealistic. The approach is based on a single-product company, so substitutive and complementary relationships within the program are not recorded. This is also somewhat unrealistic. The exclusive goal of profit maximization is assumed, which is very doubtful in practice. The used marginal-analytical calculation method is completely unsuitable there, because infinitesimal small changes and their effects are not realizable.

A further development is provided by the Lambin model, which allows a dynamic view of several variables of the marketing mix and also takes into account the advertising activities of the competition.

Advertising budgeting is carried out through *optimization* based on marginal revenues and marginal costs. The profit-maximum advertising budget is therefore available when the combined marginal costs, i.e. marginal advertising and other marginal production costs, are exactly the same as the price. With variable prices, the use of advertising certainly leads to a change in the form and position of the price selling function. To that extent there is an advertising budget height with different constellations, with which the profit-maximum price-quantity combination is reached. The optimum is given where the partial marginal yields of the instruments balance each other out.

However, a continuity and differentiability of the functional relationship is assumed. Likewise, no restrictions are taken into account that may be located in other areas of the company such as production. The one-sided objective of profit maximization is assumed. Likewise, only quantitative advertising objectives are considered. In addition to advertising, only pricing policy is included as a sales policy instrument. Moreover, competitive activities are completely neglected.

2.4.5 Critical review of budgeting techniques

For experience-based budgeting techniques, it is true that some of these methods, as explained, are subject to the danger of procyclically oriented budgeting and logical circular reasoning.

In many cases an analytical connection between advertising as an input variable and the output variable of the procedure is missing. Thus the profit is more dependent on numerous other factors than on the advertising, especially on the cost items. The same applies to the contribution margin, which is just as significantly influenced by the costs. Sales/volume and turnover/value are also dependent on numerous other factors which are caused outside of advertising.

In this respect, there is a risk of misallocation of the budget, but in any case, the optimum advertising budget level is likely to be more or less missed by a wide margin. Also the pure competition purchase is misdirecting, because nevertheless the success of the competition is just as dependent on various other sizes than advertisement as this is also the case with the own company.

The determination of a fixed amount of money is just as little useful as a target-task view, which assumes a known, functional connection between advertising input and target output.

The information is usually quite rough and the references underlying the statement are simplified. For example, no impact delay, direct carry over effects or impact transfer, indirect carry over effects are considered. Similarly, temporal impact networks, e.g. in the form of market resistance, are not taken into account.

For model-based budgeting techniques, a static approach of only one short-term advertising period regularly prevails. In fact, however, it is necessary in terms of forward-looking planning to include effects of current activities on future periods or influences of future periods on current activities in the decision on the advertising budget.

Often, profit maximization is also considered a restrictive goal of the company. In fact, however, all possible forms of objective setting are encountered, but certainly not profit maximization. This fails already alone because of the formal conditions necessary for it. Therefore, no company can maximize profits, even if it wanted to.

At the same time, the existence of complete information about all relevant environmental data is assumed. In view of increasingly complex marketing conditions, this is not even close to being the case. In addition, the limited processing capacities of the decision maker human being speak against the achievement of this premise.

The functional relationships between input and output are assumed to be constant and differentiable. Instead, they are to a large extent not even known, let alone the nature of their relationship. Advertising in particular is characterized by elementary qualitative criteria which largely elude quantified recording.

Market forms of either monopoly or polypoly are assumed, but not the oligopolies that are widespread in real life. Apart from the fact that absolute monopolies do not exist in a world of alternatives, polypolises are also mostly permeated by monopolistic substructures. No statement is made in the models for these practical mixed forms.

In the company under consideration, mono-production is taken as a basis. However, this is the blatant exception nowadays. Almost all suppliers make products available for several markets in order to better exploit their traditional know-how or to reduce market risks.

No marketing instruments other than advertising should be available. However, it is now sufficiently known that the other marketing mix instruments are capable of making at least the same contribution to the sales success of products as advertising. Therefore, this assumption does not refer to reality.

Finally, a given advertising method is assumed in campaign design, media selection and usage. This excludes the possibility that the efficiency of advertising can be increased by changing the creative implementation, by using other advertising media and carriers as well as by media-technical measures. However, this is often the goal in view of limited budget resources.

2.4.6 Allocation of budget funds

The advertiser's available budget must first be divided into three proportions, one for classical offline and one for non-classical offline, one for online advertising media. This distinction is based on a historical development. The former have fixed price lists which are used as a basis for standardized invoicing in a large number of cases, at least officially, whereas non-classical advertising media are not subject to fixed price lists but are invoiced individually in each case. Classic advertising media have also included 15 % agency commission for advertising agents in their price lists.

Although these areas are still occasionally budgeted separately, problem orientation is increasingly replacing media orientation for advertisers. Rather, a task is then defined, e. g. new launch, relaunch, line extension, and a total of funds is allocated to it. The areas for which these funds are then used should be measured by the comparative performance of the individual media and not by abstractly defined budget limits.

Practically no serious offline campaign can be based solely on classical or online or non-classical advertising media, but requires a mix of communication instruments. This involves a rough allocation of funds to these three areas. The fine-tuning only takes place during the realization phase. Despite the strong trend towards non-classical advertising media, it must be emphasized that building and maintaining brands is in fact only possible through the use of classical advertising media.

Within the classical media, the alternatives of advertisements, spots and posters are available. For each of these media there are specific strengths and weaknesses, which are worked out in a performance profile. Their individual suitability is determined by comparing them with the requirement profile resulting from the advertising objectives. The ranking of the media is derived from the degree of correspondence between the performance and requirement profiles.

Accordingly, it must be decided whether only one type of media should be used or a combination of two or more types of media. It must be taken into account that certain media performance values should at least be achieved for an activation. This in turn requires a certain width, frequency and equipment of the media use. Due to the high costs involved, only large budgets are able to finance more than one classic media genre. In practice, the lower limit is assumed to be € 4 million/p. a.

The budget is then divided according to pre-development and switching costs. The preliminary development costs budget covers all costs incurred in the commercial (marketing information) and technical (production) development of advertising measures. It concerns the conditions for the employment of the advertisement, represents however still no advertising measures and has therefore fixed cost character. The placement cost budget covers all costs which advertising executional organizations, i. e. broadcasters, publishers, tenants, receive for the booking of advertising materials in their advertising media. Only then the actual distribution of the advertising messages becomes possible. In addition, there are the costs in non-classical advertising.

Advertising investments in Germany in 2018 in the area of classical advertising (above the line/A-t-l) amounted to around € 36 billion. This corresponds to slightly more than 1 % of GDP (€ 3,388 billion) and is also slightly less than in previous years. The spreadable volume of this was € 15.82 billion, or around 44 % of the total. This amount is also slightly declining.

Television accounted for the largest share (€ 4.591 billion advertising revenue = 29 % of A-t-l), followed by daily newspapers (€ 2.386 billion = 14 %), free sheets (€ 1.856 billion = 11 %), trade journals (€ 1.739 billion = 11 %) and online/mobile/ digital (€ 1.638 billion = 11 %). This was followed by outdoor advertising (€ 1.150 billion/7 %), consumer magazines (€ 0.965 billion/6 %) and radio (€ 0.790 billion/ 5 %) (remainder together 6 %/with rounding differences).

This contrasts with the non-classical advertising sector (below the line/B-t-l), which stood for around € 20 billion in advertising investment in Germany in 2018, or around 56 % of total expenditure, with a slight upward trend.

Sponsoring accounted for € 5.0 billion (25 % share of B-t-l), catalog € 4.45 billion (22 %), search engine advertising € 3.79 billion (19 %), promotional items € 3.58 billion (18 %) and direct advertising € 2.97 billion (15 %) (all data rounded according to the Central association of the German advertising industry ZAW (Werbung 2019). However, the allocation of digital advertising to A-t-l or B-t-l, as carried out there, is questionable, possibly resulting in a third category OMD. Depending on the measurement method, up to 45 % of the total is specified by interested parties.

2.5 Advertising period and timing

There are various postulates regarding the time required for advertising. Theoretically, it is recommended to advertise *anti-cyclically*, i.e. when the business situation is not so good, to stimulate it by increased advertising or, when the business situation is good anyway, not to overheat it unnecessarily by withdrawing advertising. In this regard it is problematic that in recession usually no money for advertisement is available, and in the boom the supply of advertising budget is easy, so that the time employment practically rather takes place *pro-cyclically*. Besides according to seasonal emphasis advertising should be pro-seasonally, whereby a temporal delay effect of the advertisement in relation to the sales effect leads to the fact that the advertising season is temporally pre-aged the sales season.

In addition the advertising measures must be co-ordinated also spatially. So it can be meaningful to use all measures in the same area or to provide separate space-measure combinations. In general, it must be ensured that the advertising area is largely congruent with the realized or intended distribution area. Thus, there should be neither underfilling, i.e., distribution areas which are not covered by advertising through distribution gap, nor overfilling, i.e., the advertising covers areas which are not distributed through spatial *misscatter*. It is conceivable to achieve a uniform coverage, but also a selectively increased coverage, e.g. in conurbations or distribution areas to be newly established.

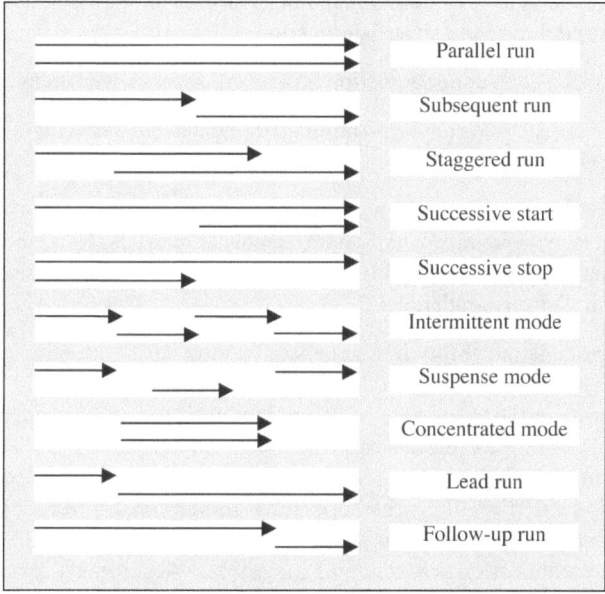

Fig. 13: Options for advertising timing (Source: own illustration)

An important aspect of all advertising measures is without doubt their spatial and temporal coordination. Within a certain advertising period, the media can be used in different time sequences. A general distinction can be made between the following (*see figure 13: Options for advertising timing*):

- *Parallel* run, i.e. two or more communication instruments are used completely simultaneously running side by side,
- *subsequent* run, i.e. a following communication instrument replaces a previous one and is immediately connected to it,
- *staggered* run, i.e. two or more communication instruments run for the same length of time, but start and stop at different times, resulting in a temporary overlap,
- *successively* starting, i.e. communication instruments are deployed one after the other and then expire together at the same time,

- *successively* stopping, i.e. communication instruments expire one after the other after they have been used simultaneously,

- *intermittent* mode, i.e. two or more communication instruments alternate continuously and without interruption

- *suspending* mode, i.e. two or more communication instruments alternate discontinuously with interruption,

- *concentrated* mode, i.e. communication instruments are only activated to a limited extent during the advertising period

- *leading* run, i.e. one communication instrument acts as a lead-in to another one,

- *follow-up* run, i.e. one communication instrument acts as a follow-up to another one which is ahead.

The advertising period regularly results from the advertising task itself. Usually it is a budget year, more rarely half-years, tertials or quarters. Here, the flexibility, exact responsiveness, of the media to business requirements must be considered. This results in various gradations.

The exception is the ability to react exactly to the day. A time lag of up to one week results from technical production precautions which have to be taken for advertising use, i.e. the production of artwork or digital pre-production. But also due to the reaction time of the parties carrying out the advertising as publishers/broadcasters/tenants. A time lag of up to one month results from more complicated technical production requirements, e.g. three-dimensional advertising material, processing, and longer intervals between the use of advertising material, e.g. with monthly publication frequency of magazines. Accordingly, responsiveness is limited. Even longer intervals are required for certain media, such as public television broadcasters or popular magazines in the case of four-color ads. It is therefore important to plan accordingly in good time by including these lead times.

In the case of new product launches or relaunches, it must be ensured that advertising only begins when the new or varied product is actually available. A certain amount of lead time may be advisable to provoke curiosity for the product as a teaser. A certain amount of advance notice is also useful for building up distribution, because the actual unavailability of products can easily turn into bad will on the part of customers. Often special opening motifs or better advertising material are used to dramatize the first appearance. Likewise, in the introductory phase the contact dose is often increased compared to the remaining time.

As it is often not possible to cover a whole year due to limited budgets, a "summer break" is usually taken. This is based on the experience that during the summer vacations in schools and companies many decision-makers are not in the circulation area of the advertising media occupied. The temporal stretching of the vacations due to numerous vacation days leads however to the fact that over the whole year more or less evenly distributed, persons are in organized spare time. Incidentally, titles subscribed to in the print sector are highly likely to be "read up". Nor can the summer slump be verified from the sales figures for many of the products.

Pulsating advertising is recommended to a greater extent, i.e. several insertions/occupancies should take place shortly after each other, then one can take a break, whereby the memory is largely retained. After this pause, advertising starts again to update the company/brand and quickly raises the reminder to the initial level again. However, there are also findings to the contrary, which rather assume the need for constant penetration.

It is also conceivable that advertising intensity will increase over time, if one believes in the recency effect, which means that the messages closest to the time of purchase are processed best, or that advertising intensity will decrease if one believes in the primacy effect, i.e. the best processing for the earliest messages. The media can start at the same time or with a time delay, i.e. successively one after the other (see below).

Since there are external overlaps between advertising media, i.e. a target person uses more than one advertising medium, the insertions can be staggered in a way that, due to the circulation period of the advertising media, an advertising presence in the target group is guaranteed during all times. Often there are also specific reasons for the insertion of the advertisement based on external deadlines such as gift date, order period or end of year.

However, the overview of the insertions should not hide the fact that the impression of the distribution plan does not reflect the real situation, but is only seen as such by advertisers or advertising agencies. However, this often leads to inadmissible conclusions about public advertising penetration. In addition one must always keep in mind that the vast majority of advertising rushes past the target persons unnoticed. And the advertising that is noticed quickly falls into oblivion if it is not renewed at short intervals. And the noticed advertisement does not have to lead to the impression as advertising impact or even to the purchase as advertising success.

2.6 Advertising area and density

However, exact spatial control of the media is very difficult, so that even major incongruities can hardly be avoided. Conversely, in the case of fractional media landscapes, such as private radio, daily newspapers or outdoor advertising, it is often difficult to achieve comprehensive coverage. In this case, it makes sense to use tariff combination of media which are organized in such a way that they cover larger areas with several parallel advertising media almost without gaps or overlaps. The following gradations result for the advertising area (*see figure 14: Options for advertising coverage*):

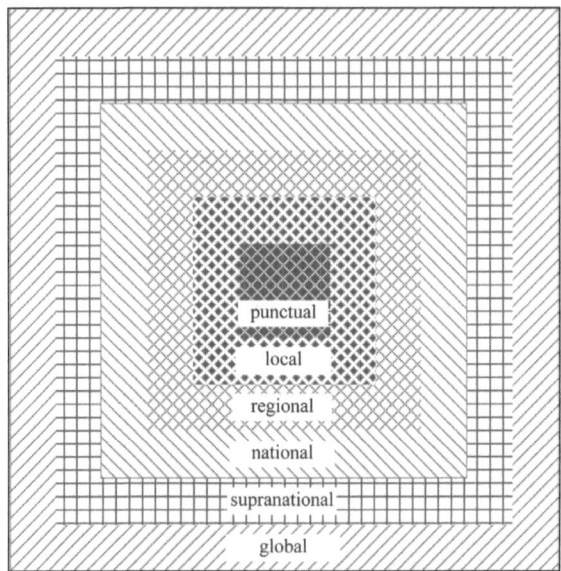

Fig. 14: Options for advertising coverage
(Source: own illustration)

- *Punctual* advertising employment takes place in direct spatial environment of the supplier. This is relevant e. g. for trade and crafts enterprises with a point of sale. Accordingly, only media that can be controlled selectively are indicated for the application, all others do not correspond to the task.
- *Local* advertising assignment is carried out with a narrow spatial limitation of the catchment area. This is relevant e. g. for small and medium-sized companies. Only those media are considered for the application which can be controlled locally or selectively.
- *Regional* advertising is used with further spatial expansion. In marketing, the Nielsen areas are often used as a basis. As media both those, which are regionally as well as locally and punctually controllable, are considered.
- *National* advertising employment takes place only within the borders of a country. However, in view of the increasing internationalization of markets, this is rarely the case. As media those come into consideration, which are national, regional, local and punctual controllable.

However, the emphasis is on *supranational* advertising. The ERPG approach of Perlmutter is usually used as a basis. According to this approach, the extent of the advertising can be divided into home-country oriented/ethnocentric advertising, which is designed domestically but is also used in foreign markets, foreign oriented/polycentric advertising, which is designed and used separately for each advertising market, economic area oriented/regio-centric advertising, which is designed and used within relatively homogeneous international regions, e. g. EU, North America, Asia, and *global* coverage through geocentric oriented advertising, which is designed and used uniformly in all countries. A practiced compromise is the lead country concept. Here, for a larger regional unit or the world market as a whole, one country and thus one branch or the head office itself assumes the position of coordinator and "primus inter pares". All other countries then adapt these activities. This is a compromise between sufficient uniformity of marketing on the one hand and consideration of market-specific characteristics on the other. Lead countries are usually determined by their domestic market volume.

Market management is usually based on differences/similarities in the cultural marketing environment of the countries to be promoted (*culture-bound products*). As a theoretical construct, culture can only be captured indirectly via indicators. There have been many efforts to achieve this, the oldest and most common approach comes from Hofstede. It operationalizes culture through the dimensions masculinity or femininity, uncertainty avoidance or acceptance, high or low power gap, short-term or long-term concept of time, and individuality or collectivism. Assuming these dimensions, advertising in countries with similar cultures can be the same, but must be different in countries with different cultures. The only exceptions to this are so-called *culture-free products*, i.e. those which are to be advertised uniformly and internationally, regardless of culture. The existence of cultural differences has given rise to a controversial discussion that is being conducted in the context of international marketing communication.

With regard to market cultivation, the alternatives are successive or simultaneous market penetration (*for context see figure 15: Alternatives of international market penetration*). The so-called *waterfall* technique means that new foreign markets are only opened up slowly and after an extensive search for information, successively country by country over the time. The so-called *sprinkler* technique, on the other hand, is used when a company wants to develop as many countries as possible for foreign sales in a short time by simultaneously entering several markets. A feasible compromise is the alternating combination of waterfall and sprinkler strategy. This is suitable in case of clustering effects such as the existence of similar target groups in some of the targeted country markets, different technological, political and social conditions as well as diverging market structures in some selected countries and the existence of different levels of market entry barriers.

Within the defined advertising area, the media can be used with varying density (*see figure 16: Options for advertising density*). A general distinction is made between:

- *Spatially constant* coverage, i.e. the entire advertising area is uniformly covered by one or more media,

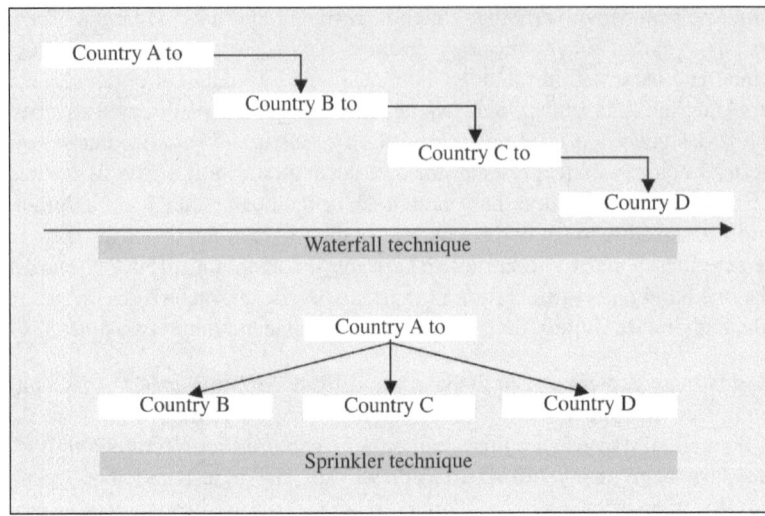

Fig. 15: Alternatives of international market penetration (Source: own illustration)

- *room-thinned* cover age, i.e. starting from a desired basic cover, partial rooms are left out, this is usually necessary for budget reasons,
- *space-compressed* cover age, i.e. starting from a desired basic cover, partial spaces are covered several times, this usually refers to metropolitan areas.

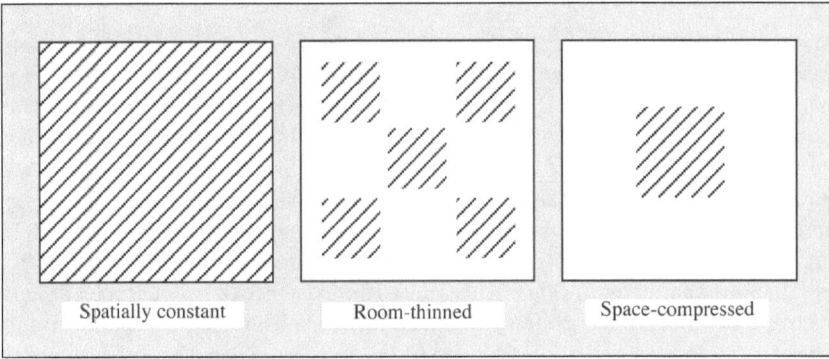

Fig. 16: Options for advertising density (Source: own illustration)

2.7 Meaning and representation of the brand

Professional marketing is impossible without a brand, also marketing communication is a bit difficult without a mark. Regularly the forming of a brand is at least the implicit goal of advertising. So it is advisable, to have a closer look at the brand phenomenon.

2.7.1 Brand content

The following are generally *definition criteria* for a brand:

- Uniform presentation, although varying almost imperceptibly over time. This does not mean rigidity in appearance, but on the contrary a continuous flexibility, which adapts to trends without losing its distinctiveness.
- Consistent or improved quality, quantity and pricing. This means the effort for a constantly increased efficiency, a quantity dimensioning more in line with demand and thus a more favorable price performance ratio for an offer, which is aimed at and ensured by scheduled activities.
- Manufactured goods for differentiated mass demand. This means that it concerns products of the same kind in principle, whose profile is cut by certain offer characteristics on intended market segments. This makes it difficult to include raw materials and semi-finished products and restricts services.
- Trademark for consistent identification. This means that all communication activities are uniformly marked with an independent trademark, whether on the equipment, the product itself or in advertising material. This trademark is also called a logo.
- Property promise through systematic communication. This means that substantial advertising activities are used to spread consistent messages about the specific performance of the brand offering, which from the public's point of view are to be understood as guarantee statements.
- Appropriate availability. The degree of distribution in the defined sales area/channel can range from ubiquity, as in the case of cigarettes, magazines, soft drinks, chocolate bars, to exclusion, for example in forms of contract marketing.
- High awareness and recognition in the market. This means a sufficient degree of formal brand awareness combined with high familiarity in terms of offer claim, benefit promise and image appeal within the target group.

Opinions are divided as to whether success is a criterion of the brand article or whether it is only the result of the successful use of the other characteristics. The same applies to the criterion of ecology as environmental compatibility, which is a constitutive prerequisite from a modern perspective. Offers which meet these criteria are called brands/branded articles. They are an indispensable prerequisite for the possibility of any kind of marketing.

Following, a somewhat shorter definition (based on Bruhn):

- The brand in the broadest sense is a designation for companies or goods or services which indicates their origin to users in order to distinguish them from those of other origins.
- At the same time, the brand forms the personality of a product, which complements or reinforces the buyer and makes his values recognisable in the social environment.
- The branded article is a marked offer, precisely product/service, which is formally known and familiar in the relevant market.

2.7.2 Brand characteristics

Building a brand involves considerable investments. Accordingly, there must be significant advantages in the market which justify this costly strategy. As such brand characteristics the following are to be called on the *supply* side:

- Creation of a means of communication from the manufacturer to intermediate or end customers. The existence of a brand enables the dialog between the supplier and his customers, because without a profiled offer the common communication basis is missing.
- Conspicuous differentiation from competitive offers. The conciseness of a brand allows the positive differentiation of one's own offer from those of the competition and thus its highlighting through recognizable performance characteristics.
- Formation of preferences in favor of the own brand, thus discrimination of the competition. The brand allows the formation of preferences which present one's own offer more favourably than that of the competition and as a result lead to a desirable devaluation in fair parallel competition.
- Possibility for target group marketing. Finally, due to its distinctive profile, the brand enables the segmentation of the overall market through the use of a differentiated set of marketing instruments.
- A prerequisite for securing or expanding sales. Due to the high level of market exploitation, the sales base can be sustainably secured and possibly even expanded. It can be assumed that a high proportion of the demanders will buy the product again at regular intervals.
- Achievement of pricing leeway. This binding in turn allows the resulting lower price elasticity of demand to be used to exploit higher revenues in the market without customers migrating to competition.

- Market plannability and probability of plan fulfillment. The high level of investment involved in launching and maintaining a brand becomes more easily bearable against the background of plan reliability by the brand.

On the *demand* side, the following brand characteristics are added:

- Orientation aid in the diversity of the product range. The formation of a ranking within objectively similar offers makes it easier for customers to find their way through the increasing variety of goods and services. Brands thus create an overview of the market and help to categorize the alternatives.
- Individual satisfaction of demand. On the demand side, this results in the possibility of a targeted choice of benefits by choosing exactly the brand which best meets one's own objectives among several brands with a concise and competent profile.
- Recognizability and the chance to straight rebuy. The marking of such preferred offers enables the recognizability of this particular offer and thus offers the chance for repeat purchases.
- Security with the purchase. This overview creates purchase security with regard to the amount of money to be invested to the extent that a brand is consciously preferred to others because of its previously known performance profile.
- Building brand loyalty. This in turn enables conscious loyalty to an offer when subjective expectations and brand performance match. This product satisfaction can even lead to exclusive use.

A problem is that every buyer actually prefers only a few from all existing brands per category. When it comes to purchasing the decision is made only among these brands. Therefore in the long run, it is important for manufacturers to survive to belong to this relevant set of brands with as large a multiplicity as possible of potential buyers in each time and at each place of the purchase decision. This requires intensive marketing efforts like:

- Creation of availability as presence in the available set under all brands of the universal set through appropriate distribution measures,
- improvement of the level of awareness as presence in the awareness set through the choice of suitable media,
- increasing the degree of familiarity as presence in the processed set/consideration set by selecting suitable content messages,
- increase of acceptance/competence as presence in the accept set/choice set through sustained, often personal communication,
- establish preference/respect for choice/presence in the evoked set by offering concrete, attractive benefits,
- retention of customers on an emotional, technical or legal level as presence in the loyalty set.

New products in particular only have a chance of being included in the evoked set/loyalty set if they succeed in simultaneously displacing a brand already present there, or in establishing a new market, and thus a new set, which is extremely rare. This is because consumers do not expand their evoked set just because of a new offer, but rather delete a previous offer. In turn, the existing suppliers defend themselves against this. The market leader has the greatest protection against crowding out.

2.7.3 Brand name development

One of the reasons why the brand is so important is that it is associated with the product throughout its life. In the simplest case, the company name can be used, which may be provided with appropriate product information. Otherwise a new brand name must be found:

- *Descriptive* brand names with semantically conditioned force of expression make a concrete statement as to the product, they are however little independent and original, therefore basically only insufficiently protectable, probably however by market validity, and due to linguistic barriers abroad only rarely applicable.
- *Associative* brand names with phonetically conditioned expressiveness say more or less directly something about the product performance and evoke certain associations, they are easily protectable and internationally well applicable, as long as they do not evoke country-specific undesirable associations.
- *Artificial* brand names are purely synthetic words which initially remain without any concrete meaning and say nothing about the product, are easily protected and, taking into account linguistic, cultural and associative requirements, can be used internationally very well. Since they have no discernible semantic or phonetic connection to the product, the brand must first be loaded with content which is meaningful in the sender's sense in order to develop its acquisition effect.

As the first step for development of the name serves a study to verify the underlying marketing strategy. The brand as the name of a product concretizes the associated marketing strategy and must therefore fit exactly.

This is followed by a review of the supplier's brand portfolio to determine whether existing, used or unused, but protected or protectable brands can be transferred to the new product.

If this research remains unproductive, the next step is to analyze the positioning of the brand in order to obtain clues for search fields of product names. Furthermore, company guidelines must be explicitly taken into account as restrictions.

Only then do creativity techniques come into play and the results of database searches are used. Also conceivable are computer-supported procedures, with which associatively fitting word stems, syllables or letter groups are searched and systematically combined. In this way, a large catalog of possible brand names is created.

The internationalization of brands in particular poses serious problems. This set is then subjected to a linguistic check, whereby this is required for each language area which is intended to be used later. This already significantly reduces the number of possible brand names. The subject of the check is the barrier-free pronunciation of the brand name.

Then a semantic check is performed. This is about the desired understanding of the brand name. Thereby a goal-oriented selection according to coherent meaning takes place.

Subsequently, a brief search is carried out in accordance with trademark law, after which all suggestions which are already protected elsewhere or cannot be protected at all are dropped. A variety of requirements is placed on the brand name, including that it is memorable, clear, easily recognizable, unmistakable, language-related, identifiable by product and service, shortsyllabic, melodious, positive, suggestive, attention-grabbing and activating, permanent and supraregional.

The remaining brand names are then tested to see if they correspond to the desired association in the target group. This usually requires creative support in look & feel, e.g. in the form of graphic grid, typography, color mood, design/equipment, logo, slogan/jingle, in order to make the tonality and visuality of the brand perceptible.

The remaining brand names are then subjected to a detailed legal analysis and, if possible, registered for each country which is or will be a sales territory. The remaining brand name is then registered for protection.

The *mark* can be, according to its form, above all the following:

- *Word* mark, which is expressed by the text, e.g. Samsung, Siemens, Sony. The word mark is difficult to protect, even with typographic design.

- *Figurative* mark which is expressed by an independent symbol. The image of a product is usually not sufficient for registration.

- *Combined word and figurative* mark as a permanent combination of graphic and textual elements. This is frequently encountered and very independent.

- *Color* mark which can be defined from the standardized color classification systems Pantone, RAL or HKS. There distinctiveness is important.

- *Olfactory* mark which is equally protectable if it has distinctive character, either originally for perfume, deodorant, soap, etc. or derivatively for luxury goods such as spirits, chocolates, etc.

- *Tasting* mark monopolizing decided taste impressions.

- *Tactile* mark which protects the haptic impression of a product or packaging.
- *Audio* mark, which results from the sound image. It is defined by musical notation. In addition, there are numerous modalities such as noise, dynamic, timbre, instrumentation, etc.
- *Three-dimensional* mark, it is created by physical representation of the trademark such as the VW logo.
- *Motion* mark, e.g. cutting symbol with two fingers in Twix, T-sign in Telekom-IPO.

It is important that the trademark remains effective even when modified, i.e. enlarged, reduced, negative, positive, monochrome, multicolored.

The brand represents a significant proportion of the assets of each market-oriented company. These assets largely consist of intangible company value, of which the brand value is usually the most significant. In this respect, there is a great interest in protecting the brand from any dilution or attack. This is a central task of product management. Brand value also plays a major role in many strategic business decisions. Since it is immaterial, it is important to approach this value using operational measurement methods for financial brand equity and/or behavioral brand strength.

The most valuable international brands include Amazon, Apple, Microsoft, Google, Visa, Alibaba, Tencent, Facebook, McDonald's, Mastercard, AT&T, Verizon, Coca-Cola. The most valuable national brands include SAP, Telekom, BMW, Mercedes-Benz, DHL, Siemens, Aldi, Adidas, Bosch, Audi (Source: BrandZ).

3. Advertising campaign formatting

Campaign formatting represents a crucial interface in communication management. This is where the conceptual view is abandoned in order to carry out the actual communiqué design, i.e. to determine how the message is presented in concrete terms. In any case, it is necessary to look at it from the perspective of the intended target audience. And this only is interested in the benefits promised to them by an offer, how these benefits relate to competing offers and which needs are satisfied by them.

3.1 Determination of target groups

The focus of marketing communication is usually on the B-t-c sector/business to consumer, but in fact the B-t-b sector/business to business has a high potential in view of the much larger transaction volume. Every consumer transaction is predated by multiple producer and distributor transactions.

3.1.1 Business target groups

Business target groups are often manifold, depending on the characteristics of the markets, the role of actors on these markets and the decision-making relations among these actors. This makes advertising efforts very complex and complicated.

3.1.1.1 General market characteristics

For a closer look, it is helpful to first consider the general characteristics of the B-t-b market most important:

- A manageable number of suppliers and a limited number of demanders, therefore high market transparency,
- typically stable, long-term market partner relationships of the more or less always same players,
- supply-side reputation and demand-side trust are decisive factors for buying or not buying,
- often detailed, long pre- and post-negotiations, especially in view of the economic importance,

- superficially formalized decision-making, but here too it is still predominantly people who decide,
- high project values with often discontinuous business development, therefore high risk bearing,
- mostly short distribution channels as direct sales by disintermediation to commercial intermediates and end customers,
- high dependence on aftermarkets with a "bullwhip effect", whose fluctuations have an increased impact,
- frequently customer-specific service provision (lot size = 1) with the consequence of a lack of fixed cost degression,
- complex hardware-software combinations with a high service share of business volume,
- multiple influence of external third parties like experts, consultants, etc. on the purchase decision,
- often formation of provider coalitions such as working groups, cooperations, etc.,
- order placement even for small amounts of money strictly formalized by tender, usually in triple pitch,
- highly international markets due to geographically dispersed demand for mostly specialized products.

These are overarching characteristics, but in the B-t-b sector there are types of business with a very different profile. These include plants, systems, processed and unprocessed products and services.

3.1.1.2 Main market actors

Various players are active in the B-t-b sector. These are essentially the following:

- *Manufacturers of finished products* in industry produce complete products across all stages of the value chain and sell them either directly or indirectly to resellers or to processors as original equipment manufacturers/OEMs,
- *raw material growers/miners* in the agricultural sector and extraction represent the first stage of the value chain and sell their products, in normal case commodities, to commercial processors/converters,
- *parts manufacturers* (third party suppliers) produce semi-finished products from raw materials over one or a few value-added stages and sell them to commercial processors,

- *component manufacturers* (second party suppliers) produce semi-finished products on the basis of delivered parts, supplemented by their own performance shares over several of their own value-added stages,
- *system manufacturers* (first party suppliers) produce finished products based on components, supplemented by several of their own value-added stages,
- *importers or exporters* of semi-finished and finished products as well as online suppliers of semi-finished and finished products and suppliers of unbranded merchandise are treated equally,
- *resellers* (dealers) purchase finished products and sell them without substantial processing or treatment to commercial end users via wholesale or private customers via retail,
- *industrial service providers* create independent or product-related services for commercial customers, mostly in the form of medium-sized companies,
- *craftsmen* create technical repair and maintenance services for commercial customers, mostly in small-scale operations,
- *freelancers* (professional service) contribute supplementary commercial or technical consulting services for commercial customers,
- *sales agents* accompany the flow of goods in the supply chain by crediting and securing in finance, by transport, reloading, storage and disposal in logistics or by data provision, processing, compression in information.

These actors partly are in complementary relationship to each other and work symbiotically together in value chains, but partly they are also in substitutive relationship and fight for their share of importance in the value chain. This leads to a competition of business models. In this respect, the respective interests are decisive for the communication goals.

To generate decision-making characteristics, mainly three approaches are common (*see figure 17: Typologies of organisational buying behavior*).

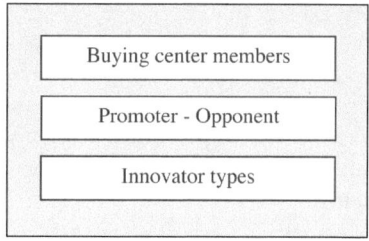

Fig. 17: Typologies of organizational buying behavior

3.1.1.3 Decision-making relations

Buying center

Purchasing decisions of a certain size are typically no longer made by individuals but by buying centers. Such committees consist of different persons who perform different functions in procurement. It is also conceivable, however, that a member takes over several functions at the same time or one after the other or that several members share a function. Individual functions can also be assumed by external parties.

The analysis involves identifying the members of the buying center, examining the information behavior of the participants, their decision-making process and the influence of the individual members on this decision. The analysis also focuses on role expectations that other participants have of the individual buying center member, the responsiveness of the individual members and the information content for a contact. The following types can be distinguished in the buying center (Webster/Wind) as a hybrid organizational form which is not specifically anchored in the organizational structure.

The *gatekeeper* is responsible for collecting information, identifying purchasing alternatives which come into consideration and thus preparing the decision. Information that cannot pass this gatekeeper does not even reach the closer assessment. It is therefore highly important for suppliers to ensure that promotional information forming the basis for decision-making actually reaches the buying center. The gatekeeper function is often performed by a staff unit, but this can also be the secretariat.

The *decider* takes over the final selection. This is usually a person in a leading position with positional power, who sanctions the work of the committee with his vote. Depending on the degree of interference in the operational level, he or she exercises more or less formal influence on the procurement decision. The decider issues the purchase approval, disposes of and manages his own budget, can release funds and has veto power. The decision-maker generally focuses on the effects of procurement on the company and the business result.

The *buyer* handles the pre-selection by putting a project out to tender and inviting potential partners to bid. He also formally concludes the contract, conducts renegotiations in detail and monitors the purchase process, including all preparatory and follow-up work. Often the purchaser also only has an administrative function. Organizationally he belongs to the purchase department and settles routine transactions also on his own.

The *user* initiates the decision-making process by signaling the need. He defines requirement yardstick and availability date. In addition he judges the suitability of the found solution afterwards. Because he is an experienced user with regard to minimum quality, his operational behavior is important for the entire procurement action. He is personally affected by the project, both in case of success and failure. Consequently, he concentrates on fulfilling the function and wants to have concrete benefits. Occasionally the function of the initiator is distinguished from this. This is always the case when the demand requirement does not come from the user himself but from another source.

The *influencer* biases the evaluation of options and the decision in favour of an alternative by means of professional competence. This often involves an external consultant or an employee of an internal service department who is not directly affected by the consequences of the decision and can therefore make an allegedly unprejudiced assessment.

It is usually problematic that the persons belonging to the individual functions cannot be identified in advance and their actual share of the decision remains blurred, although this information is of the utmost importance for the conception and also the choice of media in marketing communication. A rather rational decision making process is generally assumed, although this is doubtful in practice.

Role understanding

Different views of roles can be observed in B-t-b decisions. The Promoter-Opponent concept (Witte) distinguishes between people who support innovative purchasing decisions against technological, economical and environmental resistance and those who want to block them, either because of barriers of will or for ideological, factual or personal reasons. The former are promoters, i. e. people who promote change, the latter opponents, i. e. people who hinder, delay or at least fractionate change.

Both groups rely on certain positions. *Power promoters* have decision-making power due to their hierarchical position in the organization. They are usually internally legitimized to conclude binding contracts. They can thus significantly influence processes by means of orders, sanctions against obstructors and support of driving forces in direction and speed. They are less concerned with technical and organizational details than with their effects on the company as a whole.

Specialist promoters, regardless of their hierarchical position, are characterized by specific expertise. They therefore influence decisions based on their technical legitimacy. Specialist promoters are typically located in the middle management.

Occasionally, a further distinction in form of *process promoters* is made, who ensure that decisions are implemented in the organization. These persons are very familiar with the processes inside the company and use this knowledge to influence the enforcement of the decision there.

Promoters are people who take the initiative, get involved and do not just fulfill their duty with prudence and composure and observe all relevant regulations.

Rarely do power and specialist/process promoters appear in personal union. More often, however, they appear as a team, which gives them a special effectiveness.

Opponents stand in contrast to this. They inhibit the first acquisition of new purchase objects or sources just as promoters enforce them. Analogously to these one differentiates *power opponents*, thus persons, who obstruct decisions by power basis, possible is this as

- rewarding power through the ability to promote loyal individuals,
- punishing power through negative sanction for possibly disloyal persons,
- legitimacy power over hierarchical authority towards employees,
- identification power through informal persuasion of others,
- expert power by withholding or granting necessary knowledge.

Specialist opponents are persons who hinder decisions by means of specialist knowledge, this is made possible by

- training which is particularly suitable for the procurement project and offers a knowledge advantage,
- professional experience, which is closely related to the procurement project and creates an experience advantage,
- assignment of specific tasks within the company so that domain knowledge is created,
- relevant knowledge from outside the company, e. g. from hobbies, part-time work, secondment, etc.

Finally, *process opponents* are people who hinder decisions by knowing internal organizational processes. This results from

- long retention period in the company with high transparency of the structural and process organization,
- multiple job rotations, so that different areas in the company are known and familiar,
- informal voting among colleagues who are affected by the procurement decision,
- engagement in internal or external interest groups with negative expectations.

Essentially, however, the influence of the individual parties involved in the decision remains hidden. It probably also changes from case to case, or the attitudes and behavior of the actors concerned are not always consistent. Clearly, there are cases where attitude and behavior are supportive. These are reliable promoters. And also those in which attitude and behavior are disabling. These are clear opponents. However, the following cases are difficult to assess:

- *Covered opponents* with an obstructive attitude, but at the same time supportive behavior. These are people who give the impression that they support an upcoming decision, but actually hinder it. Because of this "camouflage" these persons are difficult to identify.
- *Hidden promoters* with a supportive attitude but at the same time disabling behavior. These are people who support a pending decision, but do not consider it opportune to report it to the outside world. Therefore, they cannot easily be identified and promotionally contacted as supporters.

Innovator types

In the special case of innovations, the reaction concept distinguishes between the prototypes of the clarifier and the simplifier. These innovations relate to both new suppliers for the company and new products or processes. Therefore, there is both sales relevance in the acquisition of new customers as well as sales preparation with a product launch.

The "fact-decomposing" *clarifier* (Cox) is interested in as much information as possible for his decision, which he then sifts and processes to arrive at a well-founded result. He is interested in the most complete and rounded assessment possible of the solution offered for himself. All aspects relevant for the application in the company are examined in order to reduce the decision risk. Therefore a detailed, meaningful address is important.

The "image-collecting" *simplifier*, on the other hand, is immediately interested in condensed information which is easy for him to process. He does not depend on the completeness of his information status, but only on the presentation of key data as information chunks, which are considered important and allow an overall impression of the options offered. For this reason, the benefits of using the innovation should be emphasized on each contact.

As a mixed type there is the *reaction neutral*, to whom a balanced relation of selectively deepening information with simultaneous preservation of an overall overview is important.

It is significant that the same arguments which are of the highest interest to the clarifier, namely detailed information on data, facts, figures, bore the simplifier. And vice versa, those arguments which are highly interesting for the simplifier are far too general for the clarifier. It is therefore important to clarify which type of respondent is assumed to be the target person in order to adjust the advertising argumentation accordingly.

3.1.2 Consumer target groups

To characterize private target groups a large number of criteria are common, which hereinafter will be clarified (*see figure 18: Private target group demarcations*).

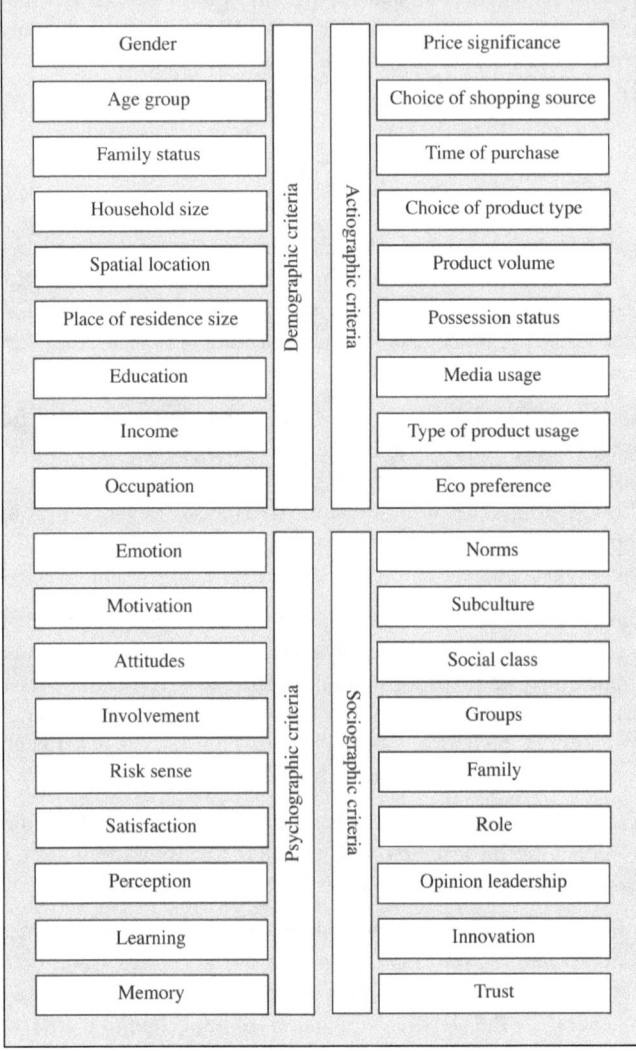

Fig. 18: Private target group demarcations

3.1.2.1 Demographic demarcations

In the B-t-c sector, demographic, actiographic, psychographic an sociographic criteria are considered for target group demarcation. Demographic criteria are those which are objectively recognizable in a person from the outside or can be specifically recorded by collecting data from that person. The following are examples of such criteria.

The starting point for segmentation by *gender* is that there are gender-specific purchasing decisions. That is, those which men make independently as well as purchase decisions which women make independently. This applies to gender-specific products such as razors, body care products, clothing, etc. However, it must be taken into account that gender-specific behavior is increasingly disintegrating; men adopt feminine values, women masculine ones. In same-gender partnerships, the specific behavior dissolves anyway. In many cases, gender-specific segmentation is also prohibited, e. g. unisex health insurance rates, or is considered discriminatory, e. g. product-unspecific erotic advertising.

In the case of segmentation according to *age group*, it is assumed that the relevance of products for consumers depends primarily on their age. Examples are toys, OTC/over the counter drugs, pharmaceuticals, etc. In this context, especially "best agers" gain relevance due to generative changes. First of all, they are many in the baby boomer generation and enjoy a longer life expectancy, secondly they have considerable free purchasing power, e. g. still solid retirement pensions, less purchasing needs, and thirdly they are also willing to spend this purchasing power on themselves instead of saving, e. g. childlessness, well supplied children, held back demand. However, addressing this segment is problematic because biological and mental age diverge. Best agers feel significantly younger and are objectively fitter than according to their calendar date. In this respect, a high degree of sensitivity is required.

The starting point for the segmentation by *family status* is the assumption that there are male-dominated, female-dominated and family-related purchasing decisions within the family. Male-dominated decisions concern products which are shared within the family/community but fall within the traditional male competence, e. g. insurances, investments, automobiles, and women-dominated decisions concerning products which fall within the traditional household competence, e. g. household goods, food, decoration. In addition, there are products decided by the family community, mostly larger, expensive, durable purchases such as real estate property, vacation travel, private school. However, this traditional family model is dissolving, both in terms of structure and time stock. In addition, children influence the decisions to buy products which affect them, such as game consoles and the like.

The segmentation according to *number of children/household size* is based on the consideration that many products are increasingly decided by children alone, for example in the context of increasing pocket money/gifts of money or at least strongly influenced, for example, technical consumer goods such as telecommunications equipment, computer games, leisure activities, etc. However, the proportion of households without children is also growing, as it is unfortunately still difficult for women in particular to reconcile children and work. To this extent, the number of children per household is decreasing and the parent's age at which children are first born is increasing.

In the context of segmentation by geography, purchasing decisions are considered to be influenced by *spatial location*. For example, the consumption of fish is more pronounced in northern Germany, whereas the consumption of pasta is more pronounced in southern Germany. This results in geographical segments. This is even more true in an international context. There are two hypotheses. One alternative states that the marketing conditions are converging more and more. According to the *generalization* hypothesis, geographically based segments would be a temporary phenomenon and would dissolve of their own accord. The other alternative states that the marketing conditions are becoming more and more fractional, not only across borders, i.e. the differences are not only present, but even increase which follows the *focusing* hypothesis. Then there would be good reasons for a geographical segmentation. Both hypotheses can be partially confirmed, but it depends on the situation, which one applies in the individual case (see below).

The segmentation by *place of residence size* is based on the assumption that purchasing decisions are different in urban areas than in rural ones. This can be confirmed empirically in many cases, although moderating variables such as education, income, occupation, etc. have an effect. The retail landscape in urban vs. rural areas has a further influence. However, these differences are levelling out in view of the increasing spread of e-commerce, which can be used almost independently of territory. An example of segmentation is the rates of motor vehicle liability insurance. These are more expensive in urban areas than in rural ones because the probability of accidents is higher there.

The segmentation by *education* can be used as a criterion on its own or combined with occupation/income. On the one hand, this will probably be based on the promotion of "smarter" products, on the other hand on freely available purchasing power. The former has an influence on the advertising of products, the latter on their design. The freely available/discretionary purchasing power is calculated after deducting all fixed expenditures from the available/disposable purchasing power. It has been observed here for years that this hardly changes in real terms. Rather, a money illusion is common. However, certain products are restricted according to educational level, e.g. student subscriptions. In the context of educational "escalation", however, this criterion is becoming less and less differentiating. For example, the proportion of high school graduates is just under 50% of an age cohort, while the proportion of university graduates is already just under 40%. The social goal is also to increase both rates significantly (Bologna agreement).

Income is seen as an important criterion for segmentation. This refers to the disposable/discretionary purchasing power after deducting all taxes and duties from gross income and after adding all allowances and transfer payments. This determines not only the quantity of possible purchases, but also the quality of the product types. In Germany, there is a tendency to see a spread of extreme values between the super-rich, mainly by property income, and the poor because of lack of retirement income, single parent status, strokes of fate on the one hand and a thinning of the middle class on the other. The latter is caused by the capping effect of taxes and contributions on the middle class and social benefits in the context of macroeconomic redistribution. Other influencing factors are the relative propensity to spend which is higher for lower incomes, the spatial distribution as in Germany the west-east and south-north slope, the type of product under consideration, e.g. with possibly saturation effect, etc. Certain products are also restricted by income, e.g. in social housing. The recording of income is problematic. Due to a widespread lack of willingness to provide information and the ability to determine income, this can only be recorded by means of information in surveys, although the reliability of the data is poor, or indirectly by means of indicators in social external classification. Purchasing power can be derived approximately from the income tax statistics of the tax office districts. These recording uncertainties are of considerable importance, especially since income is often used as a segmentation criterion.

The segmentation criterion *occupation* is closely related to education and income. In this respect, it is questionable whether it is suitable as an independent variable, although it often serves as a segmentation criterion because it is comparatively easy to capture. However, the grid used here, such as blue-collar workers, small/medium/upper clerks, self-employed, civil servants, other occupations, is very coarsely knit and does not adequately reflect the differentiation of occupational reality. In addition, access to certain products is also restricted according to occupation, e.g. civil servants' allowances in health insurance.

3.1.2.2 Actiographic demarcations

However, demographic target group descriptions are too general to be able to determine sustainable demarcations in today's differentiated lifestyle societies. It therefore makes more sense to start with purchase decision-oriented criteria, as far as these are available as data master.

The *price significance* refers e.g. to the preference of certain price ranges when purchasing or to the purchase of special offers according to price-performance ratio. The general price interest is promoted by price reductions from manufacture and trade level and also increases by better access of the target persons to information media. This criterion is often met by a certain tonality of address, which often has a disconcerting effect.

The *choice of shopping location* refers, for example, to the preference for certain forms of retail or individual business premises. A polarization can be observed, on the one hand in up market outlets with preference position, in which the service component of the offer is promoted, and on the other hand in down level outlets with price-quantity position, in which the price component is emphasized. Business locations in between have hardly any chance of survival, they are stuck in the middle.

The *time of purchase* refers, for example, to seasonal sales as preferred dates for fashion items. The choice of the pre-season for vacations or subscriptions to publishing products should also be considered. In some cases, income/purchasing power reasons are also decisive. The restrictions to be accepted in this respect are considered by target persons to be minor in view of the benefits they can access. Early adoption of innovations often has a positive effect on the social environment.

The *choice of product type* refers, for example, to the purchase or non-purchase of certain product groups. For example, convertibles are preferred by other buyer segments than jeeps or large-capacity limousines, vegan products by others than meat products, etc. In this respect, target groups can be defined quite clearly. At the same time, however, one often moves in market segments of manageable size. It is also unclear whether the product type selection is to be seen as original or is based on other target group criteria such as age, gender, profession, etc.

The *product volume* refers, for example, to the purchase and consumption volume. Thus, large packs are mainly purchased by intensive users and bulk consumers, while small packs are purchased by extensive users and single households. In this respect, similar intervals between purchases can be given. Possibly the product volume also indicates a partially commercial activity, for example in the case of DIY store products, which are often bought by concealed craftsmen.

The *possession status* refers approximately to real estates, automobiles, gardens, pets, etc. Within these characteristics it can be graded again, e. g. lawn mowers for owners of smaller or larger gardens, pet products for owners of dogs, cats, rodents, etc. This not only refers to the current status, but also to foreseeable status changes. A wide range of secondary statistical sources are available for the ownership status, e. g. official statistical data, geodata.

Media usage refers, for example, to the type and number of media which can be used to address the user and the intensity of their use. Media such as opinion-forming press for the info elite or social networks play an important role. A distinction can be made according to the type of use, e. g. linear and non-linear TV, intensive or extensive internet use. The classic media are obviously among the losers, digital media among the winners.

The *type of product use* refers, for example, to differences in the private or commercial use of one and the same product such as household electricity vs. industrial electricity, diesel fuel vs. heating oil, road salt vs. table salt, etc. In this respect, there may be considerable differences in the response to advertising measures. The distinction is usually based on sovereign control interventions in the market, for example for social reasons or to protect lobby groups.

Eco preference refers to the by now widespread trend for regardful consumption. This results in behavior patterns in various product fields, such as sustainable cultivation, certified clothes, plastic-free packings, etc., but also in the professional business in terms of environment, social, governance (ESG). Especially striking however is the strong trend towards meatless nutrition. Roundabout 10 % of the total population describe themselves as vegetarians, about 1 % as vegans even abstaining from all animal products, like eggs, milk, honey, fish, cheese, etc.

However, labelling on the basis of objective criteria is rapidly losing its importance because it only represents characteristics and not causes. Thus a change from a stratified to a lifestyle society has taken place. This means that groups of people are no longer necessarily united by a similar demography/action, but by an identical lifestyle with heterogeneous characteristics. Only psychographic and sociographic criteria can now take this into account.

3.1.2.3 Psychographic demarcations

Psychographic criteria are based on the personality inventory of private consumers. This offers the possibility for differentiation, especially according to the following elements.

Emotion means activation, which is often a prerequisite for a change of behavior. There are involuntary or arbitrary stimuli, whereby image stimuli are attributed a special activation effect because they are easier to perceive, better understood, have longer retention. Emotion plays a role, for example, in convertibles or sports cars within the car market. Advertising should arouse emotions, but it must not be allowed to overdrive, as this would impair the communication performance.

In general, *motivation* is an energized drive. Primary motives are innate, secondary ones are acquired, instrumental motives are based in the person, extrinsic ones are in their environment. Motives can be conscious or unconscious. Two or more motives can be harmonious or conflicting. For example, motivation often leads to the purchase of additional products by enthusiasts in the field of hobby. Usually a hierarchy of motives in the form of a pyramid of needs (Maslow) is assumed.

Attitudes are opinions about objects and persons. They have a knowledge component, a capability component and an action intention component, but not necessarily a chain of actions. In between lie moderating variables such as purchasing power, availability, price level, etc. The sum of attitudes is called image, whereby self-image and external image are to be distinguished. This supports, for example, the purchase of ecological products out of social responsibility.

(High) *involvement* is the result of an intensive analysis, thorough information gathering and a well-considered decision for a purchase object on the part of the prospective buyer. Frequently, an attempt is made to turn a low-involvement object into a highly-involvement object through advertising, since this has a greater impact. This is seen however often system-critically. Involvement is, among others, decisive for hobby products.

The *perception of risk* results from financial factors such as purchase price, commitment period, etc., functional factors such as quality, features, etc., social factors such as acceptance, profile, etc., and psychological uncertainties such as identification, self-image, etc. These occur before and especially after the purchase as cognitive dissonances and require advertising influence. One way to achieve a desired reduction is for buyers to give preference to certified products or products with test results/return options, etc.

Satisfaction generally arises when the subjective expectation of a product before purchase and the experience of this product after purchase resp. in the case of services also at the time of purchase coincide. Neither enthusiasm nor even more dissatisfaction is tolerable. Satisfaction leads to repurchase, unless constructs such as variety seeking are opposed. Vendor loyalty leads to the preservation of desirable consonance or avoidance of unpleasant dissonance.

Perception always takes place actively by the person, subjectively in his view and selectively in the choice of information. Information chunks bundle stimulus elements onto one stimulus, e.g. logo, key visual, jingle, because otherwise the universe of stimulus elements cannot be mastered. Perception can be conscious, unconscious or, illegitimate, subconscious. It is supported by images, colors, movements, etc. and thus segments media-advertised persons from others.

Learning comes from understanding product messages. Products are often so complicated and complex that advertising is equivalent to a learning situation. This can be due to the nature of the product, but can also be artificially induced in order to achieve a conscious willingness to engage in discussion. However, advertising-based learning is always only possible in combination with entertainment, whereby the question arises as to which element should dominate. Learning is especially important for buyers of products in need of explanation and is achieved, for example, through high contact frequency in the target group.

Memory means the storage of learned contents in order to be able to recall and update them when necessary. Messages which are not anchored in the memory cannot be retrieved or only unreliably retrieved in a concrete buying situation. In this respect, a high message penetration and its grounding at the point of sale/POS are necessary to ensure that the target group makes planned purchases from a manufacturer after problem solving, by product group or by product.

3.1.2.4 Sociographic demarcations

Sociographic criteria are based on the social environment of the demanders. This is a differentiation according. among others, to the following elements.

Norms set framework conditions within a culture and ensure social cohesion through sanctions, positive if adhered to, negative if violated. Norms are codified by law, but are usually unwritten and informally communicated within a culture. They form the "cement" of a society; if they are lost, anarchy prevails, if they are too tight, individual freedom suffers. Buyers may feel more or less committed to these norms, e. g. when buying pirated products, if persons lack purchasing power but the products are highly attractive to their peer group.

The *subculture* divides a society according to ethnic, such as race, religion, nationality, etc., generative, such as children, young people, seniors, etc., and spatial criteria, such as urban center, suburb, rural region, etc. Subcultures show peculiarities in comparison to the prevailing culture, but are predominantly harmonious with it in terms of social order. They close each other off well, so that people there can be separately advertised by providing them with subculturally adequate products, e. g. for kids, for gays, for immigrants.

Social classes divide a society vertically into upper, middle and lower categories. A pyramid shape is implicitly assumed, but in fact an hourglass shape is created. It is conceivable to identify with one's own social class, e. g. workers' ethos, or to approach the social class above ("keep up with the Jones'"). In this respect, buyers of "layer-loyal" products differ from buyers with a "product career" ambition. The permeability of the layers is questionable.

Groups are comparatively homogeneous majorities of persons. Membership groups can be defined by formal acceptance or purely factual membership, e. g. club, family, workforce, whereas reference groups are not, however, give an indication of one's own behavior, whether it is directed toward rapprochement or dismissal. Groups offer orientation, this plays an important role especially for less consolidated persons or if there is a lack of subjective market overview. Examples can be found in the fashion industry, e. g. jeans or sportswear.

The *family* is usually the formative group. Different stages of the family life cycle can be distinguished according to age, marital status, household size, occupation, purchasing power and possessions over time, as well as varying proportions of decision-making depending on the area of competence in female-dominated, male-dominated, jointly, separately. However, the steering effect of the family is increasingly dissolving and informal groups are dominating. A co-evolution of supply with the life cycle can be found, for example, in the financial services offered by banks, insurance companies and building societies.

Roles are assignments of behavioral patterns by society to individuals. Role-consistent behavior is expected, also with regard to consumption. If two or more roles are assumed, conflicts can arise, either due to society's reluctant expectations of a person or as a result of inconsistent own behavioral motives. The role behavior is also expressed in purchasing, e. g. status-underrepresented products vs. status-overrepresented products.

Opinion leaders are persons/organizations which have a multiplying effect on messages in their social environment. They are also often heavy users. However, their identification is either difficult or their integration is expensive. In this respect, a two-step communication process is assumed by the provider, first directly to opinion leaders and only then indirectly to target persons, according to a two steps flow. Both sub-target groups have different message content and forms of address. In modern form, opinion leaders can be found as influencers in social media.

Innovators are persons with low risk aversion. They appear in the early stages of diffusion or even initiate diffusion processes. They form the first adopter category, followed by early followers, early majority, late majority and latecomers. Innovators exhibit personality traits such as low risk aversion, positive attitude towards change, intensive information behavior, etc. They are often opinion leaders and as such receptive to privileged information. It is difficult to identify them, but seems possible by addressing them in special interest media.

Trust means the predictability of a supplier from the perspective of his customers. This is derived from the supplier's reputation in the target group, positive experiences with the supplier, supportive opinions of third parties, etc. In view of the fact that consumers are often overwhelmed by a highly differentiated range of products, trust offers welcome security. The trust in a product/sender is bundled in the brand. Thus, for example, brand buyers differ from buyers of generic goods.

Typology is created by combining the elements of lifestyle, values, activities, interests and opinions. In this respect, psychological and sociological criteria are combined as artificial types (so-called personas), which represent a sufficient number of real persons with similar personality traits. This results in a reduction of complexity, which in turn leads to a more pointed approach. This is often the basis for conception and media planning. Examples are Social milieus/Sinus or Roper consumer styles/GfK (see below).

In recent times, *neurological* target group criteria have become common. These are based on a tripartition of the brain in the brain stem as a balance system for safety, social acceptance, etc., the diencephalon as a dominant system for performance, profiling, etc. and the cerebrum as a stimulus system for inventiveness, variety, etc. Each person has an innate priority of one of these "sub-brains". Messages which address one "sub-brain" simultaneously inhibit the other two. In this respect, a target population can be effectively neurologically segmented. Indicators provide reliable information about brain priority.

3.2 Benefit promise in advertising

The benefit promise concerns the advantage effect from the use of an offer and is of central importance, because it is the equivalent for the amount of money to be used for the purchase. The individual benefits can, by following a means-end laddering, be reduced to a few final benefits *(for context see figure 19: Optional endbenefits)*:

	Internal drivers	External drivers
Security priority	Performance benefit	Trend benefit
Independence priority	Connoisseur's benefit	Prestige benefit

Fig. 19: Optional endbenefits (Source: own chart)

- *Performance benefit* ("There you know what you got"),
- *connoisseur's benefit* ("To be more than it seems"),
- *trend benefit* ("Wanting to belong"),
- *prestige benefit* ("Want to show it to everyone").

This is based on the theory of the means-end-chain. According to this theory, the end benefit results from a successive chain of goals, which in turn serve as a means of achieving higher-level goals. A promotional address is now the more promising, the more highly within the means-end-chain the offer use is anchored.

An example for the awarding of telecommunications lines is the following:

- *Concrete benefits of the offer is fast Internet connection,*
- *abstract offer benefit is information advantage,*
- *personal benefit of the offer is more efficiency at work,*
- *psychosocial benefits is career opportunity,*
- *instrumental benefit of the offer is professional performance,*
- *final offer benefits is self-realization.*

Another, very concise example comes from an American advertising copywriter (N. N.). He reports that in spring he always walked to work in the morning and on his way through Central Park in New York regularly passed a blind beggar who asked for charity with a sign saying "Help the blind". On his way back in the evening, he casually looked in the collection box every now and then and registered an extremely meager yield. One morning, the copywriter approached the blind beggar and asked whether he could actually live on this income. No sooner did he answer him, the people are just hard-hearted. This fate did not let go of the copywriter. The next morning he had made a new sign and persuaded the blind beggar to show it instead of his old sign. In the evening, the copywriter came by again and asked the blind beggar with interest how the daily receipts had developed today. The beggar was thrilled, and countless silver coins were collected in his tin. Curious, he asked the copywriter what he had written on the sign. He enlightened him: "It's spring, and I'm blind."

The benefit is of central importance because it is the superficial equivalent of the amount of money to be sacrificed when purchasing a good. Subordinate arguments have no chance if there is already a lack here. Given the generally high quality of the market offer, almost only additional benefits are considered relevant, i. e. security, individual, social and ideal benefits, because basic benefits are assumed to be consistently fulfilled anyway. Good advertising is characterized by the fact that it always places this benefit in the center of the address and implements it expressively and impressively, but allows the claim to offer to take a back seat.

Example soap Fa

Fa was introduced by Henkel in the early 1950s as a fine soap and by 1958 was already number three on the market. But by 1967, the market share had melted dramatically to 2.5 %.

Fa was positioned as "beauty soap" (fine soap of new style) and "cares for the skin with fragrance and freshness" (claim). The reason why was its moisturizing effect. In the mid-1960s, the brand was still extremely well known, but not very attractive because deodorant and cosmetic soaps had been launched in the meantime and had passed Fa by. Henkel was faced with the choice of either withdrawing Fa from the market without a sound or trying to make a fresh start.

There were two options for a relaunch: either an advertising update of the brand, at that time with the ambitious goal of doubling its market share (i. e. 5 %), or a relaunch of the brand.

Henkel, like all major branded companies, is rather risk-averse and decided on the update option. The contract was awarded to the then very well-known advertising agency TC-E, which also presented the campaign completely finished for approval

The successful deodorant segment was led by "Rexona", "8×4" and "Banner", the no less successful cosmetics segment by "Lux", "Camay", "Palmolive" and "CD". Behind them were suppliers such as Unilever, Colgate and Procter & Gamble.

The deodorant segment had deodorant body care as a benefit in addition to fragrance, and the cosmetics segment had cosmetic skin care in addition to fragrance. The fragrance and freshness segment was occupied by Fa alone, but it stagnated.

A change to deodorant soap or cosmetic soap seemed too risky to the decision-makers, but the mere updating perhaps did not sufficiently exploit the brand's potential.

The idea was therefore to expand the positioning of the brand and thus make it more attractive to experience. In essence, the idea was to combine scent with freshness, i. e. not to offer scent as a generic product property, but to use scent to specifically solidify the freshness component and make it attractive again.

The question remained as to how this could be achieved. The advertising agency came up with the idea of positioning Fa as a fresh soap with limes. The starting point was a souvenir purchase by then creative director Gunter Ott during his then very exotic Caribbean vacation, Royall Lyme, a scented and aftershave soap with natural lime essences.

Henkel, however, had great reservations about this approach, as it would ultimately completely jeopardize Fa's remaining market position. Limes were also completely unknown in Germany and were at best classified as "unripe lemon". And body care products with a lemon fragrance, on the other hand, could only be found in cheap curd soaps. And, and, and. Also the auxiliary argument, limes were straight in the trend in the U.S. as exotic addition, did not sting. Nevertheless, the idea was pursued further and finally led to the groundbreaking Fa campaign.

For this purpose, the instruments communication and product were activated. The core target group was young women between 19 and 39 years of age, modern, open-minded, interested in many different things, fashion-conscious and sporty. The advertising objectives were:

- *Clearly emphasizing the product advantage of limes in the form of a clear message. Credible presentation of the specific product promise of freshness to potential customers. High emotional identification of the target group with the product message. High attention and recall values for the advertising material through concise design. Easy to understand and quickly communicable messages.*

The advertising was implemented using three visual elements (key visual): girl, ocean, lime. The product slogan was: The new Fa with the wild freshness of lime. The actresses were young, sun-tanned, blonde girls, as in the vacation cliché, and should provide identification. The ocean was initially an unlocatable sea and symbolized freshness. And the limes formed the reason why for the promise of freshness.

Magazine ads, outdoor advertising (18/1 posters) and TV spots were used as advertising media. In the latter, the concise and dynamic jingle composed by famous jazz musician Klaus Doldinger played an important role.

An olive-green-sun yellow marbling of the soap bars served as product signalization, which also dramatized the freshness visually. This was difficult to achieve from a production point of view, but it was finally accomplished.

The relaunch took place in 1968, a time of new beginnings, which led to escapism, the escape from everyday routine into attractive dreams (this explains, for example, the enormous success of the "Camel" and "Marlboro" cigarettes launched at that time).

By 1970, Fa was already number two in the market again. Step by step, the mono-brand was developed into an umbrella brand for other products such as bubble bath, Fa Soft and deodorant spray, which were advertised with the same key visuals. In the mid-1970s, however, competitors followed this obvious recipe for success with brands such as "Atlantik" or "Irish Spring".

Fa, however, continued its communication strategy unchanged. The actresses were also allowed to be shown topless, except on Bavarian television. They also dominated the picture more strongly, and the abstract ocean was concretized by the clear Caribbean water of the Seychelles. All in all, one of the success stories of advertising to this day.

Example Cetebe (GSK)

The market for vitamin C preparations is the second largest within the OTC/ over-the-counter drugs market. Powder and effervescent tablets dominate as dosage forms. Cetebe is a high-dose vitamin C preparation with long-term effect, which is offered pharmacy-exclusively. The Cetebe capsules contain "time pearls" which release the vitamin C throughout the day and thus supply the body with vitamin C evenly from morning to evening. This is because excess vitamin C is otherwise immediately excreted by the body via the kidneys and bladder. The "time pearls" have coatings of different thicknesses, so that the stomach acid breaks through them with a time delay and releases the active substance contained in them by retarding preparation. Cetebe was introduced at a high price. No name effervescent tablets were sold in comparable quantities for one tenth of the price.

Since the mid-1990s, the market as a whole has not experienced any increase, and the cetebe business has also stagnated. A significant increase in distribution was no longer possible. However, brand awareness left much to be desired.

As a displacement of the low-price preparations could be ruled out, the market was split into two parts: (cheap) preparations without long-term effect on the one hand and Cetebe with long-term effect on the other. Insofar the argumentation emphasis lay not on the expediency of concentrated vitamin C supply, this is anyway sufficiently well-known, but on the fact that the body exhibits a vitamin C saturation level and surplus supplied vitamin C is immediately again excreted. Only a preparation with long-term effects, such as Cetebe, is therefore able to supply the body with a higher dosage of vitamin C by delivering the overdose in small doses throughout the day. In this way, the supply remains continuously below the saturation level and thus actually benefits the body. At the same time, it is a typical convenience product, as it only needs to be taken once for 24 hours.

This product performance was illustrated by a graphic performance curve over time, side by side between Cetebe and a conventional vitamin C preparation without long-term effect. This product advantage was symbolized by the "capsule watch", i. e. an analogy of the hands of a watch through the Cetebe capsule, which in turn contains the "time pearls", and a rotating dial with hour indexes.

The target group were existing users of vitamin C preparations who were to be convinced of the superior product performance of Cetebe compared to the preparation they had been using since then. The main advertising medium was a 21-second spot, plus 4 seconds of mandatory text, at pre-prime and primetime on various TV-stations with reach priority. The advertising agency was Grey.

Sales were significantly increased as a result, the market share rose to over 50%, the supported brand awareness to almost 70%. At the same time, the recommendation rate by doctors and pharmacists increased.

3.3 Style components in advertising

The style component concerns the actual creative design. The following elements are used as design elements (*see figure 20: Style components in advertising*).

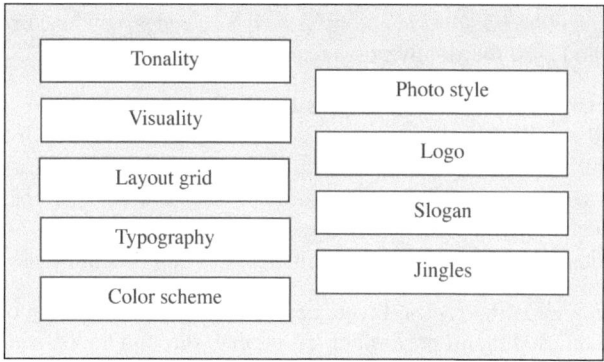

Fig. 20: Style components of advertising

Tonality/Tone of voice is the style of addressing the target persons in the communicator's self-image. There are considerable differences here. Some advertisers address their target persons on a first-name basis, e. g. soft drinks, sportswear, others present themselves in a very distanced way, e. g. technical products, some argue in a strongly convoluted way in order to reinforce competence, especially with low-interest products, others try to remain generally understandable, especially with complex products. In any case, the choice of tonality sends eminently important signals, the use of which requires careful consideration.

Visuality/Key visual is the core image used to illustrate performance in "big pictures". Such pictures should be particularly memorable. A legendary key visual was the apple bite in the "Blend-a-med" campaign. It compressed the complex advertising message of the health of teeth and gums into a single scene which, generally familiar, symbolized on the one hand the awareness of the problem and on the other hand the problem solution through the product itself. In addition, there is usually an auditive support as acoustic device, in this case an oversized loud cracking sound of an apple bite.

The *layout grid* is a concise as well as functional layout according to design-determined principles of order. This supports the recognizability of a sender. Usually this division is fixed in extensive CI booklets (for corporate identity, but better CD for corporate design) and declared binding for all concerned. For this purpose, all common formats and advertising media are "declinated" and described with regard to certain graphic factors such as image/text relation.

Typography concerns the selection and arrangement of fonts according to character set, style, point size, etc. At the latest since the spread of DTP programs (desk-top publishing) in offices and households, even laypersons have become aware that there is a whole range of different character sets, and that these are also available in different cuts and sizes. The same applies to text arrangement. Both elements have a decisive influence on the appearance of advertising media, and should therefore be selected and used with care and stringency, i. e. uniformly determined and used for all advertising appearances.

The *color scheme* includes an impression defined as a corporate color, which can be found on all advertising materials including packaging, trade fair stands, etc. This color is usually specified according to HKS or Pantone color scales or in DTP color management systems. The different meanings of the colors must be taken into account. Even nuance shifts can lead to irritations here. In detail, it is useful to differentiate according to font, image, markup or font parts.

The *photo style* is the typical image perception for a sender or an offer. It supports the unique selling proposition of the product through the optical staging. In most cases, famous photographers are used for this purpose, who create an unmistakable picture atmosphere with their handwriting. One can think of Ben Oyne with his stills, Annie Leibowitz in the Amexco campaign, Peter Lindbergh or Herb Ritts in fashion photography and Reinhard Wolf in food photography or Helmut Newton in people photography. In addition, it can also be a specific pictorial style as a commitment to a typical illustration style which promotes the conciseness of the appearance, or a video style, e. g. director Ari Kaurismäki.

As a memorable sign, the *logo* summarizes the advertiser's sender signal. It can be a word, number, image or combined sign. Its use also has concrete legal consequences as to trademark protection. In this respect, the logo may not be changed unplanned. It is usually found at the bottom right-hand edge of advertising media and is spatially linked to the slogan to create a condensation of advertising message and sender.

The *slogan* is the core statement to the addressee, summarized in one sentence. Catchy, coherent slogans are extremely difficult to find, but provided they are sufficiently penetrated, they become firmly established in people's minds, e.g. Volkswagen, Deutsche Bahn, Esso, Clausthaler.

Jingles serve the additional emotional background of the advertising message. Depending on the type of product, they have a considerable advertising impact, e.g. Intel processor. One might think of the evergreen series of "Levi's 501" ("the original"), the "Langnese" cinema spots ("like ice in the sunshine"), the "Aral" campaign, etc. It is not uncommon for pieces of music from the advertising to become hits, e.g. at "Coke", "Bacardi", which then update the image component of the advertising message with each sound playback in the course of the audio-visual transfer.

3.4 Requirements for good practice advertising

In view of the imponderables of advertising implementation, calls for patent remedies for creativity are constantly being made; however, "good" advertising cannot be standardized in any way. Every advertising statement must rather be developed anew in an original way, because otherwise it does not fit. This is why all patent remedies for creativity are misleading, because "rules for good advertising are crutches for lame creative people" (W. Butter). Nevertheless there are some clues.

3.4.1 Basic principles

Alienation

Good advertising often works by alienating normal situations. Because the everyday is boring and therefore not suitable as an eye catcher. Only the surprising creates attention. In the meantime, the audience is so well versed in dealing with advertising that the exaggeration of the advertising message is reduced to the presumed reality. Here are two spot examples.

A heavy thunderstorm in the night. The little girl lies anxiously awake in her bed. The lightning flashes dangerously, thunder rumbles and she looks for protection. So she grabs her doll and makes her way across the house to the garage. The father looks after his daughter as a precaution. When he doesn't find her in her room, he sets off on a worried search. Finally he finds her in the new Ford Mondeo, because it really provides security.

The big TV show Britain's got Talents, a chubby, only moderately groomed man enters the stage, Paul Potts, a car phone salesman. He is wearing a €50 suit which fits badly, the jacket is too tight, the sleeves are too long. He stands clumsily alone on the huge stage. "What are you here for today, Paul?" is the peers' question. "I just sing an opera," is his short answer. The three jurors look at each other suspiciously. The man sweats, he has bad teeth. "Okay. We're ready when you are." At the same time, you see pictures of people watching the TV show on notebook, desktop or cell phone. Everyone is skeptical, even mocking. Then the music begins. Nessum dorma, the aria of Prince Kalaf from the opera Turandot. Paul Potts starts to sing. And it is a moment of goosebumps, an overwhelming voice, everyone is absolutely thrilled, the audience is raving, some are crying with emotion. His comment: "My dream is to spend my life with what I feel I was born to do". "Life gives you unique moments. It's nice that we share them with others. Deutsche Telekom. Experience what connects".

Reduction

Good advertising usually also means reduction. In other words, the signal range is reduced until nothing can be left out without affecting the transport of the message. On the other hand, almost all advertisers want to communicate each and everything which their product is capable of doing. However, the public's interest in advertising messages, which can be assumed to be low, and the general overload of information stand in the way of this. Therefore, instead of everything, nothing comes across at all. Insofar, single mindedness is required. Here are two spot examples.

Two little boys sit on the steps of a house. They play driving a car, upright hands stretched forward on an imaginary steering wheel, imitating the sound of an engine with their voices. In between, one boy reaches for a likewise imaginary gear stick, interrupts its sound and starts again with a lower tone. The other boy, however, keeps the sound without a shift pause. A text chart appears, pointing to the new Golf with continuously variable direct shift transmission. You see the two boys again. One of them has given up the game in frustration in the meantime, the other one still holds the engine tone, but already visibly strained. The picture of the new VW Golf DSG appears, which is what it is all about. And then you see the two boys again. The boy who has chosen the Golf with continuously variable transmission is getting more and more strained and starts to run red. He can't catch his breath because his car doesn't have any gear shifting breaks, but the power is transmitted constantly from the engine to the drive axle. This is followed by the VW logo.

3.4 Requirements for good practice advertising 91

You can see a dark, exclusive bar, subdued background music, an attractive young woman is sitting at the counter. A well-dressed man sits down next to her, places his car key conspicuously on the counter and casually says: "400 HP, 12 cylinders, 296 topspeed – tomorrow evening 7 p.m.?" She puts a large start key next to it and answers: "10,877 HP, 330 topspeed, tomorrow morning 8.43 a.m. – track 7". Tilting screen, you can see the woman walking along the platform as the driver of an ICE train. The engine shed gate opens, the ICE slowly rolls out. Textchart: Train driver at the railroad: Not a job like any other. 7,500 jobs, 500 professions, apply now. Again tilting screen, the macho is obviously dismayed. To be on the safe side, the woman asks: "Everything OK?"

Addition

The best advertising is the one which does not pretend that everything is in the given presentation, but gives the recipients the opportunity to complete missing parts of the message by adding their own. In this way, a much more sustainable learning and memory effect is achieved than by simply specifying all the information facets. Of course, this effect is extremely difficult to accomplish. Therefore another two spot examples.

A family leaves their house with suitcases packed and walks towards their VW Passat parked in front of it. A small, white dog trots along beside it. The family loads their luggage into the car. The man opens the tailgate and naturally expects the dog to jump in. But the dog trims. It recognizes the Passat Variant TDI and defiantly remains seated. The man calls "Rufus" and points energetically at the car. But the dog remains stoically in its seat. The man takes out a small squeaking toy to lure the dog. But it lies down only dismissively. A text chart appears indicating that the Passat Estate TDI can cover 1,370 km with one tank of fuel without stopping for gas. Of course, the dog has long since realized this and suspects that if it jumps there now, it cannot go for more than thousand kilometers. And this is something which should be avoided if possible.

One sees an Austrian village at the turn of the before last century. The villagers have an arduous life in the country. On the village road a Mercedes C-class car from another time is driving. It has the latest brake warning system installed, which detects dangers before they arise. So two girls play, unfamiliar with cars, guilelessly on the village street, the Mercedes approaches and the automatic brake system responds, you can see the indicator lamp on the dashboard lighting up. The children leave the street. A little further on a little boy with black hair pulled into his forehead plays with his wind kite. He is so engrossed that he does not pay attention to the approaching car. The automatic brake system is expected to respond again, but on the contrary, the car accelerates and runs over the little boy. His mother looks on in horror and shouts alarmingly "Adolf!, Adolf!" Then you see the town sign, Braunau am Inn, the birthplace of Adolf Hitler. The new

Mercedes recognizes dangers before they arise. The boy lies dead on the ground in the shape of a swastika. The Mercedes-logo and claim follow.

(However, for understandable political reasons this spot did not go on air, but was only a competition entry).

Trojan horse

After all, good advertising is based on the allegory of the Trojan horse. It is superficially nice to look at, but at its core it is incredibly combative. Above all, this means that entertainment in advertising must by no means be an end in itself, but always only a means to an end, to cleverly package information units which cannot otherwise be effectively conveyed, so that, through the fun of what they perceive, the target persons absorb what they need to know about the product. Also, here are two spot examples.

Late in the evening, a young woman impatiently waits for her husband in her apartment. She kills time. When he finally comes home, he stops embarrassed in the door frame. She looks at him firmly. He apologizes: "Sorry, but I had a car breakdown". She is visibly skeptical and asks back: "With your Mercedes?" He nods affirmatively. Then she slaps him in the face. A text chart appears ("According to ADAC breakdown statistics, a Mercedes only breaks down after more than 1 million kilometers"). Then a second text chart follows ("So come up with something better").

A little red-haired girl jumps playfully through the supermarket. She stops at a hen's egg tray, shaking one egg after the other, expecting a usual surprise. But nothing can be heard. So she looks up expectantly to an angular Edeka shop assistent in a white coat and asks curiously: "What's in there?" Without batting an eyelid, he answers strictly and off the cuff: "13 % protein, calcium, iron and vitamins A, D, B1 and B2". Frightened by this detailed information, the girl takes refuge behind her mother's shopping cart. The shop assistant remains astonished behind. "Edeka, we love food". Logo and jingle follow.

In this context there is always a controversial discussion whether an entertaining form of advertising is a prerequisite for a message to be perceived by target persons or whether this entertainment only covers up the actual message and thus has a counterproductive effect. It seems clear that every advertiser is anxious to make the various amazing capabilities of his product accessible to the demand, but it also seems clear that hardly anyone else is really interested in this. In this respect, an entertaining component in advertising is indispensable to attract the attention and interest of the target persons. However, the form is very important. Entertainment as an end in itself, however popular it may be, is inefficient in advertising because advertising is purpose-bound communication and the purpose of advertising is clearly not to entertain the recipients. Entertainment, however, which helps to better convey the intended message, is highly welcome.

3.4.2 Points of reference

Other necessary, although in as such not sufficient, but widespread conditions for successful advertising are listed below.

Advertising must be *unique and unmistakable* in order to positively differentiate the own offer from the relevant competition. Any possibility of confusion between the communication measures of an advertiser and those of competing advertisers must be excluded as far as possible. Otherwise, advertising means at best unproductive use of funds, at worst, if there is agreement within a product category, even support for direct competition.

Advertising must be *continuous installed*, since only constant, consistent exposure will lead to learning outcomes. In order for the profile of an offer to develop and maintain in competition with all other information which has to be processed daily and is usually far more important, advertising measures must be planned for the long term.

Advertising must convey *content* that is plausible and can be argued interpersonally. It is not enough to offer only aesthetic formalities. At the latest when the target group realizes that there is little substance behind the beautiful façade or something completely different than assumed, the enthusiasm decreases noticeably. In the long run, therefore, only content can captivate.

Above all, advertising must *generate purchase security as equivalent of the amount of money paid*. And the higher the purchase price, the more so. This security is based on trust, which can only be gained if there is no doubt that the product really has the promised, particularly appreciated and consciously sought-after properties.

Advertising has to be *flexible created* in order to respond to current market and demand trends without compulsion. Instead of rigidity, adaptation to current trends is required without losing the typical appearance of the product. This can only be achieved by a step-by-step, well-considered, almost imperceptible approach, so that changes can be made without irritating the target group.

Advertising must focus on a *central message*, because with the widespread assumption of low attention, several messages have little chance of getting across effectively. This core statement is the concentrate of all advertising efforts with the goal of consolidating the type-defining characteristics of an offer with the public, to create a better understanding and memory of the advertising statement.

Advertisement is to if possible *prove the core statement,* because one is inclined to face advertising statements skeptically. The proof must be credible and consistent, i.e. it must really serve to fully support what is claimed. It is also helpful if the evidence is comprehensive and varied.

Advertising must provide a *justification for the choice* of an offer which is convincing and comprehensible. So it must explain why and how the particularly advantageous characteristics of an offer come about. Thus a choice decision becomes interpersonal communicable, because now rational arguments are available instead of hard to convey feelings.

Advertising must *make the benefits of the offer tangible*, because only the promise of benefits encourages people to take an interest in the offer. A desirable offer creates a high attraction on the market. Ultimately, only this benefit is important for the public. The more directly and plausibly it is presented, the higher the appetite to buy and also the willingness to pay.

Advertising must *make the brand clear* as the sender in order to channel the affective attention to the right offer. It must be possible to clearly trace all ascribed positive characteristics back to the name of the sender. Just as people are distinguished from one another by names and not by vague, misleading descriptions, products are only distinguishable and consciously selectable by their brand. In this respect, sender identification is of central importance in advertising.

And finally and above all, advertising must be *eye-catching*, because this is the necessary prerequisite for any successful advertising. In order to penetrate the consciousness of the target persons and to stimulate further engagement with the advertising content, the implementation must be designed in such a way that it stimulates discussion. Only then can the communicative core message be sustainably processed.

For orientation for the fulfilment of the conditions mentioned a simple example: the Bettl.de introduction spot.

This spot truly does not belong to the category of creative highlights. But it is nevertheless exemplary, because it very precisely implements the conditions of successful advertising and thus follows the tradition of, for example, Blend-a-med spots. The problem with mattresses is that they are extremely low interest, which is why the mattress market has been so sleepy for so long. As soon as you show a mattress in its surroundings, this inevitably draws attention away from the product, the same applies e. g. to car tires. Therefore, the scene was kept very reduced, neither color nor tone allowed any distraction. The dialog was precise, in fact high, proven quality at a very low internet-based price. This was followed by the proof from Stiftung Warentest judgement. When another mattress later won the next comparative test, the sales volume achieved in the meantime was taken into account ("best sold"). The permanently displayed logo clarified the sender and the text contained an explicit call to action ("order") for the website visit. A high switching frequency at the best transmission times ensured that nobody missed the message. Bettl became market leader. Here the description of the TV spot:

The scenery is puristic, white hollow, no props, two white covered bedsteads, on the left a bed cover with drapery, on the right the smooth one. On each bed lies a young man, on the left in a slightly cramped, on the right in a relaxed position, on the left the buyer of a common mattress, dressed in gray, on the right the buyer of a Bett1 mattress (dressed in colour). Their dialog is underlaid with a quiet scale melody, it runs for 22 seconds.

The following spartan dialog is created, left begins:

"I bought a new mattress." – "Me too."

"I didn't take the decision lightly." – "I did."

"It cost me a fortune, but... quality has its price." – "The best mattress ever tested costs € 199." (Later: The mattress most sold in Germany only costs 199 €.)

The statement appears as text super, likewise the test seal "Stiftung Warentest" as well as later a stamp with "over 2 million sold".

"Nah, nah, nah." – "Yes."

Off screen: Order now very simply at bett1.de.

4. Media of classical advertising

The classical advertising media of adverts, spots and posters are used as mass media in print, electronic and outdoor advertising. Each category can be subdivided manyfold as shown in the following.

4.1 Advertising material adverts

Print advertising may take place in newspapers, magazines and other print titles as well as directory entries and special forms. These are explained in the following (*for context see figure 21: Characteristics of print advertising*).

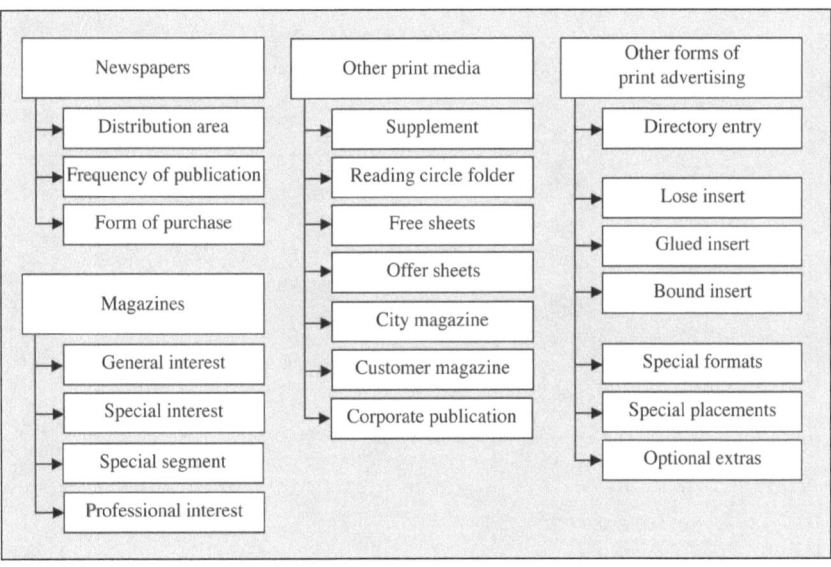

Fig. 21: Characteristics of print advertising

4.1.1 Newspapers

Newspaper advertising has been traditionally the largest media genre in Germany. Daily newspapers are those print titles which are published locally to regionally, are predominantly purchased by subscription usually in single copies and are published regularly on weekdays. In terms of content, these are mostly political-cultural newspapers, although there are also specific subforms such as local newspapers, church newspapers, etc. There are three different newspaper formats:

- Nordic format with eight columns of text (approx. 570 × 400 mm/H × W),
- rhenish format with seven columns of text (approx. 530 × 360 mm/H × W),
- Berlin format with six text columns (approx. 470 × 315 mm/H × W).

The column width is uniformly 45 mm in the advertisement section and 52–70 mm in the text section. The newspaper is usually divided into three "products", the 1st product with national editorial content, the 2nd product with local editorial content and the 3rd product with the advertising section, which is often disparagingly referred to as the "advertising graveyard". For the 1st and 2nd products, minimum formats for adverts are usually specified, and in addition, two- and multi-page text-enclosed adverts are considerably more expensive there, but also benefit from the general greater attention paid to the advertising section. Local advertisers and those who work without an advertising agency are generally granted a local rate reduced by the intermediary commission.

Normally, the sheet area of the newspaper which can be used for printing is limited all around the type area. This leaves a white margin on all four sides, which for technical reasons cannot be printed or can only be printed at great expense. In many cases, the center margin, i. e. the right edge of the left page and the left edge of the right page, can still be used for double-sided panorama ads in the form of fretted printing.

The readership of daily newspapers is usually outdated compared to the local population. Circulation and reach figures are in sharp decline. About 90 % of the content is viewed deliberately, without a sideline; the average reading time is about 40 minutes. Daily newspapers have a high credibility and radiate this with an ever smaller basis on advertisers in their object.

Total editions of newspapers can be limited in their configuration mostly to district or local editions. However, such partial occupancy is always disproportionately expensive, so that it must be examined in each individual case whether full occupancy is not nevertheless more cost-effective, despite the associated misallocation to areas which do not belong to the advertiser's catchment area.

4.1.2 Magazines

Magazines have an important function within the mass media for advertising. The magazine differs from the newspaper mainly in that it appears

- at least once a week, in bound, stapled or stapled processing, with independent cover, with a higher page number, in a smaller format, usually DIN A 4-like, than the newspaper, including a large four-color component, on better paper, mostly at a higher price.

Magazines are available in an almost unmanageable variety of titles. A simple glance into a station pressstore illustrates the market variety, and even at the kiosk around the corner, which by no means carries all the titles freely available for sale, all that remains is a small peephole for the eye and a small reach-through gap for money and goods contact.

In general, different types of journals can be categorized, namely

- *General interest* titles, mainly current affairs magazines, program guides and news magazines, they offer a wide variety of topics in their editorial content, i.e. multithematical and multisectoral,
- *special segment* titles, which address demographically defined reader segments, such as women, parents, children, young people, men, etc., i.e. multithematical and monosectoral,
- *special interest* titles which offer a special coverage of topics in the editorial content, such as needlework, fashion, sports, cars, gardening, society, health, art, etc., i.e. monothematic and multisectoral *(for context see figure 22: Categories of journals)*.

	Mono-thematic contents	Multi-thematic contents
Mono-sectoral contents	Professional interest publication	Special segment publication
Multi-sectoral contents	Special interest publication	General interest publication

Fig. 22: Categories of journals

In addition there are *professional interest* titles such as technical periodicals, monothematic and monosectoral, whose use is job-related and does not originate from private information interest, knowledge need or hobby. These are available for practically every industry, and usually only by subscription. Professional interest titles are industry-oriented, e.g. trade, function-oriented, e.g. sales or topic-oriented, e.g. computer. They can be delivered by alternating mailings according to subject focus, at certain intervals, according to criteria such as professional group, postal code or even unsystematically.

Germany is internationally considered the classic magazine country par excellence. However, this is less to do with the fact that Germans are so well-read, but rather with the fact that the electronic media have been tightly restricted in terms of advertising for decades. However, as there was previously an ever-increasing need for advertisers to access target persons through the media in the course of undiminished economic growth, this demand could only be met mainly through adverts. But it usually makes no sense to fill a print title with advertising alone. Rather, it requires the editorial environment as a reason to buy and read. The proportion of adverts in a print title can hardly be increased permanently beyond 50% without provoking the readers' unwillingness to buy. Since, on the other hand, the scope of print titles is also limited by the copy price, the only chance left was to establish more and more new magazine titles, whose editorial staff could then handle more and more advertising pages. This development has only been reversed since the early 1980s, when the first private television and radio stations were able to go on air. Since then, there has been fierce cut-throat competition between electronic and print media, making the advertising business increasingly difficult.

What's more, the function of general interest titles is now largely taken over by the full-service programs on television, which also report more up-to-date and impressive news. As a result, the circulation of this type of magazine is stagnating. This also applies to the special segment titles. By contrast, circulation figures for special interest titles continue to rise steadily. This is also plausible, since the voluntary or involuntary shorter and shorter working hours lead to more and more spare time, which should be filled. This task is usually performed by a more or less intensively pursued hobby. But to keep up to date with it, a sound information base is required. And this is provided by mostly elaborately designed, special interest titles.

Magazines build up their distribution rather slowly, offer a high reproduction quality, are at least as special interest titles well controllable in their circulation, but have long booking periods, however stand-by booking with a discount is also possible, and are therefore particularly suitable for image-building and learnable message content. Advertising media contact can also be repeated as often as required due to the magazine's characteristic as a statuary medium.

4.1.3 Other print titles

In addition to newspapers and magazines, there are many other print titles which can be considered for use in advertising. *Supplements* are regularly published, thematically specific, illustrated supplements to at least one carrier object as a supplement with additional editorial focal points which are not or not covered in detail in the carrier object. They are free of charge and are regarded by readers as part of the carrier objects. They are classified according to carrier object as magazine and newspaper, publication frequency weekly, monthly, quarterly, editorial topic, relationship between supplement and carrier object, i. e. one or more publishers, one or more carrier objects and target group national, regional, upscale, experts, age, etc. In most cases, these are program supplements, entertainment supplements and specialist title supplements.

Reading circle folders usually supply fixed subscribers on a weekly basis with folders consisting of 6–10 copies of magazines according to individual compilation of the content in a folder. The price is determined by the selection of titles and the topicality of the content. A distinction is made between the first, second, third folder and fourth folder, each one, two or three weeks later than the week of original publication, which become more and more affordable as the time interval between them increases. The folder offers additional advertising possibilities through stickers and inserts.

Free sheets are characterized by the fact that the advertising section predominates. However, the editorial section is becoming increasingly important to the reader. Publishers are responding by expanding the scope, subject matter and quality of their publications. Freesheets are distributed to readers/households free of charge, they are financed exclusively by the income from advertising. The distribution areas are very limited locally, in large cities often even to individual districts. If a reliable, area-wide distribution service is available, a particularly intensive penetration of the area is guaranteed, i. e. freesheets end up in practically every household. They are usually published by the company which also publishes the local daily newspapers and, if necessary, operate the local radio stations. However, the actual use of freesheets is controversial. This is based on the assumption that newspapers delivered free of charge to households are therefore less appreciated and possibly disposed of finally unread. However, advertisements are presumably used intensively by local retailers because of their informative character. Problematic could be also the value impression of the setting, then it is feared that qualitatively high-level offers are pulled down by an unfavorable vicinity ("pork belly ads") in their image.

Offer sheets do completely without an editorial section. But they offer private people the possibility for free insertion. The financing is mainly based on the sales price. Tradespeople can also use these newspapers as advertising media, albeit against payment. The success is considerable. However, the question of the influence of the possibly negative environment, depending on the product category, on the image of the advertiser also arises here.

City magazines have emerged from alternative papers of the scene or pure event calendars and have newspaper character. They are partly distributed free of charge. The editorial content consists mainly of local reporting, reviews of films, books, DVDs, announcements of events, etc., which are relevant to young, rather critical target groups. For advertisers which offer corresponding products, this offers the possibility of a very targeted, authentic media contact. The situation is similar with (professional) school and student magazines. Typical examples are Prinz (10 local editions), Fritz (13 local editions), Coolibri (3 local editions) or Marabo (Ruhr area).

Customer magazines are obtained by retailers against payment, but are passed on to their customers free of charge as a service.

It has to be thought of titles like:

- *Pharmacy review, Day + Night, Family + Food, Health journal, Paperback magazine, Lucullus/Butcher post, Shoe service magazine, Neuform courier, Clivia, Baby and the first years of life, Baker flower, Diabetic guide, Health, Household journal, Journal for perfect household, New pharmacy illustrated/Health journal, New health, Guide from your pharmacy/Amphora, Senior citizen guide.*

These reach considerable circulation figures and have usually councellor function and attain thus an enormous spreading.

With *corporate publications* in form of magazines is to be thought of e. g. Lufthansa Magazin, DB mobil, Gazette (Swissair) or CEO (PwC). These titles are mainly used for relationship management and usually publish high-quality, confidence-building information about the sender and his products/services. In some cases, it has been possible to offer them for a fee, e. g. Room/Ikea, in others they are distributed only to interest groups, mostly via newsletters. They are often used for sales promotion, cross-selling between company services and cooperating partners.

All titles are published regularly, often at longer intervals. They are financed by advertising and commissions from tie-in activities with partners. The editorial work requires professional handling. Other special title groups include denominational papers, association papers, etc.

4.1.4 Directory entries

Entries in directories are mainly entries in residents' address books, official and local telephone directories, branch telephone directories, etc., namely those which go beyond the mere minimum entry and represent informative additions or advertisements. Advertising is possible there on the cover pages and by highlighting in the directory in bold. In addition, extended entries are possible as a supplement to the minimum entry, e. g. on headers and footers. Users of these directories are both business people and private individuals looking for specific factual information. In this respect, entries in these directories have a high attention effect. In addition, the market significance of the provider behind the entry is often deduced from the conspicuousness of his entry. General advantages lie in always high contact numbers and ranges of coverage, the long edition duration as constant reference book, the favorable price performance ratio and the absolute inexpensiveness. Of disadvantage are the limitation of the advertising space and the lack of topicality, which makes the medium rather inflexible. Moreover it has become obsolete.

4.1.5 Special forms of print advertising

Besides adverts, other forms of print advertising are also possible. The *lose insert* is attached loose to a carrier object. Format and weight restrictions resulting from the general terms and conditions of business of the publishers must be observed, as well as higher postal charges for the subscription circulation share resulting from the tariff of the advertising medium. A distinction must be made between editorial supplements, which are available for advertising, and advertising supplements, which are used by a single advertiser and are additionally produced by the publisher or delivered to him ready for use.

The *glued insert* is attached to an advertisement page, also as a sample, in such a way that it can be detached by interested parties and used, for example, to request information or products in a store or by postal delivery. Tip-on cards are dot-glued to a free carrier ad, and designed tip-in cards are additionally integrated into the print motif underneath. Their importance however is decreasing.

The *bound insert* is firmly attached to the carrier object and can be delivered to the publisher ready for use, also as brochures. Again, there are format and weight restrictions. Depending on the choice of paper in quality, composition, surface, weight, etc., an editorial impression can be achieved, but in this case, the addition "advertisement" is required if there is a risk of confusion.

In order to achieve increased attention, special forms of advertising in print can also be used. *Special formats* refer to all formats which are not rectangular but are otherwise geometrical flex format advertisements, e. g. L-shaped. Also conceivable are two or more ads on one page as chessboard ads. In both cases, advertisers can benefit from the presumably increased attention of readers for such special formats. Adverts, which may give the impression of editorial work to the unbiased reader, must be clearly marked "advertisement". In addition, special formats such as cover gatefold with a fold-out page in the magazine cover, inside gatefold with an inside fold-out page, inside rolling gatefold with an one-sided fold-out or french door with a half pages fold-out are also possible.

Special placements refer to all places in an advertising medium which are expected to attract special attention. In most cases this refers to placements on the front page as a title scoop or in the title header of the press medium. However, special placements in relation to the editorial office are also conceivable, such as in the text section of a newspaper, depending on the minimum format, usually 1/4 page, or enclosed by text all around as island ads or enclosed by text on two sides as corner field ads. It is worthwhile to arrange a constant special placement with the publisher and to fill it regularly.

Optional extras affect all colors which are not produced as part of the four-color set, but are additionally printed as a 5th or additional color. However, this is quite costly and therefore rarely worthwhile. A distinction must be made between additional colors, which are generated within the four-color set from one or two colors to increase the attention effect of a black-and-white ad (b/w). This also entails additional costs of approx. 30% per color compared to b/w. Spot colors are used to highlight areas or elements in adverts. Other optional extras include scented coatings, glued-on product samples ("sachets"), spot colors, punching and folding, scratch-off fields, etc.

Furthermore the following forms are possible:

- Advertisement sections, i.e. several consecutive pages, possibly with section discount,
- panorama ad running across the center spread of the magazine,
- tunnel ad running across the center gutter not across the full pages, but only part of the page,
- L-ad which is not rectangular, but L-shaped,
- island ad enclosed by editorial content on all four sides,
- satellite ad, i.e. several separate ads on the same page, but usually a minimum volume is required for this,
- title puller as placement on the front page of the advertising medium with a small ad,
- handle corner ad as placement at the bottom right of the right-hand page of the print object, limited in format size,
- flexformat ad, i.e. editorial text runs around the ad, requires special agreement with the publishing house,
- shadowprint, i.e. the ad is placed behind the text,
- china cover, i.e. the booklet has an advertising cover on part of the page,
- closed ad, i.e. the ad is closed on one side and the pages are not cut open,

- multi cover/blister cover with the inclusion of product samples, etc. on the cover page,
- booklet within the booklet as bound-in insert with independent stapling, addressed by name in case of subscription magazines,
- scented varnish ad, which releases scent particles trapped by rubbing,
- metallic ad in gold, silver, copper as fifth special color,
- signal colors/luminous colors as fluorescent paint,
- checkerboard ad with top left and bottom right placement on one page,
- geographical split with two ad motifs in split run according to Nielsen areas,
- mechanical split with two ad motifs alternately in split run over the total circulation,
- Nielsen partial placement only circulated in one/not all Nielsen areas.

4.2 Advertising material spots

Electronic advertising may take place in different forms of television, radio and movie theaters. These are explained in the following (*see figure 23: Characteristics of electronic advertising*).

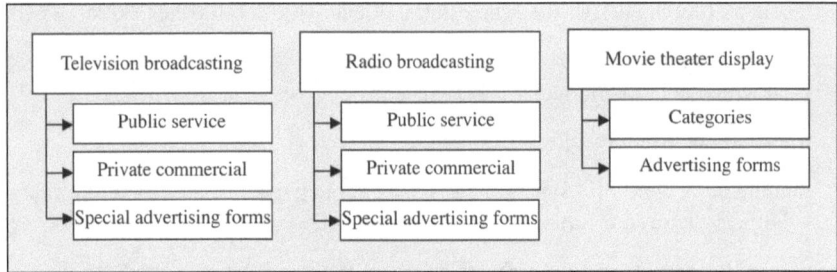

Fig. 23: Characteristics of electronic advertising

4.2.1 Television

TV as an advertising medium is becoming more important and has superseded print because of the superior possibilities to present goods and services especially for daily and daily mutiple private personal or household use.

4.2.1.1 TV-station landscape

Spots take place in television, radio or movie theaters. For decades, television has been of comparatively little importance due to *public service broadcasters* and the state-contractually limited advertising time of 20 minutes per working day, only between 6 a. m. and 8 p. m. But this is gradually changing with the emergence of *private commercial broadcasters*, although it is repeatedly claimed that the shortcoming is due less to a lack of routine than to the German mentality. The first commercial was broadcast in 1956 on 1st German TV-station ARD for the product Persil/Henkel on Bayerischer Rundfunk. The first color commercial was aired in 1967, the first privately-owned TV-station went on air only in 1984 (SAT.1/PKS).

Traditionally, public service broadcasters book all spots for the entire next year until end September of each year. Cancellation and rebooking are only possible to a limited extent after this date. These broadcasters collect all registrations and determine whether or not they exceed the upwardly capped volume of the total possible advertising time. If this is the case, airtime is rationed, but this is mostly unrealistic nowadays. This results in a predetermined placement in advertising blocks, with exclusion of competition being promised per block. A rebooking is then only possible to the extent that broadcasting slots become available. If there is no overbooking, which is regularly the case, the wishes of advertisers for specific placements per month, weekday, time of day, commercial block, space can be largely met, at least outside main seasons. ARD and 2nd German TV-station ZDF report considerable unsold advertising time quotas, and even the private commercial broadcasters do not use their whole disposable allotments. In addition, the volume of TV spots is expected to continue to stagnate, if not decline, because their impact is being questioned. Editorial work and advertising must always be separated by visual and auditory signs. Advertising is regularly only permitted in a block, whereby a block consists of at least two spots. The break between program and advertising must be 3 sec. long at least in full picture. The blocks should be at least 20 minutes apart; in live broadcasts, the natural breaks can be used for advertising. The number of breaks however is depending on the length of program.

Private stations are already administratively far more accommodating, because they have to get along completely without broadcasting fees as a state compulsory levy on the possession of equipment in the household and are financed solely by advertising revenue. In the course of increasingly dense networks with distribution via antenna, cable and satellite with actual connection as technical range, a shift from ARD/ZDF to private stations such as RTL, SAT 1, Pro 7 has taken place. This has led to drastically increasing costs for broadcasting. In this respect, criticism of the editorial level of these stations is also misplaced, because private stations, in contrast to public broadcasting, do not have a programming mandate but rather an advertising mandate, i. e. program is necessary to fill the breaks between advertising blocks as stipulated in the state treaty. The advertising share is limited to 20 % of the broadcasting time, i. e. to twelve minutes per hour. The placement of the spots can largely be agreed individually and at short notice up to two days before broadcasting, whereby the order of bookings is taken as a basis for the surcharge. The rating values of the viewer research already show the absolute and relative viewing participation on the day following the broadcast. If an owner's private stations have a market share of more than 30%, they should cede broadcasting time to third parties in order to ensure diversity, although the calculation of the market share basis is disputed. In fact, however, a duopoly has emerged, with the Bertelsmann group on the one hand mainly with RTL, RTL II, Super RTL, n-tv, Vox and the Permira/KKR group (formerly Kirch), which is somewhat larger in terms of advertising volume, on the other with mainly SAT 1, ProSieben, Welt, Kabel 1, Sixx, etc. Together these account for approx. 80% of the TV advertising market, ARD/ZDF hardly play any role at all. Currently, the following stations, among others, are on-air in Germany:

- public service-TV:
  - through full programs: 3sat, arte, BR, Das Erste, hr, MDR, NDR, Radio Bremen, rbb, SR, SWR, WDR, ZDF,
  - through divisional programs: ARD-alpha, KiKa, One, Phoenix, tagesschau24, ZDF Info, ZDF neo.
- private commercial-TV:
  - through general programs: dctp, DMAX, kabel eins, ProSieben, RTL II, RTL, SAT1, Vox,
  - by special interest channels (selection): Anixe, Astro, Bible, Disney Channel, ERF, Eurosport 1, HOPE Channel, kabel eins doku, MTV, n-tv, N24 Doku, NITRO, ProSieben MAXX, RTL plus, SAT.1 Gold, sixx, Sky Sport News, spiegel.tv, SPORT1, Super RTL, Tele 5, TLC, TOGGO, Viva, Welt, etc.,
  - through pay TV channels, teleshopping channels, channels with foreign license.

The advantage of ARD lies in the regionalization of the eleven programs, which can only be imperfectly compensated for by local windows of private stations and conurbation-TV. The disadvantage, however, is the relatively high proportion of demand-inactive, very old or young viewers. This is due to the airtime of advertising alone. Late in the afternoon and early in the evening, when advertising is permitted by public broadcasters, target groups with purchasing power are generally still busy earning or at least spending money, are on their way home from work or doing their housework because they have just come home. In any case, they mostly have no leisure time to watch animating commercials. This is rather true for pensioners, students, unemployed, etc., who in turn lack purchasing power. This is also the reason for the demand for the fall of the 20.00 o'clock limit on ARD and ZDF. This has already been achieved implicitly today, through patronage broadcasts in the opening and closing credits of editorial contributions, even on Sundays and public holidays. The ban on certain interrupt advertising has

4.2 Advertising material spots

also been softened, e. g. commercial breaks between "Heute" and "Heute Wetter", as has the separation of advertising from the program for at least three seconds to fill the picture, e. g. "Best minute" newsreel clock. Short spots have a higher price per second as dysproportional tariffing.

Television advertising thrives on the combination of moving pictures with background sound. This increases both the impression and the memorability. However, block advertising leads to unwanted interference, i. e. spots with a high impact are superimposed over spots with a low impact which are broadcast in the same advertising block and are close to the time period. Furthermore, television advertising as a transitory medium is time-bound to the broadcast, so that a repetition or temporal shift of perception is not possible.

The number of channels which can be received terrestrially, i. e. via *antenna*, wired bound i. e. via *cable*, and orbitally, i. e. via *satellite*, is already enormous. Since the total time for television use has not increased significantly, it is divided among more and more channels, with the consequence that the viewing time per channel shrinks, and thus the chance of reaching the target persons switched on there. The competition between advertising media is increasing considerably, since digital television is offering dozens of new, largely ad-free channels. The consequence is that the advertising volume per station must be further increased in order to reach any significant target groups at all. The consequence of this is that viewers resist this excess of advertising influence by evading. Zapping means the deliberate switching off of a channel with the beginning of the commercial break there by remote control, skipping the automatic hop of commercial breaks during the recording of programs and flipping the fast switching through of channels on the stalk for more and more spectacular programs. In addition, there are numerous secondary activities which distract attention (so-called mental zapping).

It may therefore be assumed in future that rating-related spot costs will be incurred, which are calculated on the basis of the reach data determined by audience research. The price/performance ratio will remain more or less constant; high ratings mean high tariff prices, which are, however, justified because of many viewers, and vice versa. To that extent only a minimum tariff price is firmly computed, the remainder is performance-based. If minimum range values are not kept, an appropriate number of free compensation spots takes place as it is already presently practised. For planning reasons the ratings can be segmented demographically according to household size, gender, age group, schooling, net household income and occupation.

108   4. Media of classical advertising

4.2.1.2 Channel graduation

The television programs can be classified according to different aspects (*see figure 24: Types of TV broadcasting*):

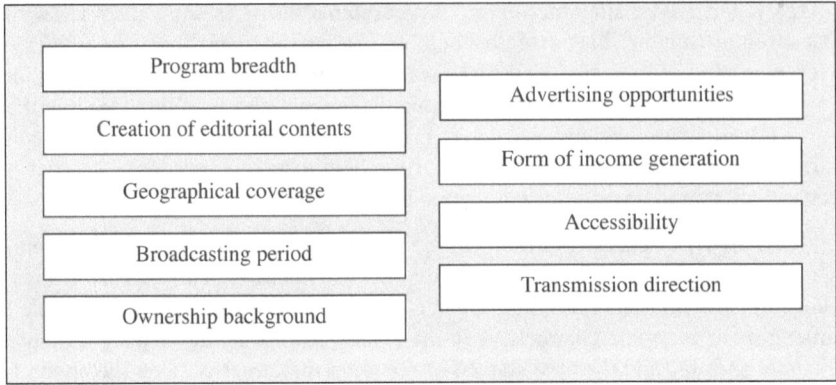

Fig. 24: Types of TV broadcasting

- In terms of *program breadth*, there are full programs which follow the proven pattern of current affairs magazines, and special interest programs which follow the pattern of special interest titles, e. g. Welt, n-tv, DSF.

- As to the *editorial content*, there are in-house programs which are produced by the broadcaster itself, bought-in programs which are purchased from third parties with a certain amount of lead time, and sheathed programs which are pre-produced for third parties and are used several times in parallel.

- According to *geographical coverage*, a distinction is made between international programs which are broadcast across national borders and into which country-specific "windows" can be latched, e. g. MTV, national programs which are only broadcast within the national borders but can also be received in foreign areas close to the borders, regional programs which are broadcast for the inhabitants of one part of the country, e. g. III.-ARD programs, and local programs which are even more limited in geographical terms, e. g. metropolitan area TV.

- A distinction with regard to the *broadcasting period* can be made between full-time programs, which are broadcast around the clock, and part-time programs, which are only broadcast on a daily basis.

- According to *ownership*, there are public-law institutions with sovereign sponsorship and control, for which broadcasting fees must be paid in the case of technical reception, and private commercial stations, which belong to private legal or natural persons and require a public broadcasting permit and frequency allocation for operation.

- According to the *advertising opportunities*, there are ad-free stations which are financed exclusively from licence fee income as pay-TV, ad-financed stations which are financed exclusively from advertising income as free-TV, and dual/mixed forms which are financed both from broadcasting fees and advertising income, e. g. ARD/ZDF.

- According to the *form of income generation*, there are fee-financed programs for which only the reception possibility obliges to pay the fees, and contribution-financed programs which are time-dependent fixed charged as pay per channel, e. g. Premiere, or usage-dependent variable charged only with registration as pay per view. The usage can be determined by the broadcaster through a program framework, can be individually arranged in terms of time as video on demand or can be repeated in narrow time intervals as video near demand.

- As to *accessibility*, there are public programs which are generally accessible, and non-public programs which are directed to an auditorium limited in time and/or space, e. g. on-board TV, hotel-TV, POS-TV.

- Finally, with regard to the *transmission direction*, a distinction can be made between programs with one-way communication, as is still common today, and those with two-way communication as interactive-TV, which allow a feedback by means of camera setting, product ordering or requesting advertising material, etc.

With *interactive-TV*, signal reception takes place via open and closed networks by means of a settop box which can be activated according to internet protocol. A closed circle of subscribed users is provided with a fixed program offering with high technical quality via broadband network against payment, e. g. Magenta-TV, WaipuTV, Joyn, while I-TV makes any program content open and freely available on the network via streaming. The distribution can take place from a central server or in the peer-to-peer principle. Use is possible on individual or unicast demand or near demand as multicast or cyclic service. The business model is based on subscription fees or revenues from combined advertising. Mobile devices are increasingly being considered as end devices.

4.2.1.3 Special forms of TV advertising

Special forms of TV-advertising include all forms which take place outside the regular advertising blocks originally reserved for advertising. Due to the large number of incidences of these special forms of TV advertising, only such a negative definition is possible, but no positive definition.

The reasons for the use of special forms of TV advertising lie in particular in the aspects of competition, attention and legal framework. Regarding the legal framework, "regular" spot advertising is restrictively defined by state treaty provisions. However, two important requirements have been abandoned over the course of time, which have given broadcasters considerable room for maneuver.

Firstly, the requirement that advertising must always take place in a block of two or more spots, and secondly the requirement that all advertising must be visually and acoustically separated from the program surrounding it. The other requirements, however, remain unchanged, in particular the requirement to separate program and advertising, the obligation to clearly label advertising, the requirement of fairness, as no misleading about the type of program, and the prohibition of interference by advertisers with the program content.

It is known from advertising blocks that they often lead to interruptions in or withdrawal from television use by spectators. In this respect, the attention for commercial breaks remains limited. However, since advertisers depend on the attention effect of television advertising to assert their products and since this implies ever higher costs, they have a strong interest in finding ways to shift the use of the program to the broadcast of advertising. At present, this seems to be possible only outside the regular advertising blocks.

The exemption from the obligation to broadcast advertising blocks also relieves advertisers of interference effects, because otherwise the spots within an advertising block not only compete with the preceding or subsequent program, but also with each other.

The special forms of TV advertising can be divided into different areas, such as program sponsoring, split screen, station-specific advertising formats and cross-spot advertising formats, as well as on-air promotions (*see figure 25: Special forms of TV advertising*).

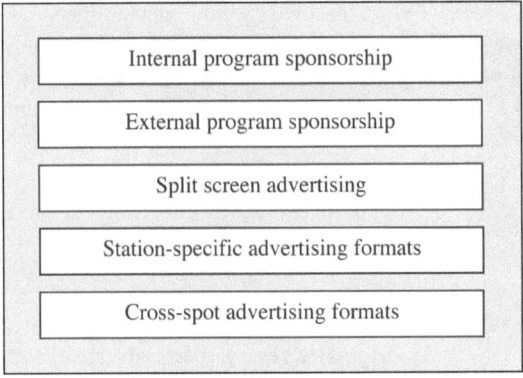

Fig. 25: Special forms of TV advertising

Program sponsorship

Program sponsorship is understood to be the contribution of a natural or legal person or an association of persons not involved in broadcasting activities or the production of audiovisual works to direct or indirect financing of a program in order to promote their company name, their brand, the image of the person/association, their activity or their services (based on Bruhn). A distinction must be made here according to whether the sponsor exerts influence on the editorial content as internal program sponsoring or does not exert any influence on it as external program sponsoring.

Internal program sponsoring has mainly the form of game shows. This also involves fine-tuning program content and placements according to the wishes of the sponsor. Gameshows must be marked with the addition "permanent advertising".

In the case of *external* program sponsorship, the sponsor's reference can consist of the name of the sponsor, the company emblem or the brand. Full video is also permitted. The sponsor notice must be short, it may only last until the external financing is clearly visible, usually no longer than seven seconds. Neither the picture nor the sound may refer to special advantages or features of the product. This is because sponsored programs must not encourage the purchase of a sponsor's product or the use of his services. News and programs on political events are not allowed to be sponsored, but weather reports may be sponsored, e. g. ZDF and Union Investment. Political, ideological or religious associations are not allowed to sponsor. Nor may products for which advertising is prohibited appear as sponsors. This means that manufacturers of cigarettes or other tobacco products are barred from acting as sponsors.

Program sponsoring is possible as exclusive sponsoring or as co-sponsoring, i. e. in association with one or more other sponsors, e. g. Champions League. It is also possible to sponsor several programs in succession, e. g. "Kulmbacher Filmnächte". Public broadcasters are legally equivalent to private commercial broadcasters.

Moreover, it is questionable whether the term program sponsoring is applicable in a definitional sense, because sponsoring is a barter transaction of money or material resources against the public, whereas the forms of advertising usually referred to as program sponsoring mean the normal purchase of advertising, albeit in special forms. In this respect, the term patronage is probably more pertinent, because here it is not third parties which appear in the media and thus create publicity, as is typical for sponsoring, but the media themselves are paid for the broadcast.

In the case of external program sponsoring, a distinction must be made between numerous forms such as indicative before the beginning of the broadcast, abdicative after the end of the broadcast, reminder before and/or after commercial breaks, program trailer when the program is announced, daily sponsoring or theme sponsoring analogous to the program clock, theme evening sponsoring.

Split screen advertising

With split screen advertising, the screen is divided into two areas, with advertising and program being transmitted simultaneously in one window each. The windows can be set up separately and may overlap in a corner or be set into each other. The best known are certainly the split-screen advertising islands towards the end of the transmission of Formula 1 car races. This allows the viewer's attention to be better drawn to the advertising block.

Partial occupancy of the broadcast image with advertising is permissible if the advertising is clearly optically separated from the rest of the program and marked as advertising. The split-screen advertising shall be credited in full time to the total duration of the spot advertising, regardless of the size of the presentation. This also applies to treadmill advertising. Split screen advertising is not permitted in broadcasts for children and in the transmission of church services.

The advantage is seen in the fact that the parallel transmission of editorial content helps to prevent viewers from wandering off within the advertising blocks. In fact, however, it is doubtful whether this is capable of capturing the viewers' interest. However, the more dominant the program which is actually of interest, the more the advertising message must be pushed back at the same time, which in turn limits the attractiveness for advertisers.

As to the execution one can differentiate between different forms of image splitting, such as sole spot as a single split screen spot, advertising clock before the news, preminder before a split screen, diary combined with program notice, credits advertisement or ticker advertisement.

Station-specific advertising formats

This involves special forms of TV advertising of various kinds, some of which are created exclusively for the station. They are used to offer advertisers unique advertising formats. The most common forms are advertising programs, patronage with naming for the program, insert special advertising, logo morphing, spot premiere, single spot as a one-spot advertising block, TV sweepstakes, notice board or virtual advertising with subsequent insertion of advertising.

Cross-spot advertising formats

These are special advertising forms which have lost their spot character. These include continuous advertising programs and teleshopping:

- A *permanent advertising program* (infomercial/telepromotions/long-run advertising program) is an editorially prepared, independent program section with advertising content, which must be identified as advertising before the start of and during the entire transmission and must be at least 90 seconds long. In the case of continuous advertising programs, the advertising character must be prominently recognizable in the foreground. The advertising must constitute a substantial part of the program. The broadcaster is obliged to clearly distinguish this program from the rest of the program by announcing it as "permanent advertising" before it begins and marking it as such throughout the entire transmission period. For this purpose, the word "permanent advertising" or "commercial" shall be permanently displayed at the edge of the screen. The lettering must stand out clearly from the background of the current program. Permanent advertising for children as target group is not permitted. Permanent advertising programs may also have the character of a regular program and thus have a fixed program position, e. g. in the low-frequency, low-cost night or morning programs.

- *Teleshopping* can take place on independent TV shopping channels like QVC, HOT or as spot advertising on other channels. Teleshopping spots outside the shopping channels must be clearly recognizable as such and clearly distinguished from other parts of the program by optical means. As in advertising, no techniques of subliminal manipulation may be used. Teleshopping windows must be identified visually and acoustically at the beginning and for the entire duration as "advertising program" or "sales program". The costs incurred by the viewer when ordering must be clearly indicated. Like television advertising, teleshopping spots must be inserted between the individual programs as hinged commercials. If the context and character of a program are not affected, the spots can also be inserted into the program as commercial break. Here too, the general legal conditions, such as compliance with the protection of minors and the rights of stakeholders, are a prerequisite. Teleshopping may not encourage minors to conclude purchase, rental or leasing contracts for goods or services. In a program not exclusively devoted to teleshopping, teleshopping windows must last at least 15 minutes without interruption. No more than eight such teleshopping windows may be broadcast per day, which together may not exceed three hours. The quality of teleshopping spots is sometimes doubtful.

4.2.2 Radio

The extensive liberalization of broadcasting at the beginning of the 1980s also led to the emergence of numerous privately owned radio stations which are solely financed by advertising revenues. Due to their technical range through feed-in to cable network, antenna beam and/or terrestrial frequency, their reception is space-bound. Radio has a rather limited suitability as a basic medium for advertising and often receives little attention as background music. In terms of content, simple, appealing messages are suitable for advertising, and in terms of form, atmospheric and lively performances, especially music. Without optics, however, the lasting memory effect is usually missing.

The number of people reached by radio varies considerably according to time of day and day of the week. On weekdays in the morning, families at breakfast and car drivers on their way to work are reached intensively. In the morning, the radio is usually only playing in the background. At lunchtime there is another peak. In the afternoon, pupils are also reached when they are doing their homework. Late in the afternoon there is another intensive reception on the car radio. In the evening the radio is almost completely replaced by the more attractive medium television. Accordingly, the tariff prices for spots fluctuate depending on the time of day occupied, the day of the week and the season. The socio-demographical audience structure according to gender, age, education, profession, household management, net household income, etc. is usually derived from the station's tariff according to surveys in market media analyses.

The spots are usually 15 seconds long, but it is also possible to create optionally longer or shorter ones (every 5 seconds). Advertising is limited to max. 90 min./day on an annual average for public broadcasters and is not permitted after 8 p.m. or on Sundays and public holidays. For private broadcasters, advertising is limited to max. 20 % of daily broadcasting time, including 15 % as pure spot advertising (= max. 288 min./day). It must be broadcast in blocks usually three to four minutes long. Since the creative output of the vast majority of radio commercials remains stuck at a rather low level, a great deal of imagination is required for the design, or, if this is not possible, a large budget, in order to penetrate the perception of a sufficiently large number of listeners according to the law of large numbers.

The mechanics of audio-visual transfer are helpful here. Audio-visual transfer means the phenomenon whereby the image component of commercials which are highly penetrated by TV and cinema is supplemented by the image component of the recipient's mind, even if only the sound component is given ("movie in mind"). This allows a budget-friendly extension of advertising pressure, because after a certain start-up time, cheaper radio spots add the visual component to the overall message.

Just think of the "Intel" logo in your mind, and you can "hear" the corresponding sequence of sounds. The same applies to slogans like "Toyota. Nothing is impossible." Just listening to the Bacardi music alone creates a dream of beach, sun, palm trees, vacations, etc. in the mind.

An increase in attention can be achieved by various special forms of advertising on radio:

- The *patronage* is the recognizable sponsorship of a program by an advertiser with advertising reference mostly at the beginning and at the end of the program, but without direct editorial influence on contents.

- In case of a *sponsor program*, the broadcaster provides the advertiser with broadcasting time for the independent creation of programs, which the advertiser uses for his own purposes in coordination with the editorial concept of the broadcaster following the program format and extensive legal restrictions.

- In a *tandem spot*, two advertising broadcasts are coupled in such a way that a longer spot as full version is followed by a shorter one which refers to it as reminder, with advertising from other providers taking place in between. Likewise, a shorter spot as teaser can be followed by a longer one as full version which it announces.
- The *dialog spot* is a combination of pre-produced content and live announcement by a speaker in the studio or on location.
- In case of the *moderated spot*, there is an introductory announcement to the advertisement by the speaker in the studio before the pre-produced content runs out.
- Many broadcasters also offer the option of combining *editorial content* such as time check, weather report, traffic news, etc. with an advertising announcement.
- *Live advertising* means announcement of the advertising text by the moderator live in the studio, i.e. without pre-produced sound.
- Further possibilities are the integration of the advertising announcement, usually in shortened form, into a telephone promotion, i.e. a live game for listeners with a call-in, or into a promotion game, i.e. a combination of advertising and action on site, usually at the POS, by means of a mobile broadcasting station for live transmissions.

The individual radio stations can be divided into different *radio formats*, in descending order of importance in Germany, as follows

- Adult contemporary (AC) is the most successful radio format, oriented towards the taste of the broad masses, pop standards and current hits, short moderation/service parts, competitions,
- contemporary hit radio (CHR) with current fast chart hits, limited playlist, long music tracks, humorous moderation, low information content, frequent competitions, especially for young people,
- middle of the road (MOR) featuring balanced music and word parts, harmonious melodies, detailed news, sophisticated editorial content, calm moderation, partly by moderator personalities,
- melody with German hits, evergreens, folk music, relaxed moderation, promotions,
- oldies on international or national basis, factual moderation,
- album oriented rock (AOR) featuring rock music, also widely unknown titles, little information, mainly for men,
- classic with popular moderation,
- jazz with well-known titles, sophisticated editorial content, cultivated moderation,
- easy listening offers relaxing, also international music for chilling out, low word share, quiet moderation.

4. Media of classical advertising

For the electronic media TV and radio, *Figure 26* provides an overview of the *structure of important electronic media.*

	Income generation	Formal objective	Content creation	Broadcast character
Public service television	Mixed financing (Fees + advertising revenues)	Fulfillment of state-approved program mandate	Content according to demands of whole society	General interest/ Special interest
Private commercial television	Advertising financing	Profit generation for shareholders	Editorial environment for advertising	General interest/ Special interest
Shopping television	Sales revenues/ Commissions	Profit generation for shareholders	Creation of an animating sales environment	Special segment
Digital (pay-) TV	Subscription fees	Profit generation for shareholders	Content according to subscribers' preferences	Special interest
Public service radio	Mixed financing (Fees + advertising revenues)	Fulfillment of state-approved program mandate	Content according to demands of whole society	Mainly general interest
Private commercial radio	Advertising financing	Profit generation for shareholders	Editorial environment for advertising	Mainly general interest
Digital (pay-) radio	Subscription fees	Profit generation for shareholders	Content according to subscribers' preferences	Special interest

Fig. 26: Structure of important electronic media

4.2.3 Movie theater display

With the revival of film culture, the movie theater has experienced a new upswing as advertising medium. The conditions of perception are excellent, due to the concentrated, oversized reproduction without ambient brightness and largely without distraction. It is particularly popular with people under 40 years of age who are otherwise difficult to reach via classical media.

It is important to note that cinemas can be divided fairly clearly into different target group-specific *categories*:

- Family cinemas have a wide range of programs (so-called middle of the road),
- action cinemas are mainly located in large cities and are preferred by male youth,
- studio cinemas show sophisticated, international films which fits with older audience,
- art cinemas are theatrical in character and are therefore located above the studio cinemas (older audience with better income),
- program cinemas show frequently changing programs and are mainly located in large cities,
- sex cinemas show a program which is not suitable for young people,
- multiplex cinemas offer more than seven screens under one roof,
- cityplex cinemas with three to six screens under one roof,
- $1 cinemas for films shortly before video exploitation and therefore at low admission prices,
- IMAX cinemas with particularly high reproduction quality in picture and sound.

However, these distinctions are becoming increasingly blurred. This is because new formats in large cities are cinemas with gastronomy, entertainment, etc. Program-independent there are also:

- Drive-in cinemas with parking lot projection,
- cinemas with comfortable restaurant atmosphere,
- smoking cinemas which are very rare, otherwise smoking is prohibited in the cinema hall,
- troop cinemas in the immediate vicinity of barracks/soldiers' hostels,
- wandering light games with mobile, changing location.

As *advertising forms* in the film theater different ones come into consideration:

- Cinema spot up to 30 sec.: The running time is four consecutive weeks, the costs are billed to the second. The minimum length of spots is 13 seconds, for which a digital master is supplied. This is copied by distributors for various advertising film credits. A standardized background music or soundless playback is possible, although not common.
- Cinema film with more than 30 sec.: The running time is one cinema week from Thursday to Wednesday, the costs are billed to the second. A digital master is provided for this purpose. In addition, a voluntary self regulation release must be obtained from the distributor.

The cost of cinema advertising is based on the number of viewers in the relevant hall and the selected time zone. Coming from the base price, the screening is more expensive in February (+ 5%), March (+ 15%), April (+ 5%), September (+ 10%), October (+ 20%) and November (+ 15%) and cheaper in January (– 10%), May (– 20%), June (– 30%), July (– 30%), August (– 20%) and December (– 10%).

Advertising films require not only the switching costs to be incurred but also the coverage of production costs. This is because showing an advertising film always presupposes the existence of such a film in the first place. A warning should be issued here against amateur productions which are rather amusing. One should consider that with such creations one stands in the environment of highly professionally produced films, so one can only lose.

The projection is usually done on location on a digital basis via satellite. A cinema master is delivered online via dropbox, Wetransfer or offline via data carrier/blue ray for playback or copying on site. Sometimes 35 mm film projectors are also used, which is ideal for mute slides/slide animations of local advertisers.

The general advantages of cinema advertising are its high importance for industries subject to other advertising restrictions, low material usage, short-term/flexible booking, easy cancellation and, above all, a high content reference.

The screening takes place in blocks before the pre-program with trailer/teaser and between the pre-program and main program. The screening costs are calculated according to the average number of visitors per week and cinema hall/screen as classified IVW levels (information community to determine the distribution of advertising media).

4.3 Advertising material posters

Posters are available as stationary, mobile and special forms of outdoor advertising. There are several forms of stationary outdoor advertising (*see figure 27: Characteristics of poster advertising*).

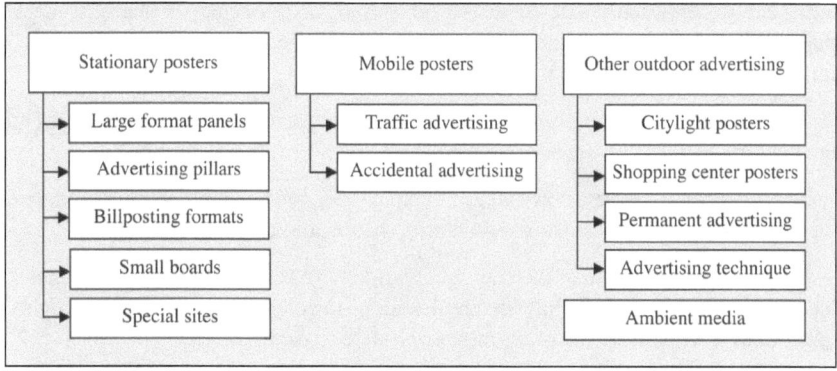

Fig. 27: Characteristics of poster advertising

4.3.1 Stationary outdoor advertising

Large format panels are poster boards in 18/1 sheet format (i.e. eighteen times 1/1 sheet = DIN A1), which are mounted on private property. Outdoor advertising companies lease this space to install and operate billboards. This has to be approved by the respective municipality. The posting period runs usually one decade of 10 or 11 days, and the decades run in three staggered blocks: "A" for posting on Tuesdays or Fridays, "B" three or four days later, and "C" another three or four days later. There are 32 decades per year, the decades at the turn of the year are 14 days long.

A coverage ratio of 1 billboard per 3,000 inhabitants is considered very good coverage, the minimum coverage should not be less than 1 : 4,500. If not yet occupied, the poster panels are to be booked individually with the tenants like DSM, Moplak, AWK, etc. Poster panels of different tenants are exchanged among them, so that only one contact person is required for the organization. For some time now, format-proportional 40/1 sheet formats have also been available. Such super posters are mounted at selected locations at least three meters above the ground, at right angle to the roadway and very clearly visible.

Advertising pillars ("Litfaß") are located on public ground and usually are occupied all around by one advertiser. The format is 18/1 to 24/1 sheets, the height varies, but on average 3.6 m. The administration of the city/county has assigned the arrangement of the occupancy to tenants. An effective organization is not completely simple here because of the always only proportionate visibility. A remedy is a 3-part repeat of an identical motif, which is glued all around.

Billposting formats are columns or boards on public ground, which are jointly occupied by several advertisers, each of whom attaches posters in a proportionate size. For this purpose, it is necessary to accept all the places on site, which in large cities can exceptionally also be displayed as half, third or quarter share. General places are suitable due to their in principle small gracefulness only very limited for branded companies.

Small boards are stop points in 4/1 or 6/1 sheet format. They are often placed near shopping areas, in front of house gables and at traffic junctions.

Special sites are other, non-categorizable carrier forms on building site fences, on exhibition grounds, on riders, on tension bands and as 3D locations.

It is assumed that 90 % of the adult population have contact with a poster panel at least once within a decade, but what really sticks in advertising memories is highly questionable in view of the often inappropriate corporate design.

4.3.2 Mobile outdoor advertising

Mobile outdoor advertising happens on *public transportation* as trams, subways, suburban trains and buses. For this purpose, surfaces are provided on the outside, for example on the vehicle's hull, on the front sides or on the roof, as well as inside, for example on the side walls, the windows or on the ceiling, which can be occupied by advertisers. If one is willing to renovate the exterior of a vehicle after the end of the advertising period, full painting is also possible. Public transportation advertising is widely accepted and reaches more mobile, active, consumer-oriented people.

The occupancy possibilities are manifold. For hull advertising, a strip of 40–60 cm width is placed under the windows of the vehicle.

It is also conceivable to paint the entire vehicle or only the area below the window line, furthermore to stick the rear surfaces or the roof wreath. The duration of the advertising is usually one year, plus expenses for the installation and removal of the advertising as well as for the renewal of the sticker from time to time. In any case longer running times are recommended, at the beginning on several vehicles at the same time. Despite a very high range and contact frequency as well as a very good spatio-temporal controllability, public transport advertising has been neglected for a long time. This is mainly due to the difficult creative design.

Furthermore, cabs and long-distance transporters of private and public companies are considered as commercial outdoor advertising media.

4.3.3 Special forms of outdoor advertising

Among the special forms of outdoor advertising are various types. *Citylight posters* are illuminated panels protected behind glass at public transport stops. Due to their extremely good visibility, they are visible from the bus stop as well as from passing traffic, are comparatively expensive and yet booked out for a long time. The format is 4/1 sheet. Also citylight posters are comparably equipped places which are not located at bus stops but in public places, city information facilities, train stations, etc.

Shopping center posters are poster spaces in the parking lots of shopping centers and supermarkets. Here, potential customers can be given a final advertising push before entering the store. This is particularly useful for impulse purchase products in the consumer goods sector.

Permanent advertising refers to facade, roof and gable advertising, as well as other sign advertising. These forms of outdoor advertising are mostly used to mark the place of business or as reminder advertising at frequently visited locations.

Advertising technique includes aerial, e. g. large banners, bandelores, skywriters, light as illuminated advertising and moving advertising as text displays, advertising on clock pillars, weather displays, in showcases, video pillars, on roll-over screens, video screens, etc. It is intended to arouse demand and inform potential customers where and how it can be satisfied. In addition, advertising technology usually serves to promote prestige and image. The simpler and more concise the advertising message is kept, the higher is its chance of assertion. Recently digital out of home advertising (DooH) plays into it, above all in the form of video screens in the public area as electronic newspaper, occasionally also combined with WLAN/Beacon technology, QR imprint or the like.

Ambient media as collective term includes all advertising formats, which contact the target group planable analogously "out of home". Mainstream ambient media is continuously created, stunt ambient media is unique. Examples are the following:

- Gastronomy: free postcards, drink coasters, mediatables, pizza boxes,
- fitness center: locker poster, mirror stickers, advertising banners,
- cinema: cardboard stands, popcorn bags, toilet posters,
- school/university: coffee to go cup, welcome bag, displays,
- point of sale: shopping cart posters, mall-TV, floor graphics,
- street: city scooters, show trucks, station-TV.

This also includes forms of special outdoor advertising, such as in airports, amusement parks, telephone booths, etc., and other outdoor advertising which cannot be categorized in more detail, such as on construction fences, on exhibition grounds, on riders, on tension bands and as 3-D sites. Further advertising promotional items are to be called, which are distributed as articles of daily use free of charge generally or purposefully and carry advertising prints of the sender. Finally also sample distributions are to be thought of, as they take place, except from POS, also in the remaining public.

In recent times further, as innovative designated advertising forms step in additionally. So for example:

- Agricultural posters on agriculturally used areas at airports, on slopes, etc., beer coaster 3rd party advertising in the gastronomy, i.e. not for beer brands, envelopes and mailing bags, shopping carts, airport baggage belts, floor advertising in retail, cell phone design tops, in-flight advertising as videos or magazines, manhole cover advertising, kindergarten gift bags, store radio/instore-TV, parking spotlights, ship advertising on outdoor areas in the harbor or on ferries, school advertising media, toilet advertising on walls, cisterns, wake-up call by telephone free of charge, but with advertising, bench with advertising imprint, fuel dispensers at gas stations.

4.4 Classical media profiles

The performance of classical media can be evaluated quite differently. Therefore, the performance profiles of the treated media are shown below:

- With regard to the *function for the users*, a distinction must be made between more entertaining and more informative media. The perceived topicality of the messages is also of influence.

- In terms of the *usage situation*, a differentiation can be made between domestic and non-domestic usage, but also according to whether the usage is focused or more casual.

- In the case of the *function as an advertising medium*, a distinction must be made with regard to the size of impact it creates.

- This in turn is closely related to the *possibility of representing* sound, image, movement, color, text, placement, etc. simultaneously.

- According to the target group environment, the different *selection possibilities* of the users are noteworthy, which can be more or less subtle.

- With regard to the *use of time*, there are more flexible or more rigid media.

- Associated with this is usually the unlimited or only limited operative *availability* of advertising time/space.

- According to the *reach* as number of contactable persons, there are narrower or broader scattered media.

- Finally, the media are more or less suitable for independent *campaign development*.

Performance profile of newspapers:

- Function for the users: current information, news, also reports from the region or local area,

- usage situation: different in the daily routine, at home, in means of transport, at work, before shopping, at the end of the day, etc., in each case freely selectable, but conscious reception of information,

- function as an advertising medium: use of the environment through current product offers/information, possibility to re-update product/brand names, local reference through actions, credible,

- representation options: static display of image and text, mainly black and white, possibly additional color, only limited print/paper quality, therefore more suitable for concrete offers and promotions, less for image,

- target group environment: narrowly defined areas as a result of good structuring, with a broad-based approach in those areas,

- time commitment: use presumably once a day, rapid obsolescence, short insertion deadline,

- availability: arbitrary at all release dates, rather low production and activation costs,

- reach: high reach in the distribution area, quality represented by subscriber share, high contact density,

- campaign structure: due to a high degree of internal overlap because of the large proportion of regular readers, the campaign can be easily managed in terms of time and region, but above all it can be run quickly.

Performance profile of magazines:

- Function for the users: entertainment, information of general interest and with a fixed thematic focus, opinion forming in global subject areas, high personal and socially exploitable benefit through life support, background information, topicality, etc.

- usage situation: domestic atmosphere, means of transport, reading circle, usually targeted concentration, anticipation, often in-depth, intensive, repeated use, usually without a sideline, sometimes collective effect, undisturbed reading behavior,

- function as an advertising medium: development and expansion, consolidation of brand recognition and image, through detailed information targeted addressing of readers as opinion leaders within a communicatively important group is possible, use of the magazine's competence for its readers, placement possibilities, gaining sympathy,

- presentation options: static presentation of image and text, color in high print quality, direct editorial influence possible, thematically oriented, positively experienced environment, for in-depth, image-oriented, complex messages,
- target group environment: good target group selection through socio-demographics via interest ties and opinion formation, especially for special interest titles, addressing of multipliers possible, in some cases regional split or partial occupancy possible, but more expensive,
- time commitment: due to weekly, fortnightly and monthly publication frequency, short-term campaigns with low frequency can be used, repeated use, usually several reading phases,
- availability: arbitrary for all publication dates, partly special placement possible, medium production costs, long lead times,
- reach: high quantitative reach possible with qualitatively interesting target groups, high accumulation and contact density, but limited reach for special interest titles, limited target group selection for general interest titles,
- campaign structure: possible through consideration of internal overlaps, use as a basic or supplementary medium, systematic structure with a high subscription rate, but relatively slow, image generation and maintenance.

Performance profile of outdoor posters:

- Function for users: brief information, statuary advertising medium,
- usage situation: on the street, in passing/driving, fleeting impression, subliminal, peripheral out of the corner of the eye, rather random,
- function as an advertising medium: building and consolidating awareness, brief information about the product, strengthening and steering existing willingness to buy towards a concrete offer, "bigger than life",
- representation options: by fleeting impression a concentration is necessary in picture and text (just placative), therefore catchwords, slogans, holistic design necessary, little information transport,
- target group environment: no socio-demographic selection feasible, addressing also mobile population groups, fine-grained local control possible,
- time commitment: minimum runtime 10/11 days (decade), multiple use probable, at least arbitrary possible,
- availability: due to high demand and limited number of billboards waiting times, rather high production and placing costs,
- reach: depends on the contact density by pedestrian frequency and contact chance by job quality, therefore not to generalize,

4.4 Classical media profiles

- campaign structure: especially in supporting function, mainly for convenience products, articles of daily use, less for products in need of explanation, but short, concise and simple messages.

Performance profile of television broadcasting:

- Function for the users: entertainment and general, largely up-to-date information,
- usage situation: in a familiar atmosphere, part-time job, mostly only accompanying medium,
- function as an advertising medium: through multi-sensory address ideal possibility for the presentation of brand and product use, identification ability, impact, emotionally preparable through dramatization,
- presentation options: moving images and sound, multi-sensory address, need to present important information in a short time, for audiovisual mini-messages, application demonstrations, topics requiring little explanation, appetite appeal, visual appeal, a picture is worth a thousand words,
- target group environment: very limited selection possibilities, high scattering losses, use of individual stations, regional programs (1st German television/ARD) also possible, both age and youth oriented,
- time commitment: only one viewing opportunity at the specified broadcasting time, basically no repeatability, little influence on placement for 1st (ARD) and 2nd German television (ZDF),
- availability: almost arbitrarily to book, theoretical limitation by maximum advertising time with public law as well as private commercial broadcasters, blocking of commercials as disadvantage, high production costs,
- reach: range per activation relatively low, due to fluctuating viewers, but high accumulation with sufficient frequency,
- campaign structure: only achievable through high frequency and contact accumulation, otherwise reach superficially, but high forgetting effect through interference, use as basic medium requires high contact dose.

Performance profile of radio broadcasting:

- Function for users: music, entertainment, current information, possibly magazine/educational offer,
- usage situation: domestic leisure or workplace atmosphere, car radio, all day long, not fixed in time, but rarely conscious,
- function as an advertising medium: utilization of the positive basic mood through a mix of entertainment and information, spontaneous appeal, support of existing

familiarity and awareness, but competition with the editorial environment, generally high risk of forgetting the spoken word,
- representation options: only acoustic advertising effect, by secondary use concentration on the substantial is necessary, frequent company/product naming remains important,
- target group environment: limited selection possibilities, target group focus in the daily routine due to program environment, e. g. classical housewives, and usage situation, e. g. car drivers, very good local controllability,
- time commitment: one-time contact at the given broadcasting time, not repeatable by listeners,
- availability: limited by maximum advertising time per day/block even for private stations, commercial blocks as a disadvantage, low production and switching costs,
- reach: relatively low per activation, due to fluctuating audience, high accumulation after a few spots, possibly several times a day activation is useful,
- campaign structure: only achievable through high frequency and contact accumulation, current purchase impulses/reactivation, audio-visual transfer, i. e. use of learned image-sound elements by reminding the user of the image, even if only the sound element is reproduced.

Performance profile of movie theaters:

- Function for users: entertainment, fascination, mediation and triggering of emotions,
- usage situation: largely controlled environmental conditions, usually in the company of partner/clique, large temporal dispersion, although daytime/weekday are focal points, mostly late afternoon/evening,
- function as an advertising medium: through multisensory address ideal possibility to record advertising in a relaxed atmosphere, strong impact, high concentration, competition from main film,
- representation options: picture and sound, ideal multi-sensory address, embedding in very emotional frames possible, comparatively inexpensive,
- target group environment: "young" medium, concentrated addressing of an active, open-minded target group, very good local control,
- time commitment: only one-time viewing at the specified screening time, repeatability possible but unlikely, statuary medium,
- availability: largely freely available, production cost problem, except for existing artwork and co-op advertising,
- reach: absolutely small but qualified reach, if young target persons are interesting,
- campaign structure: regularly only useful as a supplement to other media.

4.5 Requirements for media selection

Inevitably, the question arises as to which of the media mentioned is the best for insertion. Unfortunately the "best" in this sense does not exist, but which medium is the best depends solely on the respective advertising task. And this is as individual as every advertiser himself. However, it is possible to create a checklist of requirement criteria which should be decisive for the selection. There are quantitative as well as qualitative criteria (*see figure 28: Requirements for media selection*).

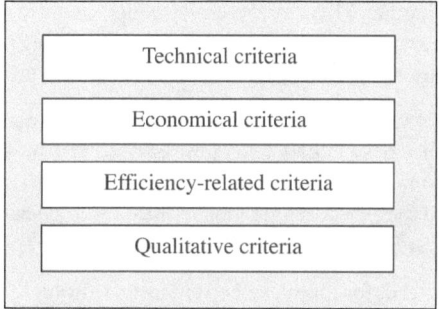

Fig. 28: Requirements for media selection

4.5.1 Quantitative criteria

Quantitative criteria include technical, economical and efficacy criteria. *Technical* criteria of media selection mainly concern the following:

- *Booking deadline* as the time interval between booking and activation of a medium. Newspaper adverts, for example, can be booked very flexibly with a minimum of two days' notice, whereas posters must be booked up to 90 days in advance for the positions sought.
- *Targeting* means the fine tuning of a medium to the target group. Here, for example, posters are completely unspecific, they are seen by everyone (or not), while cinema is used to restrict the audience to younger people.
- *Periodicity* means the length of time the advertising medium is used until it is renewed. Newspaper adverts are very short-lived, but also up-to-date, and advertising for means of transport is only useful in the medium term.
- *Location* refers to the spatial variability of the medium. Posters, for example, can be booked right down to the individual location; with other media, greater compromises in the catchment area must be accepted.
- *Covering area* means the spatial spread of the medium. The mentioned media can be controlled partly down to the local area, partly up to the global area.

- *Person* refers to the typical user of a medium. Posters can hardly be categorized here, for example, whereas the situation is different for radio or cinema spots.

Three of the most important *economical* criteria for media selection are as follows:

- The *advertising costs* result from the media's tariff prices. Appropriate discounts are to be deducted from the list prices given.
- The *budget framework* represents the amount of money to be used at least for one medium. Usually senseless is the unique booking of adverts or the allocation of only one poster place. Therefore it does not make sense to split small budgets between several media. Then every advertising medium lacks the ability to assert itself against the masses of other incoming messages. Instead, a certain advertising pressure should be built up by concentrating on one medium.
- The *production costs* are technical preliminary costs which arise before an advertising medium is switched on. These should not be underestimated. For example, the artwork for an 18/1-sheet poster easily costs € 15,000, i.e. these costs are incurred before a single poster has even been posted. For advert artwork, the costs are between € 8,000–15,000, for radio spots approx. € 5,000.

Efficiency-related criteria for media selection are manifold:

- *Penetration* refers to the presence of an advertising medium. For example, daily newspapers and thus the adverts they contain are present everywhere in the catchment area, but cinema advertising is only accessible to people who have paid admission.
- The distribution of the medium is important for the *accessibility* of the target persons and depends, among other things, on the potential advertising pressure, the controllability of the use and the responsiveness of the target persons through the medium.
- A *repeatability* of the advertising medium contact is equally important. In principle, this is not the case with TV commercials, for example; the chance of contact exists only at the time of broadcast and cannot be repeated.
- *Overlaps* between media genres influence the contact density. For example, adverts in several local daily newspapers are certainly not perceived by one and the same person, so that there is a small external overlap, whereas this person may well perceive the poster and radio spot together.
- *Multiple contacts* offer the possibility of systematically building up advertising pressure and are high for media with a high proportion of regular users, e.g. daily newspapers, or low for media with a high proportion of changing users, e.g. posters.
- Finally, *progression pace* means the speed at which contacts are established. This is high for short-lived advertising media, e.g. newspaper adverts, and low for long-lived advertising media, e.g. transportation advertising.

4.5 Requirements for media selection

Those requirement criteria are to be selected, which are the most important for the respective advertising task, e.g. reservation period, goal, budget framework, spreading and structure speed. Against it the preferential medium is placed, e.g. daily newspaper. If the preferred medium fulfills the selected criteria or if the criteria correspond to the media profile, the requirements and performance profile match and the media selection is consistent. If there is no agreement, it should be examined first of all whether a medium other than the preferred medium fulfills the requirements better, then this medium should be used, or secondly, it should be examined whether reductions/alterations in the requirements are acceptable (*for context see figure 29: Intermediary comparison of classical advertising*).

++ very good, + well, - poor, -- very bad	Newspaper	Magazine	Televison	Radio	Movie theater	Outdoor poster
Booking deadline	++	+	-	+	-	--
Targeting/Misalignment	+	+	-	-	++	--
Periodicity/Duration of presence	+	+	--	--	--	+
Location/Place of reception	++	-	-	-	++	++
Covering area/Delimitability	++	--	-	-	++	++
Typical user community	-	+	-	-	+	-
Advertising costs (absolute)	--	-	-	++	++	-
Budget volume required	--	-	-	++	++	-
Production costs	-	-	--	+	-	+
Penetration	+	+	+	-	++	-
Accessibility/Usage	+	+	++	++	+	++
Repeatability	+	++	--	--	--	+
Contact density/Overlaps	+	+	+	++	-	+
Cumulation/Multiple contacts	++	++	-	-	-	-
Progression pace	++	+	++	+	-	--

Fig. 29: Intermediary comparison of classical advertising

4.5.2 Contact quality

However, these criteria do not yet give any indication as to whether the advertising actually leads to contact with target persons. Therefore, the criterion of contact quality is based on the attempt, if it is not possible to collect the advertising contact directly, to record it at least indirectly via indicators which provide information about the probability of the advertising contact. Such indicators are mainly the following:

- *Proximity to the medium* as dispensability of the advertising medium carrying the advertising material. User loyalty is measured by the willingness to dispense with the medium. "Indispensable" media therefore have a higher authority, which benefits the advertising integrated in them and thus the advertising message.

- Truth content as *credibility* of advertising statements. This applies above all to dominant advertising media/advertising material such as posters. Conversely, the competence of the advertising medium or the editorial environment can radiate on the seriousness.

- *Novelty character* as topicality of the medium. The hypothesis here is that media which promise news enjoy a higher speculative attention than others.

- *Relaxation* as an entertainment effect. Here, animating environments come off more favorably. However, this can also result in an undesirable distraction from the advertising content.

- *Regional reference* as local relevance. It correlates strongly with the spatial distribution of a medium. However, this does not necessarily mean that the advertising environment is adequate, but can also make "big" products "small".

- *Familiarity* as a turn towards a medium. The higher the authority of a medium, the more likely it is to be accepted as far as advertising statements are concerned. This experience is also expressed in the type of purchase and is higher for contract customers with subscription.

- *Information content* as the ability to interpret a medium. However, taking into account the importance of key stimuli and non-thematic, atmospheric information which is directed at the belly rather than the head, this judgement is relativized.

- *Exposure* as the actual reaching of target persons by a medium. Here it is assumed that the higher the advertising share, the lower this exposure is, because the more the medium is then avoided.

- *Perception* as perceptibility of an advertising medium. Statuary media have an advantage, because the information delivery is determined by the audience (print media), whereas in transitory media the medium itself determines the time of information delivery (TV/R).

- *Apperception* as actual processing of the advertising message of the medium. This can only be speculated about, because it cannot be reliably proven which advertisement effort results to which effect on attitude and behavior.

- *Extent of use* as regularity of usage. Advertising media which are aimed at users who are loyal to the medium are presumably more efficient in this respect. However, the interval for renewal is also decisive.

- *Intensity of use* as multiple contacts. Advertising media which offer multiple contact opportunities are presumably at an advantage here.

- *Advertising openness* as acceptance of advertising media. Media with a high proportion of advertising-open-minded users are at an advantage here, as they are assumed to be more receptive to advertising messages.

- *Image share* together with the reproduction/reception quality. This is particularly important in view of the findings of imagery research.

- *Editorial share* in relation to advertising share. Assuming a general reactance to advertising, those media have a higher chance of using media in which advertising is also perceived as a waste product of the editorial department.

- *Features* as criteria of form, e. g. special advertising formats, length in seconds, color/multicolor, format (page count), etc. The more variable the equipment can be selected, the better the specific conditions of communication can be addressed.

- *Placement/timing* and the possibility of influencing it. Likewise, specifics of media use and sender can be taken into account by skilful control of the advertising.

- *Harmony* of product character and media character. The greater the connotative correspondence, the better the suitability of the advertising medium is considered.

- *Function* as commercial or dominant. Here, commercial advertising media have an advantage because they combine the attention of editorial staff and advertising, while dominant advertising media such as posters depend on stimulating them only from within themselves.

- *Usage environment* which depends on the place of use, time of use and period of use. The more flexible these are, the better.

4.6 Media selection for classical advertising

With the selection of advertising media several goals are aimed at. Firstly, the user base of the selected titles/stations/spaces should match the defined target group as closely as possible, whereby media-technical misallocation should be avoided. Secondly, to cover the defined target group as completely as possible with the selected titles/stations/spaces. Thirdly, the most frequent possible contact between the selected media and the defined target group, i.e. the implementation of a wide range of advertising impulses. And fourthly, the most cost-effective realization of coverage and contact intensity with the selected media in the defined target group, i.e. the best price-performance ratio.

4.6.1 Market media analyses

For the execution of the advertising medium selection market media analyses are to be emphasized, which raise extensive and meaningful data for the medium use (in the following shortened and appropriately changed after crossvertise.com) (*see figure 30: Types of market media analyses*).

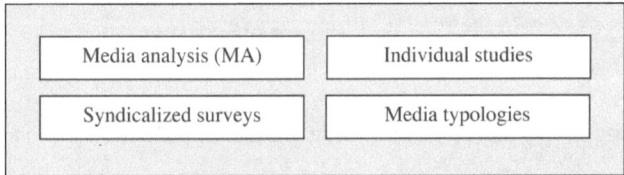

Fig. 30: Types of market media analyses

MA

The Media analysis (MA) is conducted by the AG.MA working group media analysis annually as an advertising media survey and investigates the media consumption behavior of the population and thus provides information on a uniform basis for editorial research as well as media data research. The main focus is on data on reach and usage structures of advertising media. The MA takes place in different tranches, such as for press media, radio, daily newspapers, posters. It is carried out jointly by several market research institutes, in particular Enigma, GfK, IFAK, Ipsos, Marplan, USUMA, MMA, TNS Infratest and TNS Emnid. It is conducted twice a year in January/July. The basic population is the German-speaking population in private households at the place of the main residence in Germany aged 14 years and over. Media included are radio, cinema, online, posters, popular magazines, TV, newspapers. Markets include computers, shopping behavior, leisure behavior, online, travel.

Syndicalized surveys

There are also syndicalized surveys which bring together several initiators, usually publishers and/or broadcasters. This is to rule out the possibility that the results are distorted in one direction or another. In addition, the costs for each initiator are lower and thus easier to bear. One such survey is the VUMA, another the LAE.

Consumption and media analysis (VUMA) is a single source survey on media and consumption data. Twice a year, 7,500 people are surveyed on leisure time behavior, attitudes, opinions, target group models and topic interest. Initiators are the publishing houses Bauer and Springer, the survey is conducted by Ipsos, Ifak, Marplan as market research institutes. The analysis takes place in two areas, classic from 14 years onwards and youth from 12 years onwards. The basic population is the resident population in Germany. Included media are city light posters, yellow pages, cinema, online media, popular magazines, radio, daily newspapers, TV. Markets include cars, health, household appliances, Internet, cosmetics, fashion, food and beverages, telecommunications and consumer electronics.

The readership analysis decision-makers in business and administration (LAE) is a survey, which is conducted every two to three years by the LAE Association in cooperation with 13 publishing houses. The focus is on the analysis of corporate information as well as business and media usage behavior. The subjects of investigation are online media, popular magazines, daily newspapers, weekly newspapers in the areas of society, politics, business, science and culture. The research is conducted by the institutes CZAIA Mafo, IFAK, Marplan, TNS Infratest. The population is about 2.2 million people. Markets concern sales, R & D, finance, investment, investment decision makers, marketing, microelectronics, production, travel, administration.

Furthermore there are joint studies which are executed by two or more initiators. Examples are the following:

- *Jugend-MA as media analysis with 3,000 interviews every three years, covering 16 magazines in the youth market, initiators are the participating publishers, young people aged 12–21 years are interviewed,*

- *Kinder-LA as reader analysis with 3,000 interviews at irregular intervals, covering 20 magazines in the children's market, clients are the participating publishers, children aged 8–14 years are interviewed,*

- *LA-Medizin as study with 1,350 interviews every two years, approx. 50 medical journals, clients are the participating publishers and advertisers, doctors are interviewed,*

- *Konpress for denominational titles with changing case numbers and survey, approx. 30 weekly magazines of the denominational press, initiators are the participating publishers, a cross-section of the total population aged 14 years and over is surveyed,*

- *KLA for customer magazines with 5,000 interviews three times a year, approx. 15 customer magazines from food trade, drugstore, pharmacy and Raiffeisen Cooperative bank, initiators are the participating publishers, a cross-section of the total population aged 14 years and older is surveyed,*
- *AOL for land press with 1,500 interviews three-yearly, approx. 25 agricultural technical periodicals, clients are the participating publishers of the organization-bound land press, questioned are representative persons, who live in agricultural full-time farms.*

Individual studies

Individual media studies focus in terms of their topics on the content of the respective publisher/broadcaster objects, including attitudes towards brands (in-depth), consumer data and demographics, such as the following:

- *The Allensbach advertising media analysis first class analyzes the consumer and media usage behavior of those persons who, according to their status, i. e. education, income, social class, are among the top ten percent of the population. It is published annually in September. The basic population is the German population aged 14 years and older in socio-economic status 1. Included media are advertising journals, cinema, customer magazines, online media, popular magazines, radio, TV, newspapers. Markets include computers, photography, leisure, money and capital investments, hobbies, culture, fashion, politics/social affairs, travel, sports, telecommunications.*
- *The Allensbacher computer und technics analysis (ACTA) comes from the Institute for public opinion research and is conducted annually in October. The basic population is the German population from 14–64 years of age. Media included are cinema, online media, TV, magazines, newspapers. Markets include computers, information technology, online media, telecommunications, TV, consumer electronics.*
- *Markenprofile is a readership and consumption study by G & J Publishing house and is conducted annually among up to 10,000 people representative of the resident population aged 14–64 in private households in Germany. It is a face-to-face and single-source survey. Characteristics collected are awareness, sympathy and willingness to buy as well as media usage data for 140 magazines, 7 newspapers and 16 television stations. The survey is conducted by MMA, IFAK, Ipsos, ISBA. Markets include computers, funds/money investments, fashion, food, online media, insurance.*
- *The Kommunikations-Analyse (KA) is published by Brigitte magazin among German-speaking women between 14 and 64 years of age for consumer mag-*

azines and advertising television. Relevant topics are cosmetics/body care, retail, electrical household appliances, drugs/remedies, globalization/sustainability, society, consumer habits, brand/price awareness, shopping locations, brand/communication behavior, consumption-controlling characteristics such as attitude, consumer climate. The survey is conducted by MMA, Ipsos market research institutes every two years. Included markets are electrical household appliances, food/drink, trading companies, Internet/e-commerce, cosmetics, fashion, wellness/health.

- *Communications networks (CN) is a single-source study which primarily examines the use of TV programs, online offerings, daily/weekly newspapers and consumer magazines. The client is Focus magazine, the survey is conducted by TNS Infratest, MMA once a year in September and is representative for the German/German-speaking population between 14 and 69 years living in private households in Germany. The markets include books, financial services, business travel, mobility, fashion, online media, telecommunications, consumer electronics.*

- *The Online Reichweiten Monitor is published semi-annually in February/August by AGIREV to research the German online advertising market. The study focuses on the share of internet users in the German population in private households between 14 and 69 years of age, the sociodemography of these users, their usage habits, thematic interests, e-commerce and reach of online advertising media. The initiator is the Arge Internet Research, the implementation is carried out by the institutes Ipsos, GfK, NFO Infratest.*

- *The study of the Arbeitsgemeinschaft Online-Forschung provides Internet facts about online media and the online advertising market and is published four times a year. The focus is on the analysis of online reach and the determination of structural data on the user population. The analysis is carried out by Ipsos, IFAK, TNS Infratest, MMA, representative for the German resident population aged 14 years and older.*

- *The ARD/ZDF online study is conducted by the public media commission as a fundamental study on the development of internet use and the handling of online offers. The population is made up of all German online users aged 14 years and over.*

Media typologies

Media typologies go one step further and include as an additional criterion living environment characteristics either AIO approach for attitudes, interests, opinions or VALS approach for values and lifestyles. These are operationalized by criteria such as leisure behavior, style preferences, brand orientation, etc. In detail, general and media-specific typologies are to be distinguished. The latter are usually based on the advertising media of the respective advertiser. Probably the best known and also one of the largest regular surveys of publishers is the TdW (see below). Another large and well-known publishing house survey is the outfit typology of the Spiegel publishing house. Another typology concerns car buyers (Bauer).

As example serves the *Media user typology* (MNT), which was last carried out in 2015 as a telephone survey for television and radio users. The aim is to provide a clear description of media target groups with insights into the lives of viewers and listeners for the purposes of programming on the part of broadcasters. The research is based on a typological segmentation in which homogeneous groups, the media user types, are formed from people with similar characteristics. The criteria used are the degree of modernity of these types on the abscissa, from traditional to modern, and their level of aspiration on the ordinate, from simple to differentiated. There are overlaps between the types, and the distance between the types characterizes their degree of similarity/difference in terms of leisure behavior, music preferences, thematic interests, values and life goals.

As basis serves the German-speaking population aged 14 years and older:

- *Fun-oriented (10%), intensive stimulus seekers, carefree, self-referential and insecure, adolescent behavior, predominantly younger.*
- *Determined (10%), dynamic doers, assertive, self-confident, experience-oriented, predominantly male and younger.*
- *Modern established (10%), active, critical and liberal, with a sovereign basic attitude, culturally affine, interested in a variety of subjects, predominantly male and younger.*
- *Family oriented (15%), optimistic, self-confident, with a demand for individuality, sociable, well organized.*
- *Escapists (13%), focus on their own environment, adaptable, existential and wait-and-see, predominantly male.*
- *Committed (9%), broadly interested, active and open-minded, high cultural affinity without striving for demarcation, predominantly female.*
- *Domestics (8%), high need for security and continuity, strong attachment to home, orientation to private environment, secular, predominantly female and older.*
- *Highly culture-oriented (8%), active leisure pursuits, mainly in non-trivial cultural environments, well educated and demanding, predominantly older,*
- *Retired (6%), passive lifestyle, thrifty, low interest spectrum, predominantly single households, predominantly male and older.*
- *Traditionals (11%), value-conservative post-war generation, high importance of security, harmony, modesty and faith, predominantly female and older.*

Another media typology is the *Outfit typology* from Spiegel publishing house (last Mk 6, 2015). The basic population are German residents aged 14–64 (around 50 million), the sample size is around 10,000. The survey is conducted with structured questionnaires, orally, with presentation of the brand logos, and in writing as self-completion. The sample is divided into approx. 8,000 randomly selected persons and approx. 2,000 from quota selection. The survey is conducted by the Marplan, Ipsos, Sinus and ISBA institutes. Relevant product groups are clothing, shoes, accessories such as jewelry, watches, glasses, writing utensils, also based on the Sinus-Milieu lifestyle analysis typology. The focus is on attitudinal variables for the aforementioned product groups. The results are based on the scaling of descriptive characteristics, brand significance in the product fields, according to awareness, ownership, willingness to buy, and media user groups. From this, the subjective importance of the respective product, the attitudes towards the brand and their purchase preference incl. choice of shopping location are derived. In addition, consumption priorities, sociodemographic characteristics, personality traits and media usage are recorded. These data are subjected to a factor analysis with 65 dimensions, from which the interesting superfactors are drawn. Individuals are assigned to the types with the highest value on one of the superfactors.

The result is seven male and seven female clothing types, each with around 25 million people with internally similar attitudes, motives and preferences with regard to fashion based on the measurements. The male types are

- *the Fashionable (12% share of male population), the Average (8%), the Fashion hunter (14%), the Demanding (10%), the Pragmatic (19%), the Indifferent (23%), and the Rejecting (14%).*

The female types are

- *the Thrifty (12% share of female population), the Sovereign (23%), the Exclusive (13%), the Pragmatic (14%), the Individualist (21%), the Fashion enthusiast (8%), and the Invisible (10%).*

The media usage of each of these types is shown, so that it can be seen how the respective type can be reached through advertising media.

Further typologies are the following:

- *Car buyer typology (Bauer media group). Basic population is the German resident population aged 14 years and over, with a sample size of around 9,600. The study aims to create car buyer types on the basis of the purchase decision process. The core sample consists of people who intend to make a purchase within the next two years. The focus is on purchasing motives such as economy, environment, safety, comfort, family, prestige, etc. and sociodemographic data as well as media usage behavior. As a result, nine car buyer types are created by means of cluster analysis. For media planning, this makes it possible to define individual types as a target group and to target communication measures specifically at them by using advertising media which are used more than average by the buyer types corresponding to one's own target group in the field of automotive (affinity).*

- *Typology of desires (TdW/Burda publishing house) (last in 2013, thereafter merged into Best for planning). The basic population are German residents aged 14 years and over, the sample size is approx. 20,000 people. Approximately 1,800 brands in 400 product areas together with single source media usage are surveyed with the aim of typologizing lifestyles according to consumption and media habits. The characteristics covered are psychographics, socio-demographics and behavior. Media usage refers to reading behavior based on 170 magazines/newspapers, reading locations, television usage (station/intensity), radio usage (station/intensity), cinema usage, online usage based on 100 websites. Market sectors considered are automotive, cosmetics, home technology, fashion, finance, food/beverage, gardening, health, leisure, living, shopping, travel. The aim is to create improved media plans based on this typology.*

As general, in this respect overarching typologies, the Sinus typology of social milieus, the Sigma milieus and the Roper consumer styles (GfK) should be mentioned here. If market and media data are collected and processed together, one speaks of *single source* analyses. If, in addition, several media categories or even all media categories beyond magazines, TV, radio are covered, these are called multi-media or all-media analyses.

These data serve as basis for further processing, namely the validation by fine structure countings, the ranking by media performance values, mediaplan combinations and media plan optimization (*see figure 31: Steps for media planning*).

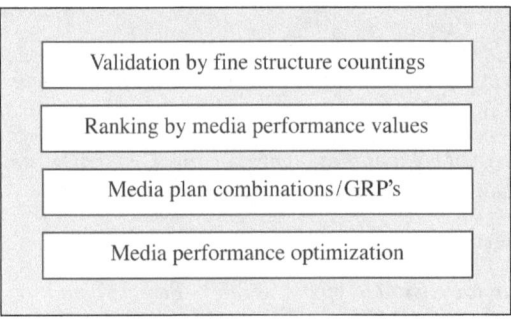

Fig. 31: Steps for media planning

4.6.2 Validation

The goal of media planning is to select those advertising media which seem to be most suitable for reaching a defined target group. This requires several steps of media planning, first of all the evaluation of the advertising medium and target group. Such a validation can be done by three approaches, whereby these are only auxiliary criteria for the formal representation of reality:

- Based on demographic criteria,
- by reference to attitude, opinion, interest and behavior,
- based on characteristic personality traits.

The collected data basis also helps to check a pre-conceptually defined target group and provides indications for corrections. If non-demographic characteristics serve as criteria, computer counts can be used to obtain a picture of the demographics of the target persons, who thus gain more concrete information for further processing. In the same way, several sub-target groups can be selected and compared with each other and viewed in relation to the population. The resulting characteristics can be used to fine-tune the target group definition. Segmentation runs can also lead to the definition of a target group. For this purpose, different questions of analyses are evaluated and focal points identified, which are then used as definition characteristics. Finally, an evaluation as trend media counting over time is possible in order to understand and use share movements. The results can be output in various forms with regard to all criteria. In the narrower sense it concerns thereby less media than rather still marketing planning.

In order to do justice to the differing importance of different sub-target groups, these can be included in the further calculation by *weighting people* with different proportions. In practice, this is done by weighting the target person characteristics considered less relevant with a multiplication factor < 1. In this way, it is also possible to differentiate between decision-makers, buyers, users and influencers. Often men are weighted down as non-purchasing from this point of view.

Furthermore, the differing importance of *media types* can be taken into account by *weighting* them. Above all, this attempts to balance the potential advertising effect of several media according to format, reproduction quality, contact depth, concept harmony, content, etc. Although this attempt remains imperfect, it is still better than the assumption that every invested advertising Euro is equally efficient, no matter which medium, equipment, environment, etc. is chosen for it.

Finally, the advertising print can also be provided with a *minimum frequency* so that advertising medium contacts below a certain response frequency are not taken into account or only with a devaluation factor. There is a widespread view that frequencies < 6 do not have a lasting advertising effect in print advertising. This is just as controversial as the assumption of different impact curves. In detail, the following *effect functions* are distinguished:

- Linear assumes a constantly increasing advertising effect with the number of contacts,
- progressively assumes an advertising effect which increases noticeably with a high number of contacts,
- degressively assumes an advertising effect which hardly increases with a high number of contacts,
- logistically assumes an advertising effect which is initially progressive with the number of contacts, and later degressive,
- concave-convex assumes an advertising effect which is initially degressive with the number of contacts, and later on progressive,
- single-stage assumes an advertising effect which occurs suddenly with a certain number of contacts,
- stair-like assumes an advertising effect which increases discontinuously with the number of contacts.

Often an *effective range* is defined between an impact threshold and a saturation point. This is based on the hypothesis that contacts in the target group below the impact threshold do not lead to an advertising effect due to under-stimulation, while contacts above the saturation point represent waste due to over-stimulation. However, this is a very mechanistic view of things.

The calculation of the individual target group criteria can be done *additively* (OR-method) or *multiplicatively* (AND-method). Especially with AND-methods, the combination of several selection criteria quickly leads to a remaining sample cut-off quantity which is no longer sufficiently meaningful. The practical lower limit is seen here in absolute terms in about 200 cases, a limit which, however, already implies a considerable variance and therefore gives rather clues than valid results. But even these are much more valuable than having no data at all. In practically all cases, however, at least a factorial weighting is required to adapt the structure of the resulting sample to that of the population. This calculation is performed automatically by the computer counting program and is also shown as a case number. The cause lies in unfulfilled quotas during the survey, in refusals to provide information, loss of addresses, falsified surveys, etc. This redressement adapts the structure of a random sample to that of the population to be depicted by cell weighting of the cases and thus, starting from the actual sample, by extrapolation of "artificial" cases first fully exploits the sample size and thus makes it compatible with other representative surveys.

The results of the structural runs are output in five forms:

- Firstly, *horizontal percentages*, i.e. the share results of several sub-target groups add up to 100% as a sum for each criterion per line.

4.6 Media selection for classical advertising

- Secondly, *vertical percentages*, i.e., the structure results of each sub-target group add up to 100% as a composition across all criteria per column.
- Thirdly, in *absolute numbers*, i.e., the results are given per row/column as real case numbers.
- Fourthly, as *extrapolation*, i.e. the results are shown per row/column as an extrapolated sample survey on the underlying population.
- Fifthly, as an *index* (base = 100), i.e., for each criterion, each sub-target group is shown in relation to the average of the population.

These different forms of presentation make it possible to characterize an existing target group in a very meaningful way. Now, the most important thing is to find out which advertising media can be considered the most efficient in relation to the task defined in the input data. This question is answered in the form of a ranking.

4.6.3 Ranking

Numerous computer planning programs are available for ranking the advertising media. In detail, they offer performance features such as tariff files, price maintenance functions such as updates, target group processing, structure counting, ranking countings, plan evaluations, graphic output and other special features. Corresponding data is provided as a free service by the publishers, who thus practically provide a service which advertising agents are tacitly or explicitly rewarded by their customers. For this purpose, the data sets are made available to media planners in clouds for their work and updated at regular intervals.

Input data of this software are program type, client, date, file, advertising material equipment, multidimensional target group criteria and weightings. Output data are case numbers before and after case or person weighting, target group share of the total population, advertising media, advertising placement costs, sorting criteria and rankings. The result is a ranking of the advertising media in such a way that the best-rated title or station appears at the top of the list, followed by the next highest rated advertising media in descending order. On this basis, a clear determination of the advertising medium to be preferred is possible. However the term "best" is to be interpreted ambiguously, because very different expectations are placed on the performance of an advertising medium. Therefore there are also different performance values for its evaluation. The performance values mentioned are only statistical indications. They cannot reflect the actual performance of the advertising media. Rather, they are historical data determined from representative surveys. The performance values can be divided into at least four terms, reach value, contact intensity, affinity score and cost-efficiency (*see figure 32: Media performance identifiers*).

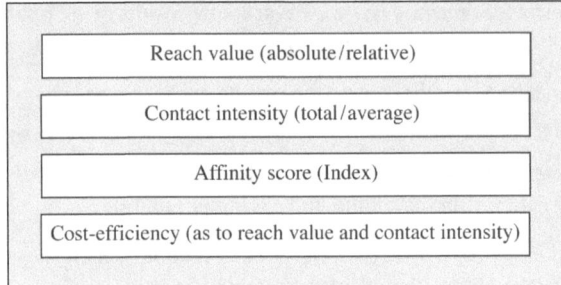

Fig. 32: Media peformance identifiers

4.6.3.1 Reach value

Reach value is the number of target persons who have at least once the chance to get in contact with an advertising medium and thus with the advertising material contained therein, specified as opportunity to see/OTS, opportunity to hear/OTH. This chance is calculated on the basis of secondary statistical data from the past. The effective reach is only achieved above a specified minimum contact frequency or between a defined impact threshold as the lower and a saturation point as the upper limit. The absolute number is also shown as a percentage of the achieved out of all target persons (= reach in %). Accordingly, high reach values mean that the advertising message is widely distributed within the target group.

The *increase in reach* in the case of multiple occupancy of an advertising medium is also referred to as the C-value (= cumulation) and is high with a high proportion of fluctuating and few core/exclusive users of an advertising medium. In addition, the increase in reach indicates how quickly the user base is collected after the initial insertion, e.g. quickly for print in the case of program magazines, but slowly for hobby titles. A distinction is made between the C1 value for single activation, the C2 value for double activation, etc.

Readers per number indicates the number of readers (print), determined by survey, reached by an average issue of a title in the last publication interval. Similarly, there is the listener/viewer per day (TV/R) or visitor per week (cinema) value. Purely statistically, the summary reader per issue value is calculated, i.e. average number of readers of an issue, analog average number of listeners during 1 hour of radio program or viewers during 1/2 hour of TV program. The reader per copy value indicates the average number of people who read the same physical copy of a newspaper/magazine. The technical reach is determined by the connection density of receiving devices (electronics) or the distribution area of copies (print).

Internal overlaps are caused by people who use several issues/broadcasts of the same advertising medium over time. This only becomes relevant for the plan combination, since the ranking is always based on only one switch-on.

External overlaps are caused by persons who use several advertising media in parallel. This is relevant for mediaplan combinations. These are couplings of two or more advertising media belonging to the same advertiser, which generate a combination discount when used together. The external overlapping of these media leads to multiple contacts. Persons to whom internal and/or external overlaps apply are only considered once in the net coverage, but according to their incidence in the gross coverage. The gross reach of coverage is therefore the range of coverage including all internal and external overlaps.

4.6.3.2 Contact intensity

Contact intensity means the total number of advertising media contacts with target persons. This can also be shown as average contact frequency per person or as the sum of the absolute number of advertising media contacts within the target group. It is only of limited importance in the ranking, namely in the case of tariff combinations which generate external overlaps. Their reach is less than their contact sum, because the reach value is understood as net reach, i. e. after deduction of the external overlaps between the advertising media combined in the rate combination, while the contact sum represents the gross value, i. e. the sum of the contacts of each individual advertising medium included in the rate combination. This effect is of great importance when several advertising media are combined into mediaplan combinations.

The *contact dispersion* indicates how many people are addressed within which time periods. In the case of print, for example, it is fast for program magazines and slow for hobby magazines.

The *contact distribution* indicates how the number of contacts is distributed over all persons reached according to frequency and varies around the average value according to contact classes. Thus, the same value for an average contact can be achieved by distributing the contact classes very differently. The necessary addition represents therefore the variation of the contact classes around the average.

The *contact dose* indicates the desired minimum number of contacts with target group persons, which is regarded as condition for the advertising fulfillment.

4.6.3.3 Affinity score

Affinity is the percentage share of the reach of target persons in the total reach of an advertising medium and thus a measure of its misallocation, i. e. scattering losses due to contacts via occupied advertising media with persons who do not belong to the defined target group. This value is also shown as an affinity index in relation to the share of the target group in the total population (= index 100). High index values mean disproportionate affinity and vice versa, i. e. a high proportion of defined target persons in the actual user base of an advertising medium and vice versa. In this respect, special interest titles/stations (SI) have an advantage over general interest titles/stations (GI), which indeed reach more users in absolute terms but also more "irrelevant" users in relative terms. This is particularly important for small target groups. For example, the number of target persons reached when a GI title/station is occupied will certainly be higher than for an SI title/station. At the same time, however, the GI advertising medium reaches irrelevant persons to a large extent, while the SI advertising medium has a lower level of misdistribution. The former therefore has the higher range, but also the greater scattering losses. These in turn have a concrete effect on the cost-performance ratio.

4.6.3.4 Cost-efficiency

The cost-efficiency relates the performance values reach and contact intensity to the booking costs. This is done by calculating the 1,000 user price as costs per *1,000 target persons* reached at least once as readers, viewers, listeners or the *1,000 contact price* as costs per 1,000 potentially realized contacts in the target group.

The performance values range and contact intensity are known from the database. If the respective tariff prices according to the contract year and discounts of the advertising media for the given equipment are added, the profitability can be calculated. A high degree of profitability is of decisive importance for small advertising budgets. Advertising media with the same reach or contact intensity thus lead to different profitability with different tariff prices. Conversely, advertising media with the same tariff prices with different reach or contact intensity also lead to different profitability.

In addition, in the print sector there is the 1,000 circulation price as costs per 1,000 copies of a title or in the electronics sector the 1,000 device price as costs per 1,000 TV/R receivers technically accessible by a transmitter, whereby several devices per household can be installed. Further measures of cost-efficiency are the

- Price per 1 % reach in the target group, as low as possible,
- number of contacts per € 1.000 advertising budget, as high as possible,
- cost per 1,000 users at effective range, lowest possible value.

4.6.4 Mediaplan combinations

The media-technical objective usually cannot be realized by using one advertising medium alone, but requires the parallel use of several advertising media. For this purpose, mediaplan combinations are created, which consist, in addition to possibly obligatory advertising media, of those which qualify from the ranking.

4.6 Media selection for classical advertising

However, in addition to the purely quantitative view, this always requires corrections which take qualitative aspects into account. Thus, titles/broadcasters regularly place themselves far ahead in terms of price-performance aspects, not because they provide a special qualitative media performance, but because they provoke high profitability through low tariff prices, e.g. yellow press titles. These advertising media may have to be excluded just as much as those which, due to their editorial orientation, show an unsuitable harmony with the target group despite high cost-effectiveness. Conversely, it is precisely this argument which can lead to the inclusion of relatively uneconomical titles, because their mathematical disadvantage is more than compensated for by the far greater thematic proximity. Although these corrections prevent optimization, they are very valuable from a heuristic perspective. Ultimately, however, they distort the elaborate objectification of market media analyses by subjective criteria.

Based on these considerations, mediaplan combinations are formed within the budget limits and again counted in terms of their performance values. Each plan combination thus receives values for reach, contact intensity, affinity and profitability in relation to 1,000 users/1,000 contacts. On balance, the best result in the preferred value is selected. The target values in terms of reach are calculated as (*see figure 33: Advertising placements and materials*):

		Advertising placements	
		once	two or more
Advertising materials	sole	Single reach	Quantiplucative reach
Advertising materials	multiple	Cumulative reach	Combined reach

Fig. 33: Advertising placements and materials

- *Single reach*, i.e. a simple insertion in a single advertising medium,
- *accumulative reach*, i.e.
    - two or more insertions in a single advertising medium with net reach shown by eliminating internal overlaps from the gross reach (so-called cumulation),
    - one insertion in each of two or more advertising media with net coverage shown by eliminating external overlaps from the gross coverage (so-called quantuplication),

- *combined reach*, i.e. two or more insertions in two or more advertising media. The net reach in this most common case is calculated by deducting the internal and external overlaps from the gross reach.

The influence of *multiple insertions*, i.e. the booking of an advertising medium with multiple frequency, thus leads to the following consequences with regard to

- reach to give preference to advertising media with a high proportion of fluctuating user groups, because advertising media with changing user groups reach more users on balance than those with constant user groups,
- contact intensity for the preference of advertising media with a high proportion of constant users, because advertising media with a constant user base generate more contacts with the same users on balance than those with a changing user base,
- cost-efficiency for development depending on reference value, analogous to reach as 1,000 user price or contacts as 1,000 contact price, influenced by the publishers'/broadcasters' discounts on times/quantities,
- affinity to increase in value, if growing users are target persons and vice versa.

The influence of *multiple occupancy*, i.e. placement in multiple advertising media with one insertion each, thus leads to an increase in value in the

- reach to give preference to advertising media with little external overlaps with others in the plan, i.e. a high proportion of exclusive users, because the disjunctive core user groups of several advertising media add up to a higher net reach than if the user groups overlap,
- contact intensity to give preference to advertising media with high external overlaps with other planned, i.e. low proportion of exclusive users, because overlapping user communities of several advertising media achieve multiple contacts which are not given with disjunctive user communities,
- cost-efficiency see above, but influenced by tariff price differences,
- affinity to the increase in value, if growing users are target persons and vice versa.

The plan options can be stated separately with regard to all target group criteria and all performance values, so that a precise structural analysis of the media performance is possible. This concerns e.g. Nielsen areas for comparison with distribution focal points. It is also possible to divide the data into contact classes within the framework of contact distribution.

In this respect, there is an insoluble conflict of objectives between the number/the share of reached target persons and the sum/the average of contacts achieved by advertising media. Typically, a plan combination with good values in terms of reach and 1,000 user price has at the same time bad values in terms of contact intensity and 1,000 contact price. This follows from the law of accumulation, i.e. weak reach growth coincides with strong contact growth. If this applies to several mediaplan combinations at the same time, no conclusive result can be obtained. For a given budget, a desired advertising impulse can therefore only be realized alternatively either by booking a certain number of advertising media in favor of reach with one insertion, or by booking an advertising medium over a certain number of periods in favor of contacts, or by every possible combination in between, whereby an increase in reach is inevitably at the expense of contact intensity. Unless, as the only way out, the advertising budget would be increased, because only then both partial goals can be realized simultaneously. Since such increase possibilities of the financial means are lacking practical relevance however and beyond that the budget is assumed during planning as fixed, a compromise with priority setting is usually necessary, particularly since there are effective thresholds for ranges and contacts. If necessary, the planning data may have to be changed, i.e. the target group may have to be defined more narrowly, the advertising period may have to be tightened or the amount of advertising material reduced.

Parallel to this planning dilemma of reach and contact, also the variable efficiency fluctuates. Either a plan is characterized by a particularly favorable 1,000 user price or a particularly favorable 1,000 contact price, or perhaps a good compromise between the two. Harmony exists with regard to the relationship of all other variables to each other.

Reach will be preferred over contact intensity when the advertiser is concerned with the rapid dissemination of a message, e.g. when launching a new product. Conversely, contact intensity will be preferred over reach when the advertiser wants to let learn the content of his message in the long term, e.g. with products in need of explanation. If none of these goals is clearly in the foreground, the GRP value can be used as practical compromise as a benchmark.

4.6.5 Gross rating points

Gross rating points (GRP) as gross contact sum per 100 target persons provide an indication to make inconsistent results of the evaluation comparable. The multiplicative linking of reach and contact intensity to the GRP value creates clarity here, if one criterion alone does not enjoy clear priority. The plan alternative with the highest GRP value represents the one to be preferred overall. By referring to the budget total, the profitability can also be calculated.

Advertisers often define benchmarks in order to keep pace with the advertising pressure of strategic competitors or to guarantee absolute value for money as price per GRP. Since the media usage of the competitor is known from competitive intelligence, its performance values in the own target group can also be calculated. Again, the GRP value is used as a measure for the advertising pressure. If one holds the own media usage against it, the relative advertising pressure of the competition in relation to the own target group can be determined. If this in turn is put in relation to the respective market share, overspending as well as underspending in relation to competition and market share may result, which can be consciously maintained or changed.

In addition to these heuristic procedures, which are dominant in the reality of advertising, there are also those of mathematical calculation of mediaplan combinations. Here, individual advertising media are not subjectively planned, but the planning itself is carried out by a computer program. Individual advertising media can be set and further candidate titles can be nominated. After the input has been specified by priority criteria, budget limit, frequency, object frame, effect curve and discount situation, the optimal combination of advertising media under the given conditions is then determined by statistical calculation. Theoretically, there are three procedures for this purpose:

- *Design models* of the plan structure with mutual inclusion of new advertising media in the plan list and examination of possible improvements in the defined performance criterion, mathematically the quotient of marginal benefit and marginal cost,
- *iteration models* of plan improvement with mutual addition of new advertising media to an initial plan with examination of efficiency increase, mathematically the quotient of marginal cost and marginal benefit,
- *permutation models* of the environment check of an initial plan for improvement of the cost-performance ratio by changing it.

Optimization programs are of negligible importance in practice. Apart from the exorbitant computer processing times they lead to rather schematized results. It is very likely that the media planner will still make subjective revaluations. In addition, there are further limitations of the media comparison. Above all, this results in the as yet unsolved dilemma of comparing the effects of different media genres. In order to determine the most effective medium, it would be necessary to be able to precisely quantify the advertising effect of each medium and compare them with each other. One starting point in the direction of contact quality is the identification of advertising media/multiple contacts with magazines. For this purpose, the statistical number of users of advertising media per interval as readers per issue is set in relation to the number of people who claim to actually have advertising media contact as readers per page. An index represents the degree of deviation by which the advertising material (adverts) is below the advertising medium (magazine) reach because the advertising medium is used but the advertising material is not perceived. In the same way, it is determined to what extent the advertising material is above the advertising medium contact because there have been multiple contacts with the advertising material in one advertising medium.

4.7 Optimization of media performance

The conventional possibilities of media planning are equally available to all advertisers and advertising/media agencies, they are therefore not able to work out a comparative competitive advantage. In addition, the virtually exploding range of advertising media requires an individual profile in each case. Both interests lead to a more flexible handling of the media implementation. Under the term media optimization, publishers give their customers leeway to achieve an edge.

This is particularly obvious in the most hotly contested media genres of television and magazines. In private *television*, for example, there is the possibility of booking or cancelling spots at short notice. This allows current developments at the advertiser, in his field of competition, with his customers or in his environment to be taken into account. Budget increases or cuts can also be partially absorbed. The most important aspect is certainly the possibility to rebook placements. Here, it is about to find the optimal placement depending on the auditorium, time of day and editorial environment. For this reason, the first time a booking is made, only the airtime is reserved, which can be adjusted in due time. Since the program clock of the broadcasters repeats itself weekly, and in some cases daily at fixed times, the rating figures from audience research can be used to determine how many people with certain demographic criteria have then watched television. These values are recorded every second and displayed every minute. The disadvantage is that only limited information is available on the attitudes and behavior of viewers. Nevertheless, it is possible to compare the data of viewers of certain programs, which are shown by date and time, with those of the defined target group and to book spots if there is as much congruence as possible between the two. The result of this placement can already be followed on the day following the broadcast based on the ratings and leads to the retention of this placement or to its change. These results are then followed up until a relative optimization of the placement is achieved. Since the tariff prices of the placements also vary over time, the profitability calculation is also important in addition to this coverage consideration, i.e. the change of performance in relation to its costs. In addition, parts of the program are also shifted, for example as a result of current influences, or are newly added, for example. in the case of sports events. Therefore a fast reaction is required, which is guaranteed by online connection of the media agencies with the broadcasters. For example, rating figures show that the first and last placements within an advertising block have the best chance of escaping zapping. Since this is always aimed at several advertisers simultaneously, the time factor is crucial. The know-how needed for this requires a high degree of specialization, which has led to the training of media agencies, which are actively supported by the media departments of advertisers.

In *magazines*, such media optimization is only possible to a limited extent. One instrument is issue-related circulation reporting. Since the advertising prices for all issues of a title are usually constant throughout the year, but their circulation fluctuates, a more favorable 1,000-circulation price can be achieved if high-circulation issues are booked, e. g. before Christmas, Easter. At the same time, however, these magazines are more voluminous, so that the competition between adverts for the attention of the readers is greater. In addition, the figures relating to the issues are always past values whose prognostic suitability is questionable. It is known, for example, that magazines are purchased very much on a cover-related basis and that the magazine circulation is therefore subject to fluctuation. In addition, the optimization does not help if the less expensive issues are outside of the relevant advertising period. If advertisements were to be billed according to issue-related circulation, this speculation would also be invalid. Then the positive effect of theme specials in magazines, which are being offered more and more frequently, and print promotions, such as editorial theme sections with product placement, can also be checked.

Just how difficult such differentiation is, by the way, is shown by the various reader terms which are used:

- Exclusive readers read only one publication in a category, double readers/multiple readers use two or more publications within a category. First-time readers purchase a publication and also read it mainly. Second/third readers only read a print title, but as co-readers do not buy it. Core readers regularly read a publication, operationalized by stating that they have read at least ten of the last twelve issues. The broadest circle of readers implies all persons who claim to have read at least one of the last twelve issues of a publication. Random readers are only reached by a publication on a case by case basis. Some readers purchase a print title on a contractual basis by subscription, some on a free basis via retail sale and others receive a print title in the reading circle folder.

According to the MA definition ("media currency"), a reader of a magazine is a person who has read or leafed through this magazine in whole or in part. It is not sufficient to look at the title page alone, this is only considered a "reader" in the case of daily newspapers. The periods of time on which this survey is based differ according to the type of magazine. The expected memory capacity is taken into account. In the case of monthly magazines, people are asked about the last year, in the case of fortnightly titles about the last six months and in the case of weekly titles about the last three months. In other words, the usage of the last twelve issues of a magazine is surveyed in each case. In the case of daily newspapers, the usage within the last two weeks is investigated, whereby the viewing of the cover picture is used as a criterion for the broadest reader circle. All these persons are assigned a reading probability for the relevant press medium which is above zero.

A viewer is defined as a person who has used the respective program/station continuously for at least 60 seconds (so-called minute convention) within half an hour. Reach is not determined by questioning, but by technical measurement. For this purpose the GfK Telemeter records television activities in approximately 5,640 panel households to the second. The media unit is defined as half hour during which the reported stations broadcast advertising. The times of day are 18.00/17.30–20.00 hours for ARD/ZDF and 15.00–24.00 hours for private stations. All persons are considered to have been reached by media technology if they switched on the television set for one minute during the respective half hour period, regardless of whether commercials or editorial stuff were running at that time.

4.8 Special features of business advertising

Business advertising concerns the addressing of people in their capacity as professional representatives. This means that advertising to professionals has a fundamentally different meaning than advertising to the general public. In this context, advertising is understood more as job-related information than as a seductive appearance. Accordingly, the content and style of address are also different from that of addressing the public. Primarily business-relevant arguments are offered, whereby the style constants often pick up on end-customer advertising, if present. However, the contents refer to performance, sales success, test market result, cost savings, etc. These arguments are no less emotional in professional advertising, even though they are apparently rationally interpreted. This is perfectly acceptable, since it is undoubtedly still people who are being courted, who are driven more by emotions than by reason. The variety of media genres is reduced to print media, especially newspapers and magazines, e. g. Lebensmittel-Zeitung, Textilwirtschaft. Within this media genre print, but there is an almost unmanageable number of titles. However, since professional advertising is usually based on a sectoral breakdown, this selection is actually reduced to a few titles per sector.

Professional interest titles can be divided into several categories. Depending on their content, they are

- Practice-oriented, cross-industry specialist titles,
- industry-related specialist titles, i. e. objects whose editorial content is oriented towards the information requirements of a specific economic sector,
- cross-industry, function or occupational group oriented specialist titles, i. e. those which deal with problems of functional areas or occupational groups and are used in companies in many sectors, e. g. social services, education and training, health care/medicine, business, trade, traffic/transport, crafts/industry/other trades, agriculture/forestry/horticulture/animal husbandry/hunting, authorities/military, tax/business/legal professions,
- principle- or product-oriented specialist titles, which are oriented towards technological principles, process engineering, product and material applications,
- scientific specialist titles which are aimed at target groups in research and teaching and are largely financed by subscriptions instead of adverts,
- export specialist titles whose aim it is to make the range of services available abroad.

Examples are

- *Deutsches Ärzteblatt, Lebensmittel Zeitung, Textil Wirtschaft, Horizont, Ärzte-Zeitung, Computerwoche, MM Maschinenmarkt, Markt&Technik, Allgemeine Hotel- und Gastronomie-Zeitung, Elektronik, fremdenverkehrswirtschaft/FVW, Deutsche Verkehrs-Zeitung, Automobilwoche, Pharmazeutische Zeitung, Top Agrar, Lebensmittel-Praxis, Immobilien-Zeitung.*

These specialist titles can also be delivered by alternating mailings according to subject focus, at certain intervals, according to addressee criteria or unsystematically.

However, the specialist advertising budget is regularly insufficient to finance an allocation of all relevant titles. In this respect, a comparison of the individual advertising media is necessary. However, unlike in the public sector, there are usually no meaningful market media analyses available. However, there are data specific to advertising media which, if viewed with the appropriate caution, nevertheless provide informative insights.

An important point of reference is, in the absence of any other survey of reach, the circulation. If this is IVW-tested, it can be considered sufficiently reliable. The IVW mark is a kind of seal of approval for the correctness of the reported circulation. Publisher's own figures, on the other hand, are subject to great imponderability.

Using the known circulation, different advertising media can be compared with each other over their 1,000 circulation price, i.e. it can be calculated how much 1,000 copies of a specialist title cost. The lowest 1,000 print run price represents the best price-performance ratio. However, the number of copies says nothing about the number of readers. This is because each copy of a specialist title is most likely to be used by more than one person, e.g. via distributors in the company. However, it is the number of users, i.e. reach, in particular which is important for assessing the price-performance ratio. Because a specialist title which is used by more people at the same tariff price works more efficiently than one which is used by fewer people. Apart from a few exceptions, the only information available on reach is from the publishing house, which, like any market research, is subject to more or less distortion.

However, it is not only important how many people are reached by an advertising medium, but above all which ones. This requires information about the user community. And this information is separated according to industry, hierarchical level and function. This provides information about whether the intended target group, i.e. the people who are intended to receive the advertising, are actually reached. More precisely, it is the chance of being reached by adverts in a specialist title, because the mere presence of advertising in an advertising medium by no means says anything about the fact that these users actually become aware of the advert, they rather only have the chance to do so, i.e. an opportunity to see (OTS).

4.8 Special features of business advertising

Usually there are one or more *"mandatory" titles* per industry, which are read by practically all relevant decision makers. However, this raises the problem of determining decision-makers in the context of multi-personal purchasing processes. Due to their work-specific content, specialist titles are usually a compulsory reading for professional decision-makers. They help them to recognize market trends, to become aware of innovations, to grasp industry interests, to increase qualifications, etc. Accordingly, advertising therein has a higher chance of attracting attention than in the audience. In this respect, contact with advertising media can be equated with contact with advertising material.

Publishers often have results from *user surveys*. As part of ongoing market research to optimize editorial content, these surveys as copy tests collect data on user acceptance. In the context of these surveys, which take place anyway, questions are also asked about the attention, interest and conviction of advertising. Publishers occasionally announce these data, which provide information about the advertising contact opportunities.

The review of *test copies* of specialist titles also provides decisive information. This provides information on parameters such as paper and reproduction quality, page count, ad share, editorial style, etc. It is therefore absolutely essential to request such review/working copies from the publisher. Better still, a temporary free briefing is recommended in order to get a first-hand impression of the character of the medium.

Finally the *tariff prices* are important for the decision about the advertising insertion. It must be taken into account that these costs are often comparatively low in relation to the costs of the artwork. This is because extensive preparatory work is required before an advert can appear in a business journal. The content of the advertisement has to be conceived, the design has to be specified, the individual design elements have to be implemented, e. g. photography, and produced ready for printing, e. g. preprint. Since the resulting ad always says something about the sender's self-image in addition to its purely factual message on relationship level, one must be careful not to save money at the wrong end. In this respect, costs of €8,000 per motif can easily run up. On the other hand, the insertion costs of some business journals are comparatively low.

Furthermore the following criteria are relevant for the evaluation:

- Competent editorial staff, clear thematic plans, recipient and reader structure analyses, IVW examination, reach analysis, modern contemporary design, price flexibility, willingness to negotiate/discounts, detailed, well-designed media documentation, high proportion of paid on total circulation, no color or bleed surcharges, feasibility of special advertising forms/cross-media offers, favorable price per mille, absolute number of copies, favorable thousand copies price, counting service, possibility for ad copy tests, adverts of important competitors in the title, EDA evaluation (recipient file analysis), high paper and print quality.

Due to a certain dependency of business press on the industry advertisers, they are sometimes prepared to make far-reaching concessions. Thus, considerable discounts compared to the price list can often be agreed. Furthermore, placements on the front page are possible. Company-related news can also be printed in return for adverts in the editorial section of another issue. There is also the possibility of interviews, cover stories or company portraits. Copies of these issues are made available to advertisers. Occasionally, there are also free multiple insertions to simulate advertising volume.

With regard to advertising timing, there are usually seasonal peaks in each business area, which require advertising at this time for presence reasons alone ("show the flag"). These include national and international trade fair dates. In addition, there are special editions which address specific topics and are available for booking. Finally, there is the order time, e. g. for confectionery in early summer for the Christmas business, in order to effect any updates.

Nevertheless, professional advertising often serves as an alibi. The possibilities of direct contact, in personal sales, via direct mailings or telephone contact offer more individual, better acquisition opportunities. Often, professional advertising only serves as a contact bridge to all customers, whereby A- and B-customers experience additional activities.

4.9 Media implementation

In the course of media implementation, multiple steps are involved. Of particular importance are the choice and justification of the advertising media equipment and placement as well as the advertising period and flexibility. In addition, there are tasks in the area of media purchasing and its working materials, media invoicing and its conditions as well as in the course of media processing (*see figure 34: Steps on media implementation*). These elements are explained below.

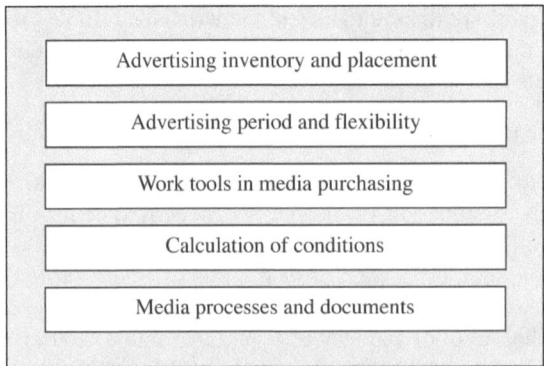

Fig. 34: Steps of media implementation

4.9.1 Advertising inventory and placement

The advertising material equipment can be determined in the print sector by format and color, in the electronics sector by length and special formats.

For *adverts*, the formats are 1/1 full page, 2/1 cross page or even more pages as an advertisement section, etc., or page-part as 1/2 page, etc. up to 1/64 page or similar. With regard to color, a distinction is made between single-color black and white (b/w) and multi-color (b/w + 1 additional color, b/w + 2 additional colors or 4-color). Occasionally, special colors are also used, such as the corporate color or gold/silver. The extent to which the application of scratch-off areas, scent markings or adhesive dots for product samples, reply postcards, etc. is useful must also be checked. This also applies to fold-out pages like gatefold, rolling gate, fold-out page, french cover, etc. or other folding techniques.

Posters are based on sheet formats, starting from 1/1 sheet (DIN A1 = 59 × 84 cm). Popular formats are multiples of this, e. g. 4/1 sheet for citylight posters. The most common format is 18/1 sheets as large format billboard. Here, it is particularly important to ensure that the quality of perception is maintained despite external influences such as weather, vandalism, detachment, etc. There are appropriate control procedures and monetary compensation for this, whereby it must be ensured that such possibilities are also used by those responsible. Furthermore, it can make sense to use unusual designs such as 3-D posters or coupon posters, which are very expensive to produce.

Spots on television and radio are measured by length in seconds. Common lengths are 7, 15, 20, 30, 60 seconds, slight over- or underruns are effectively billed by broadcasters. Special forms refer to the special design and/or placement of spots and are becoming more and more important in order to avoid the uniformity of the legally required advertising blocks. One example is program sponsoring, these are game shows or direct response spots. An important, often neglected element is the sound component, here mainly as background music.

Cinema advertising does not only consist of cinema spots and films, but can be combined with many other forms of advertising. These include back-printed tickets, posters in the entrance area, edgar cards for distribution, mirror stickers and sanitary posters, interior posters on walls and steps, video walls via beamer, door and floor stickers, flyer dispensers, stand-up tabs, printed popcorn bags, drinking cups and trays, sampling, etc. In this respect, the relatively isolated situation in the movie cinema can be well used for multi-channel addressing, especially since the visitors are still relatively homogeneous.

With regard to the placement of advertising *press media* usually prefer placements at the top or bottom edge of the page as well as in the corners, in accordance with the typical viewing pattern on the pages. Right pages should also attract more attention than left pages, and placements in the upper part of the page should be larger than those in the lower part. The effect of ads placed next to an editorial contribution (1/1 page or page-part formats) is considered to be greater. Ads in the front part of an issue are, according to primacy effect, considered better than those in the back part. In the case of magazines, placements on the cover pages at the front, at inside front cover opposite the table of contents, at inside back cover as the last inside page of the magazine or at back cover are often aimed for because of the presumably higher attention. For newspapers, placements in the title page header on the front page are particularly sought after. In the case of specialist titles, placement on the title cover is also possible. If a press medium contains special topics, placement within these topics or specials is particularly worthwhile.

Placement is naturally of particular importance in the case of *outdoor media*, as it essentially determines the extent of contact between target persons and advertising. For poster panels, there are elaborate billboard evaluation procedures which ensure that the price-performance ratio enjoys priori. Higher tariff prices, which are usually divided into three price categories, then also mean better visibility.

In the case of *electronic media*, there is a need for block advertising on television and radio as well as in the cinema. This is not unproblematic, as there are interference effects between the spots in a block, i.e. of several advertising messages broadcast in a row, only the message with the greatest impact will probably be remembered by the recipients and neutralize the effect of all other messages. To prevent this, two ways out are seen: the highest possible advertising penetration by budget or the strongest impact via creativity, both of which are difficult to achieve. At least in the important medium of television, zapping as switching to another, supposedly ad-free TV channel is an additional complication. In this respect, it is recommended to aim for a placement as the first or last spot in the commercial break. The first spot has the best chance of escaping the zapping, and the last spot has chances because viewers switch back to the original channel in anticipation of the program's continuation. Increasingly, TV stations are synchronizing their commercial block times, so that it is also possible to show a parallel activation during important commercial events as so-called roadblocking.

4.9.2 Advertising intensity and flexibility

For a given advertising area and advertising period, different intensities of communication may be required (*for context see figure 35: Options of advertising intensities*):

- *Constant advertising intensity* means that the media usage in the entire advertising area remains at a constant level during the entire advertising period,
- variable advertising intensity means that the use of media is on a continuously *rising level* or *falling level*, this is referred to as back loading or front loading, the choice depends on whether the primacy effect or the recency effect is preferred,

4.9 Media implementation

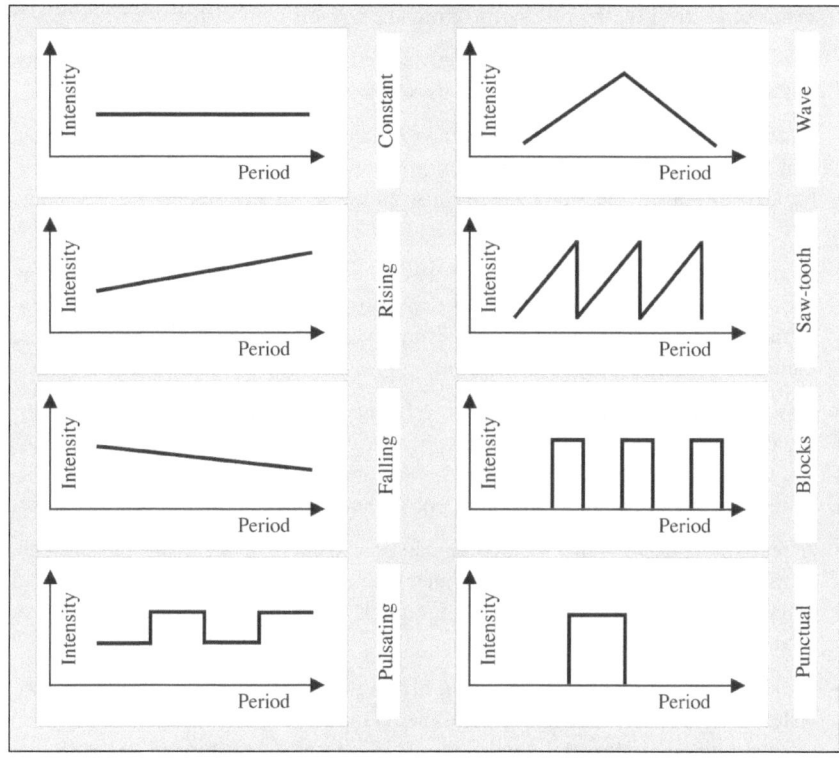

Fig. 35: Options of advertising intensities (Source: own illustration)

- *pulsating* advertising intensity means that the media use takes place at regularly or irregularly changing intervals on a regularly or irregularly changing levels, this is often the case with seasonal businesses,
- rising and falling *wave-like* advertising intensity means that the advertising is aimed at a peak season period with a development effect and an aftermath effect,
- a *sawtooth shape* means, that the advertising intensity is rising to a certain level and then immediately stops to start again on a significantly lower base, the idea behind this is, that the impetus bypasses the interjacent low-level period to the next high-level period,
- *blocked* advertising intensity means that individual activity flights are placed, between which periods without advertising appeal remain,
- *punctual* advertising intensity means that advertising is only carried out during one limited period of time, e.g. a seasonal peak as a burst.

In terms of flexibility, the following application levels can be distinguished:

- *Exactly to the day* implies an extremely short reaction time. The prerequisite for this are appropriate concepts which make this rapid deployment possible.
- *Exactly to the week*, the reaction time exceeds one day. This is due to the fact that appropriate technical production precautions are required before use, e.g. for artwork, or the reaction time of those carrying out advertising must be taken into account, e.g. at publishing houses.
- *Exactly to the month*, the reaction time exceeds one week. This is due to more complicated technical production precautions, e.g. in the case of three-dimensional advertising media, or to longer intervals between the use of advertising media, e.g. until the publication date.
- The media's response is more likely to be medium-term *exactly to the quarter*. This means that it is only possible to respond to changing environmental conditions to a very limited extent. The reasons for this are both the need for internal organizational preparation and the need to notify the external availability of measures.
- A reaction time of *half of the year* can easily occur if there are no strategic framework plans available for changes in the environment, but these have to be developed first. In this case, even a quick reaction does not help to achieve greater flexibility in implementation.
- *Yearly exact* corresponds to the usual media planning intervals. It allows a consistent, efficient and well-considered media mix. No consideration can be given to changing environmental conditions. This is reserved for the operative media.

The different level is achieved either by the breadth of the address according to the number of communication instruments or the depth according to the penetration per communication instrument or by a combination of both.

4.9.3 Work tools in media purchasing

The most important tools in media purchasing are the factsheet, the advertising media rate and the media data.

Media purchasing is carried out differently depending on the type of media. Print will be discussed here as an widely used example. For press media, an information sheet (so-called electronic factsheet) should be created for every eligible title. It contains information about the following:

- Publisher address for advertising planning and production, circulation differentiated and most possibly IVW-tested, frequency of publication, readership structure by industry, hierarchy level, function, content in editorial focus, booking by competitors, year of publication for market persistence, tariff costs of common formats.

4.9 Media implementation

With regard to the criterion circulation, a distinction must be made between different *circulation terms* as follows:

- Print run as the number of copies which comes off the printing machine (less waste), subscription run as the number of copies sold on a fixed contractual basis, also as member copies or as part of a collective subscription, reading circle run as the number of copies which are processed in reading circle folders, single copy circulation as the number of copies sold at POS and sold circulation as the number of copies which are actually sold (single copy sales less returns), circulation actually distributed as the number of copies sold and distributed elsewhere, circulation distributed free of charge as the number of copies distributed as free copies but not sold, residual, archive, specimen copies as the number of copies which do not reach the readership, controlled circulation as the number of copies which are reported by the IVW as sold/distributed, guaranteed circulation as the number of copies which the publisher guarantees as a minimum in his tariff, binding circulation as the number of copies which are sent for further processing after printing, reader circulation as the number of copies which are saleable/distributable, returns as the number of copies which are not sold in the circulation interval and are returned to the publisher as complete issues, partial returns of only the title page or head returns of only the logo receipt.

This means that all important data are available at a glance. It is important that they are constantly updated. For this purpose, it is necessary to evaluate the updated, valid tariffs, i.e. the publishers' price and conditions lists. It is therefore necessary to always regard all tariffs of potential publishers available in the latest edition.

An *advertising medium tariff* generally contains the following information (using again print as example):

- Sequence number of the price list and period of validity, general terms and conditions which are accepted when the order is placed, basic prices for the most important formats, these usually contain 15 % agency commission as remuneration for advertising agencies, surcharges on these basic prices, e.g. for bleed, i.e. use of the entire area beyond the type area of a page, spot colors, i.e. those which are not or cannot be created from the four-color set, special formats, e.g. non-rectangular, etc. discounts in the form of number and unit discounts in scales, whereby the number discount refers to the number of insertions within a contract year, the unit discount refers to the cumulative quantity of these insertions and the respectively more favourable discount rate can be claimed, prices for multi-colour adverts, practically all colors can be built up from the four basic colors cyan, magenta, yellow and key/CMYK, column width and number of columns per page, height and width of the trimmed booklet format and format of the type area which leaves the unprinted edge of a page all around, plus bleed, i.e. motif reserve all around, page content in millimeters. This is important if the price is calculated in millimeters, the gross price per page, i.e. if a 1/1 p. page is advertised, and price per millimeter, this information refers to a millimeter height in the respective column width, advertising deadline for booking an issue, delivery deadline for the submission of artwork, cancellation date, a place which has already been booked can be cancelled up to this date, topic plan of the editorial department, this is important in order to be able to utilize synergy effects between editorial reporting and own ad insertion, partial booking information, because some publishers offer the possibility of separate booking according to federal states or Nielsen areas, express booking for last-minute ad placements and local rates which apply to local advertisers who place ads without an advertising agency, prices/editions/placements for lose inserts, these are only attached loosely to the carrier medium, stickers, these are glued onto one side of the carrier medium, and bound-in inserts, these are an integral part of the carrier medium, technical data for inserts, stickers and bound-in inserts, e. g. maximum and minimum formats, paper quality, paper weight, terms of payment and discount, place of publication (usually the publisher's headquarters), address of the advertising management, guaranteed sold circulation, publishers increasingly give credit if this circulation is not reached, circulation of reading circles, if available, copy price, if a specialist title is not only available by subscription.

In the event that such rates are not available or it is not known which advertising media are eligible for booking, there is another important tool in the form of *media data*. There the following information is provided (staying with print as example):

- Brief description of the advertising medium, organ (association, etc.), publisher (name, address), editorial office (name, address), advertising management (name, address), current year, publication frequency, publishing house (postal address, telecom connections, bank details), publication schedule, editorial plan, first day of sale, subscription price (copy price), scope analysis (editorial office, advertisements), content analysis (editorial focus), advertisement control (IVW), print run, actual circulation, sold circulation, subscribed circulation, single copy circulation, free copies, remaining/archive/voucher/working copies, geographical distribution analysis (federal states/Nielsen areas), recipient analysis, if available by industry, economic sector, specialization, occupational group, size of economic units, etc.

4.9.4 Calculation of media conditions

A central element in media purchasing is naturally the calculation of media prices. In the case of newspapers, the advertising rates vary from title to title and can be found in the respective tariff. It is important not to assume the stated circulation of the newspaper, since the same copy of a newspaper is always used by several people, i.e. 1,000 copies reach far more than 1,000 people, because one and the same copy is used by several members of the household, for example.

The basis for calculating is the *advert price*, i.e. the price for 1 mm height in a column width of usually 45 mm (mm-price). Different basic prices may apply for the same newspaper for different sections and/or issues. The rate shows common ad formats as fixed prices, e.g. 1/1, 1/2, 1/3, 2/3 pages. Page-wide ads run across the entire page width, page-high ads run analogously across the entire page height as strip ads.

A calculation example for newspaper adverts is as follows:

- ad format: 2 columns per 150 mm (W × H)
- mm-price: 4 €
- ad price: (150 mm × 4 € per mm) × 2 columns = € 1.200 total.

Continuous small ads, i.e. those which are not designed, are charged according to the number of words or possibly lines used plus cipher fee. The usual classification is by category such as finance, opportunities, cars, real estate, official announcement, family, education, tourism, etc. Commercial advertisers are possibly to be marked separately.

With regard to discounts, a distinction must be made between repeat and quantity discounts. The respectively higher discount can be claimed. The repeat discount depends on the number of insertions except for classified ads and is usually graduated between 5–20 %, the quantity discount depends on the total advertising space taken up for the same advertiser. Discounts are granted for all ads in a contract year determined by the advertiser. With skilful negotiation and a certain minimum volume, it should be possible to negotiate a bonus or a discount e.g. as free insertions with the publisher at the end of the year.

Several local newspapers are often united under one organizational roof as advertising ring/tariff community. If two or more newspapers under one roof are jointly booked with adverts, it is possible to take advantage of a combination discount.

The basic format for magazines is 1/1 page and multiples thereof (2/1 p., etc.) or a fraction thereof (3/4 p., 1/2 p., etc.). The ad formats are located in the type area with an unprinted margin all around, printed in bleed up to the paper edge, and the margin on the right on the left side are also printed, have portrait or landscape formats, etc. The mechanical display split allows two or more identically equipped motifs to be alternately switched within issues. The geographical split allows two or more equally equipped motifs to be distributed to different circulation areas, usually Nielsen areas.

Advertising rates are calculated linearly across different formats based on the area occupied. In addition, there is occasionally a surcharge of approx. 30–35 % per color, whereby this is always based on the entire page, even if only page formats are used. Repeat, quantity and combination discounts apply to all inventory.

Booking is made by means of an advertising order, the content of which is determined by the tariff of the advertising medium. The advertising deadline is usually three to four weeks before the publication date, and at the same time this is also the cancellation date for advertising orders placed earlier. In contrast the print copy deadline is the date by which the contractually agreed advert template must be received by the publisher at the latest.

In the case of poster advertising, the positions are divided into three *outdoor tariff groups*, depending on the quality of the location. This again is determined by factors such as location, pedestrian frequency, visibility, etc. The calculation is based on the sheet price per day, i.e. price per 1/1 sheet per posting day. Volume discounts are calculated on the basis of board decades, i.e. the number of boards and decades used. Booking and cancellation deadlines are 90 days before the start of posting. Orders 180 days before the start of posting are usually invoiced with a special discount.

Television spots are calculated on the basis of prices per second. These vary according to month, weekday, time of day and commercial break. The television stations work with a fixed time line as so-called "program clock" with daily recurring thematic focuses, in some cases covering several days at fixed times. By coordinating editorial and advertising content, synergies can be achieved in the placement between program and advertising. Advertising breaks between two programs are possible at any time, interruptions within a program depend in their frequency on the program duration. The assignment is carried out via TV-marketing companies (IPA-RTL, Seven One, etc.), which take over the purchase of advertising time for their associated broadcasters and, in some cases, the sale of print media advertising.

The costs for *radio spots* depend on the time of day, most expensive between 7.30–10.00 a.m., also at noon, cheapest after 7.00 p.m. and on weekends. The prices can be seen in the respective tariff, which also shows the terms and conditions of business in addition to the price list. It also contains information about the program format of the station with sound colors such as classical, rock, oldies, etc. and the editorial timelines. This information is decisive for the evaluation of the station or its audience and the placement of the individual spots, since the respective program content in turn allows conclusions to be drawn about the audience.

A major threat to the media performance of radio broadcasting is zapping, i.e. the switching through of stations, which causes a high fluctuation of listeners. For this reason, a comparatively large number of repetitions is required to reach the same people several times with a commercial. Often, local program windows are also broadcast in by supra-regional stations, which allow individual content for the local environment on an hourly basis within a mantle program which is otherwise identical (so-called syndication).

Various special forms of advertising can be used for *cinema advertising*, mostly the spot/film combined with on-site promotions in the foyer. However, the amount of advertising per screening is limited, as is the length of each cinema spot to two minutes, although usually it is only 30 seconds long. The booking is usually hall-related. The screening costs depend on the size of the room and the duration of occupancy. The screening takes place in blocks before the pre-program and between the pre- and main-program. Placement orders are not concluded with individual cinema tenants, but only with national advertising marketers. These can also refuse orders due to content, origin or technical reasons. Above all, lead times must be observed.

In recent times, some controversially discussed conditions have been added. For example, TV stations are offering *media agencies* discounts in kind, i. e. free postings in the event that contact cost per mille guarantees are not reached. It is questionable, however, whether these quotas are actually passed on to their clients, the advertisers, because they alone are entitled to them, or whether they are used by the media agencies to acquire new clients by offering low prices, which would mean embezzlement. Likewise, kickbacks from the media to the intermediaries, the media agencies, are common as goodwill for their commission. Here too, it is questionable whether and to what extent these are passed on to advertisers. The same applies to initial booking discounts or share deals, i. e. discounts on the budget share for an advertiser in an advertiser's total budget. Therefore, there are efforts to pay out discounts only on a customer-related basis and in cash to achieve more transparency.

4.9.5 Media processes and documents

Media processing is based on five plans: the media plan, the distribution map, the cost survey, the prepayment overview and the production schedule (*see figure 36: Media processing documents*).

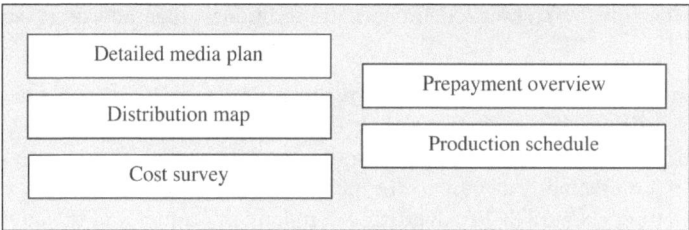

Fig. 36: Media processing documents

The media implementation is based on an approved *detailed media plan*, which contains the following information:

- Title of the selected advertising media, number of insertions per advertising medium, timing of the insertions per advertising medium, equipment according to format, colors, special forms, motifs inserted, references to special agreements, costs of the insertions individually and in total.

The *distribution map* gives an overview of the temporal distribution of all advertisements in all advertising media in the form of a calendar. It usually has the following structure:

- Header, usually divided into weeks and provided with the dates of the installation of each week, head column with indication of the advertising media, end column with indication of the costs per advertising medium and the sum of the costs, heading with indication of advertiser, brand, product, budget year, division for motives, equipment, actions.

The individual insertions are marked with crosses in the week of the respective publication date or bars for the duration of the advertising medium circulation.

The next document of the purchase within the media implementation is the *cost survey*. This reflects the financial campaign situation. It contains in detail:

- All advertising media used, the format, color, time/duration, bleed, type, etc. of the advertising media, the frequency of use, the regular costs according to the price list as gross prices, the individual discounts, these depend on the combination of the placement in two or more advertising media combined in one rate combination, thus providing the advertiser with an incentive to use his own advertising media instead of competing media, furthermore from the contract year for which discounts are agreed, in each case a period of time, the start of which is determined by the client at his own discretion, then from the affiliation of the advertiser to a corporate body, this is important for a group discount and from individual negotiations to determine the net prices per advertising medium after the discounts mentioned (so-called 1st net), the net-net prices after deduction of the agency commission (so-called 2nd net), the sum of the cost items of all advertising media, the discount amount deductible on advance payment (usually 2 %) (so-called 3rd net), the additional value-added tax (so-called 4th net).

This results in the next step in the *prepayment overview*. This is only necessary if an advertising agency is involved. It ensures that the funds required for the placement are available on time and in the correct amount. Because the media agency is contractually debtor to the publisher/station/tenant it is not ensured that the actual client, i.e. the advertising company as customer of the advertising agency, is solvent as well as willing to pay, there is a risk that the agency will be called upon for amounts for which it is not responsible. Therefore, it makes sense to ensure that the required funds are available in time. There is the deadline of the withdrawal date with publishing houses. A cancellation of an order after this deadline is no longer possible.

The prepayment overview of the advertising agency informs the advertiser, usually monthly, about the budget amounts which will soon be due for insertions. It is broken down by advertising medium, equipment, frequency, payable net per advertising medium, payable net per publisher/station/tenant, covered period and payment date. The advertising agency will submit advance payment requests for the following month to its client by the cut-off date and check whether the advance payment for this is made on time. In doing so, the client usually settles all amounts due for the following month in one sum. In any case, this deadline must be before the deadline for the advertising agency. Only if the necessary funds for the settlement of the placed orders are available on the account of the advertising agency, it will leave the intended bookings. Otherwise, it will ask its client whether there has been an oversight or whether the insertion should be cancelled. The procedure of booking insertions with advertising media as early as possible in order to achieve favorable placements there requires a complete tracking of deadlines and costs in order to avoid expensive breakdowns. At the same time, the advertising agency has larger amounts of liquid money at its disposal, since payment is only due after the insertion of the advertising media, while maintaining discount advantages. From this investment profits with mediators and/or capital commitment costs with clients result.

The fourth plan is a *production schedule* as overview of the templates to be submitted. In detail are specified in it:

- Advertising media which are to be used, selected equipment of the insertion in format, color, publication dates, production process of the advertising media, required insertion templates, motifs to be inserted with time allocation, shipping address, if necessary with shipping method, deadline for template submission.

Even in retrospect, there are possibilities for exerting influence, especially in three ways. Firstly, the technical quality of the advertising material must be checked, i.e. the print quality of the advert, the transmission quality of the television or radio spot, the reproduction of the cinema spot and the status of the outdoor poster site. If something is irregular, there is the necessaty to raise a complaint. Advertisers are usually accommodating, so that a price reduction or partial or complete free replacement can be expected.

Secondly, the placement of the advertising material must be controlled. Although a certain space for the advertisement is booked, the publishers reserve the right to change placements for technical reasons (pagination). With posters, booking implies a certain space and the right to be able to occupy it with advertising. The same applies to TV and radio spots on private commercial stations and cinema advertising. However, there is always the objection of the change for technical reasons on the part of the organization carrying out the advertising, which must then be proven by it.

And thirdly, the billing must be checked. It must be checked whether exactly the prices have been calculated which are shown in the current tariff and all the discounts due as well as the negotiated individual conditions have been taken into account.

5. Online advertising

Online advertising is establishing itself between classical advertising and non-classical advertising as an increasingly dominant third sector. This can be divided as follows: Information technologies in the sound area, text area, data area, graphics area, fixed image area, moving image area, animation area, storage media, and transmission networks/Internet with services such as WWW, e-mail, etc., these are the focus of the following.

Interested parties are already claiming 45% of all advertising expenditure for online media. This is certainly speculative, as these expenditures are difficult to estimate and many ads are also very small-sized, e.g. advertising portals such as Immoscout. The expenditures in the more controllable areas speak a different language and range at about 30% share. It is undisputed, however, that the share of online media is very likely to grow.

The internet provides various services, the use of which is relatively simple, since for each of these services corresponding programs can be called up on the computer. The best known service is certainly the World Wide Web (WWW). But there are also a lot of other internet services. Online media can thus be plausibly categorized into non-web applications using other protocols than *http/s*, web 1.0 applications *half-duplex and/or vertically* and web 2.0 applications *full-duplex and/or horizontally* (*see figure 37: Forms of online media*).

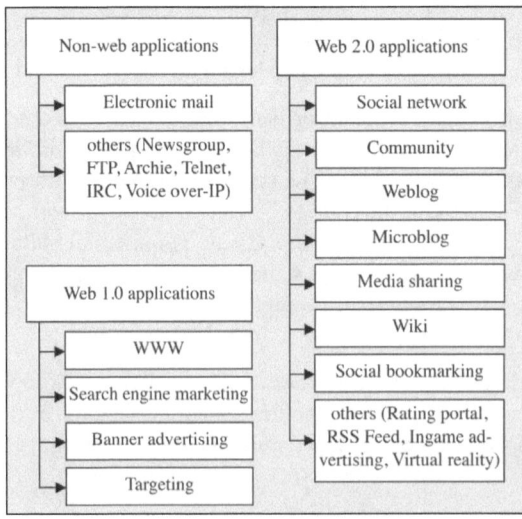

Fig. 37: Forms of online media

5.1 Non-web applications

The dominant non-web online application is for sure electronic mail. But besides that, there are several other applications, which are going mainly to be displaced by web-applications. Examples are file transfer protocol, newsgroup, internet relay chat and others.

5.1.1 Electronic mail

The most widespread service is certainly the electronic mail (e-mail). It uses the internet service e-mail as a means of transport for direct advertising messages to transmit messages and information with a time delay between two or more communication partners. As with the sending of conventional letters, the sender must compose a message, which must be provided with the the e-mail address of the recipient. It is sent to the "post office" mail server of the sender, which sends the electronic mail to the mail server of the recipient. There it is temporarily stored until the recipient starts his e-mail software and practically looks into his mailbox. In addition to sending messages to individuals or groups, it is also possible to send texts, digital data for graphics, images, sound files, etc. and electronic newsletters by e-mail.

5.1.1.1 Design of acquisitional e-mails

The header part of the e-mail contains the addressee, copy recipient and subject. This information is used for transport purposes. The text part of the e-mail contains the actual message. E-mails are extremely fast. By bypassing the conventional "snail" mail, the messages reach the recipient within seconds, regardless of their physical location. It is possible to receive a reply at the same speed. E-mails as such are free of charge. Dispatch and delivery can take place around the clock ("24/7"). Various protocols are used for transmission such as simple mail transfer protocol, post office protocol, Internet message access protocol and multipurpose internet mail extensions.

However, one must bear in mind that e-mails are regularly not data-protected. Theoretically, a system administrator ("postmaster") can read the e-mail at any node it passes through while it is being sent. Therefore, confidential data should be encrypted. The exact number of e-mail addresses is not known, since the operators assign names for server addresses using wildcards for individual letters/digits, which allow addresses to be generated internally from any combination of numbers and digits just as much as needed. Thus, there should be two to three e-mail clients attached to each address, but it is not known which of the addresses assigned to users are actually used and which are idle.

Attachments should be avoided with e-mails; they increase the volume of data and are suspicious of viruses when opened. Also, CCs should not be sent, as this gives the impression of mass mailings. Links directly to specific landing pages are helpful. These websites are ideal for personalizing the message. A callback button allows the sender to be contacted.

To check the functionalities, it is advisable to send a test mailing to your own address. Test elements are sender address, subject line, format, headline, time of dispatch, etc. The best dispatch date is the middle of the week, the best time is the late afternoon. Preview, content entry and archive functions are helpful.

Apart from the fact that the mass distribution of e-mails violates netiquette, this is also legally not permitted, at least in the B-t-c area and in the case of otherwise non-existent business relationships, because retrieving e-mails costs the recipient time and effort to download them from the e-mail server. Nevertheless, e-mail advertising can be considered highly interesting, as it allows very precise targeting in the distribution. In practice, permission marketing is used, i.e. the willingness of interested parties to be included in an e-mail list is checked. This not only avoids the legal inadmissibility, but also prevents otherwise possibly unrecognized misdistribution. Newsletters are sent out regularly and essentially contain editorial information on which advertising messages are based. Subscription is made by filling out a registration form on the newsletter editor's website for permission. In this respect, a high degree of target group accuracy can be achieved for advertising. At the same time, the strict legal framework is adhered to.

5.1.1.2 Newsletter management

Newsletters especially are regular mailings to a predefined group of addressees, who have subscribed. Newsletters may only be sent if the recipient has given his or her consent, which must be revocable at any time as double opt-in. Spam is defined as unsolicited impersonal and commercial e-mails. In order to prevent this, the requirements of data economy, the possibility of revocation at any time by opt-out and the provider identification, as implemented in permission marketing, apply. The goal is the realization of a progression over time from anonymous e-mail address to interest profile, personal e-mail address, name and postal address. With growing trust, such a step-by-step approach is possible.

Link tracking is a check to see which contents meet the greatest interest. Clicks on hyperlinks which are integrated into the newsletter and refer to a website with further information serve as a basis. This can be collected, stored and further processed anonymously or on a personal basis. Profile data is used to individualize the newsletter through dynamic content, composed of different text modules, or for special mailings. It is possible to automatically adapt the dynamic content to the click behavior of the user.

Campaign management first requires the determination of the e-mail frequency weekly or fortnightly. Then there must be addresses to which the e-mails are to be sent. Such e-mail addresses can be generated by purchase, rent or exchange. Purchase requires that the addressees have given their consent to being contacted. Renting presupposes that it is possible to leave the distribution list at any time. And exchange presupposes that the own subscribers have agreed to it. Freemailers or lottery portals, but then unselected, as well as permission addresses of address publishers also serve as address sources.

An own e-mail distribution list is set up via the own homepage to registration templates e. g. pop-up windows, and incentives or sample mailings can be used to reinforce this. The address input requires checking the correctness of the input, i. e. only valid characters, at least eight characters long, the @-sign must be followed by at least five characters. The registration confirmation can be made by single opt-in, i. e. simple registration of the interested party, by confirmed opt-in, i. e. registration of the interested party with confirmation to this address or, regularly, by double opt-in, i. e. registration of the interested party with confirmation to this address and subsequent confirmation for activation. In all cases the interested party will receive regular information afterwards.

The announcement of the newsletter takes place online as well as offline from e-mail addresses of customers, reference to the newsletter in usual correspondence, via classical media, packaging, events, etc. This requires an exact target group determination via profile data from the registration and response data from the interaction behavior. This also enables an individualization of the message. The subscription can be promoted by incentives such as information advantage, price discount, privilege, etc.

Dispatch is carried out via an application service provider. Users can be encouraged to recommend the service to others. In case of bounces, the address must be verified or deleted. An autoresponder can automatically generate response e-mails with standardized content under a given e-mail address. The software provided by the supplier can be programmed individually or used as a complete solution. The connection to existing, mostly CRM or ERP systems is also important.

In order to create the newsletter, it is first necessary to determine the format. This can be a pure text format, HTML format (Multipart) or PDF format for animation, sound, etc.

The naming of the sender is mandatory, the subject line should be kept as meaningful as possible to increase the probability of opening. The sender's name, address, authorized representative, telephone number, e-mail address, commercial register number and sales tax identification number are indicated in the imprint. It is useful to include a data protection notice and mandatory to include an unsubscribe notice.

The newsletter consists of header, text and footer. It should be clearly structured. The font size should be at least 11 points. Short texts are preferable, but the colors red and blue should be avoided. Links must not be abbreviated, nor should exclamation marks and percentage signs be used, otherwise suspected spam can lead to suppression of the mail. It is helpful to check the plausibility of the input, e.g. only valid characters, with an appropriate correction note.

Response management includes help for forgotten passwords, the possibility to log off and the identification of keywords for autoresponders. Autoresponders are used, for example, for order confirmations, general terms and conditions, price lists, FAQs, order forms and operating instructions. Success is monitored via response rates of various types, such as bounce rates, i.e. undeliverable e-mails, opening rates, click through rates and conversion rates into information request/order. Other variables are costs per thousand on the basis of all recipients and costs per click on basis of all recipients who clicked a link as well as costs per order.

Qualitative data are obtained by means of surveys on recipient satisfaction, by asking for reasons for unsubscribing, by analyzing click behavior, and by customer profiles and ratings.

5.1.2 Other non-web internet services

Besides e-mail advertising there are also other services available, such as file transfer protocol, archie, telnet, internet relay chat or voice over-IP. These are explicates in the following.

Newsgroups are automatic directory systems for discussion posts. In these groups one can communicate with people who are currently dealing with certain topics of any kind in order to get information or exchange information with like-minded people. Often, these lists also maintain an archive in which older discussion contributions can be traced. Communication takes place via the usenet using network news transfer protocol (NNTP), asynchronously, i.e. with a time delay:

- In the case of open lists, it is possible for anyone to participate in the discussion. To be accepted as a participant, an e-mail is sent to the list server address and refers to a specific discussion group. This means that one is registered there. To contribute to the discussion group, one may send an e-mail with the own contribution to the list address. All participants registered in a discussion list now receive this e-mail by forwarding it via these list addresses.

- In the case of moderated lists, the discussion contributions are first sent to a moderator, who checks them with regard to certain principles of the discussion list and their suitability of content for the relevant topic. E-mails which are technically unsuitable or uninteresting are not forwarded. This may lead to a higher quality of the published contributions, but at the same time there is also the risk of a certain, even if only unconscious, censorship.

- In the case of non-public lists, participants are not automatically included in the discussion group. Instead, a letter of acceptance is to be sent to the list administrator. The list administrator then decides on the inclusion, which will reduce the number of discussion members and increase the presumed level of their contributions.

The *file transfer protocol* (FTP) is a cross-operating system protocol for transferring text and binary data between different computers connected to the internet in a peer to peer system. By using this protocol, it is possible to download files and programs to the own computer via internet or to play them on other computers. Each computer can act as both client and server (so-called peer to peer). FTP is thus in competition with the WWW, which is also suitable for the distribution of information, but is superior to it in terms of its multimedia capabilities. Files or software are downloaded via FTP servers, which manage an immense archive. In some cases, a password must be entered beforehand. Then the user only has to click on the desired file/software and specify the directory to which he wants to copy it.

To find the desired files/software, *archie* serves as a search machine. This server has an archive of all FTP servers and their respective contents, so that one can use Archie to find out where a desired source is located. Gopher helps the user to access the various resources of the internet. The search for this information starts at an entry point in the search space, from there it goes via links to other Gopher servers which hold potential information. However, this service is being superseded by the WWW.

Terminal emulations (Telnet) allow the user to log on and pilot remote computers as hosts whose programs can be started and used. The own computer works as a terminal on the remote computer, without the remote computer being installed as its server. The screen content of the remote computer is rather sent to the own computer, processed and displayed there. To use this function, appropriate software is required both on the own and on the remote computer. In some cases, a password is required for access. Telnet opens up great possibilities for teleworking, but its use is purely command-oriented and therefore not very user-friendly. In this respect, the WWW is dominant.

Internet relay chat (IRC) offers a simultaneous, real time communication on the internet. Users log into an IRC server deploying a client under a pseudonym or their real name, open a new conversation or join a conversation which is already in progress. This synchronous dialog takes place around the clock, because people from all time zones can participate. One can also send files to each other. Today, chats are mostly WWW-based.

Internet phone & video (voice over-IP) enable the simultaneous speaking, listening resp. watching of the communication partners. Users log on to an internet phone server and all users who are also present are displayed on their screen (e. g. Skype). The communication is started by clicking on the desired participant. A data compression method is used to send digitized voice and video images through the internet. In addition to the visibility of the partner, the advantage lies in the comparatively low costs, since the internet access is usually located in the local area of the user, so that international long-distance calls can be made at flat rates. However, the connection quality is limited. With teleconferencing (e. g. Zoom), more than two participants can communicate with each other. All conference topics are represented by a video image, the dialog follows either via a text box or audio.

5.2 Web 1.0 applications

World wide web (also web/WWW) is a graphic-capable, multimedia and service-integrating surface of the internet. Its universal user interface allows access to the entire range of information there. Different information in texts, graphics, pictures, videos, databases, etc. are combined into a whole. The hypertext transfer protocol/http of the WWW regulates the communication between the browser programs which can display hypertext documents and the web servers. Hypertext can be used to provide structured information on the internet in order to make the wealth of information available in a clear and concise manner. Individual words in the text can be underlined or other image elements can be used as links within the website or hyperlinks to other websites. A mouse click establishes a connection to the computer to which the address of the link as uniform resource locator points. Every object on the internet is uniquely defined by its URL. This simplifies navigation and makes the WWW very user-friendly. Another advantage is the ability to design a graphical user interface. The overwhelming popularity of the WWW means that it is often equated with the internet par excellence and not actually seen as one service alongside others. The page description language of the WWW is the hypertext markup language. This is used to define the logical structural elements of a page such as headings, paragraphs, etc. and to determine the integration of graphics, images, tables, etc. The page layout is created by interpretation on the client side using a web browser.

5.2.1 Website presence

The website presence includes different conceptional dimensions as well as usability aspects. Moreover the website is a central advertising medium in many cases by insertions on the respective webpages.

5.2.2.1 Conceptual dimensions

The conceptual dimensions of the web presence concern in detail the domain name, content, design and user guidance.

Domain name

One of the most important decisions in this context concerns the choice of the right domain. This does not necessarily have to correspond to the company, but it must be memorable, positively associative and clearly writable. When registering, possibly varying spellings should be reserved and then set up with a redirection to the correct URL. This also applies to different end domains (.de, .com).

A complete URL consists of the service, e. g. WWW, the protocol, e. g. http, the actual domain address and the level domain, e. g. de. The service indicates which online service currently is used, the protocol indicates the technical connection base, the level domain provides information about the origin or content of the website, e. g. com, biz, net, org. Anyone can register as many domains as they like, the registration is done by an internet provider. The rule of temporal priority applies in principle. In order to increase the number of possible URLs, numerous new top level domains have been introduced, and the domain addresses have also been made more flexible, e. g. only two letters. If there is no temporal priority, a domain may still be subject to legal action. For example, a company can demand that its name be surrendered as a third party domain if the vast majority of users expect the company to be at this address and not the actual holder with temporal priority. Confusion with brand names should also be avoided, and a brief check on trademark law is possible.

The check of free domain names is done under denic.de for .de domains or at a web host. Domains which have already been allocated can possibly be purchased, e. g. via sedo. For particularly sought-after, generic domains, the search term and domain name match, e. g. the term "marketing". Two-word domains are also possible, usually connected with a hyphen, e. g. "marketing-domain". More than two words may be confused with search engine spammers. Second level domains bear the host name, third level domains are composed, e. g. "de.tt" for Audi tt coupe.

Contents

A website is characterized by contents of text and image, emotional elements as personal address and colors as well as interactive elements like hyperlinks, contact options, configurator. The texts should be provided with a short summary at the beginning. Enumerations and subheadings help with the necessary structuring. It is important to ensure easy readability and avoid unnecessary jargon.

Important text elements are the headline with a recommended maximum of six words and otherwise self-explanatory, the subline/skyline to explain the headline, a teaser as opening credit, the actual continuous text, first with the important facts, then with details, then in-depth, and a formulation active, i. e. verbs instead of nouns, in the language of the target group, without filler words, without nested sentences, with short words and paragraphs for each new thought. Pictures should be authentic and have a subline, picture and text should not double but complement each other. The reading speed on screen is much slower than in print, also the resolution is much lower, so that keywords should be used. Content is usually first roughly scanned and searched for relevant information, the processing depth is low by scanning. Core elements of the text are then captured, the reading speed is reduced by skimming. The most important content is then read at a comparatively low speed and captured in full.

The typography should use familiar fonts, Verdana is often used, the font size should be 9–11 points, capitals should be avoided. The line spacing should be 120 % of the text size. The line length should be set to 45–55 characters or eleven words. Line breaks should be with hard separation. Black on white or blue on white have proven to be the best font colors.

Graphic

For the graphic web presence, a screen layout with design grid, typography and technical elements such as loading time, technical presentation are characteristic. The design of websites happens according to the criteria of information and functionality as well as aesthetics and entertainment. Texts are entered in HTML or xHTML format. Cascading style sheets apply to the design of color, form, arrangement and grouping. Color selection must be done using a calibrated red-green-blue monitor to avoid color distortion. A maximum of three colors plus black and white are reasonable on one page. Complementary colors, i.e. those that complement each other to form basic colors and are opposite each other in the color wheel, should be avoided. The font size must not be set too small, texts should always be left-aligned. Short lines and paragraphs are to be kept, because you "see" differently on screen than in print. A sans serif font should be used.

The page design is at least created in a minimum resolution (1,024 × 768 pixels), which is important for end devices with small screens such as laptops, netbooks, etc. Technically possible is also a responsive page design which adapts to the respective screen format. For the reproduction of animations, the browser must be supplemented by plug-ins, which, if otherwise unavoidable, should be implemented as a download offer on the site.

The website is considered a platform for directly addressing target groups by displaying product- and/or company-specific information in the form of texts, graphics, videos, etc. The design of the website depends on the target group and the intended message. In addition to the graphics, the functionalities are particularly important, e.g. the integration of an e-mail connection. The entry page, which also provides an overview of the entire website offering, is called homepage. It is often decisive for staying on the website or moving on to other sites. The website is usually divided into different sections which are displayed on the homepage.

Only a few websites are still static, i.e. with HTML programming. Changes then require a change in the source code, which in turn requires programming skills. Also the complete navigation must be adapted in each case. Wysiwig editors, e.g. Macromedia, offer a relief here, where the displayed page text is used instead of the source code, but this can lead to errors. More common are content management systems (CMS). These work on the basis of templates as website frames in which the contents are placed. The linking and translation into source text is done automatically. Enhancements also allow, for example, search engine optimization or multimedia content.

Important is the structure of the website and the individual web pages. The website is usually structured according to parts as header, e.g. logo, actual content and footer with e.g. contact details, terms and conditions, partners. The start page is the most important one. Since it usually carries little content, it is not found sufficiently by search engines. Useful contents of a homepage are an overview of the site content, links to subpages and note on the e-mail address. The structure of the subpages should follow a common structure which is characterized by the user's visit of thousands of other pages.

When designing graphical user interfaces, developers should orientate themselves on predefined standards from a style guide. This applies, for example, to the arrangement and sequence of menu items. The user's technical conditions, such as browser, screen resolution, transmission capacity, etc., should be adjusted to general standards, in case of doubt rather at the lower level. The use of colors, the arrangement of the screen as well as the linking and the use of multimedia elements such as audio or video are subject to a high degree of freedom of design. In general, frame pages should be avoided if possible. Horizontal scrolling should also be avoided. The contrast between foreground and background is important.

Terminology should be appropriate for the target group and headlines, keywords, etc. should be highlighted. Longer texts should be avoided, alternatively they can be offered for printing. References to authors and persons responsible for the website need mentioning under the imprint obligation. Furthermore, link collections, about us pages and FAQs are desirable. Short loading times are recommended for files. The screen resolution should be specified. Hints for unavoidable plug-ins and system settings must be given. If contents are spread over several web pages, they should be provided with an overview.

Visitors should also be informed about the further use of input data and the effect of cookies. In the case of security-critical input, a note on secure transmission ("https") should be included. Guiding texts should be placed to the left of short input fields or above longer input fields. Related input fields should be grouped to each other and each input field should be of an appropriate size. For standard input fields, frequently occurring values should be preset, e.g. Mr./Mrs. Required and optional input fields should be visually separated. Checkboxes and option fields should be arranged in columns. If there are several option fields, list fields should be used as pulldown menues. Buttons and input fields should be labeled meaningful, related buttons should be identical in their dimensions and placed flush. Plausibility checks are helpful to avoid input errors. Likewise, incorrect input should be pointed out. It should be possible to change already entered data without problems. All input data and overviews should be printable, possibly also in summary form. Forms must be designed user-oriented.

User navigation

To ensure that users do not get lost in the variety of offers, guidance through the website by means of navigation elements such as orientation, scrolling, paging and orientation elements such as sitemap, icons are required. A navigation bar with control commands serves this purpose. Also a given linkage of the pages is appropriate, in order to consider didactical aspects with the use. The own URL is announced in classical media, in advertising material of the company and in the business stationery.

No more than seven anchor points are recorded by users per website. The positioning of individual elements must therefore be based on standards. The highest attention is at the top left of the page, the lowest at the bottom right. Important elements are the page name, the home logo to get back to the start page and the marking of the already visited, the not yet visited and the total number of links which can be visited, usually highlighted in color. In addition, there is an error-tolerant full-text search, which ignores upper and lower case letters, letter transpositions and the like. Up to 27 characters for search words are common. The search should only refer to the internal area, not to the WWW as a whole, since the user will then be "lost". It only makes sense with larger presences.

Often only a part of the entire page is in the visible area. Since scrolling should be avoided as much as possible, a part of the page is therefore not perceived (so-called iceberg effect). This can be counteracted by paging, i.e. a page layout in such a way that scrolling is not necessary. It is also helpful to use metaphors, i.e. familiar environments on the website, such as pinboard, icons, etc. The website logo should be placed on the top left or right, it should have a link to the home page. The positioning of the navigation elements should remain identical on all pages. A distinction can be made between primary and secondary navigation. A sitemap should provide an overview of the entire web presence.

The navigation bar appears at the left or right margin or at the top, with no more than ten dots. Sub-points for refinement are called up by pull-down menus. The search is always done by words. If possible, a test should be carried out with probands as to usability. If possible, no more than three clicks lead to the target page, i.e. short navigation paths and flat site structures. A navigation overview is also helpful for orientation or breadcrumbs, i.e. the display of the path to the called page so that one can jump back directly. The contact page should offer different ways for contacting. Sometimes a callback option or a toll free phone number is offered.

It is important to display the page correctly in different browsers and in different resolutions, most often 1,920 × 1,080 pixels. Only a few users have different browsers installed, so that they can use different resolutions and functionalities. Therefore, the browser representations should be tested in advance, and it is also important to minimize loading time. Data compression methods can be used for this purpose. The bandwidth of the internet access is from experience no longer a problem nowadays. Helpful are offers for downloads on the site, e.g. user manuals, handbooks, software, games, wallpapers, videos, recipes, case studies, white papers, virtual factory tours, forums, picture galleries, expert interview podcasts, glossaries, test results, etc. Pictures of contact persons also work well.

Software ergonomics generally make numerous demands with regard to dialog systems, such as

- appropriateness, i.e. the user should be enabled to fulfill his task completely, correctly and with manageable time expenditure,

- self-description, i.e. the answers and feedback should be comprehensible either immediately or on demand,

- conformity to expectations, i.e. an interactive system should meet the expectations of the use by uniform designed, following generally valid conventions, correspond to the knowledge of the respective application area, etc.

- error tolerance, i.e., simple errors in operation should be avoided or intercepted by the program and the user should be given instructions on how to avoid operating errors,

- controllability, i.e. the user is responsible for controlling the system, which includes the ability to undo work steps,

- individualizability, i.e. a system should be adaptable to the preferences and characteristics of users within certain limits,

- learning support, i.e. the user should be instructed and supported in the application of the system.

5.2.1.2 Usability of webpages

There are a number of recommendations for the design of websites. For example, frame pages, i.e. separate screen frames, should be avoided wherever possible. Text terminology should be designed to suit the target group. Headlines, keywords, etc. should be highlighted. Longer texts should be avoided, alternatively they can be offered for printing. Furthermore, link collections, "About us pages", FAQs, etc. are desirable. Short file loading times are just as important as barrier-free access. The screen resolution should be specified. Hints for required plugins and system settings should be given.

Usability tests ensure that the functionalities are maintained. Methods used for this are logfile analyses, which record which navigation elements and pages were called up in which order and how long the dwell times on the individual pages are. Logfiles contain all information which is transmitted from the user's browser to the server in the http header during a usage process, such as URL, file, time, IP number, operating system, browser type, etc. The data is cleaned of hits from irrelevant entries (frames), from search agents, internal accesses, etc. Then, data are compressed with assignment of users to IP addresses for visitor identification and path completion.

In addition, further information about the user/usage can be obtained. For this purpose, session IDs represent a temporary marking of the client browser at the WWW server. Cookies are small text files in ASCII format, which are written by the server to the random access memory of the user's PC and permanently mark the browser. Log-in is understood to be input data for personalized registration, whereby the visits can be assigned to the user to create an individual user profile. In the case of integrated e-mail functions, meta data are collected, including information on the e-mail program, operating system, subject line of the e-mails, e-mail address, etc. In the case of form entries, transaction data are recorded.

In addition, primary studies through video analyses are carried out, which can be used with selected users, e. g. as eye movement measurement. Thus, facial expressions and gestures of the user can also be observed. However, this requires a relatively high technical effort. Individual and group interviews provide information about the evaluation of a website. Questionnaires and evaluation forms allow metric measurements, possibly also as online questionnaires. Laboratory tests, on the other hand, are problematic; they lead to so-called heat maps by means of eye tracking, for example.

General *success factors* for the web presence are as follows:

- Ease of finding the e-mail address of specific contacts, ease of finding the phone numbers of specific contact persons, ease of finding the postal address of the company, contact forms available, phone callback button available, complaint option available, newsletter is offered, RSS newsfeed possible,
- ability of the homepage to captivate the visitor, ability of the homepage to make the time fly while usage, ability of the homepage to offer entertainment, adaptation of the homepage to the needs of business clients, coherence of the homepage with other communication tools,

- breadth and depth of information offered, quality and comprehensibility of information offered, structure of the information, timeliness of the information, possibility to download information, newsboard display, information about the company, information about job offers, linking to partner companies,
- clarity of the layout, manageability of the menu items, menu bar available, harmonious color scheme, comprehensive design, high-contrast font, understandable links, navigation support, home button available, full-text search function, possibility to choose different languages, fast page construction.

A central requirement for every website usability is the *accessibility*. There are a number of conditions for this. For example, equivalent alternatives of other modalities must be available for images, sounds and videos. Texts, images and graphics must be clearly recognizable for those with defective vision, even without colors. The HTML page description and the CSS page design must be used according to their specifications. Language peculiarities such as abbreviations or language changes must be indicated. Tables may in fact only be used to display tabular data. Internet offers must be usable largely browser-independently. Time-controlled content must be controllable by the user. Automatic updates or forwarding must not take place. Access to user interfaces, e. g. through database connections, must be possible without hindrance. It must be possible to use the entire range of functions of an internet presence independent from the input or output device, e. g. by navigation without a connected mouse. It must also be possible to use the website with older software, possibly by waiving functionalities. All technologies used to create the web pages must be fully documented. The user must be provided with orientation aids. Navigation must be clear and comprehensible, e. g. by specifying hyperlink targets, site maps, search functions.

While this requirement was originally aimed at providing only disabled people with access to internet content, it has since been proven that all measures which help disabled people are also helpful for the use of internet content by everyone else.

5.2.1.3 Website as advertising medium

A website consists of several web pages or documents such as files, resources, which are connected by a uniform navigation in hypertext mode. It begins with the homepage or, upstream, the welcome page. Hyperlinks allow to switch between the documents and between different web pages or even websites with a mouse click.

Web presences are usually programmed in the platform-independent page description language HTML. Server-side scripting languages like Perl, PHP, VBSkript, etc. or programming languages such as Java are often used. There are also client-side scripting languages, e. g. Java Script. Server-side scripts/programs preferably produce HTML text as output, which is interpreted by the client-side browser. The web presence can then be called up on the screen.

A web presence is addressed via a URL, which is unique for each site. The data of the web presence is stored on a web server, which is often operated by a web host center and rented to users as web space.

The basis for the design of a website is a suitable user model, i.e. a profile of the presumed visitors of the presence. The visitors are generally anonymous, but in some cases cookies still provide the possibility of successively profiling each individual user. For this purpose, information about the respective visit is stored in the browser of the user's computer and reactivated when the same presence is accessed again. In this way, information is cumulated which allows an ever better impression of the user profile. Above a certain threshold, individualized information offers can be generated on this basis, which correspond to the manifested interests from the respective user profile.

The internet presence is a typical pull channel of communication, i.e. only participants who are already somewhere in the network can be reached. Therefore a provider must constitutively first of all arouse the attention of the participants and direct it to his own presence. There are several possibilities for this. First, the presence can be pointed out via other communication channels offline, such as adverts, TV spots, brochures, business papers, etc. Secondly, the participants can refer to their own presence in other presences, usually in exchange for mutual cross-linking. Thus, the more frequently these sites are visited, the more users are reached. This is the strength of portal sites, the most frequently used entry pages to the internet, because they create multiple contacts through high traffic. And thirdly, it has to be ensured that the own company is properly represented in the search engines, by means of appropriately indexed keywords.

Now, a single visit to an internet presence is already quite good, but only the repeated visit by one and the same user is really useful. Therefore addresses can marked in the browser, to which one wants to return, as bookmarks. But this requires a motivation to return. This is achieved primarily through service offers to which multiple access seems worthwhile. However, the distribution of messages to identified users by e-mail is also conceivable, but the undifferentiated sending of messages as spamming is prohibited, at least with regard to private individuals, and also violates the self-imposed rules of conduct on the internet, the netiquette.

The initially widespread, pure fascination with modern technology, i.e. the aimless, random surfing, has long since been replaced by the targeted search for specific sites. In this respect, the reliance on random contact with one's own presence is built on sand. Instead, a conscious channeling of access is required.

Important to be considered for the design of online advertising are the following:

- Concise URL, short and memorable, perfect functionality, no error messages, especially not in case of typing errors, fast loading times, mainly for convenience, few images, easy handling with no more than three click levels to get to the desired page, informative content, not "art", competent reaction to inquiries, short response time.

The following are to be avoided if possible:

- Necessary plugins to display a website, long intros without usefulness, forums and guestbooks, mostly useless, because they are anonymous, external links, the user is away from the presence and may not come back, counters without any utility value, except for the competition, site signs ("under construction"), news tickers, distract from important content, forms, if they are difficult to understand or otherwise complicated.

5.2.2 Function of the search engines

In order for a website to be found, its entry in search engines is essential. These are used intensively to find the information you need in the confusing vastness of the internet. Users enter the search term(s) in a database, which then searches all entries and lists the addresses in which the search term(s) occur(s) or which are related to it. Relevant aspects are the type of search engine, the search engine marketing, the search engine optimization and the search engine advertising.

5.2.2.1 Types

Three types of search engines can be distinguished:

- *Full-text search engines* automatically crawl through all accessible websites 24 hours a day, 7 days a week and save their headings and parts of the texts stored there word for word and pack them on a server. When a search request is made, the search engine scans this server stock and displays the corresponding hits. This requires a definition of the search field that is as exact as possible, because otherwise a confusing number of hits will result. It is therefore advisable to use restrictive formulations, e.g. using AND operators when searching. Full-text search engines are particularly suitable for detailed searches for special information, provided that the restrictions and specifications are chosen appropriately. Examples are Google, Altavista, MSN, Ask, etc.
- *Web catalogs* are compiled by editors who index web pages, i.e. assign keywords to the contents, which they then place in a catalog. This catalog is hierarchically structured. During a search request, this web catalog is searched by keywords. Accordingly, the search can be made very efficient. There are hardly any irrelevant hits, but not all keywords are included by far, so that not all relevant websites can be evaluated. Nevertheless, this is the best choice for getting closer to a subject area. Common web catalogs are WEB, DINO, Yahoo, etc.

- *Meta search engines* do not keep their own database, but search several full-text search engines, web catalogs and other special databases in parallel. This allows access to a huge amount of information, but the usability of the data depends on the appropriate limitation of the search term. However, these services are very well suited for obtaining an initial overview of a subject area. Common meta search engines are Metaspinner, Apollo, Metager, etc.
- *Special search engines* mainly concern purchasing. Examples are systems for price information like Idealo and others, shopping like Kelko and others, price comparison like Check24 and others.

When the text is indexed by search engines, the title of a page is first recorded and evaluated by the search engine. This title is the most important criterion in determining the relevance of a search result for the user's query and decides whether the own address is displayed at the top or bottom of a search list. The following sections of the text are also recorded by the search engine. The table of contents, which is supplied with the output of the address list, is automatically generated. Thus, the wording of the first paragraph of a page is important, although this wording does not necessarily have to be visible on the screen. Metatags, which describe the content of a page but are not made visible by the browser, can be used to identify keywords as more relevant than perhaps actually given in the text.

Directories allow the entry of website owners in corresponding categories. For this purpose, there is usually a registration form which allows for a characterization of the site in addition to the content. For this purpose, registrants should provide a short description of the page content, which will be displayed in a result list of the directory user together with the address upon request. In order to be placed as high up in the result list as possible, it is helpful if the title of a website contains the keyword specified by the user. Placing it high on the result list makes actual use more likely, since users usually select the list from the top and stop searching as soon as they find the information they think is appropriate. Therefore, the lower an entry is placed on the list, the more likely it is that it will not be called up again because the underlying information problem has already been solved. The registration is checked by the employees of the directory provider and then added to the directory.

Hybrid search engines offer additional directories with the pages from the main index. This prevents content from not being found because it has been assigned to the wrong index. In hybrid search engines, it is therefore possible to switch between directories and search again and again.

The entry in the various directories is time-consuming. Service providers therefore offer to take over the entry in the common search engines. Also possible is the automatic registration by appropriate registration software, however no fine tuning of the entry is possible, so that substantial chances are given away. However this saves time and money. Website optimizers improve the ranking by website analysis via visibility of the content, log file, technical analysis, by optimizing the website, by registering it for indexing and observing the ranking rules when changes occur.

5.2.2.2 Search engine marketing

Search engine marketing (SEM) affects the rule-conformal production of relevant contacts over placements on the search result sides of the search machines. Search engines use search robots (so-called crawlers) to capture all URLs available on the search engine and follow the links there up to a certain depth, usually up to the third click level, in order to reach further pages. All collected pages are analyzed and indexed. Horizontal search engines search all websites, e.g. of a country or a language. Vertical search engines search only in one subject area. Meta search engines search in the results of search engines and display them according to their own order criteria.

The pages found by the crawler are regularly transferred to a central indexer, where they are processed into a searchable index. From this index, user queries are answered according to the ranking criteria of the search engine with an ordered list of URLs and their descriptions. The indexing depth indicates the extent to which links are followed from websites at the top level of the hierarchy. The indexing frequency indicates how up-to-date the content of the website is. However, the largely existing dynamic content is usually not found.

The aim is to achieve the best possible ranking in the search result lists for a web presence. However, the criteria for evaluating the relevance of results vary from search engine to search engine. These criteria are kept secret in order to make index spamming more difficult, which attempts to achieve top rankings by manipulating data. The quality of the results is determined by the number of search engine result pages (SERP) delivered or the range of use of the search. The number of search engine result pages indicates the capacity of the search engine, the usage range indicates the number of users within a certain period of time.

5.2.2.3 Search engine optimization

Search engine optimization (SEO) deals with the technical optimization of the traceability and assignability of websites. This optimization can be done onsite, i.e. by measures on the site itself to improve the position of search results in response to queries e.g. by higher keyword density, or offsite, i.e. by linking/referencing web pages to/from third sites in order to achieve greater relevance e.g. by Google Pagerank 0–10. Google's market share is just under 90% in Germany and about 60% in Europe. In Google, sources are searched for about 200 different criteria, which are secret in detail.

A search engine friendly web design increases the probability of good rankings. This includes the following elements:

- Focus on the top web crawlers Google, Bing, Baidu, Yahoo, Yandex, Ask, AOL, links within the site, as only the pages linked to the home page can be found, the title tag as the title of the website displayed in the browser bar, this should already contain the most important terms of the site, specific title tags should be used for all main pages, the integration of the search terms into the text, high link popularity due to many cross-references and a long duration of the domain, a flat hierarchy of the site structure, as the links are only followed up to a certain depth, the so-called deep web however is not reached.

The deep web is created as a result of crawlers being locked out by website operators, e.g. by means of captchas, non-expressive metatags, password protection for the pages, dynamic programming, e.g. by means of databases, real-time page content, lack of links to and from other pages, paywalls, campus licenses, etc. These important contents thus remain "hidden".

The following elements however are detrimental:

- High server downtime as time during which the server of the website is technically unavailable, copied content on several webpages, links from low quality pages, identical meta tags on many subpages and participation in link networks.

5.2.2.4 Search engine advertising

With search engine advertising (SEA), the purchase of advertising placements is made, which appear before the organic search results when defined search terms are entered and must be marked as "advertisement". Payment is implemented per click, i.e. each advertiser offers a certain amount of money for a placement in the paid rankings and defines a budget limit for a period of time. The relative amount of the bid determines the ranking, the address is shown until the budget is used up by clicks on the link. The advertiser can then decide to increase his budget or not to place any further bids. Usually two to five related search terms are defined. The importance of this is very high, since most people use search engines to provide an overview on the internet, especially before purchasing decisions are made. Most users also only pay attention to the links on the first page of SERP.

However, there is also click fraud by competitors. Indications of this are a high number of page views from abroad, pages which are accessed via changing IP addresses and cannot be identified, increased page views where visitors to the site leave the site immediately after accessing it, and clicks which are executed at unusual times. Other indicators are extremely low conversion rates, i.e. conversion of the click into a desired activity, visits to pages which do not have their own advertising material, frequent cancellations of purchases, and technical conditions which deviate conspicuously from the norm.

5.2.3 Banner advertising

The most common form of advertising on the WWW are banners as display advertising. There are different types of banners according to their layout mainly simple and elaborated integrated banner ads, new window ads and layer ads.

5.2.3.1 Integrated banner ads

Integrated banner ads are those which lead the user from the website to the online offer of an advertising company with a click on the banner. This includes the following *simple* integrated banner ads:

- Static banner ads allow only one click by the user, which opens the advertiser's linked website. Since banners, like other advertising media, are often seen as a disruption to actual media use, they sometimes appear in disguise. The sizes are standardized to half size banners (234 × 60 pixels), full size banners (468 × 60 pixels) and super banners (728 × 90 pixels), but there are also special formats.

- Skyscrapers are not scrollable, but use the entire right side height for a vertical advertising bar (120 × 600 pixels), also conceivable as a wide skyscraper (160 × 600 pixels).

- Hockey sticks are placed in an L-shape at the top and right edge of the website.

- Scroll ads represent a clickable advertising space at the edge of the screen which scrolls along and cannot be closed.

- Rectangle/Midpage ads are directly integrated into the editorial content of the advertising medium and cannot be clicked away by accident or on purpose. Due to their size, they offer extended creative possibilities in design, comparable to island ads in the print sector. Sizes are 180 × 150 pixels, 300 × 250 pixels, 336 × 280 pixels and 240 × 240 pixels.

- Fake banner ads simulate a computer message, e. g. an operating system error, to attract attention to their message. Whether this is helpful is doubtful at all.

Elaborated integrated banner ads allow additional functions within the banner field:

- Animated banner ads consist of repeating single image sequences similar to a cartoon film, which allow smaller animations without further software technical requirements. Thus, a high attention of the user can be achieved. They also work by clicking on them, but require high storage and transmission capacities. The limitation of the file size therefore often leads to inadequate creative solutions.

- HTML banner ads allow the use of selection boxes or pull-down menus familiar from the software. In this way, individual information offers, e. g. programs such as small games, databases, which are kept in stock by the advertiser, can be selected directly from the banner. For this purpose, it consists of several images, form elements and texts, which are inserted in the source code of the page of the advertising medium. No plug-ins are required.

- Nanosite banner ads are completely functional websites in mini format. They contain interactive elements with functionalities. All content is displayed in the banner window, not in a new window. The individual elements are linked to each other. However, the programming is quite complex. They are based on Java or other languages, so it is possible that not all potential users are technically reached. They allow database queries and transaction processes without leaving the advertising medium, e. g. as mini-shops.

- Transactive banner ads allow users to dispose of the content of the banner without having to leave the website they are actually visiting. Therefore, extensive functionalities are built into the banner, including transaction options.

- Richmedia banner ads allow the inclusion of multimedia elements such as 3-D animations, video clips, audio sequences, interaction possibilities, etc. The data transfer capacity is sometimes limited by jerky images, low resolution, etc. Sometimes plug-ins are required.

- Microsites are self-contained, multi-page advertising appearances on highly frequented websites. This allows sufficient information to be transported without the user having to visit a new website. Thus, no change to the homepage of the advertiser is necessary.

5.2.3.2 New window ads

New window ads automatically appear in a browser window which opens and include various forms:

- Pop-up ads automatically open a new browser window of any size above the currently viewed web page during the loading process, so they do not interrupt the intended navigation on the web page. Pop-up ads are a "softer" form of interrupt advertising, but users may have clicked them away before the window is finished, so that short loading times and an attractive presentation of content and design are important for success. Often an additional benefit is associated with this.

- Blow-up ads are a variant of pop-ups. They inflate themselves only gradually to their final format when the page is called up.

- Interstitials are faded in between two called pages during the usual page layout on the screen and temporarily take up the entire format similar to TV commercials. They cannot be clicked away because they do not require a separate browser window. After a certain amount of time, the fade-in disappears by itself, unless the user activates the interstitial to get to an attached website. The transfer unpleasantly extends the loading time and interrupts the use.

- Superstitials load in the background, while the user continues to navigate the site undisturbed. As soon as they are fully loaded, the advertising message appears in large format. It is also possible to integrate multimedia elements such as animated flash spots, graphics and sound.

5.2.3.3 Layer ads

Layer ads are located one level above or below the content page and do not appear in an opening window. This includes the following:

- Floating ads seem to float above the viewed website and can be hidden.
- Expanding ads increase their size as soon as the user touches the banner, when the mouse pointer leaves the area, it returns to its original size
- With the mouse move banner an advertising banner appears directly next to the mouse position, which moves with the movement of the mouse pointer.
- Comet cursors are cursors which change their shape as they are moved over web pages and banners. The change can take the shape of the logo of the advertised product, for example. This can achieve a high recall effect, but the user must download the appropriate installation program from the internet as a prerequisite.
- Pop-under ads are only visible as the last image on the screen when the browser window is closed, because they are located below the other windows.
- Sticky ads consist of buttons which, regardless of scrolling, always remain optically in the same place on the screen, usually on the right-hand edge.

Banner ads are placed on general interest sites such as portals with high reach but also high wastage, or on special interest sites with correspondingly less circulation but higher target accuracy. The delivery of advertising is carried out by

- rotation of different advertising materials on the same advertising space,
- rotation within a website on different web pages,
- network rotation within a group of multiple web presences,
- time-dependent delivery of advertising media.

5.2.4 Special forms of web advertising

Since these conventional forms of banner advertising reach the limits of effectiveness through reactance analogous to classic offline advertising (so-called banner blindness), special forms of advertising are increasingly used:

- Breaking news are clickable forms of advertising which are usually integrated in tables of contents, navigation bars or other content and contain short messages. It is also conceivable to integrate this up-to-date information in the banner, where it runs through the format, similar to a ticker text.
- E-mercials are full-screen advertising spots based on HTML5 technology, which are usually coupled with interactive logos of the advertising customers.
- Streaming ads also enable moving image advertising and are interactive. They are delivered via ad server and are clickable in the usual advertising formats.
- With DHTML banners, a free object moves across the webpage, at the edge of the content or across it. It is also possible to add content, e.g. competitions, which combine a high fun factor with product, brand and company information. The advertiser also receives user data, for example through high score lists.

In addition, there are some forms of advertising which pursue more far-reaching approaches than the pure use of advertising media:

- Cross-media applications involve the use of classical or non-classical media types in parallel with online advertising. Thus, advertising messages can be distributed via TV commercials or press adverts simultaneously to the presence on a website. This makes it easier to reach the target audience. Advertising media which carry several offline and online offers can also be combined to cross-media offers for advertisers at a package price.
- With web promotions, a website operator passes on content from his website to other website operators. These are mostly databases as guest books, discussion groups or event calendars interspersed with advertising. The person taking over the content sets a link to the corresponding content of the provider, the presentation of the content can be adapted to the appearance of the person taking over the content. The acquirer pays a fee for the transfer to the provider.
- In the case of web sponsoring, a reference is made on a website to the sponsoring of another website, e.g. theme websites with only implicit sender naming, a delimited theme offer or a web event. This also includes the mentioning of the brand name and/or logo in a suitable topic environment as placement.

In affiliate programs, a program operator, the merchant, places the banner of an affiliate on his website. Payment is made in the form of commissions for the orders forwarded via this banner. This enables much higher revenues than by selling the space for banners. However, one must pay attention to the seriousness of the affiliates in the selection process, otherwise there will be negative spillover effects. This is often depending on the affiliate network.

5.2.5 Targeting

Instead of this undifferentiated scattering, defined criteria can be used for targeting:

- *Behavioral* targeting is based on the previous surfing behavior of the users and segments them according to areas of interest usually based on cookies, network monitoring or log-in data, but fields of interest are often narrowly defined.
- *Contextual* targeting is based on the thematic environment of a website as to affinity, which fits particularly well with the advertising message, based on search queries and e-mails.
- *Semantic* targeting is based on search word entries and assigns content to single words, word combinations, phrases and texts although there are semantic boundaries due to homonyms, e.g. "art" as a method or a skill, "lead" as guidance or heavy metal.
- *Predictive* targeting is based on statistical algorithms from survey data on the extrapolated web properties of users usually according to user profile, socio-demographics, living environment, etc., thus intending to minimize wastage.
- *Regional* targeting concentrates on certain areas, cities, zip code zones, etc., especially as geo-targeting based on the IP address it can be estimated from which area a user comes from or where he is currently located.
- *Re*-targeting addresses users who have interrupted an interaction on a website after leaving this website on to another website usually within an advertising network. The goal is the completion of the interaction, prerequisite for recognition are, if allowed, cookies on the user.
- *Technical* targeting delivers advertising media tailored to the respective hardware and software environment. Parameters are browser type, network bandwidth, usage times, etc., possibly with limitation of contact frequency.

Measurement basis are logfile analyses, cookie messages, registration/login data, web bugs (transparent 1 × 1 pixel) etc. However, there are also limits by cookie deletion/deactivation, incomplete user profiles, low database/click rates, data protection, adblocker, etc.

5.2.6 Measuring success of web advertising

Measuring the success of online advertising, like any advertising efficiency measurement, is not without its problems. A distinction can be made between advertising media-related, advertising material-related and user-related key figures. *Advertising medium-related* measured values are above all the following:

- Hits indicate how many individual data of a site have been queried, be it HTML pages, graphics or similar, readable by the number of lines in the logfile.
- Page views/page impressions represent the number of retrieved individual pages, whereby only content pages are counted. It is a measure of the visual contact with individual pages.
- Visits are related visits of individual users to a website by calling up one or more web pages of a site's offer. A visit is a technically successful page access of an internet browser to the current offer.
- Error log is an evaluation of the error codes during access to optimize the website.
- Abandonment rate is an evaluation of the pages from which a website is left.

Advertising material-related measured values are mainly:

- AdClicks are the number of uses of advertising-bearing hyperlinks which lead to the website or to other information of the advertiser.
- AdImpressions are the number of visual contacts with advertising media on the internet.
- Click through rate is the percentage of clicked ads out of all visited websites.
- Exposure duplications are the percentage of visitors who see an advertising banner more than once.
- Banner reach is the number of users with at least one visual contact with the advertising material.
- Banner frequency shows the intensity of visual contacts per user.
- Viewtime is the period of time during which a potentially advertising part of a web offer is visible.
- Stickiness is the dwell time on a specific website determined from frequency, duration and range.

Advertising user-related measured values are above all:

- Referring pages determine from which website the user came and where he went to from the site.
- Entry pages/exit pages are the inflow and outflow pages of a website, e.g. indexed via search engines.

- Navigation patterns aim to detect the movement patterns of users within a website.
- Visit length includes the length of stay from the first to the last page view within a visit.
- Unique users are the number of different visitors to a website.
- Conversion rate is the percentage of transactions out of all visitors or visits to the site.

However, the informative value of these measurements is limited in several ways. For example, internet offers are accessed via decentralized proxy servers instead of via the provider's server, if the websites are frequently accessed. These accesses cannot be measured because they are not entered in the logfile of the provider's server. The situation is similar when using cache memory reserved in the user's PC and providing content locally without contacting the provider server when the content is called up again. Similarly, firewalls, which are standard equipment in networks, have a distorting effect because only the firewall IP address appears in the log file instead of the real internal IP address used for actual data retrieval. Furthermore, many providers manage stock IP addresses which are assigned to different users according to availability (so-called dynamic IP addresses). This means that a correct identification of the users is no longer possible. In addition, offline reader functions offer the possibility of viewing web pages and thus also advertising content located there without being online, i.e. the time-related identification of the advertising is falsified. If users dial in directly to the advertising-bearing page without being connected to it via links, the measured values are also incorrect. If a website consists of several independent elements as frames, the structure of a page is evaluated as a multiple hit per frame.

In order to create a "hard online currency", this is standardized by IVW measurement procedure which at least ensures comparability of the communicative data thus collected. It is essentially based on the measurement criteria page impressions and visits.

5.3 Web 2.0 applications

The WWW in the form of Web 2.0 applications includes the trend from mass communication to individualized communication by personalization, from push to pull communication with user generated content (UGC) and from one-way to interactive dialog communication. At the same time, the user makes content available to others and uses content from these others. This is mainly done by

- *networking* for the self-presentation of users, their networking among each other in groups resp. of content and users via Internet platforms e.g. Facebook, Xing, LinkedIn,

- *blogging* by providing authoring tools for creating weblogs, hosting blogs and categorizing them, including RSS feeds and microblogs, e.g. Twitter,
- *file sharing* by providing online storage space for systematizing content and for searching and displaying information, e.g. YouTube, Flickr, Shazam, also as wikis,
- *tagging* for central archiving and ubiquitous availability of bookmarks and their keywords, e.g. Stumble-upon, Digg, Reddit.

The most common of these are briefly presented below, although there is an increasing overlap between these forms. All are based on the following principles. The internet serves as a platform, the focus is on harnessing collective intelligence, user-generated content prevails, lightweight programming modules like apps are available, the applications are terminal-neutral and there is a well-developed user interface.

To simplify matters, a distinction is often made between three types of internet-based media:

- *Owned media* such as the own website, the Facebook fan page, a Youtube channel, a Twitter account or a weblog,
- *paid media* like search engine advertising, banner advertising, sponsoring, etc.,
- *earned media* such as fans/followers in social networks, positive product reviews, positive user contributions, etc.

5.3.1 Social network

Social networks are user communities of web services which either remain limited to certain groups of people or include everyone, examples are Path, Stayfriends, Foursquare, etc. Each member can set up a personal page as profile to present himself or herself to other members with various visibility settings. An easy receiving and sending of messages is possible via contact lists/address books according to certain personal characteristics. The aim is to send internal messages and to form communities of interest.

Social networks are financed by membership fees and primarily by advertising/sponsoring. Companies can maintain fan pages there to spread brand messages and increase traffic on their site by linking to them. This is particularly worthwhile for advertisers because very meaningful user profiles are available and the users are closely meshed and communicate intensively. Although this commercial use of member data is coming under increasing criticism, especially from a data protection perspective. It is difficult to measure success, but it can be measured by "listening" to keywords such as technical terms, brand/company or trend topics. A sentiment analysis as to tonality is important, which is difficult in the case of irony, idioms, abbreviations, slang, common spelling mistakes, double negations, ambiguities, etc. Especially important is the identification of opinion leaders. Minilytics can be used to measure Facebook, e. g. by "likes" from fans or friends of fans in absolute and relative values, reach as number of people who are linked to or subscribe to the page, people who post about it, etc.

Within the professional sphere, career networks like Xing, LinkedIn have established themselves. These are about professional contacts and getting to know "interesting" people, maintaining contact with former or remote colleagues, business partners, potential customers, etc.

5.3.2 Community

Online communities are organized groups which communicate and interact with each other on the internet, e. g. Gutefrage, Chef, Motor-Talk, HiFi-Forum. A social platform serves as the basis; the exchange takes place in detail via e-mail, forum, chat system, instant messaging, blackboard or file sharing network. The prerequisite for this is the registration and creation of a user account. Mostly pseudonyms are used, sometimes guest access is also possible. Commercial proprietary communities take over the setup and administration of the structure, sometimes also the moderation. Open systems allow communication from and to different networks. The contents is topic-oriented, e. g. games, travel, sports, often knowledge management (wiki) and voting/rating are also included. Developer communities (e-collaboration/open source) are also widespread.

5.3.3 Weblog

Weblogs (so-called blogs) are frequently updated websites on which content of any kind is displayed in chronologically descending order, e. g. Wordpress, Blogger, Weebly. All contents are usually connected to other websites by links and can be commented on directly by the user. Weblogs can be organized thematically and assigned to categories. Author is either an individual person or a group. The term weblog is composed of world wide web and logbook. An own software (blogware) for creating posts ensures that anyone without web space or programming skills can create an internet presence in the form of an electronic diary as an author (so-called blogger). The publication is free of charge, not limited in content, but structured by categories, freely accessible, dialogical and possible on a global scale. Within the blogosphere there is a strong network among each other, communication is direct and personal.

The elements of a weblog are the contribution itself (the blog post), comments on it, permanent, unchangeable links, the permalinks, a trackback, i. e. notice to the original address about how the content was further used, a blogroll, i. e. collection of links with offered references to categories, tags, i.e. frequently used keywords, as well as the administration area and the RSS news feed function. Tag clouds automatically display the occurring terms graphically in such a way that the more frequently occurring terms appear in a larger font. This makes it quick and easy to recognize the relevance of blogs. A distinction can be made according to media between text blogs, photoblogs, audio blogs, video blogs, but also link blogs, voting blogs, sports blogs, watch blogs, etc. according to contents.

There are private and corporate blogs. *Corporate blogs* are relevant here first. They increase the presence on the internet with search engines, allow a better customer dialog, differentiate from the competition, as long as not many companies in a particular industry use blogs, enable relationship marketing, increase the reputation of a provider, improve internal communication and position the sender as an expert. Passive corporate blogs observe the blogosphere for market research purposes. In this way, one gains insights into customer thinking, recognizes trends and developments and gains competitive data. Active corporate blogs allow open commenting on products and the placement of advertising.

Independent blogs are operated by initiators outside the company. For the company, this means low costs, high reach and special attention, but also the risk of free, largely uncontrollable entries. Alternatively, moderated blogs can be used, but they must essentially avoid the impression of censorship, for example by deleting critical comments. Instead, they must prevent violations of the blogoquette, such as libel, slander, insults, etc. Company blogs can be used for employee communication, e.g. in project management, or for dialog with customers.

Different *types* of professional weblogs can be distinguished:

- Knowledge blogs convert implicit employee knowledge into explicit general knowledge. Employees make knowledge which is important for the company available to colleagues. They can comment on and supplement the contribution. In this way, employees' knowledge is retained even when they are absent. In addition, it can be accessed regardless of location. However, many employees are reluctant to contribute because they feel that they can be replaced. The difference to wikis is that the knowledge is ordered chronologically, not lexicographically.

- Department blogs are used to optimize the interfaces between departments as well as for the exchange of experiences and suggestions for improvement. This reduces e-mail traffic and facilitates, for example, the training of new employees. However, the blog must not become an end in itself as expensive toy.

- Topic blogs present the company's activities to the public. This improves the reputation of companies. However, the content of independent blogs is difficult to control and thus implies a risk.

- Service blogs are used for dialog-oriented customer communication, for example to present new products or services, to uncover weaknesses in the product or for suggestions for product improvements. However, customers may first need to be motivated to participate in such blogs.

- CEO blogs create a fast communication on the management level, especially in large companies, to shareholders and other stakeholder groups. This is especially true for ad hoc announcements. However, there is a confidentiality problem which can be solved by hierarchized password access.
- Campaign blogs support an advertising campaign cross-media or a product launch in offline media by offering target group-specific information. Brand blogs are used to present brands or existing products to increase their market value. Sales blogs support demand by providing product information. This enables the marketing of niche products in particular.
- In an emergency, crisis blogs create fast communication paths to relevant target groups and back again.

Other blog forms include CSR blogs, collaboration blogs, personality blogs, activist blogs, watch blogs (NGOs), amateur journalist blogs or trade union blogs.

All weblogs require an imprint notice, in addition the copyright and usage rights must be observed. A major problem is the "keeping alive" of the weblogs. Because they live on current entries and comments. If there is too little activity on the weblog, they quickly become uninteresting. Furthermore, the evaluation of weblogs requires a lot of time, so outsourcing to third parties is advisable. If the weblog is moderated, it should also be considered as labor-intensive. Otherwise, weblogs are inexpensive, can be used regardless of location, are easy to use and interactive, they are fast, uncensored and versatile in their content as well as platform independent. However, there is also a lot of data garbage, there are plenty of copyright infringements and distorted or falsified content. Blogs require a high maintenance effort and reflect a trivialization of the German language.

Blogs and microblogs are widely used by *influencers* as follows:

- A- and B-celebrities from sports, music, fashion, film, television, etc. with born awareness level, they are primarily in self-promotion ("social hubs"), not in thematic influence and also not about generating direct income,
- with C- and D-celebrities only self-promotion is given, they use it aggressively to stay in business or even to get into it, their influencing capacity however is limited by their limited awareness level and the fluctuation of their presence,
- public figures such as politicians, journalists, popular scientists, experts, etc. also with born awareness level, here it is mainly about idealistic influence in favor of one's own interests, not about self-promotion,
- social media stars create awareness level, they are dominantly in self-promotion, because the earning potential depends on it, they have large influence on their target groups and are a phenomenon of the medium,

- corporate/brand influencers (so-called brand ambassadors), here it is primarily about commercial influence in favor of the represented brand/company, secondarily also about positive image transfer from the brand to the person of the influencer (and the other way round).

Monetization is made through partner companies/brands, then posts are to be marked as advertising to be at least on the safe side, but also through product placements in other channels (Youtube, Instagram, etc.). Legally it is questionable whether influencer have to mark personal recommendations without payment as advertising, as it meets life experience that influencers are paid, in this respect this should to be known. Paid posts however must be clearly marked as advertising in any case.

5.3.4 Microblog

This is a form of a publicly viewable diary. It can be accessed stationary or mobile on the Internet. The special feature is that the text messages can be a maximum of 280 characters long. In addition, picture messages can also be integrated, e. g. Twitter, Jaiku. It is a real-time medium, the writing of texts is called twittering. Tweets are then the messages. Users can also subscribe to messages, the referenced repetition of such messages is called retweet. The subscribers are followers. The authors are twitterers. They can decide to which circle of followers they make the messages available. The search function can be supported by hashtags (#) in the text. This enables to track the popularity of posts. Hashtags are also used to comment on texts by cross-reference.

The tweets are displayed chronologically downwards in a log as a diary similar to weblogs. Twitter collects personal data through the registration of each participant. Revenues are generated by selling this data. This enables companies to establish and maintain targeted contact with user communities. Measured values in Twitter twazzup are the number of followers or followers of followers as discussion participants, @-mentions, favorites of supporters, frequency of hashtags (#), etc.

5.3.5 Media sharing

Here every user can upload videos/photos/audios/charts and comment other videos/photos/audios/charts, e. g. Flickr, Youtube, Myvideo, Picasa, Pinterest, Slideshare, Scribd. The media files can also be downloaded and integrated into other websites or sent by e-mail. This enables the integration into company presentations, product information, etc. It is also possible to subscribe to media files of particular other users. For marketing purposes, videos are especially helpful. These in turn are mainly offered as tutorials, for example in the form of user manuals or quick courses. Through an affiliate program, authors are provided with the downloads of their files. Commercials are often placed before videos, and can only be turned off with ad blockers. Digital photos are suitable for photoblogs or as templates for printing on demand. They can be captured, organized and accessed with image management software. Often image editing software is also embedded. Also common are virtual pinboards for favorite photos which are publicly viewable. Chart presentations are mainly used for professional or student purposes. Audios, on the other hand, are mainly used for entertainment purposes.

5.3.6 Wiki

A wiki is generally a hypertext system of web pages whose contents can not only be read by users, but also re-entered or modified online. This is based on the "wisdom of the crowds" as knowledge management. Usually, a topic-oriented design is made for general or special interests. The software for wikis, a simplified content management system, the wiki engine, is freely available, so that every website operator can set up his own wiki. Wikis are also operated in-house, for example in innovation management. They allow collaborative work on texts and use collaborative intelligence in companies, departments or projects. They can be installed on workstations, in local networks or extranets. Version management is of central importance here. A critical mass of users and contributions is required. Open wikis are usually free of advertising and are financed by donations. Closed wikis are of increasingly important relevance of internal communication. Unlike blogs, entries are organized by topic, not by time.

A variation is their use for crowdsourcing, i.e. the deliberate outsourcing of improvement activities to the online audience, for wiktionary as dictionary on WWW, wikibooks as learning material, wikiquote for quotations, wikisource for free text content resp. wikimedia for free pictures/videos, wikinews as news on WWW, wikiversity for scientific projects. Especially internal wikis serve the knowledge management of organizations.

5.3.7 Social bookmarking

Web pages saved as personal favorites can normally only be accessed from the own PC. However, these favorites can be tagged by internet bookmarks and taken over by or being exchanged with other users via servers in the extranet or intranet, so that users can point each other to interesting websites. For this purpose, such links are marked as "public". Examples are Digg, Stumbleupon, Getpocket, etc. These collaborative indexings are registered by search engines and thus improve the ranking of the referred pages via backlinks. At the same time, this is a possibility of abuse, so that bookmark ratings have been introduced. The classification can be done by keywords, categories or users. There are also favorite rankings. The lists can be followed by RSS feed. Bookmarks are thus a proven means to increase the popularity of a website.

5.3.8 Other web 2.0 services

There are many other advertising-relevant web 2.0 services, such as rating portals, RSS feeds, Ingame advertising or virtual realities as is shown here.

Rating portals are used to evaluate products, e. g. Ciao, services, companies and organizations online. Other objects of evaluation are teachers, university lecturers, employers, doctors, lawyers, etc. There are also industry-specific portals such as Holidaycheck, HRS, Trivago, etc. in tourism. Also the combination of map services and rating content, e. g. Qype, is common. Online ratings are becoming increasingly important and a large number of users consult them before making purchasing decisions. But providers also use them as a basis for improving their services. Recommendation portals only publish positive reviews, feedback portals forward reviews without publication to those affected for evaluation. In the event of abusive criticism or untrue criticism from competitors, there is a right to have the entry deleted.

Gateways to price comparison portals are often found. These access information from meta search engines in order to assign the prices of different providers to a product. In addition, there is information on delivery capability, test reports, ecology, safety, etc. Often, however, the information is outdated or not comparable. There is also a dependence on the listed providers.

RSS stands for really simple syndication and is used for the XML-structured publication of changes on websites. Providers are RSS channels which send headlines and links to indexed pages to subscribers, this is called feed. The news can then be viewed in the feed reader, sometimes as full text. In contrast to e-mails, this is a push service which does not have to be called up separately. This means that large numbers of sources, e. g. weblogs, can also be viewed undercover. The news can be integrated into own websites using RSS parsers, this is called syndication. Only content, mainly texts, but also audio and video files, are transmitted, but no navigation or functionalities. Advertising sites with RSS feeds thus receive a wide distribution among subscribers.

Ingame advertising includes the insertion of advertising messages in computer games. In static in-game advertising, product placements are programmed into the game dramaturgy to guide the action or remain a permanent component of the respective game. This leads to problems in terms of advertising law. With dynamic ingame advertising, geocoded or time-coded advertising media are also used, which makes necessary a feedback channel for online games. The advertising messages are then faded in or out depending on the advertising budget in the game and are thus campaign-capable. Variables are the duration of the fade-in, the relative size on the monitor and the viewing angle, thus creating different values with measurable efficiency variables. Adgames are games which have been developed on behalf of brand owners and are exclusively peppered with advertising, usually in the game environment. Conceivable, although not widely accepted, are also insertions during game breaks. Game forms are ego shooters, adventure games, strategy games, role-playing games, jump 'n' run games, flight simulators, business simulators, sports games, etc. These can be played by single players, also against the computer, by several players on the same computer or in a network as well as by massive multiplayer online games (MMOG) via server. The latter are usually role-playing games for which server usage costs are often incurred. The platforms for this are game consoles such as Nintendo, Playstation, X-Box as well as PCs, PDAs and cell phones. The input is done via gamepads, joysticks, speech recognition, body movement, etc. The output is via texts, subjective camera perspective, graphics (also 3-D) etc.

Virtual reality is generated, in which users can create 3-D representatives (so-called avatars) and interact with them. Like in the real world, this virtual world is interspersed with advertising messages. Companies can use "islands" in "second life", for example, to present themselves. Second life is a parallel world with its own economic cycle, its own currency, etc., the focus is on social interaction. With a free account, a visitor can buy land on private islands and settle there. Paid accounts entitle the visitor to buy islands, as many companies have done in the recent past, whereby visitors must be motivated to visit them. Social appreciation is openly shown in the virtual world because of the anonymity, advertising regularly falls through. Various criticisms, for example because of criminality, youth endangerment, lack of liability, but simply also lack of success, etc., have led to the fact that the enthusiasm for this project has decreased considerably.

5.4 Mobile advertising

Mobile online is likely to displace desktop online in private usage sooner or later. Although the principles remain essentially the same, there are specifics, which are shown in the following.

5.4.1 Multimedia opportunities

Multimedia refers to all electronic offline media which do not belong to the classical media and use the simultaneous integration of at least two presentation formats such as sound, text, data, fixed image, moving image, animation as well as their transmission and/or storage. In doing so, they make use of technical possibilities which have only recently been developed. Their dissemination is progressing rapidly.

Multimedia is generally described by the following features, although not all formats fulfill all features individually:

- *Interactivity* describes the ability for mutual communication between sender and receiver and thus the basic dialog and feedback capability. Both personal dialogs between two or more users via the medium and interactions with the medium itself are possible. This results in the possibility of the active and individual design of the communication process by the user or receiver independent of given flow patterns.

- *Multifunctionality* is characterized by the ability to handle different forms of communication via the medium, depending on the situation. The possibilities range optionally from the different types of individual communication such as bilateral/multilateral, synchronous/asynchronous, linear/non-linear to mass communication with the same information offer for everybody.

- *Topicality* means that information can be transmitted and retrieved over principally unlimited distances and independent of the temporal presence of a communication partner. Information is thus available at any time and any place.

- *Digitization* provides access to a wealth of data and programs stored on computer systems, creating a previously unknown information potential. This only becomes feasible when the data is presented in digital form.

- *Individuality* means that modularized news and information, even personalized, can be compiled or retrieved variably and flexibly from pre-fabricated modules, thus creating a pinpoint address.

- *Ubiquity* means the basically unlimited possibility of sending and receiving. Thus, in principle, access by everyone is possible for everyone. This means a technically complex, but at the same time simple form of communication for users.

Multimedia services usually combine several operators in a value-added service (VAS). Depending on the system, this may be in detail as follows:

- Content providers raise the multimedia content and package it,

- access providers allow entry to the services and ensure their use, e.g. through user registration and administration, customer care and billing, navigation,

- net providers supply the networks for the technical transmission of content using their own or leased capacities,

- carriers ensure the installation of the transmission technology through lines and switching technology or network services,

- hardware manufacturers above all provide the required terminal equipment,

- software providers allow the operating and application of programs for multimedia use,
- service providers supplement the services with their own offerings, e. g. consultants, system houses.

5.4.2 Advertising modes

Mobile communication is rapidly gaining importance ("mobile first"). It is technically based on three components, the

- *terminals*, which are, depending on the type, internet-capable cell phones, smartphones, PDAs, pocket PCs, notebooks, e-readers, tablets, etc.,
- *data services*, these are mainly SMS (text), MMS (text/graphic/status/moving image/sound), although largely obsolete, as well as mobile internet/WAP, App, instant messaging, location based service/LBS, etc.,
- *networks*, with the standards LTE (4th generation) and 5G to be mentioned.

The advantages of mobile communication lie in the localizability through user-initiated, terminal-based or network-based locating via GPS, the also international independence of location, accessibility at any time, interactivity and flexibility, identifiability, convenience and cost effectiveness. Besides equipment manufacturers and system operators, value-added service providers and service dealers are also active as players. The main problems are inconsistent screen presentation, network interruptions and a lack of data protection.

The most important forms in mobile communications are as follows:

- Mobile use of search engines and data requests, mobile information services for recipients incl. knowledge management, single-stage or multi-stage ubiquitous dialog between customers and providers, mobile forms of advertising (push/pull), mobile initiation and processing of shopping transactions (m-commerce), mobile access to auctions, payment for products from mobile devices, fast payment at the POS via NFC, multimedia entertainment applications such as music, video, video games, applications and services which take off on the recipient's location, mobile software download, mobile browsing, mobile navigation, mobile telemetry, sponsored news as branded content, couponing with QR code/group buying, promotions, voting, mobile TV, ringtones, wallpapers, etc.

Mobile advertising benefits from improved technical standards in transmission at high data rates, but also in the end devices due to display size, battery performance, data entry, faster processors, larger working memory, etc. The legal framework conditions must be taken into account when using mobile advertising. This includes a clear identification of the sender, the obligation to provide an imprint and the sending of advertising messages only with the prior consent of the recipient. When sending messages, a distinction is made between the pull model from the customer to the provider, i.e. dialing via telephone numbers, which are often expensive, and the push model from the provider to the customer, i.e. sending without request. Banner ads represent an important form of advertising, namely as

- sky lengthwise vertical on the border, wallpaper on the upper and lower border, medium rectangle in the middle, maximum wallpaper on the upper, left and right border, superbanner as stripes on the upper border, ad rectangle on the left border.

The banner should be delivered in four sizes because of the different screen diagonals. Different *display formats* are possible. Furthermore the following advertising forms are mainly considered:

- Text link, i.e. a hyperlink leads to an advertising page,

- image and text link as JPEG, also as inpage video ad with moving image,

- expandable ad, i.e. a separate screen window for advertising with a close icon (x),

- instream video ad as pre-/post-rolls, i.e., commercials before and after video content, being immediately interrupted when called, or as embedded videos, i.e. integral part of the content,

- click to video, i.e. screen window which starts a promotional video when clicked,

- interstitial, i.e. advertising which automatically appears temporarily when the page is called up, a close symbol is required,

- landing page, i.e. special page which appears when information from other websites is called up.

In each case an advertising marking at the edge is required, in high-contrast sans-serif font in at least 9 pt size.

5.4.3 Service applications

Common service applications in the field of mobile advertising are instant messaging, apps, mash-ups, location-based services, podcasts or entertainment. This is shown below.

Instant messaging is a service which allows direct, synchronous and written communication between partners. Using various proprietary protocols, short messages can be transmitted immediately between users, e.g. Whatsapp, Facebook messenger, Wechat, Telegram, Threema. Depending on the system, it is also possible to transfer files as well as audio and video streams. The prerequisite is that the communication partners are active at the same time and want to communicate directly with each other. The recipient of the message can react to this directly.

Push services bring content to the screen or hard disk of the user's computer according to previously agreed rules without the user having to pick it up from the information service provider, including stock market tickers, database content or browser updates.

Apps stands for applets, these are small programs, some with advertising as a substitute for the purchase price, which are mainly offered on smartphones/tablet PCs with mobile-relevant content, e.g. timers, analog time clocks, flight dates, recipes. Apple in particular offers an end-to-end solution, i.e. hardware, operating system software and application software are coordinated, so there are no interface problems such as time delays or crashes. This requires a certain amount of "censorship" on the part of the system integrator, who checks apps for their executability, modifies them if necessary, and only then releases them.

Mash-ups seamlessly connect existing media content. This requires open programming interfaces such as Java-script. It is conceivable, for example, to integrate maps or satellite photos with individual markers into websites, but also embedded photos or videos. This creates added value information. This information can be aggregated and processed on the server or client side, permanently or on ad hoc basis, globally or individually controlled. They are mainly used in the so-called long tail business, i.e. for digital niche products in which capital commitment is not important and therefore program diversity is possible.

Within the framework of *Location-based services* (LBS), evaluations in the local environment can be used for purchase decisions by combining them with map services as augmented reality. For this purpose, functions and information based on the geographical location of a user or object are provided to the user himself as position aware services or to another person/organization as location tracking services ("geotagging"). With pull services, the user actively requests data on his current or future location, with push services, the data is automatically sent to him or her. This combines mobile device technology as user interface, microgeographic information systems as data source and the internet as a transport route. The location is given descriptively as a name, by geographic coordinates or by radio cells. The position is determined satellite-based by GPS network, network-based by LTE/5G or indoor by NFC as combination of RFID and radio technology. Applications include navigation, local social networks, fleet management for tracing and location-based billing for ticketing.

Podcast is an artificial word from broadcast for send to many and pod for iPod from Apple. Podcasts are used to distribute audio and video files on the internet, video files are often called vodcasts. The environment of podcasts is called podosphere. The files are online accessible mp3 files which users download and play on their PC or mp3 player. In free podcasts advertising is accepted. A subscription via RSS feed through podcatchers such as iTunes is also possible. The recording takes place on computers with sound card/video card, microphone/webcam and internet connection. The software is often free of charge. Then the editing and the conversion into mp3-files are necessary. The copyrights must of course be observed. The finished cast is uploaded to the own webspace or stored at podhosters, where one can set up an account with storage space, usually free of charge. The podcast is published in podcast portals as broadcasting. Important are an impeccable sound/picture quality, a length under 20 minutes and a serious presentation.

A *Quick response code* (QR) consists of a square matrix with black and white dots and lines. These contain digitally coded information with texts, contact data, telephone numbers, order data, etc. In three of four corners there is a square, which the scanner orients itself to. This ensures that the QR code can always be read correctly, regardless of its orientation. The code contains error compensation, which ensures that the information is still readable even if 30 % of the graphic is destroyed. This also enables designer QR codes. QR codes can easily be generated with freeware programs and captured with free apps like Qrafter on mobile devices.

The cellphone has increasingly become a device of *engagements* in the sparetime of many, especially young people. This provides diverse options such as mobile games, mobile betting, downloads of screen savers/wallpapers, ring tones, streaming of audio and video content, etc., which can be smartly used for advertising functions. Besides these entertainment engagements, also creative engagements are common. Popular in this context is e. g. crowdsourcing. Examples come from McDonald's in search of individual hamburgers, Lego for new construction kits, Tchibo for merchandising products, Swarowski for jewellery design, P & G for cosmetics, BMW for car interior design, Aldi for salad snacks, etc. More over mobile devices enable a financial engagement like crowdfunding for non-profit or private purposes by collecting more or less small amouts of money in order to invest in projects which otherwise could or would not be financed. Collectively this even enables effective speculations on stock exchange.

6. Non-classical advertising

The final result of all conceptual considerations and explanations of the communication instruments is the use of advertising in media. Two large groups of offline media can be distinguished: the classical media as above the line advertising and the non-classical media as below the line advertising. At first there were only the classical media. These are placed by advertisers, i.e. publishers, broadcasters, tenants, against a binding price list, the tariff, and have an intermediary commission of 15% included in their price. However, their effect is increasingly reaching its limits. Only think of zapping, i.e. switching off the TV channel at the beginning of an advertising block, or deliberately flipping over ads as a disruption in the editorial reading process. Therefore, the use of other media is necessary, which try to reach the target persons in other ways than the classical ones. What they all have in common is that their prices have to be negotiated on a case-by-case basis and/or do not include an agency commission for advertising intermediaries. Otherwise, this group is structured extremely heterogeneously and it only makes sense to distinguish it from classical advertising, if at all, in a negative way.

Important options are public relations, live advertising, direct advertising and others such like sales promotion, product features, brand licensing or personal communication (*see figure 38: Forms of non-classical advertising*).

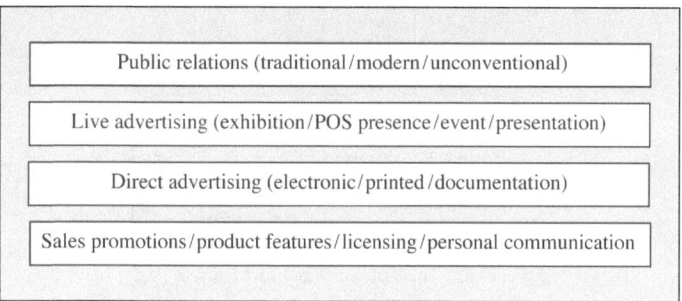

Fig. 38: Forms of non-classical advertising

6.1 Public relations

Public relations (PR) *aims to gain public trust for a sender* (company/organization) *and thus pursues psychographic instead of economic advertising goals.* In practice, however, public relations work is difficult to distinguish from (product/

brand) advertising. This is especially true if the company and the offer (brand) are identical in name. Because then public relations is also advertising and vice versa.

Public relations is the central instrument for *relationship management*. The company maintains direct, formal and indirect, informal relationships with various stakeholders who can influence the company's success. Stakeholders pursue specific, selfish interests, have the power to enforce them and, in case of doubt, do not opportunistically shy away from using it. The problem here is that different stakeholders may well have different interests vis-à-vis the company. To that extent it comes to a tightrope walk in such a way to come to meet these particular interests in each case so far that each group of interests does without the employment of means of power, because it regards its interests as reasonably interspersed, and at the same time and particularly not to leave the enterprise goals from the eye. In doing so, general decisions are to be made:

- Interpretation of the relationship as vertical, horizontal or lateral,
- priority as primary or secondary group,
- target groups as persons or organizations,
- content as formal or informal,
- intensity as strong or weak,
- symmetry as equal or unequal.

PR uses different forms of activities (*see figure 39: Forms of public relations*). Besides the traditional forms these are placements, sponsorships as well as unconventional forms of PR.

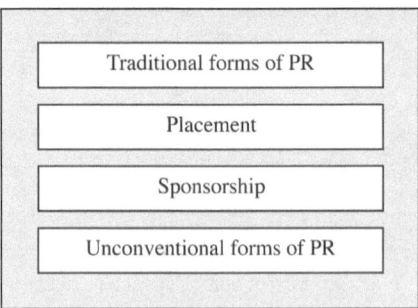

Fig. 39: Forms of public relations

6.1.1 Traditional forms

Public relations work traditionally addresses persons/institutions outside the company, within the company and multipliers as interest groups. The area of public relations work for persons/institutions outside the company, or external PR for short, includes all measures aimed at markets with which a company has business contacts. In detail, these forms include market actors, opinion leaders and internal PR.

6.1.1.1 General market actor-PR

The *sales market* players are subject to diverse activities in marketing and can be divided into several groups:

- *Dealers, distributors*, etc. constitute trade relations because these are target groups which act as sales intermediaries in the sales channel and thus limit the success of the company.
- *Customers* of goods and services constitute consumer relations because these are target groups which are the buyers of goods and services and therefore a prerequisite for any business success.
- *Interest groups* include consumer protectors, decision makers in business and administration, hobbyists. They constitute opinion leader relations, because these are target groups which act as opinion influencers in the business sector and are significant.

Moreover, there are additional market actors being target groups for public relations, such as procurement actors for raw materials and deliveries, capital and credit providers, such as banks, investment advisors, staff actors, such as labor unions, mediators, and also diverse market environment players.

The *procurement market* players are increasingly understood as value-added partners, so that the establishment, maintenance, expansion and, if necessary, the re-establishment of constructive relationships with them is regarded as significant, also in case of a relative monopoly of supply. In the context of PR, it is not the material level of the flow of services and money which matters, but the immaterial level of communication. They can in turn be divided into several groups:

- Target group *suppliers of raw materials and deliveries*

  This applies to semi-finished and finished products, merchandises, plants, systems, etc. The purchase relations concern target groups which are directly related to the company in terms of procurement management. In addition also procurement intermediaries belong here such as commission agents, brokers, etc.

- Target group *capital and credit providers, banks, investment advisors*, etc.

  These are investor relations, because they concerns target groups, which are important for investment and financing interests. It is about financial communication to private investors and the financial community such as analysts, fund managers, institutional investors, financial media, rating agencies, business journalists, investment analysts, etc. There are legally prescribed instruments for this purpose in the stock corporation act with regard to the structure of the company, accounting, appropriation of profits, the annual general meeting, in the securities prospectus act with regard to companies prior to an IPO or capital increase, in the securities trading act with regard to information on circumstances/insider information not yet publicly known, proprietary trading by members of the board of management and prohibited transactions, in the German commercial code with respect to the obligation to prepare consolidated financial statements, valuation regulations, in the stock exchange act with respect to the organization and activities of stock exchanges, admission requirements, post-admission obligations and in the antitrust law with respect to mergers and acquisitions, control of compliance with the law, squeeze-out possibility, equal treatment requirement, regulations on the offer document. These laws are enforced by small investors via their representatives as well as institutional investors such as insurance companies, pension funds, capital collection agencies, banks, etc.

An important instrument is the annual report. It is prepared for each fiscal year or on an extraordinary basis and provides information on the course of business and the situation of the company and explains the annual financial statements. The addressees are the shareholders of the company and the interested public. It contains the profit and loss account, the balance sheet, the notes and the management report. It is mandatory for large and medium-sized AGs, KGaAs and GmbHs, for eGs and for all companies, insurance companies and banks subject to the disclosure act, in some cases also as half-yearly/quarterly reports in the German leading share index DAX. The design criteria are above all appropriateness, overall impression, layout, typography, visual language, information graphics, colors, production/processing as well as spelling, morphology, syntax, choice of words, style, textcomposition, design and structure.

Other tools include mandatory letters to shareholders and ad hoc announcements for takeover and purchase offers, dividend changes, sale of core business areas, quarterly reports, etc., product brochures and image reports. In addition, there are analysts' conferences, so-called beauty contests, for discussions with financial analysts, analysts' parties with celebrities, presentations of the company to existing and potential investors, mostly in the financial metropolises as roadshows and press conferences with fact book or plant tour, as well as one-to-one meetings/chats with top managers of the company.

- Target group *labor unions, mediators*, etc.

This is referred to as employee relations because these are target groups which influence the attitude and behavior of the company's employees. An important instrument is the employee magazine/intranet. It serves the employees as a source of information, for communicating background information and information about the general structure and organization of the company, in order to make management decisions transparent. This also complies with the statutory information obligations and creates "responsible" employees. Through employee magazines/newsletters, the aim is to influence employee behavior, ensure job satisfaction, increase identification with the company and win over employees as multipliers. The promotion of dialog leads to an exchange of ideas at employee level and to the establishment of informal contacts. Problems arise in the event of loss of credibility and damage to the company's image, in the event of misjudgements by the company management regarding the state of mind, due to lack of time and/or proximity from the employee and individual misconceptions of the contents.

The *marketing environment* players can also be divided into several groups of stakeholders:

- Federal, state and local lobbies. They form governmental relations because these are target groups which determine the framework conditions for operational success.
- Public administrations, private institutions, associations, etc. These political relations are referred to because they are target groups which exert influence on providers within the framework of political decision-making.
- Residents, protest groups, youth groups, company pensioners, churches, associations, etc. These social relations are referred to because it concerns target groups which have less economic and more social relations with the provider.
- Education, science, research and teaching, students, etc. These are educational relations with target groups which are useful for the accumulation of knowledge at the PR-provider.

6.1.1.2 Opinion leader-PR

The area of public relations work for professional opinion influencers, or *multiplier PR* for short, includes all measures aimed at journalists, celebrities, teachers and the like. In detail, this includes the following activities:

- Contacts are maintained with the press with the aim of initiating, developing and stabilizing relationships and influencing reporting. This includes word and image contributions, news and image services, references, press services, and the distribution of circular letters/newsletters, literature or product samples. Occasions for contact include press conferences or meetings and visits to editorial offices. Success is monitored directly via clippings. However, the danger of increasing dependency of editorial offices cannot be denied.
- Contact is maintained with other opinion leaders through special events, editorial statements and self-promotion. The means for this are mandatory and optional

publications, video/radio productions, audio-vision technology or sound and vision, corporate advertising, etc. Special occasions for contact are charitable activities in positive cases and crisis PR and conflict PR in negative cases. To the latter the following examples apply.

A generally important tool towards opinion leaders is the *press conference*. This is held on the occasion of product launches, special economic events, new openings, crises, etc. After a precise definition of the topic, the choice of speakers takes place. Competence and eloquence are important. The choice of date should not overlap with other events. Fridays and mornings are also unpopular with the media. It is important that the event location is easily accessible, and that the choice of rooms and equipment is appropriate. The seating arrangements should also be considered. The duration should not exceed one hour. Questions should only be allowed after each or all lectures. Speakers' statements should not last longer than ten minutes. There should not be lengthy technical presentations. The order in which questions are asked is determined by the hand entries, the journalists answer with their name and editor, two supplementary questions are permitted per topic. At the end there will be a short summary, any interview requests will be recorded for separate dates, and there will be a thank you and goodbye. Press kits containing materials such as drawings, photos, text manuscripts, data carriers, etc. are distributed. In the follow-up, the non-participating press representatives will be informed, additional materials will be sent on request. The updating of the website should also be considered. The control of the press releases is carried out through distribution and resonance analyses.

Another topic in relation to opinion leaders is the handling of conflict-PR and crisis-PR. Following are some historic, but important cases on crisis-PR, which illustrate the sensitiveness of this issue.

Example Coppenrath & Wiese (2003):

In January, an 11-year-old girl who had eaten a piece of cake from Coppenrath & Wiese deep frozen-food died. Other family members had also fallen ill, so that, ultimately wrongly, food poisoning was assumed to be the cause. On the same weekend, two families also suffered from gastrointestinal diseases after eating the cake. The Hessian ministry of health warned against eating the C & W frozen cake "Feine Conditor Auswahl". Coppenrath & Wiese thereupon announced the batch number and the minimum durability date together with the exact designation of the cake concerned to the public and called back the appropriate product batch country wide. It was communicated that the recall was made in order to comply with the highest possible duty of care and that Coppenrath & Wiese would guarantee the perfect quality of the products in its own area of responsibility. However, it could not be ruled out that the goods had been affected elsewhere by improper handling, e. g. bacterial contamination. At the same time, a hotline was set up to provide information to concerned consumers. Around 1,000 calls were received here during the short period of the acute crisis. Consumers were also able to obtain information on the current situation via a website published on the Internet. Press conferences were also held.

Example Lidl (2009):

Lidl, Germany's leading discounter, was accused of spying on and video surveillance of employees and customers based on a report in Stern magazine. The company responded with an open letter, which was placed in adverts in regional and national newspapers. In it, the management explicitly apologized to the employees and at the same time clarified the causes of the behavior, namely theft and job endangerment. Interviews in the radio media had the same tenor. Other discounters and drugstores use similar practices, but were fortunate enough not to be outed. The open letter had the following text:

- *"Dear customers, dear employees, Lidl is currently confronted with accusations of having monitored employees by using detective agencies. This accusation has caused us great concern. The impression created that Lidl has systematically 'spied on' its employees is in no way in keeping with the company's lived, fair treatment of its employees. Lidl did not and does not intend to act in this way. If employees feel discredited and personally injured by the behavior described, we deeply regret this and expressly apologize for it. Theft and inventory losses are a major problem throughout the retail industry. In order to avoid inventory losses caused by theft, Lidl, like all other retail companies, used to work with camera systems and, in stores with a high inventory loss, worked with detective agencies for a limited period of time. In 2007, this was the case in eight percent of our stores. The task of the detective agencies was to obtain information in these stores to help clear up the thefts. In individual cases, the detective agencies logged additional and sometimes personal information about employees, which was not what we wanted. We have learned from the incidents and will in future protect the company from losses due to theft together with our employees. 48,000 employees are there for you every day, please continue to place your trust in us. Your Lidl management."*

Example Vattenfall (2009):

A reactor accident at Vattenfall, one of the four major energy suppliers in Germany, startled. Chernobyl had in any case made the public enormously sensitive to the subject of nuclear power. Nuclear power plants collided with the politically intended transition to renewable energies. The reactor accident at the Vattenfall nuclear power plant in Forsmark already caused a loss of confidence in 2006. The German environmental aid documented the deficiencies at the Brunsbüttel nuclear power plant, which was now affected, since 2001. The company sealed itself off because not all relevant information was available. It could not be contacted immediately due to unclear distribution of competencies between the mother company in Sweden and the subsidiary in Germany. The press spokespersons were lost in explanations in technical jargon, and the statements were not 100 percent reliable. *The company only admitted what was already publicly known. In addition, it denied the publicly speculated but clear facts. The emotional situation of those affected was not sufficiently taken into account. The whole thing ended in a communication disaster. Those responsible were recalled, but the already weakened trust of the population in the worst enemies of the energy companies, the energy companies themselves, was permanently shaken.*

6.1.1.3 Internal PR

The area of public relations for persons/institutions within the company, called internal PR for short, includes all measures which are aimed at people/staff directly bound by instructions and interested visitors. This includes the following activities in particular:

- For groups of visitors, public events are held as invitations, tours, presentations, etc. If it is a specialist public, events such as a forum, congress, conference, study trip, etc. may be considered. Welcome occasions are also company events which can be used for celebrations, visitor arrangements, etc.
- Measures for the workforce include notice boards, information for the works council and store stewards, circulars and open letters. Executives in particular are addressed by executive dossiers, discussion group offers, preferred information, etc. Formal groups such as departments, quality circles, teams, etc. are primarily addressed by company or position statements. In contrast, informal groups are difficult to record systematically. Special groups such as disabled persons, foreigners, older employees, etc. are also of particular importance. Both groups are reached through works meetings, in addition to hearings and the like. In addition, there are intranet, online magazine, employee portal/CUG, e-mail circular/information service, business TV/business radio, hotline, video presentation, etc.

Measuring the efficiency of public relations work is problematic. Media resonance analysis is used as an aid. It is carried out using various key figures such as the following:

- Affinity value indicates the content-related proximity of an opinion leader or a medium to a previously defined position,
- acceptance quotient refers to the ratio of positive, neutral or negative media contributions to a topic,
- degree of penetration indicates how often a topic, a name, an actor or a product is mentioned in the media,
- initiative quotient displays the ratio of self-controlled vs. externally controlled reporting,
- response quotient provides information on the number and distribution of reports in the various media target groups,

- text-image quotient notifies the ratio of texts with illustrations to texts without illustrations,
- topic quotient indicates the share of individual topics in the overall media resonance,
- transfer quota corresponds to the ratio of the mentions of individual keywords such as product name, message, company, etc. to the total number of publications or total circulation,
- distribution value shows the regional media presence.

6.1.2 Modern forms

Modern forms of public relations include placement, sponsoring and unconventional forms of PR. These are shown in the following.

6.1.2.1 Placement

Placement is the integration of products, or even just advertising material, and topics into the editorial process of entertainment projects. In this respect, the goal is the targeted integration of materials and services in the course of a media program for advertising purposes. These are mostly cinema, television and video films, more rarely radio or print projects.

Famous cinema film examples include the minute-long driving scenes of a red Alfa convertible across America in Dustin Hoffman's film "The Graduate", or the luring of E. T. in the Stephen Spielberg film of the same name by children with Hershey's candy, or the use of Sony entertainment electronics equipment in the Tom Cruise/Dustin Hoffman film "Rain man". In television series, the Paroli scene in Tatort episode "Zahn um Zahn" with Schimanski/Götz George is especially well-known, but also the car journeys of Commissioner Derrick (BMW on 2nd German TV/ZDF), "Schwarzwald-Klinik"-Professor Brinkmann (VW-Audi on 1st German TV/ARD) or the former hotelier Berger alias Roy Black in "Schlosshotel am Wörthersee" (Volkswagen on RTL private TV-channel).

It is quite possible to query the film and TV projects which are currently being realized at the productions and to check the integrability of certain products on the basis of a script breakdown. As a result of the high, rising production costs, screenwriters are possibly prepared to redesign scenes on request so that desired products appear in them as if they were inevitable by product plugging. This also applies to the avoidance of delicate scenes such as car accidents during car placement. There are price lists for these services, which are calculated on the basis of the negotiated broadcast dates and the resulting number and structure of viewers or performance rights.

Depending on the type of placement, a distinction is made between the following:

- *Generic placement* means the promotion of a type of goods or a branded product without its marking appearing. It is conceivable to include a Perrier bottle or a Coke bottle, which can be identified by their typical shapes alone, without the branding having to be shown. Examples in films are jelly in "Liebling Kreuzberg" (Manfred Krug) or electronic mail in "You've got mail" (Tom Hanks/Meg Ryan).

- *Corporate placement* means the forcing of an organization through action. This happened around the beginning of the 1960s, when the U.S. Space agency's NASA program met with resistance in public opinion because of its immense costs, by integrating it into the series "I dream of Jeannie", which revolved around an astronaut, his astronaut friend, both astronaut bosses, and a bottle ghost of the same name found in outer space (Barbara Eden/Larry Hagman).

- *Product placement* means the forcing of an identifiable product through targeted placement as a real prop. This is the most common form of placement and is often used as a synonym for the whole category. Product placement can refer to old products/packages/logos as historic placement or future products as futuristic placement, e.g. Lexus Coupé in the Film "Minority report" (Tom Cruise) depending on the time. Product replacement is intended to prevent unintentional placements in undesirable environments. Examples of product placement in films are Dr. Pepper-Cola in "Forrest Gump" (Tom Hanks), Starbucks in "Austin Powers" (Mike Myers).

- *Innovation placement* means the promotion of new products through scenic integration. 007 films have often been pioneers in this field, just think of the famous digital watch scene by James Bond, the navigation system in the dashboard of the Aston Martin or the presentation of the BMW Z 3 convertible as Bond car in "Golden eye".

- *Message placement* means the promotion of an overarching production theme. One might think of the "Traumschiff" series on ZDF, which, with a little help of TUI, revived the desire for sea voyages which were long considered rather antiquated.

- *Country/Location placement* means the promotion of a particular location within an entertainment project, e.g. "Schwarzwald-Klinik" for recreational stays in the Black Forest, Prague in "Mission impossible" (Tom Cruise) or New Zealand in "Lord of the rings" (Elijah Wood).

- *Music/Movie placement* refers to the establishment of a musical performance, e.g. Whitney Houston/"Bodyguard".

- *Image placement* promotes the settings for a sender, e.g. "Cast away"/Fedex (Tom Hanks) or "Top gun"/U.S. Navy (Tom Cruise).

According to the form of the placement, the following can be distinguished:

- An *on-set placement* is done passively with props, which only serve as staffage or to decorate a scene, e. g. Marlboro in "Otto – Der Film".
- A *creative placement* is done actively by props which take on an action role, e. g. Coke in "The Gods must be crazy".
- A *visual placement* is done by props which only appear in the picture, e. g. Nesquik's can in the series "Lindenstraße".
- A *verbal placement* is made by props which are mentioned in the audio track, e. g. Omega in the Bond film "Casino royal" or Whiskas in the Bond film "From a view to a kill".
- An *endorsed placement* is done by the main actor with visual and/or verbal support, e. g. the DeLorean sports car from "Back to the future".
- A *sub-placement* takes place without actor support as requisite. Other forms are personality placement, game placement, etc.

The admissibility of placements is problematic because they violate the prohibition of mentioning products/companies in programs, the avoidance of any advertising intentions of the broadcaster and the avoidance of misleading the general public about the actual purpose of a program.

Nevertheless, placements on TV against payment are legal. This applies to entertainment programs, fictional programs such as series and films and also sports programs. Excluded are news, broadcasts on current political events/news, religious services and children's television programs. However, such placements may only be incorporated into the plot of a film or program for predominantly programmatic-dramaturgical reasons. The editorial responsibility and independence with regard to content and broadcasting space must not be impaired, the program must not directly encourage the purchase, rental or leasing of goods and services, in particular these must not be strongly emphasized by special, promotional references. The broadcasts must be marked with a logo at the beginning of the program, at its end and after each commercial break, thus informing viewers about the placement. An equivalent reference must be made in radio broadcasts. To present a brand or a product in such a broadcast in advertising is prohibited as covered advertising.

It is permitted to provide marked goods free of charge as long as they have no significant value. The limit for such a provision is one percent of the production costs, max. € 1,000, and applies primarily to public broadcasters. Foreign productions only have to be marked if placements can be determined with reasonable effort; the same applies to non-internal productions in private commercial television. The obligation to label also does not apply to feature films, films and series, sports broadcasts and light entertainment broadcasts which have not been produced or commissioned by the broadcaster itself or by a company affiliated with the broadcaster, unless these are broadcasts for children or if no remuneration is paid, but only production aids and prizes are provided free of charge with a view to inclusion in a broadcast. Exceptions to this are productions before 2010.

There are placement agencies which act as intermediaries or licensors for merchandising products, as well as outfitters who maintain large warehouses for the selection of props and coordinate transport from the producer to the shooting location. Their main tasks include identifying suitable productions, reviewing scripts for placement opportunities, ensuring the availability of placement products and monitoring their advantageous deployment dramaturgy.

6.1.2.2 Sponsoring

Sponsoring includes the planning, organisation, implementation and control of all measures for the provision of financial and/or material resources by companies for persons and organisations in the sporting, cultural and social sectors in order to achieve their own marketing and communication goals in return for the sponsored party (based on Bruhn). The sponsor thus borrows external performance advantages by dedicating investment funds. The difference to the well-known patronage lies in the fact that this is done without a fixed consideration by the sponsored party, i.e. rather on an idealistic basis.

The goals pursued are of psychographic nature, i.e. they consist of image, publicity, contact, goodwill, motivation, etc. With regard to the target groups, a distinction must be made between those of the sponsor and the sponsored party. The former refer to sponsored subjects and objects, the latter to the groups of people reached by the sponsor. It makes sense for sponsoring to be included in the publicity of the sponsored person and the sponsor/organization, in the former by naming, thanking, offering a message or the like, in the latter by label/logo, testimonial, highlighting or the like. It is important to dovetail the overall communication, whereby experience has shown that considerable expenditure is required for the general conditions and exploitation. Sponsoring should therefore not be seen and used in isolation, otherwise many of the opportunities it offers will be missed.

The prerequisite for success is a commitment to sponsoring. This requires an appropriate balance between performance and reward, benefit and expense. Sponsoring topic and area should be in a plausible connection with the sponsor's communication concept. Continuity of commitment is also necessary for a lasting effect. All measures must be precisely prepared and coordinated in detail. To this end, responsibilities and authorities must be clearly defined and formulated.

A distinction usually is made between four areas of sponsoring: sports sponsoring, cultural sponsoring, social sponsoring and ecological sponsoring.

Sports sponsorship

Sports sponsorship is based on the economic dependence of sport, especially in the top-class sports sector, and is by far the most important and historically oldest form of sponsorship. It was pushed forward above all by the tobacco industry, which faced tighter advertising restrictions in many countries and was looking for ways out of this situation to still reach the media, even the editorial section in those countries. One has to think of the early Formula 1 race activities of Philip Morris ("Marlboro"), Reynolds Tobacco ("Camel") or Reemtsma ("West"). The advantages of sports sponsoring lie in the possibility of image transfer from the sport or the athlete, in target group-specific communication which is not subject to resistance to influence, as is often the case with classic advertising, in a non-commercial message environment and in the extensive bypassing of advertising bans.

The *subject* of sponsoring are products of various degrees. 1st degree products are those which have a direct connection to sports, e.g. sports equipment such as running shoes. Products of the 2nd degree are those which are at least sports-related articles, e.g. soft drinks. Products of the 3rd degree are those which are at home in the field of sports, e.g. health food. And 4th degree products are those which are not related to sports at all.

With regard to the *type* of sponsorship, numerous subdivisions are possible. A distinction can be made according to the type of sport sponsored. Particularly popular are youthful, dynamic sports, more in the individual sports such as tennis, golf, skiing. Also, a distinction can be made according to the type of sports event. Depending on the dimension, this has local, national or international significance. Since all available events are sufficiently occupied by sponsors in the meantime, own events for sponsors are invented like the former Compaq grand prix in tennis. However, the already tight schedule of the athletes sets strict limits here. Furthermore, a distinction can be made according to the level of performance. Thus there is top competitive sport, which is the most spectacular, popular sport, which is cheaper to promote, disabled sport, semi-professional sport, amateur sport, etc.

The *way* of sponsoring itself can be moneywise, in-kind or by services. Possible sponsors often are equipment suppliers, companies as sponsors, foundations, moreover federations, clubs, foundations or public/non-profit organizations. It can be concentrated only in one area or differentiated.

The *manner* of use can be isolated, i.e. without utilization in other media, or integrated. The type of sponsored event can be official, unofficial, e.g. show fights, or own-created. The consideration of the sponsored party can take place via advertising during the event, the use of predicates, such as official supplier or similar, or the use of the sponsored athletes in the company's corporate communication. The power category can be on grassroot level, performance level, e.g. junior, or top level.

Advertising can take place on the athlete himself and in the classical media with athletes. As costs result apart from the sponsor amount above all personnel costs for the organization, implementation costs, follow-up costs and commissions for mediators. The main strengths of sports sponsoring lie in the high multiplier effect via the media, in the great variety of sports with very different image characteristics and in the general interest of the population in the topic of sports. Significant weaknesses are the concentration of media interest on relatively few sports and leagues, the already strong coverage of these disciplines by sometimes extremely large sums of money and current image problems such as doping, hooligans, etc.

Cultural sponsorship

Cultural sponsoring concerns the areas of

- visual arts such as painting, sculpture, graphic design, architecture, photography,
- stagecraft like acting, opera, operetta, ballet,
- music in serious genre and the entertaining genre,
- literature in fiction and non-fiction, film, radio and television,
- preservation of monuments, etc.

Sponsoring includes the provision of financial means, for example for tours, exhibitions, projects, material resources, the announcement of competitions, the awarding of scholarships and the assumption of organisational tasks such as marketing, etc. Beneficiaries of these activities are individual artists such as authors, soloists, singers, cultural groups such as orchestras, choirs, ensembles, cultural organizations such as museums, galleries, publishers and cultural events such as festivals, cultural days, etc. The beneficiaries can be top-class, popular or young artists.

The main strengths of cultural sponsoring lie in the breadth of the possible range of applications, in the achievement of attractive image values, in the wide variety of design options and in the growing interest among demanding target groups with high purchasing power. Its main weaknesses are the low level of public awareness, the reluctance of the media to report and the occasional reluctance of creative artists to pursue commercial interests.

The type of sponsorship can be by support through financial resources, material resources or services, the type of consideration can be activ self-organized or passive. The type of sponsored parties can be cultural creators, institutions or projects. The beneficiary's performance category refers to elite art, popular art or mass art. The cultural sponsorship can be self-initiated or externally initiated. According to the number of sponsors it can be exclusive or cooperative.

Social sponsoring

Social sponsoring is a forward-looking form of sponsoring in social areas such as health, science, education, etc. via institutions. The difficult and challenging tasks in the social sector are to be improved by the provision of financial/material resources or services by sponsors, who thereby directly or indirectly aim to achieve effects for their corporate culture and communication. Examples can be found in the Philip Morris research award or the Otto Beisheim chair of marketing at WHU Koblenz. Again, these can also be self-initiated activities, whereby the boundary to donations is fluid. In the U.S., for example, this is completely normal in the field of education, as the Kellogg school of business (Northwestern university), where marketing pope Philip Kotler taught, shows.

The main strengths of social sponsoring lie in its many different approaches, in its independent conception and presentation possibilities, in conveying sympathy, in documenting a sense of social responsibility and in the reasonable price-performance ratio of these measures. Major weaknesses are the low transparency of possible sponsor offers, the low advertising impact due to media restraint and credibility problems.

According to the number of sponsors this can be exclusive or cooperative. The sponsorship can be externally initiated or self-initiated. The type of communication use is either isolated or campaign-integrated. The type of consideration is active or passive. The organization of the sponsorship can be group-related, project-related or independent. Types of project are events, campaigns or competitions. And the type of predicate may use the awarding of titles or licensing. This is valid for social sponsoring as well as ecological sponsoring.

Ecological sponsoring

Ecological sponsoring concerns the fields of activity nature and landscape, animal and species protection, ecological research, environmental education and information services. Prerequisites for the implementation, however, is a public commitment of the sponsors to take over the responsibility for defined tasks, which require a correspondingly consistent corporate behaviour in terms of these goals. In addition, there must be a strong internal motivation for the sponsored topic, an open and credible identification with ecological issues and the will for a long-term, sustainable commitment. To think of the initiative of "Uhu", at that time Lingner & Fischer, for the release of the eagle owl in native forests, or "Birkin" (Dr. Dralle) for the reforestation of native birch forests, which were financed by a donation from the sales price of the products. Here, too, the line between sponsoring and donation is fluid.

The main strengths of eco-sponsoring lie in the high level of interest and acceptance of this topic among the population, the resulting sympathy and the effective starting points for corporate communication by documenting environmental obligations and responsibility towards future generations. Major weaknesses lie in the central credibility of the commitment, which presupposes a "clean" company, negative examples are Hoechst, Shell, BP, and in the danger of overstretching this topic.

6.1.2.3 Unconventional PR

Great hopes were placed in sponsorship because it offered a new possibility of attractive, non-commercial appeal, achieved high reach through the multiplier effect of the media, was experience-oriented, selective and flexible in its application, was accepted by the target group and thus possible reactances were immediate. In view of restrictive budgets, however, the enthusiasm is noticeably waning. The lack of possibilities to control success, the risky dependency on individuals and events, the difficult target group definition, the high costs and the limited design possibilities are the main burdens. Therefore unconventional forms of PR as guerilla marketing came up.

Guerilla marketing should be surprising, shocking, breaking rules and taboos. It gets along with a very small advertising budget and relies on particularly creative ideas. Occasionally thereby the legal borders are exceeded. It concerns essentially one-time actions, so that these are unsuitable for brand building or brand care. Therefore mostly non-branded companies avail themselves of these controversial tools. The Guerilla marketing has as subforms ambush marketing, viral marketing, ambient media and buzz marketing.

Ambush marketing bears a certain resemblance to sponsoring in that it is also based on the "loan" of publicity, but in a different way from the latter, without the ambusher being willing to give anything in return. It is therefore a conscious attempt by a sender to create public attention without being an official sponsor. At the same time this is an attack on the official sponsor, usually a competitor in the industry. It is planned to mislead the public about the role of ambusher and official sponsor and to steer attention away from the sponsor and towards the ambusher. The sponsor can only protect himself against ambushes targeting his borrowed public by drafting a contract with an exclusivity clause, registering trademarks, names, signs, etc., and warning potential ambushers of legal action and countermeasures on the spot, if one is prepared for this.

Well-known examples of early, but milestone-setting ambushes are the following:

- *Kodak booked TV spots before and after each commercial break at the 1984 Los Angeles Olympics, but the sponsor of these Olympics was in fact Fuji, the competitor.*
- *Nike distributed baseball caps to spectators at national team games in the U.S. in 1994, displaying the Nike logo on the stands, but the sponsor of the national team was actually rival Umbro.*

- *Mercedes-Benz used skywriting during the New York marathon, but the event was actually sponsored by rival Toyota.*

- *Linford Christie (sprinter) attended the press conference of the 1996 Atlanta Olympics with Puma contact lenses, but the sponsor of the Olympics was actually rival Reebok.*

The direct ambushing uses protected trademarks and original image/film material, it is therefore anti-competitive. Indirect ambushing relies on presences in the immediate environment and in the media, provides services in the surrounding area or advertises with participants of the event.

Viral marketing is based on the request to target persons to spread received messages. It thus concerns the targeted triggering and control of word-of-mouth advertising for the purpose of companies and products. As a means to this end, references to websites serve as links to forward or "like" buttons. To get started, entries in search lists, guest books, blogs, free downloads or partner programs are recommended. Viral marketing works emotionally and with simple messages, it is about leaving traces and offering exclusive access to information. The means are the individualization of the message and a surprise effect. Sometimes additional benefits are offered which are not even disclosed. The approach is based on inclusion and trial & error, it is entertaining, free and innovative. The following phases can be distinguished:

- Analysis of the goals and target groups, conception of the measures, infection (so-called seeding) by creating a breeding ground with targeted distribution channels, development of the virus, usually first slowly, then exponentially quickly, and success measurement through response, views/clicks, user coverage, etc.

Advantages of viral marketing are low costs, low wastages, high attention, credibility, as well as the innovative character and fun of the activity. E-mail attachments based on recommendations are forwarded in large numbers. The mechanics require seeding, i.e. the target group discovers the campaign material itself or is made aware of it via a suitable platform.

Risks of viral marketing mainly concern the following:

- The message is spread to the wrong group of people. The connection to the originator is lost (e.g. Moorhuhn/Johnny Walker). The intended message is distorted during distribution ("silent post"). A necessary absolute critical mass is not reached. A loss of control occurs, which includes a possible negative multiplication via shitstorm/hatesites. The credibility of the campaign suffers, for example because the sender company is too much in the foreground.

The Pril promotion by Henkel showed the problem. Henkel challenged users to invent a new pril bottle design and post it on Facebook for voting. Henkel promised to launch the two best-rated packaging suggestions as a special series.

Some users then developed real horror packs with vampire depictions and the like, which were well received by the Facebook community and therefore made it to the top of the ranking. Henkel recognized the flaw in the mechanics and subsequently changed the rules of the game in such a way that a design jury was to select the two best proposals for realization from the ten best evaluated ones. This led to a controversial discussion ("shitstorm") with indignation, insulting the manufacturer and even a boycott of his products. The city of Schwäbisch-Gmünd (Bud Spencer Tunnel) or the English Football Association (Didi Hamann bridge to the new Wembley stadium) experienced similar events.

Productive applications come from McDonald's (customized hamburgers), BMW (co-creation lab), Lego (new construction kits), Tchibo (Ideas for merchandising products), Swarovski (jewelry, watches, pendants), P&G (cosmetics), Unilever (cosmetics), Apple (apps), etc.

Buzz marketing is pre-marketing and as such intended to draw attention to a new product or service even before its market presence. This is achieved by word-of-mouth propaganda with the help of private opinion leaders. These recommend the upcoming product as multipliers and receive it in advance for practice as lead users. The selection of the right buzz agents is therefore crucial for success. In this respect, buzz marketing combines various communication measures which are already known elsewhere. Related to this is sensation marketing, which seeks to attract attention through one-off campaigns.

6.1.3 Cause-related marketing

In cause-related marketing, a company promises to donate money or material resources for a previously defined "good" purpose ("cause"), provided that customers engage in behavior which is in line with the company's goals, usually the purchase of products, but indirectly also increases in brand awareness and image e.g. Krombacher rainforest project. A donation is the voluntary and gratuitous performance in the form of money or goods for a purpose recognized as worthy of support. In the case of non-profit status, this donation can moreover be claimed as tax-reduction. Companies pursue economic goals with cause-related marketing, so it is not about altruism. In contrast to sponsoring, however, the goal here is direct action by the customer. In this context, the company's social, societal and ecological responsibility (CSR) can be emphasized. Prerequisites are the relevance of the activity for the target group e.g. the "Dove" promotion for greater female self-esteem, the credibility and sustainability of the activity, the seriousness of the activity without an opportunistic "publicity stunt" and the commitment. Risks lie in an unsuitable choice of cooperation partner and public criticism by NGOs. In addition, legal aspects of the psychological obligation to buy, compassion advertising and the offer of transparency must be considered.

6.1.4 Olfactoric impact

Olfactory impact occurs via the sense of smell through odors. These can be original like coffee and chocolate or derivative only for the communication purposes. The latter is achieved by masking, i.e. covering up odours. It is used as a product concept, e.g. for scents, as a dominant signal, e.g. for soaps, for simulation, e.g. for used cars, and for signaling, e.g. for fruits. At the POS, scent columns are often placed which release scents in a controlled manner just below the immediate perception threshold. Alternatively, they can be connected to air conditioning systems. However, an evenly concentrated dose is difficult to control and depends on the number of people in the room, their distribution in the area, the air flow, etc. Applications can be found in reception halls, at exhibition stands, on airports, in sales rooms, etc. But also in hotels to help people fall asleep, doctors' surgeries to take away fear, fast food restaurants through kitchen aromas, bakeries through pastries aromas, production facilities to motivate employees, furniture stores as lamination of side smells in veneer furniture, travel agencies to convey a vacation feeling in the shop or at seminars to support learning processes. Negative aspects, however, are ethical concerns due to the danger of manipulation and annoying side effects for allergy sufferers. In addition, the subjective perception of scents varies depending on the individual's olfactory memory. The superimposition of several scents can also cause unpleasant odours.

The scent reaches the olfactory mucosa through the upper nasal cavity. Up there are about three million sensory cells, each cell is specialized in a particular scent. After recognition, the cell sends an electrical impulse, by which the scent then reaches the olfactory brain via nerve impulse. There the signal is evaluated and compared and triggers stimulation in body, mind and soul. Up to 4,000 scents can be distinguished, whose perception depends on the situation.

6.1.5 Customer clubs

Networking refers to the direct dialog with market partners and its institutionalization in the form of a network, for customers often by grouping in a customer club. Main parameters are the structure, the concept and the content of customer clubs.

Customer clubs are not necessarily set up profitably, the pay-off rather consists in increased customer loyalty. They offer services exclusive to the target group and appreciated by their members. Access is usually passive, i.e. customers join the club.

From the initiator's point of view club *goals* are primarily customer loyalty by building up economic barriers to switching and creating emotional added value, gaining new customers with immigration of interested parties straight or primarily because of the club benefits, increasing sales with existing customers, creating an efficient communication platform from the provider to its customers/interested parties and obtaining data about these individuals. At least peripheral goals are publicity and image effects, market research support and triggering a pull effect at POS.

The following are the main *motives* for customers to enter the club:

- Information search for product and/or enterprise data, communication and contact need to like-minded people, social prestige as an elevation from the masses, better use of the basic services by performance-supplementing offers, bargain search as smart shopping and private entertainment/comforts for diversion, fun, experiences.

The club services consist primarily of the elements club card, club magazine and bonus system:

- The *club card* has a legitimation and identification function and documents in the shop club membership. It is also an advertising medium and entitles the holder to use the club services. A company-related payment and credit are possible, for example in the context of co-branding with a credit company. The editor can collect member-related data via the club card. Depending on the type of card, it can be embossed, magnetic stripe or chip cards, as well as rechargeable smart cards, noncontact readable closed coupled cards or triggerable remote cards.

- The *club magazine* meets the information needs of club members. It is a basis for dialog and also serves as a constant reminder of the club. It takes up topics which are expected to be highly relevant to club members, either because of their informational or entertainment value.

- The *bonus system* manifests the concrete benefits of club membership. A mixture of material benefits, such as special prices, etc., and immaterial benefits, such as limited editions, etc., should be offered, and they should vary in the course of time, so that it always remains current.

There are generally several concepts for the design of customer clubs:

- *Open clubs* are freely accessible to everyone, regardless of customer status, without legal or financial access restrictions and without charging membership fees, for instance Camel club.

- *Closed clubs* have entry barriers for the interested party, such as admission fee, membership fee, subscription to a club magazine, etc., for instance Deutsche Post business club.

- *Enthusiast clubs* are characterized by a special emotional bond between the members and the brand/company. This is complemented by the sale of products and merchandising offers, for instance Dr. Oetker-Backclub.

- The *Lifestyle club* serves to attract and retain regular customers. The focus is on the core target group, which usually has an upmarket lifestyle, for instance Davidoff club.
- In the *VIP club*, the circle of members is limited to "important" persons, whether they are regular customers with high turnover or influential personalities from the public and business as multipliers and provide preferential treatment, for instance Frankfurt Airport club.
- The *Customer advantage club* is aimed at all customers and offers them financial incentives such as discounts, bonuses, special ordering and delivery services and exclusive offers. The barriers to entry are low, for instance IKEA Family.
- The *Pro club* has a business to business orientation. Target groups are the trade partners and sales agents or other business partners of the initiating company. The access is limited to these.
- The *Youth club* is especially addressed to children and young people as a new generation of customers, who should be familiarized with a provider/offer in time and feel preferences for it.

In any case, there is always the question of *refinancing* customer clubs. There are several concepts for this as well:

- The collection of membership fees implies a filter function. The level of services depends on the purchasing power of the target group, the equivalent offered and the level of the intended entry barriers.
- The sale of club products, e.g. limited editions for fan club members with an affinity for the product, can limit the financial investment in production, logistics and distribution. Distribution is often carried out via club stores, also with merchandising articles.
- Conceivable are also commissions for the procurement of services of third parties, e.g. tour operators, insurance companies, hotel industry, by the sale of tickets for tour operators, the distribution of products of cooperation partners which are not part of the club, but round off the club's offer.
- The sale of tickets for club events increases at the same time the subjective attractiveness of the event, if they are felt to be appropriate. Since the organization is complex, however, this often remains a subsidy business.
- Third-party advertising in the club magazine through adverts or inserts, usually by cooperation partners of the club or providers with content close to the offer, as well as advertising at events generates income, but a reasonable limit must not be exceeded due to reactance.

The club constantly needs new impulses and a high contact frequency, so that it "lives". Experience shows, however, that activities fall asleep over time or it becomes increasingly difficult to identify activities which are still attractive and affordable. A club concept must always be long-term. In this case, considerable costs are incurred, so that sufficient budgeting is necessary in advance, also resources in terms of personnel and IT-equipment must be available.

Numerous regulations must be observed as general conditions. Therefore no activities may be started without a legal examination. Customer loyalty measures cannot be carried out in addition to "normal" work. Rather, they require institutionalization in bodies/departments which are dedicated to these tasks on a full-time basis. Outsourcing to external service providers is also conceivable. The club activities should be designed in such a way that windfall profits from less profitable customers are avoided. To this end, segmentation prerequisites must be created as a fencing. This also applies to inactive members, whose membership must be adjusted from time to time.

Example Spies Hecker Profi club:

Spies Hecker is one of the world's leading manufacturers of car repair, truck paint and industrial coating. The Profi Club brings together car repair companies with the aim of exchanging information and experience.

Bonus points resulting from membership can be used for services in the areas of marketing, technology and management/controlling. In the field of marketing, means such as facade sign, posters/billboards/flyers, standardized internet presence, marketing manual, customer journal, PR package, direct mailing package, individual telephone advertising advice, interior design of the garage, partner integration on the company homepage or local events are offered.

The technical section offers resources such as technical hotline, technical information, workflow descriptions for painting, operational and workshop planning, hardware and software solutions, technical seminars or information about accessory suppliers.

The management/controlling section offers tools such as operational analysis, balance sheet analysis, cost plan, personnel management, operational planning, customer satisfaction analysis, potential and location analysis, accounting or time recording.

In addition, the provision of industry-specific software, participation in newsletters, certifications according to own standards analogous to quality, service, price-performance ratio, convenience and the exchange of information with industrial companies like car manufacturers, car insurers, are part of the club program.

Example 1. FC Märklin (children's club):

Märklin is the leading German model railroad manufacturer. For the target group of children, a kid's club is installed. This publishes a club magazine six times a year with a sheet for model railroad equipment. The members are offered to a website with password protected access, where hobby related information is available. Once a year there is a yearbook for HO gauge. Club members also have the right to purchase an exclusive club wagon, which is produced in a limited edition and usually increases in value rapidly. The club card allows price reductions when purchasing from various cooperation partners. And when visiting the trade fair, each member receives a small gift at the stand.

Example Märklin Insider (hobbyist club):

For the target group of hobbist end customers an insider club is installed. There a club magazine appears six times annually as well as in same frequency the Märklin magazine, both equipped with news of Märklin and information around the model railroad hobby. Club members receive a yearly wagon in a specially produced edition once a year free of charge. Also once a year there is a DVD with a review of events in the past Märklin year. Club members have the right to purchase one exclusive club model per year, which promises a rapid increase in value. Furthermore, there is the yearbook with interesting reports about the model train hobby. The club card allows price reductions when purchasing from cooperation partners. On the Märklin website there is a password-protected member area with additional information. When visiting a trade show, every member receives a gift at the booth. Finally, price reductions are granted on Märklin trips which revolve around the "big" real train.

6.2 Live advertising

The term live advertising usually refers to exhibitions as well as presentations and presences at point of sale and events. They can be grouped according to internal or external activities as well as regulated or free participation *(for context*

	Internally initiated activity	Externally initiated activity
Non-public (regulated) participation	Presentation	Exhibition
Public (free) participation	Event	POS-presence

Fig. 40: Forms of live advertising

see figure 40: Forms of live advertising). An exhibition is a temporary event at which a large number of exhibitors show and distribute a representative range of products from one or more sectors of the economy or economic areas or provide information about these products for the purpose of promoting sales to the general public. The focus is therefore on presentation.

6.2.1 Exhibition

Originally, a distinction was made between trade fairs and exhibitions in such a way that trade fairs are market events at which goods are sold on the basis of order samples, while exhibitions were considered to be temporary representations of the offerings of a large number of participants for information and contact, but not for sale. In practice, however, both terms are usually used synonymously. In the foreground of exhibitions is the purpose of demonstration and presentation, which is not limited to the presented offer, but shows the entire capacity of the exhibitor. This is intended to improve the knowledge, the presentation image and the readiness of visitors for action. Exhibitions can be aimed at the general public or at specialist circles such as resellers, processors, commercial users, bulk buyers, etc. They take place at regular intervals at the same location. This distinguishes them from related forms as permanent events such as sample warehouses, individual events such as special shows and events which change location such as travelling shows. They represent the highest possible concentration of supply and demand in the smallest possible space and in the shortest possible time; in this respect they have a compressed market barometer function.

Due to its geographical location in the heart of Europe and its economic significance, Germany is an important venue for events, especially in foreign trade. This development is met by the fact that information is an increasingly important success factor, the increasing variety of offers requires the exchange of experience and a personal relationship of trust, and the need to explain the products is growing. Moreover, exhibitions are multifunctional. They offer a direct response opportunity for effective feedback from the market and interested parties. There is also a very good possibility to combine them with other communication measures. Therefore, they are usually mandatory events for all serious suppliers, as well as for committed private and commercial customers. Exhibitions appeal to all human senses, ensure and increase market transparency, open up new market contacts and offer themselves as acceptance tests for new product ideas. Above all, however, they have an event and experience character which can convey information about an offer more intensively and actively than most other communication instruments. The corporate culture is also reflected in the design, location and infrastructure of the booth.

The disadvantage of these events, however, is their limited availability due to their institutionalized character with regular intervals, fixed places and long registration periods. Likewise, there is an inflationary increasing number of events, which can hardly all be attended. Thus there are universal presentations, which combine economic goods of all kinds, multi-branch presentations, which are divided into different industrial, trade, service and commercial sectors, as well as specialized presentations, which combine similar branches, customers, processes, topics, etc. There are also congresses with a conference part and markets in hobby areas as well as international, regional and local events.

Therefore it is important to choose the right trade fairs and exhibitions. The first criterion for this is their market significance. Market research figures show, among other things, visitor as well as exhibitor flows and structures, times, exhibitor sizes. They also show how the event environment match the company's participation objectives. For the former, information is available in the manuals published by AUMA (Exhibitions and trade fair committee) and DIHK (Federation of German chambers of industry and commerce), by chambers of trade, trade associations, chambers of foreign trade and by the trade fair companies themselves. This includes information such as catalogs of previously held events, the structure and nomenclature of products and services with product group classification, the development of exhibitor and visitor numbers, structural data, results of participant surveys, market and industry analyses, etc.

Exhibitions can be classified in many ways, according to their

- scope in regional, national or international,
- presentation breadth in specialized or universal,
- presentation focus,
- function,
- duration in permanent or punctual,
- location,
- representation as single-branch or multi-branch,
- direction of action for procurement or sales,
- target group in specialized or public visitors,
- significance as leading or non-leading.

Also relevant are the

- existence of a supporting program (congress or similar),
- number of exhibitors and visitors,
- media transport real or virtual,
- exhibit in original, as sample, as dummy or as showspiece,
- influence of institutionalised association or not.

6. Non-classical advertising

Leading exhibitions, i. e. market-leading events, in Germany include

- *IAA/Frankfurt, Cebit/Hanover, Grüne Woche/Berlin, Int'l Funkausstellung/Berlin, Drupa/Düsseldorf, Boot/Düsseldorf, Bauma/Düsseldorf, Hannover-Messe/Hanover, Int'l Buchmesse/Leipzig, Int'l Handwerksmesse/Munich, K/Düsseldorf, AutoMobil-Messe/Leipzig, Photokina/Cologne, Bautec/Berlin, Automechanika/Frankfurt, Int'l Möbelmesse/Cologne, Orgatech/Cologne, Ambiente/Frankfurt, Medica/Düsseldorf, Systems/Munich, Musikmesse/Frankfurt, Eisenwaren-Messe/Cologne, Electronica/Munich, Heimtextil/Frankfurt, Dach+Wand/Leipzig, HerrenModeWoche/Cologne, Spoga/Cologne, Brau/Nuremberg, Ispo/Munich, ACHEMA/Frankfurt, Equitana/Essen, Bau/Munich, ISH/Frankfurt, Hanseboot/Hamburg, Int'l Tourismus-Börse/Berlin, Spielwarenmesse/Nuremberg, Anuga/Cologne, SMM/Hamburg.*

Important *participation targets* of the exhibition organizers are as follows:

- Development of new markets, maintenance of existing markets, attention of new customers, maintenance of existing customers, company presentation, presentation of new products, consolidation of existing products, development of the sales organization, market and competition overview, profiling of personal contacts, etc.

Goals of the *visitors* are mainly as follows:

- Researching market transparency, comparing offers, identifying providers, gaining business inspirations, identifying industry trends, experiencing demonstrations, attending the supporting program, personal training, establishing and expanding business contacts, etc.

Exhibitions are extremely costly. Therefore, precise budget planning is essential. The most important *cost items* concern the following:

- Stand rent, calculated on the basis of occupied square meters, stand type and location, which also includes services and pre-sales measures by the trade fair company, costs of exhibits for demonstration models, transport, installations, etc., costs of stand construction and supplies, costs of supporting measures to actually bring visitors to the stand, as well as personnel costs for preparation, implementation, follow-up, accommodation, catering, transport, assembly and dismantling, clothing, etc.

Sometimes there is also the chance to benefit from public funding, e. g. in the case of foreign exhitions, or cost splits through cooperation.

The *cluster* of participation include the

- Minimum or maximum size of the stand in width and depth, location within the hall or in the open air area, construction method with number of floors, exhibited products for sector classification, deviations from the division grid or stand construction method and any sub-exhibitors.

The *contract conditions* have to be considered such as

- Admission, stand rental, terms of payment, withdrawal from the contract, assembly and dismantling times, information on building materials, stand height, floor load capacity, technical installations, regulations on fire protection, accident prevention, safety regulations, liability, insurance, etc.

Services of the organizer include

- Rental of stands, furniture, floor coverings, kitchens, lighting, AV and office technology, furthermore logistics services, storage space, room reservations, stand cleaning and supervision, installations of telecom connections, electricity, water, gas, compressed air ,etc., insurance, temporary staff, decorative materials, exhibitor passes, free admission tickets, parking passes, etc.

It is also important to take care of an entry in the exhibition's catalog and information system. The entry is made according to alphabet, list of goods and/or hall. In addition, advertisements are possible there. The inclusion in the supporting program should also be checked.

With regard to the *type of booth*, a distinction is made between the

- inline stand, which is open on one side only to one aisle and is arranged next to other inline stands,
- central stand, which is open on two sides to two parallel aisles,
- corner stand, which is at the end of a row and open to the main aisle,
- cross aisle, the head stand, which is at the end of a row and open to two main aisles and one cross aisle,
- block stand, which is open to all sides, and the open-air stand outside the hall.

Furthermore, the position of the booth within the area is important. This depends on the direction of visitor flow and the orientation towards hall entrances, stand neighbors, functional areas, etc. On the one hand, stand construction involves renting, leasing or purchasing the stand, which involves different business expenses. On the other hand, the *booth construction* method:

- System construction is inexpensive and easy to handle due to prefabricated, precisely fitting parts, easy transport and storage, low personnel and tool requirements for assembly and dismantling, great stability, versatility and adaptability. A disadvantage, however, is the lack of individuality in appearance, which is of utmost importance in view of the concerns of the organizational culture.
- A distinction is made between open stands, which have no exterior surfaces which obstruct visibility, semi-open stands, which partly have exterior surfaces, and closed stands, which have exterior surfaces as visual barriers.

The *construction of the booth* can be carried out by construction companies or architects after a tender or also by own contribution. The stand architecture should allow and promote a scheme of order for visitors, a verbal and visual presentation concept, the possibility of getting to know exhibits in practice and personal contact with consultants. This requires considerations regarding stand layout, floor covering, ceiling design, screens and coverings, stand and object lighting, technical setups, choice of colors, furnishings, etc. A distinction can be made between the table level for meetings and catering, the platform level for information and demonstrations, the writing level for boards and displays, and the identification level for identity and guidance system. For identification purposes, there is a corresponding distinction between distance, close-up and detail recognition.

Another important aspect is *personnel planning* and selection for stand operation. The planning includes representatives, stand managers, technical and commercial staff, interpreters, information and service personnel. Qualities such as convincing technical knowledge, sociability, confident demeanor, linguistic expression, flexibility and ability to work under pressure are of utmost importance for the selection. Prior to the event, the respective responsibilities must be clarified exactly and training and education must be provided. A daily situation meeting on site is recommended. It also makes sense to agree on a common code of conduct and to ensure that the stand looks clean and tidy at all times of the day, that there are no bottlenecks with food and consumables, that all technical equipment functions smoothly, and that standards, e. g. for VIP care or visitor registration and duty hours, e. g. according to an attendance schedule, are adhered to exactly. The atmosphere should remain always friendly and relaxed.

Finally, the *postprocessing* is also important, for example by evaluating the contents of the discussion according to products, applications, customer requirements, etc., recording the focal points of the discussion according to content, information status, need for advice, submission of offers, sampling, acquisition, etc. and the systematic follow-up by means of letters of thanks, sending requested documents, arranging discussions, processing inquiries, etc. For this purpose, and also for the purpose of market information, standardized data entry forms have proven their worth. From this, it is also possible to derive a limited control of success depending on given exhibition goals. So all in all, a wide range of activities must be planned.

Traditional exhibitions are more and more substituted by hybrid forms of exhibitions as combination of real event and virtual presentation. On the one hand, the personal contact is indispensable in communication and cannot be replaced by any form of virtual contact, on the other hand, general conditions are becoming more and more obstructive, so that personal contacts become near to impossible and have to be substituted by virtual ones or otherwise by house fairs.

6.2.2 Point of sales presence

A further form of live advertising is the POS presence (so-called visual merchandising). This includes all efforts to identify, inform and advertise manufacturer offers in the dealers' premises and in their media.

In this context, the shop window/entrance area and interior are of particular importance. Let's start with the *shop window*:

- The shop window can be designed as a stacked window with a variety of goods, a demand window with a bundle of needs satisfied, a fantasy window out of creativity, an occasion window after an event, a doll's window with dummies, a luxury window with exhibits and a department store window with a view into the sales room.
- The arrangement of the presented products is based on the principles of endless row, ordered geometry or contextual scene.
- The target persons pass the shop window in a long-distance flow on the other side of the street, in a short-distance flow coming from the right, in a countercurrent flow coming from the left or in a driving stream with private or public vehicles.

In the *interior*, purchasing decisions often only take place in the immediate vicinity of the goods placement. Here, the product presentation, supporting "furniture" such as shelves, counters, racks, etc. as well as advertising material in the form of displays, chutes, trays, etc. have a promoting effect. Acoustically, quick announcements as live spoken texts and store radio as pre-produced spots can be integrated into the editorial program. Visually, this is done by advertising on carrier bags, shopping carts, etc.

The retail media are regularly local classical media, whose use is supported financially by manufacturers, e. g. through advertising cost subsidies, or materially, e. g. through production templates.

6.2.3 Event

Events are self-staged activities which present emotional and physical stimuli through experience-oriented corporate and product events, which in turn trigger an activation process in target persons. Typical for this is their project character, the presence of the participants and their dependence on the presentation. In the context of communication, events thus represent targeted and systematic ideas for the organization, implementation and control of events. Often celebrities are used as guests, attractive locations are chosen and elaborate catering is offered. The presentation itself is usually done via multimedia and effects as light, music, decoration, equipment, etc. Frequent examples of such events are sales force conferences to motivate the sales team, events for initiated sales rounds (so-called kick-off meetings) or dealer presentations to get in the mood for product events (so-called hospitalities). Events are characterized by features such as exceptionality, experiential character, originality, topicality, immediacy, sales promotion, live experience, target group orientation, experience communication, staging, activation, dialog orientation, interactivity and communication of emotional content.

A rough classification of events leads to the following distinctions:

- Cultural events include music, theater, religion, art, scientific, tradition, technique, media,

- sports events includes olympiads, championships, competitions/tournaments, recreational excercise,

- economic events include congresses, roadshows, incentives, dealer presentations, seminars, anniversaries, ceremonies/galas, shareholder meetings, sales force conferences, open house days,

- social events include political meetings, celebrity visits, parades/processions, garden shows, openings,

- natural events include countryside spectacles, nature conservation and the like.

A distinction can be made between primary groups being present and are directly contacted as target group, secondary groups being present but are not belonging to target group and tertiary groups being not present but kept informed via media.

Public events are open to everybody, corporate events are closed. A variety of activities are required for the realization of events.

In the future, *hybrid trade events* are increasingly expected, which take place partly via physical presence and partly via virtual presentation. Reasons for this are, besides the time and cost aspects epidemiological aspects like expected pandemics similar to Corona and ecological aspects in terms of environmental stress.

Another possibility is an *in-house exhibition*. For this business partners are invited to the company location or a business hotel. This provides the opportunity to exclusively present the products and to negotiate conditions for a deal.

6.2.4 Brandpark presentation

Brandparks have the task of allowing a brand world to be physically experienced, but cannot be classified exactly. These are parks which focus on specific target groups, whose amusement offerings are thematically oriented and essentially stage the products and brand of a single company. This company usually also operates the park. Examples are the following:

- "Autostadt Wolfsburg" with the presentation of all group brands, infotainment mobility, technology, cars, vehicle delivery as well as the Transparent factory, Dresden by Volkswagen,

- "Porsche world of emotions", Leipzig and Porsche museum, Zuffenhausen,

- "BMW world", Munich as an exhibition, spot delivery, experience, museum and event location,

- "Mercedes Benz-World", Stuttgart, as a customer center with vehicle delivery and factory tours, sale of cars from employees as well as implementation of events,

- "Audi customer center" with vehicle delivery and brand museum as well as Audi forum, Ingolstadt with events, adventure tours, exhibitions, travel and youth program.

The objectives pursued with brandparks are brand-related image building, increasing customer loyalty and enhancing employee identification with their company. In addition, brandparks serve to promote sales and provide a source of additional income through revenues, which at least support maintenance of the activity. Nevertheless, their economic eligibility remains after all doubtful.

6.3 Direct advertising

Direct advertising means communication, which aims at individual addressees and/or contains a means of reaction, as to individual contact already an information offer is sufficient for the qualification as direct approach, with disperse establishment of contact that the reaction takes place towards the message sender

	Parallel sender – receiver contact	Successive sender – receiver contact
Mass media operation	Interactive-TV	Direct-response adverts, spots, posters / Web 1.0
Individual media operation	Landline / mobile phone advertising / Fax advertising / Web 2.0	Direct mailing / Bulk mailing / Household distribution / Documentation / e-mail / Newsgroup

Fig. 41: Forms of direct advertising (examples)

with the help of the means of advertising or in other defined kind and refers to an offer. The aim is to establish a dialog with potential market partners and to involve them. However, reactions are already noticeable. The forms can be grouped according to parallel or successive exchange as well as mass media or individual media approach (*see figure 41: Forms of direct advertising*). Mainly electronic and printed media are used for direct advertising.

6.3.1 Electronic offline direct advertising

Electronic offline direct advertising can be delivered through direct-response television (DR-TV) and direct-response radio (DR-R). Both include diverse forms of advertising as shown in the following.

6.3.1.1 Direct response television

DR-TV spots are initially classic TV adverts, but they are more or less dominantly provided with an invitation to react. This is the insertion/announcement of a telephone number, which usually leads to an external call center or, more rarely, to an internal telephone answering service. There are DR-TV spots which are used predominantly to advertise products and in which a telephone number is only inserted as a supplement. Or DR-TV Spots, which are predominantly used for direct sales, usually with products which are not available through other sales channels. On the other hand, certain product categories have established themselves as promising, such as image carrier devices, coins, financial investments, etc. DR-TV spots are usually designed in such a way that the address to be contacted is mentioned with a high degree of penetrance. Problems arise from the fact that the response immediately after the broadcast of this invitation is so high that queus form, e. g. long waiting loops in call centers, which leads to dissatisfaction among potential buyers, whereas at other times the call volume is very low.

Broadcast advertisements are permanent commercials which are editorially designed but serve to market-specific offers. Their entertaining presentation is intended to attract the attention and interest of viewers, which is often missing in normal commercials. In order to avoid confusion with the editorial program of the broadcaster, these programs are to be identified by the insert "permanent advertising program" or simply "advertisement". Direct contact is usually made possible by inserting a free, reduced-price or chargeable phone number. There are private television stations whose business model relies on the co-financing through advertising revenue, commission on sales volume and a share of the telephone volume. The taste quality of these programs is usually questionable. The information is provided via television, the order via telephone and the delivery by parcel service. The products are usually presented in the form of consumer advice, shown in their applications and emphatically advertised, are often not or not yet available in free trade and are rather generously calculated.

Interactive television (I-TV) takes place in full duplex communication via a broadband transmission channel and a narrow-band return channel digitally via cable and satellite. This requires a digital design of the technology by set-top box as well as a suitable input device (keyboard, remote control). Each participant is identifiable, so that he or she is not only individually addressable, but can also give feedback from his or her individual address. This can consist, for example, in reacting to information offers or ordering sales offers. Streaming services on the Internet offer a cost-effective alternative to this. Smart-TVs serve as combination of linear TV and webterminal in one device.

6.3.1.2 Direct-response radio

Direct-response radio spots (*DR-R*) are widespread. Since the important optical element is missing, the penetrance of the telephone number to be called is crucial. Usually, value-added numbers from Telekom (08 00) with an attached, easily remembered combination of numbers are used for this purpose. Sometimes, vanity numbers are also used, i.e. the combination of numbers results in the name of the sender/product by means of the letters assigned to the number keys and is therefore easier to remember. In accordance with the editorial content (so-called tone colors) of most radio stations, the products offered are audio media which are often not available in other distribution channels. However, the efficiency of this form of advertising suffers from the fact that radio usually serves only as a background medium, i.e. it does not attract any directed attention. In addition, at times of spot broadcasting like housework, driving, etc. there are often no writing utensils nearby, so that the number to be called cannot be written down. Then memory is required, but often fails.

6.3.2 Phone advertising

Direct advertising via telephone may be active (also outbound) or passive (also inbound). *Active* telephone advertising is particularly suitable for initiating contact with prospective customers/acquisition of new customers, for activating existing customers, for customer retention also after the purchase and for additional sales. The establishment of contact with prospective customers takes place for example with respondents to actions e.g. information requesters, responses from random contacts, direct new customer approaches in the commercial sector, provided that the offer corresponds to the commercial purpose and the impulse comes from the prospective customer. The latter also applies to the private sector, whereby strict consumer law requirements are made, especially an existing business relationship.

The activation and binding of regular customers takes place, for example, through remaining stock, seasonal or replacement offers, technical product, usage, storage, application or operation instructions, determination of requirements, presentation of new products, invitations to events, delivery date notifications, explanation of business conditions, advertising and sales promotion tips.

Passive telephone advertising includes, among others, the acceptance of orders, the arrangement of desired appointments and brief information in case of inquiries. The tools used for this purpose are Service 0800, answering machine/call redirection and increasingly computer-aided processing. Often there is a personal separation between sales lead generation and monetization of the contact, or the telephone is only used to generate leads, but not for the actual sale. The successful establishment and maintenance of contact proves to be extremely difficult when speaking on the phone, since on the one hand the spectrum of communication possibilities is reduced to acoustics in addition to content, and on the other hand these two dimensions are only available as a means of monitoring success. This is especially true for "cold" addresses, which, however, must not be addressed in the private sphere.

Cell phone advertising is predicted to have a great future. A broad network coverage, permanent reachability of the recipients, their localization and identification offer various starting points for direct advertising. Several networks are available, and several services in m-commerce are also offered. Current technical restrictions should be overcome quickly in the course of development. The situation is different with legal restrictions, which, as with all forms of direct advertising, are likely to be applied more strictly.

Fax advertising is generally using telecommunications by fax machine as a means of transporting direct advertising messages. In the B-t-c sector, this is only permissible if the express consent of the addressee to be faxed has been obtained or if there are already existing business relationships. In the B-t-b area, fax advertising is only permitted in the case of existing business relationships and if it can be assumed that the advertised offer can be used in the business operations of the person faxed. The design of fax advertising is limited due to the low resolution and the regularly missing colors. Frequently, the variants of fax-on-demand as fax polling, fax on demand, faxback and fax mail are encountered. Fax is still widely used in the broad fields of crafts, small and medium-sized businesses, doctors/pharmacies, civil services bureaus, etc. and generally in international communication with developing and emerging economies. So the importance should still not be underestimated.

6.3.3 Printed direct advertising

Printed direct advertising includes direct-response adverts as well as direct-response mailings. Especially the latter are quite common.

6.3.3.1 Direct-response advert

Direct adverts include a reaction request such as writing, calling, dropping by, e-mailing, with address or telephone number or with a latched reaction element such as coupon, reply postcard, voucher, etc. It is pointless to discuss whether these adverts are to be classified as classical advertising because they are the medium of the advertisement, or as non-classical advertising because they carry a response offer. In either case, a change of media is necessary, namely from print advertising to postal media such as postcards, letters or telecommunication media such as telephone, fax, e-mail. The most obvious response is a reaction element in the form of a sticker to be removed, bound-in insert to be detached or insert to be removed. This allows orders for products or advertising material to be addressed and information to be requested. Depending on their characteristics, they can accommodate more or less differentiated order details. It makes sense to code the reaction media in order to be able to assign responses to advertising materials. This also allows the identification of different issues, advertising motifs, placements, etc. However, measuring the efficiency of a direct advertising campaign only by the number of responses, information gatherings or order placements, depending on the situation as to advertising target, may be misleading. Unless a completely new offer is advertised for the first time in a single ad run. But this is far from the reality of the markets.

6.3.3.2 Direct mailing

Direct mailing is an addressed, postal advertising mail to addressees who have been selected as promising on the basis of selection criteria. Addressed, non-postal direct mailings via private letter delivery services are possible since the expiration of the postal letter service monopoly. Main parameters in direct mailings are the handling of addresses, the creative design of the mailing and the choice of non-addressed mailings.

Address handling

Corresponding addresses can be rented from address publishers or are taken from the own database. There are various weight, format and arrangement limitations of the mail pieces to be observed in order to minimize postage costs. Pre-sorting of the mail pieces on posting fulfills the same objective. The content usually consists of several parts, one of which serves as a response for information/order and whose process often runs in several phases like teaser, roll out, reminder. Modern laser and inkjet printers enable personalized letters signed in ink. Within the framework of customer contact programs, clients are systematically granted after-sales support to bridge the gap until the next need arises. The response rate is to be increased by using activation techniques, such as

- early bird at subscription price, free gift as a promotional gift, free trial with goods on display, limitation by time and/or quantity, sweepstake as a contest with predetermined winners, partial payment and/or payment target, negative option for non completion of a contract only in case of revocation.

According to the target group, it concerns private customers (B-t-c) or potential business customers (B-t-b). Prospective customer contact programs accompany prospective customers continuously to their first purchase. Within the framework of customer contact programs, customers are systematically provided with after-sales support to bridge the gap until a repeat purchase. The address handling is facilitated by the *database*. It contains specific information about:

- Order data such as order path, order value, choice of article, price category, payment method, etc.,
- order master data like customer value, returns, etc.,
- creditworthiness data such as credit rating information, reminders, etc.,
- advertising data such as type of advertising, quantity, period, etc.,
- support data such as complaints, frequency of visits, etc.

In the business-to-business area (*B-t-b addresses*), the following details are particularly useful:

- Name block with name, title, form of address, position in the company, branch office base, interest code, decision-making authority, area of activity, length of stay in function,
- address block with company name, street, P. O. Box, postal code, city, branch office, field service region, date of last modification,
- general information such as telephone number, fax number, website URL, industry key, creditworthiness data,
- interaction block with correspondence, contact matter, date of first contact, inquiry, complaint, advertising contacts, cumulative/individual sales figures, supervisor, visiting hours,
- profile data with date of company foundation, company size by turnover, number of employees, ownership structure, shareholdings, branches, industry, product range, innovativeness of the company, buying center structure,

- profile data decision-maker with name, title, telephone number, e-mail address, position in the company, field of activity and responsibility,
- campaign data with type and time of the first contact via field service, mailing, telephone, coupon display, type and time of the promotional address, advisor, responsible salesperson,
- reaction data with time and type of reaction, including complaint behavior, duration of the customer relationship, cumulative sales figures and by individual orders, level of the loyalty ladder, classification in terms of customer attractiveness and accessibility.

The following *sources* can be used as a basis for research:

- Address books, telephone directories, field service information, internal service notes, trade fair notes, own prospective customer advertising, inquiries for press publications, addresses from sales promotion campaigns, chamber of commerce directories, embassies, consulates, trade fair catalogs, exhibitor directories, participants in seminars and conferences, entries in the commercial register, exchange/purchase/rental of addresses of direct advertising companies/address publishers/brokers/specialist publishers, etc., clipping service, trader information, personal interviews, recommendations, member get member, public announcements.
- Mailing list providers from their own stock. Companies may not trade with addresses themselves, but must commission neutral third parties, e.g. a lettershop, to rent out addresses for one-time use.
- Address brokers use original sources from direct contact and external collection. These are rather small quantities, but with a great depth of selection and additional information on the address. This means low scattering losses, but also low coverage.
- Address publishers dispose of secondary sources, whose data is available in large quantities but with low selection depth. No additional information about the adress is offered. The consequence is high coverage, but also high scattering loss.
- Enquiry agencies look into original sources, mostly for contract research. Data is available there in large quantities and a high selection depth, including additional information on the address. This means low scattering loss with high coverage. However, a maximum of three characteristics, e.g. name, address, profession, may be combined.
- Online company databases such as ABCD, BDI, Dun & Bradstreet, Hoppenstedt, Kompass, VC, Who supplies what, Who belongs to whom. The costs concern quantity-dependent fees, connection time for the use of computer and database as well as an information fee per company.
- Offline databases such as CD-ROM from ABC, AZ Bertelsmann, Creditreform, Hoppenstedt, Industriedatenbank, liefern + leisten, Kompass, Markus.

In the business to consumer sector (*B-t-c addresses*), the following details are particularly useful:

- Name block with surname, first name, title, form of address,
- address data with street, P. O. box, postal code, city, office, field service region, date of last modification,
- general information like interest code, gender, age, occupation, family size, credit rating, phone number, referrer, multiplier for, length of stay at address, bank type, credit card, regional type,
- interaction data with advertising type, number of contacts, time of the last order, cumulative/individual sales, payment type, reminder data, mail order index,
- profile data such as age, date of birth, marital status, household size, number of children, family life cycle, education, occupation, income, opinion leaders, opinion followers, region type based on microgeographic segmentation, hobbies, interests, attitudes, payment behavior,
- promotional data according to type and time of the first contact via field service, mailing, telephone number, coupon display, canvassing, type and time of the promotional address, advisor, responsible salesperson,
- reaction data according to time and type of reaction, including reaction behavior, duration of the customer relationship, cumulative sales figures and by individual orders, level on loyalty ladder, classification in terms of customer attractiveness and accessibility.

Addresses from the own inventory require constant maintenance and updating, new addresses must be generated continuously. Addresses can be rented. This list broking includes the mediation of the right of use of internal company addresses of other companies via address brokers. The addresses must not be given to competitors of the owner. If address publishers are switched on, these rent own addresses for unique use. To control against misuse, dummy addresses are built in, which lead to returns to the publisher when used repeatedly. In addition, all data protection regulations must be observed, especially the strict separation between address and information parts. However, the quality of the addresses rented in this way is often doubtful despite all optimizations.

An additional address acquisition for the broadening of the data base can be done by different measures, so coupon adverts for information request, competition, recommend a friend for purchase, etc. The value of many such leads is however doubtful. Also the own investigation of foreign addresses is time-consuming and not very promising, e. g. because of up-to-dateness.

A particular advantage is seen in the extensive efficiency prognosis of direct mailing. There are various forms of success prognosis for this as follows:

- List tests provide information about the presumed quality of the address base,

- product tests provide information about the acceptance of the product performance,
- target group tests provide information about the presumed accuracy of the target group definition,
- advertising material tests provide information about the effect of the design of the direct advertising,
- regional tests provide information about the presumed appropriate delimitation of the advertising area,
- timing tests provide information about the presumed best time period for direct advertising.

It can be assumed that two days after the highest response time of a mailing, approximately half of the total response has taken place ("half-life period").

Creative design

The design of the direct mailing should meet the following requirements:
- Disposable stoppers in order to at least increase the reading chance or even create this chance in the first place,
- openers, i.e. a short introduction to the upcoming issue,
- positive reinforcers, i.e. emphasize the reader's benefit from using the offer,
- proof as short argumentation, because readers always look for security before buying decisions,
- eye's guidance over the text must be taken into account; this is done mainly through headlines and images or highlighting,
- anticipation of objections of the addressee in the text,
- phone number for contact in case of problems or questions, this creates additional confidence,
- response element such as order form, reply envelope so that it is easy to handle,
- "P. S." with the second most important argument and an appeal for action, i.e. to order or request information.

It is important to consider the usual reading curve/eye movement of a recipient, typically from top right to left, then in a Z-shape over the entire text, then back to the beginning of the text, then from the letterhead to the salutation and the P. S.

It is also advisable to keep the letterhead free of unnecessary information which does not relate to the actual request, such as bank details, reference signs, etc. The text should be kept clear and well structured, i.e. short paragraphs, highlights, etc.

The sender must stand out clearly. The same applies to the reason why the addressee is being contacted or being contacted right now. Explicitly, the necessary reaction should be given.

The writing style should work with "you", "your", not with "me", "we", i.e. should have an addressee-related form. Non-meaning salutations are to be avoided; if necessary, it is better to start with the text immediately. Two-page cover letters should not end with a sentence at the end of the first page so that the reader may continue reading on the second page. More than two pages are not reasonable for a cover letter, if possible one page should be sufficient.

Conspicuous codes on the reply medium are to be avoided as far as possible, as they may provoke mistrust among addressees. A fax reply may also be advisable, or at least permitted, for small businesses such as those in the trade. In case it is intended to limit the response to a "hard core" by way of exception, filters are helpful for qualification purposes, e.g. request postage prepayment, provide a signature, request date of birth/telephone number.

A mail order package consists of the following elements:

- Envelope design variables are format, paper quality, franking, addressing, window, sender, headline/pictures, text,

- letter design variables are the original letter, fill-in letter, offset letter, letterhead/logo, headline, salutation, text, typography, paragraphs, underlining, bold, images, signature, P.S.,

- information and reaction element design variables are reply coupon/envelope, folder/flyer, prospectus/catalog.

The cover letter is an important part of every mailing. It serves as a disposable stopper to increase the chance of reading, as an opener to get people in the mood for the topic, as an argument for the benefits of the products offered and as proof of their advantages. In addition, there are useful reaction elements such as preferential price, trial copy, invitation, etc. The reaction can be increased by playful elements such as adhesive stamps, scratch-off fields, right of swap offer, information check handover, reservation card or chance to win a prize. The P.S. is of great importance as the most important argument or appeal for action.

Another element is the reaction carrier. Conceivable for this are a reply postcard because of the easier answer possibility, the inexpensive handling and the weight advantage, or a coupon/envelope because of the greater confidentiality, the more valuable impression and the additional space. Further contact channels such as Facebook page, Twitter account, free call-in, e-mail address, etc. are desirable.

The envelope can also be used as an advertising medium, for example, to attract attention and arouse interest or to already carry concrete offers, for example on the inside.

The specific advantages of mailings are as follows:

- A personal address can be presented, which is presumably more impressive than an anonymous mass address. A more precise targeting of defined target persons is possible, which keeps scattering losses potentially low. There is freely available space for the design of content and messages, which in principle is not subject to any restrictions. The presentation is also freely selectable, so that, apart from technical restrictions, the own corporate design can be fully conveyed. The advertising material has the undivided attention of the recipient and above all does not compete with an editorial environment. Compared to the competition, a better confidentiality of offers is possible than in most other media. In addition, there are extensive test and control possibilities with any number of cases, so that inefficiencies can be detected early on. There is a relative cost effectiveness, especially if only smaller target groups are to be reached. There is a chance to react spontaneously to offers, provoking contacts and purchases. The timing of the deployment is freely selectable and does not depend on other influenced dates, such as the first day of sale of print titles.

However, there are also some disadvantages:

- The use for low interest products, which dominate in the consumer goods sector, is not reasonable, because the necessary directed attention is usually missing. Reaching broad target groups is unrealistically costly. This is mainly due to postage costs. Without prerequisites such as awareness and image of the supplier and the product range, the application is not very promising. An appealing design is difficult due to the system-related peculiarities, and the freedom of design remains narrowly limited in reality by postal regulations. It is to be assumed that the actual use of direct mail items is low, which is mainly due to the continuing flood of direct mailings. Incidentally, one can protect oneself from this by joining the DDV Robinson list/German dialog marketing association. The address quality is also problematic and thus often the cause of misdirected mailings and returns due to undeliverability.

Non-addressed mailings

In the case of non-addressed direct mailing, two ways of distribution are possible, bulk mailings by postal distribution and household distribution by non-postal distribution:

- *Bulk mailings* are printed matter or tangible advertising materials which are distributed by the postal service to all households or to persons collecting postal mail. However, there are numerous conditions of implementation to be observed. Moreover the appreciation of this form of direct advertising which reaches the house anonymously and unsolicited, is doubtful.

- *Household distributions* are settled by private delivery services and distribution columns by delivery in mailboxes in the house or to passers-by on the road. These are mostly advertising gifts and gimmicks, as well as short brochures/leaflets and above all offer sheets/flyers. With it optionally a door ringing, door signal plus personal delivery or door signal, personal delivery and explanation can be connected. This is only of limited use, since the reliability of the distribution is questionable despite numerous controls. In addition the acceptance of such unsolicited thrown in direct mail items is questionable, particularly since numerous house owners forbid the throwing in. Nevertheless, household distribution allows an exact local spread and is used intensively, especially by local retailers in their catchment areas.

In the context of the representational dialog promotion specialities are common, e. g. as product samples, stickers, gadgets, advertising gifts, calendars, play a large role. These promotional items offer a number of advantages:

- No wastage, three-dimensional design, emotional basis for dialog, personal handover, appropriation by the target person, practical value, individual design, sole attention, originality and target group specific selection.

As to advertising gifts they have to be taxed as a non-cash benefit for the donee, unless the donor already has paid 30 % tax plus surcharges and informs about it, in case the amount is less than € 10,000 p. a., otherwise this is as bribery resp. bribability not only a matter of company compliance, but indeed also of criminal liability.

6.3.4 Documentation

Documentation is understood to be all information relating to appearance, application, persuasion and confirmation, usually in printed form, but increasingly also on data carriers or in transmission networks, in order to address intermediate and end customers with sales literature in the form of brochures and catalogs, as well as sales agents/assistants with pre-sales advertising material.

6.3.4.1 Sales literature

Brochure

Brochures serve the deepened, meaningful explanation of an offer. They provide a wealth of information which is not available in other media. Often a whole series of brochures, flyers, leaflets or the like is published, ranging from a program overview to a detailed insight. This is particularly important for offers which are subject to extensive purchasing decisions, i. e. are complex and in need of explanation. Brochures are usually extensively written and richly illustrated, contain technical data, examples of use, often also editorial parts for general image building. They are available at the trading place, are delivered or sent by representatives. Their creation is usually costly and prone to errors. They are either distributed to interested parties free of charge or for a rather small nominal charge. An important form of documentation is the user manual. Experience shows that considerable mistakes are made here. It is true that they usually start with the relevant congratulations formula for reducing any cognitive dissonance. But after that, both linguistic and didactic deficiencies are common.

There are a few rules to be observed in the design. For example, pictures are considered more attracting than text, large pictures are better than small ones, and colored pictures are better than black and white. Overall, warm color tones should be preferred. People generally have a higher attention effect than products, dynamic motifs have a higher than static ones. Above all, image details are helpful in addition to or instead of full profiles. For text, larger font sizes should be preferred over bread-and-butter fonts. Emphasized text passages structure the entire text volume. Words and sentences should be as short as possible, and short paragraphs should also be used. Framed text blocks guide the reader. With designed areas, diagonal areas are better than vertical ones, vertical areas better than horizontal ones, and circular areas better than rectangular ones. In the case of illustrations, the correct selection of the image section is also important. Environment only makes sense if it supports the message, e. g. ambience for lifestyle, otherwise it only confuses. It is also important to have a high-contrast representation of both the product in its surrounding and the writing above the image.

Antiqua typefaces are more reader-friendly than sans serif typefaces. Capital letters are read more slowly because the ascenders and descenders are missing. Mixed font styles such as locked, italic, bold, etc. also reduce the reading speed. Fonts against a turbulent or dark background (so-called negative white) are generally difficult to read. In continuous text, a font size of at least 8–12 points must be observed, each line should not have more than 40–45 characters, because longer lines can easily cause a loss of overview and shorter lines lead to unfavorable breaks. The line spacing should be 10–20 % larger than the font size. Left-adjusted flutter is best readable. Shorter paragraphs are easier for the reader to evaluate than long ones. In addition, an orientation on the spoken word is helpful for the text. Ideally, sentences should not consist of more than 15 words. Each new thought makes a new sentence. Short words are easier to understand than long ones, and an active choice of words has a more emotional effect. Pictorial adjectives, metaphors and comparisons are also helpful. Abbreviations, however, slow down the flow of reading. Overall, the text should be "effortless" to read. References in the form of quotations, addresses or fictitious persons also have a reinforcing effect. With all this, the structure/arrangement of the advertising material must not suffer.

A clear didactic structure should enable the reader to take logical learning steps and thus experience a sense of achievement. For the balance of the contents, it is helpful to divide it into chapters of approximately equal length. Concise formulations with no more than two predispositions per sentence facilitate understanding. A certain degree of redundancy is also helpful, e. g. in the form of summaries, memoranda, overviews. Colors can be used specifically for their psychological effect or to mark important passages. Action sequences should be presented in tabular form to facilitate greater transparency, selective reading, better orientation and the recognition of connections. By its very nature, the tonality should not signal an authoritarian but a cooperative attitude. Technical terms should be avoided as far as possible, unavoidable technical terms should at least be explained, whereby it depends on the target group what is considered a technical term and what is not. In the case of complex descriptions, a list of the terms used can be attached; this also applies to abbreviations used. The same terms should always be used for the same things or activities. Image and text content must be coordinated. Tables, graphics, diagrams, etc. loosen up the presentation and should be used in large numbers.

Catalog

The catalog is actually a written sales pitch. It serves as a self-sales basis in the mail order business and offers a systematic and closed overview of the range of goods offered by a company. It contains product descriptions, performance data, prices, terms of delivery, etc. and usually takes the form of a book or a data carrier such as DVD. It can be a main catalog with the complete program/assortment as a universal catalog or a series of partial catalogs, which contain only target group specific program/assortment excerpts as special catalogs. In addition, there are novelty catalogs for updating the product range, all as offline media.

The catalog may be released once per advertising period or several times, possibly with reprints. If the dramaturgical design is emphasized, one also speaks of a "magalog" as artificial word from catalog and magazine or, in a weakened form, of a "catazine". The functions of the catalog are primarily market development, acquisition of new customers, customer care and activation, as well as support of the field organization or its replacement for C-customers. The catalog carries specific product offers which can be ordered with reference to ordering aids. The optimization with regard to the allocation of pages and arrangement of the goods there makes sense.

The cover page, the back cover, the inside cover, the inside back cover and the inside pages 2 + 3 are of particular importance as hotspots. Attention is directed by highlighting key articles, illustrations according to color and size, pictograms for orientation, stoppers with important arguments, etc. The catalog design follows sales aspects. For example, there are opening pages following the title page with greetings, a list of product groups, eye catchers, etc. The last pages are mostly used for disposition-related content, such as technical customer service, telephone ordering, installment offers, measurement tables, warranty, exchange possibilities, keyword index, etc. In between, there are further stopper pages, for example with special offers, competitions, response elements, etc. The allocation of the article-related contribution margin per page enables fine-tuning the article sequence and the page share of individual articles according to their profitability. The typical view of a catalog page from top left to bottom right is also significant. Other important factors are price highlighting, color selection, product arrangement and supplementation with symbols or image details. The typography is primarily designed to ensure good legibility. In the text, care must be taken to ensure good comprehensibility, for example for product descriptions.

Catalogs usually consist of a package of advertising and working materials, including an interesting mailing envelope, a personalized cover letter, an order card with action trigger, additional flyers, etc. The correct choice of the dispatch time is also important. However, catalogs are extremely expensive advertising materials due to their production and logistics costs. But there is the possibility of a robust success control by direct cost and revenue allocation or contribution margin per advertising space.

Do's for documentations are mainly

- the use of images, especially large formats, additional image details, large font sizes, emphasized text passages, short words/sentences/paragraphs, framed text blocks, antique fonts, continuous text in 8–12 pt. size with line spacing 10–20% larger, 40–45 characters per line, figurative adjectives/metaphors/comparisons, clear didactic structure, redundancies, mnemonics, recurring color scheme, usage of tables/graphics.

Dont's are especially

- excessive text volumes, small images with unclear details, small/grotesque font sizes, versal text, mixed font styles as gimmick, negative typing, abbreviations which are not explained, technical and foreign words.

6.3.4.2 Pre-sales advertising material

The pre-sales advertising material is to achieve the purposeful influencing of the sales intermediaries/agents in the sense of the sales performance. It argues in economic dimensions, in order to provide the meaning, which the sender attributes to the own commodity in the distribution channel and uses in addition also incentives with reference to advertising campaign, reviews, test result, market position, brand standing, etc.

The sales folder is usually a leaflet, seldom a more elaborate advertising piece, in which the advantages of a product are argued to retailers. Hard business data are decisive, not images as in end user advertising. Often, however, these are referred to with the aim of pre-sales, but also with the underlying motive that the retail trade will not be able to afford to do without the article in its assortment which its customers demand due to the promotional approach of the manufacturer (pull). The salesfolder serves beside the dispatch to purchase decision makers also as a hanger for the sales talk of the field representative. In fact, however, this is largely a waste of time, as only immense initial investments can persuade retailers to take up the product range. Printed salesfolders are nowadays complemented resp. replaced by digital pre-sales advertising materials. This enables a multimedia approach via video, sound, animation, etc., is however much more complex and costly.

The order sheet is the data form on whose basis orders in the trade are placed. In addition to the detailed product description according to size, taste, packaging unit, etc., it carries the global trade item number (GTIN code), which is classically read in by the dispatcher with a hand-held scanner after checking the relevant stock of goods and completed with the required number of items. Items which not exist in this order set can therefore not be ordered. The only thing which can be achieved in the head office is that new, differentiated or varied products are included in the renewed order set at the next possible date, usually for a high fee. However, this has no influence on the actual order in the sales outlets, apart from a few centrally specified mandatory articles. Therefore, separate enclosures from the manufacturer are required to point this out. Ordersheets are nowadays obsolete in large-scale trading companies because of closed inventory management systems, which take care of product logistics in collaborative planning forecasting replenishment systems (CPFR).

6.4 Supporting activities

There are numerous supporting activities in the fields of non-classical advertising, such as sales promotion, product features, brand licensing and personal communication, which are stated in the following.

6.4.1 Sales promotion

Sales promotion could be attributed to distribution policy in marketing with the same justification as to communication policy. Because it is directed towards all measures of selective activation for the increase of sales success and sales chances with reference to the target groups sales staff, sales intermediaries in sell-in and sell-out as well as end customers. Thus already the substantial characteristics of the sales promotion are mentioned.

Sales promotion is intended to stimulate a selectively increased willingness of sales partners to engage in transactions. This definition has different conceptual components:

- By "stimulation" one understands an activation by key signals. This activation can be affective, e. g. through images, cognitive, e. g. through price quotations, or physical, e.g. through haptics or tasting. The direction of activation should aim at appetence, the extent of activation should be as high as possible. For ethical reasons it is important that the activation is consciously carried out.

- "Selective" means an actionally limited activation. This limitation can be interpreted temporally, spatially or contentwise, thus refer to a certain action period, to a certain field of action or to certain products, whereby this includes benefits in kind as well as services.

- The definition characteristic "readiness for transaction" means that sales promotion is concerned with reaching economic, quantitative goals, thus not only around pre-economic, qualitative dimensions such as announcement, image profiling, acceptance, familiarity, etc.

- Finally, "sales partners" are all stakeholders in the sales area. This includes the own sales staff as well as independent sales assistants. Furthermore trade decision makers in purchasing and sales as well as commercial and private end customers.

Sales promotion is therefore the selective activation of target persons, i.e. the activation is limited and is intended to create a state of temporarily increased inner excitement and tension. The aim is to achieve economic sales success, i.e. completed purchase/sales transactions, or the increase of probability of this happening in the form of sales opportunities by improving important psychographic prerequisites for sales success.

Sales promotion is thus distinguished from advertising by the fact that it is not selective but continuous. Furthermore, advertising does not pursue quantitative but qualitative goals. And it is not only limited to the sales market, but also aims at procurement markets for personnel, finances and input materials. No differentiation is possible with regard to target groups, as these overlap. Media types like print, electronic, outdoor advertising are also used equally in both areas. This also applies to the advertising media like adverts, spots, posters.

Several *target groups* are given:

- The *sales team* (staff). This can be the sales at internal location in the residence principle or at external locations in the domicile or meeting principle. The sales staff can be employed as traveling-salesmen or freelance as sales agents.

- The *trade* (push). These can be wholesalers or retailers. However, there is a strong tendency to eliminate the wholesale level in favor of a more direct sales channel. It makes sense to differentiate

    - sell-in as pipeline filling, the target persons here are the buyers of the trade, and

    - sell-out as merchandising of the manufacturer or trade marketing of the retailers and wholesalers, the target persons are the sales clerks of the trade.

- The *end customers* (industrial and private/push). These can be households for their own use or commercial operations for further processing. In both cases, the decision to buy depends on group influences.

The following *stages* can be mentioned as concrete *objectives* of sales promotion:

- Generation of attention and contact, especially to establish new offers and update existing offers (information),
- increase of interest and motivation of own employees and external sales intermediaries and sales agents,
- triggering and implementation of the act of purchase by individuals and purchasing bodies (*see figure 42: Forms of sales promotion*).

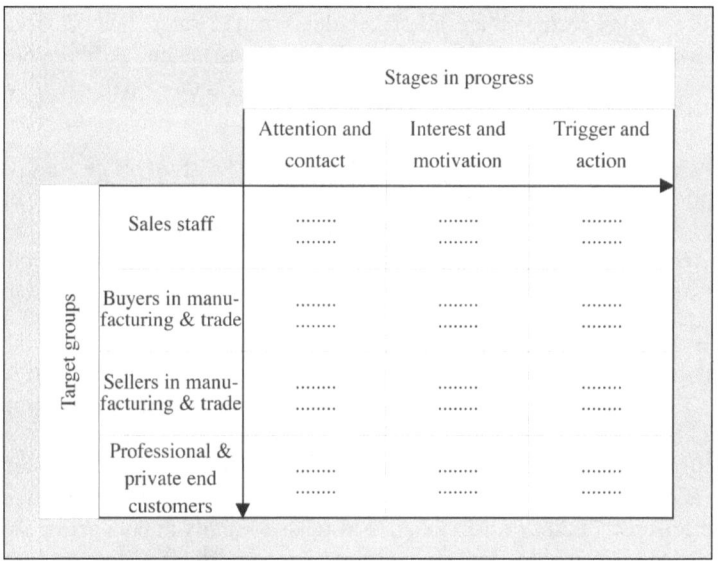

Fig. 42: Forms of sales promotion (Source: own chart)

The following twelve *groups of sales promotion activities* can be derived from the combination of objectives and target groups:

- Creating attention and contact among the sales team to transmit information from the marketing management to the salespeople in a way that they do not miss the message and are remembered as long as possible. This includes work meetings, memos or video conferencing.
- Generating attention and contact with trade staff in sell-in in order to prepare them for measures within the sales chain. This includes presentations such as a dealer congress, annual talks on the framework agreement or demonstration units such as a laptop-beamer combinations.

- Generating attention and contact with trade staff in sell-out to pass on this information to the point of sale, where in many cases the concrete purchase decision is made. This includes sales training, argumentation aids and sales manuals.
- Generating attention and contact with professional and private end customers to promote the benefits of the offer and to change or confirm attitudes and behavior. This includes sampling, e.g. tasting food products, demonstrations, e.g. by propagandists, and trade center advertising in shop windows, entrance areas or interiors.
- Increasing interest and motivation among the sales team by dramatizing the campaign content and emphasizing its importance. This includes sales competitions as round of activities, incentive systems and basic equipment such as product samples, dealer give away as door opener, etc.
- Increasing interest and motivation among trade staff in sell-in by increasing acceptance through advance payments by the activity initiator. This includes shelf maintenance, business consulting and placement management, e.g. according to direct product profitability.
- Increasing interest and motivation of trade staff in sell-out through a perceptible presence at the point of sale and a stimulating effect there. This includes product training, application aids, references to market test successes, etc.
- Increasing interest and motivation of professional and private end customers in order to get awareness at least in the short term. This includes multiple or preferential placements as offshelf or check out displays, as well as targeted risk reduction, e.g. by taking back goods, offering guarantees or product test results.
- Triggering and implementation of the promotional campaign with the sales team by supporting them in such a way that their efforts prove to be particularly worthwhile. This includes bonus and rewards systems, granting privileges among colleagues and recognition in the social environment.
- Triggering and implementation of the promotional campaign with trade staff in sell-in by creating occasions to activate and concretize the purchase. This includes offers at special conditions, e.g. discount, value date, order deadline, co-op advertising cost contribution and appeals to common interests in the sales channel.
- Triggering and implementation of the promotional campaign with trade staff in sell-out by discussing the advantageous offer and attuning to the customers' buying act. This includes favorable sales financing for higher-value products, rewards for business location loyalty of end customers and the provision of decoration services at the POS.
- Triggering and implementation of the promotional campaign with professional and private end customers through behavioral impulse towards the execution of the act of purchase. This includes among others limited offers, special prices (price-off) and product additions with the same package (on-pack).

It has to be considered that sales promotion is by no means only bound to the instrument advertisement. Rather, at least the integration of the sales tools is also given. If we look at it consistently, we can even see the importance of an *independent marketing instrument* which integrates different marketing mix areas. Here are some examples:

- Sales promotion which can be assigned to the product range include product training, covered private label policy, launch campaigns and product equipment,
- sales promotion which fall into the pay category include bonus catalogs, discount systems, forward-looking function takeovers and sales financing,
- sales promotion being assigned to the sales area, for example contract field service, sales channel selection, preferential placements at the POS and propagandist deployment,
- sales promotion which can be assigned to the advertising sector include events, trade advertising, POS advertising material and pull advertising.

6.4.2 Product features

Product features include the acquisitional use of the product cover, which also fulfills other functions.

Design refers to the development of new and the optimization of existing, industrially manufactured or to be manufactured products and product systems for the physical and psychological needs of the target group. This is done on the basis of aesthetic, economic and ergonomic analyses using form, color, material and design. Design is an important differentiation factor in view of technically more and more similar products and expresses its own cultural demands on the social environment. It should achieve the efficient design of cost and benefit, whereby the function determines the form less and less. Miniaturization thus allows the primacy of ergonomics. Design distinguishes itself from craftsmanship through the separation of design and execution as well as through the series-production capability of the approach, and from art through its functional orientation. The implementation of the most advanced, just accepted design also brings about an evolution of the sense of taste.

Styling includes the design of goods in terms of taste and functionality, as far as this is inseparably connected with the product. It is characterized by size, shape, material, surface, color, symbolism and their combinations and ideally at the same time increases the utility value of the goods. Modern production enables even small special series.

Design and styling are therefore of great communicative importance in the market. These represent a planned design work with strong aesthetic references and have several dimensions. The practical dimension is concerned with facilitating usability through ergonomics, especially styling. The aesthetic dimension refers to perceptual judgements through impression, especially design. The symbolic dimension covers the communication performance of a product, especially through labelling. The integration of product features into the communication and marketing strategy of a company is achieved by the function of design management.

Another important aspect is the *packing*, which cannot sensibly be used apart form the product resp. the *packaging*, which is separable from the product. These have central functions in marketing going far beyond design as to packaging styling as to packing. The following are especially noteworthy:

- *Rationalization* concerns the logistics function, i.e. transport improvement, shelf/storage control, robustness and stackability of the unit, the dimensioning function, i.e. quantity division, container size, filling standardization and shelf space utilization, as well as the information function, i.e. merchandise management, application sphere and mandatory data affected.
- *Facilitation in use* concerns dosage, multiple use and visibility of the content.

Beside these vital functions, of course also *communication* functions are concerned. They refer to the presentation, i.e. impression in the target group, differentiation and identification, the sales facilitation, i.e. conspicuousness and advertising message, as well as the quality award, i.e. branding, manufacturer's labeling and product designation.

Equally important are disposal claims for the return of used recyclable materials into the value material cycle.

6.4.3 Brand licensing

Licensing involves the licensee's permission of commercial use of property rights for products and services by third parties against payment to the licensor. In addition to the atypical product licenses (also brand licensing/license trademark), there are several types of advertising licenses, which are more closely related to the right to use certain signs/symbols of others in one's own advertising without modification. This requires prior examination of their affinity to the connotative character of the sender/offer as well as their distribution and relevance in the target group. It is conceivable to use media figures such as comics as the most well-known form of character licensing. Then the allocation/acquisition of usage rights in the form of names and/or images of VIPs as celebrity licensing. Furthermore the use of events as event licensing, especially in the field of sports and charity. A special form is the allocation/acquisition of exploitation rights to publications for by-products and to publications about celebrities. The income of the licensor usually consists of a minimum fixed guarantee and a variable profit-sharing. In addition, the licensee has to bear the costs for the mediation of the rights of use, the training in advertising design as well as options to extend or expand the use. Unauthorized exploitation of property rights entails high penalties depending on their value.

6.4.4 Personal communication

There are no patent recipes for the optimal conduct of a personal communication. It is rather the case that each person is best served by his/her own personal style in which he/she intuitively acts with confidence. All communicative signs can be considered as personal influencing factors of *oral* communication. These are audible in the form of vocal and non-vocal signs, or they are at least visible in the form of clothing, hairstyle, cosmetics, etc. The more congruence there is between the sender and receiver with regard to these signs, the more likely and better communication is to take place.

With *language* as an influencing factor, several codes can be distinguished:

- A restricted language code contains short sentences, simple sentence links, predominantly main sentences, concrete language, small vocabulary, hardly any foreign words, faulty grammar, gestures as a substitute for missing words.

- An elaborated language code, on the other hand, contains complex, complicated sentences, person-oriented formulation, logical argumentation, abstract, large vocabulary, use of foreign words, correct grammar, few, purposeful gestures, working by analogy, comparison, example.

In addition, various paralinguistic *variables* can be used. These are (best forming in each case)

- voice tone (rather sonorous), volume (not pushy, not shy), pausing (dramaturgical), speech tempo (rather engaged, dynamic, proactive), modulation/rhythm (accentuated), breathing technique (not short of breath), pronunciation (clear, high German), word choice (verbal rather than substantive), sentence structure (no nested sentences), flow (logical concatenation).

Furthermore besides oral signs, even much more important are signs of

- physics like haircut, cosmetics, clothing, etc.,

- proxemics like distance, relative position, touches, etc.,

- kinesics like posture, eye contact, nodding, head shaking, smiling, etc.

Body language results from the combination of the influencing factors facial expressions, gestures, head and eye posture. Facial expressions include e. g. frowning, raising eyebrows, lowering the corners of the mouth, pressing lips together, chewing lips. Since these are involuntary reactions, good conclusions can be drawn about the psychological situation of the interlocutor.

Gestures include all expressions of the body, such as clenching hands, holding palms down, arm movements, rubbing nose, stroking chin, smoothing clothes, hands in trouser pockets, hands on hips, fingertips pressed together, crossed legs, rocking feet, standing with legs wide apart, hands clasped behind the head. By far the largest proportion of communication units is thus non-verbally based.

The *head posture* expresses itself e. g. as head tilted to the side, head emphatically raised, pulled in between the shoulders, lowered, sideways swaying back and forth. The gaze posture can also be revealing, e. g. sideways out of the corner of the eye, looking past the other person, looking into the eyes, looking through the other person.

Social distances in conversation are also revealing. They concern the instinctive territorial behavior of the human being and are club-shaped around the body towards the front. Distinctions are made between the intimate distance (approx. 70 cm), the personal conversational distance (approx. 120 cm), the social perceptual distance (approx. 220 cm) and the public distance (approx. 400 cm) from the partner. Distances are also violated by the placement of personal objects, e. g., briefcase on the desk of the conversation partner.

Watzlawick stipulates in general, apart from the already mentioned axiom 1 (s. a., "One cannot not communicate") four other relevant axioms.

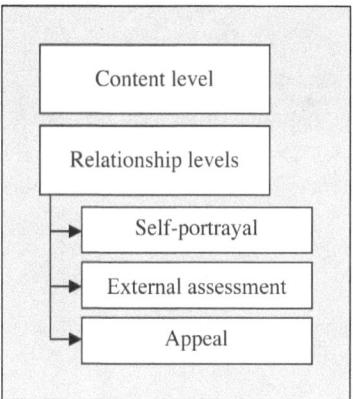

Fig. 43: Layers of communication

Axiom 2 is: "Every communication has a content aspect and a relationship aspect in such a way that the latter determines the former and is therefore a metacommunication" (*see figure 43: Layers of communication*).

Here is an example from Watzlawick: Driver and passenger are in the car, the passenger says to the driver: "You, the traffic light in front is green!"

On the factual level, this is about the objective presentation of facts to the addressee of the message, in this case the simple fact that a traffic light shows green light. But inseparably connected with it as subtext it always includes the relationship levels with the aspects of

- *self-portrayal of the message sender, here the statement that he is probably in a hurry and does not want to miss the green phase of the traffic light,*
- *external assessment of the message addressee by the sender, in this case the opinion that he/she must help the driver to get along better,*
- *appeal to the message addressee, here the request to him/her not to dawdle until the traffic light turns red again.*

Depending on how this statement is interpreted by the addressee, he answers on one of these levels:

- *Related to the subject quite harmlessly with "Yes, really practically this phased traffic lights."*
- *Reluctantly, for example by "I am not color-blind and driving faster is forbidden here."*
- *In a spirit of partnership, for example, by "Don't worry, we're right on time."*
- *Or obediently by "Yes, I think I'll speed up a bit."*

- Axiom 3 is: "The nature of a relationship is determined by the punctuation of communication processes on the part of the partners."
- Axiom 4 is: "Human communication uses digital (written/oral) and analog (non-verbal) modalities." Digital communication has a complex and versatile logical syntax in sequence, but a semantics in meaning which is inadequate in the field of relationships. Analog communication, on the other hand, has this semantic potential, but lacks the syntax necessary for unambiguous communication.
- Axiom 5 is: "Interpersonal communication processes are either symmetrical or complementary, depending on whether the relationship between the partners is based on equality or difference."

Depending on how the first message is received, the reaction which has taken place does not correspond to the original intention, and depending on the situation, a conflict may arise. In the private sphere, this means frustration on both sides in the worst case, in the business sphere it means concrete inefficiency, and in the advertising sphere it simply means lost money.

6.5 Intermediary comparison of non-classical advertising

An intermediary comparison for non-classical advertising is much more difficult to make than for classical advertising. This is mainly due to the heterogeneity of the media to be evaluated. As consequence, the following media are assumed to be the most important:

- Online media with non-web advertising, web 1.0 advertising, web 2.0 advertising, mobile advertising,
- public relations with traditional forms, placement and sponsoring, unconventional forms,
- live advertising with exhibition, POS-presence, event and company presentation,
- direct advertising in electronic, telephone and printed direct forms as well as documentations,
- sales promotion, product features, licensing, personal communication.

The classical media advertisements in newspapers, magazines and other print titles, spots on television, radio, movie theater and posters as stationary and mobile outdoor advertising as well as advertising technique include therefore at least the above-mentioned non-classical media.

The next consideration relates to the evaluation criteria of these media. Here, too, it is very difficult to categorize, but the following criteria should be used as a starting point (*see figure 44: Intermediary comparison of non-classical advertising*):

- *Product advantage* means the extent to which a medium is able to present and advertise the specific advantages of an offer. This is also important for its suitability for positioning.
- *Interactivity* means whether the medium allows a two-way communication or only an one-way communication. It is assumed that two-way communication is more effective per se.
- *Multisensory response* means whether the medium in question addresses more than one sense of perception in parallel. It is assumed that the parallel addressing of several senses is more effective.
- *Link to the purchase decision* means how close the medium is to a purchase decision in favor of the advertised product in terms of factual, formal, spatial and temporal aspects. The closer, as the more effective it is estimated.
- *Setting emotionality* refers to the extent to which a medium allows or does not allow an experience-oriented design of the advertising message. The more emotional the environment, the better a medium is assessed.
- *Presentation area/time* refers to the amount of information and feelings which can be used in a medium. The more liberal this framework is, the better it can be used for effective advertising.

6. Non-classical advertising

	Product advantage	Interactivity option	Multisensory response	Link to purchase decision	Setting emotionality	Presentation area/time	Inevitability of contact	Target group control/exhaustion	Flexiblity in usage	Demonstration possibilities	Topicality/reactivity	Pre sales fitness
Traditional PR-forms												
Placement												
Sponsorship												
Networking												
Exhibition												
POS presence												
Event												
Brandpark												
Direct-TV/-Radio												
Phone/Fax												
Direct response advert												
Direct mailing												
Catalog/Brochure												
Pre-sales advertis. material												
Sales promotions												
Product features												
Brand licensing												
Personal communication												

Fig. 44: Intermediary comparison of non-classical advertising

- The *inevitability of contact* records the extent to which it is possible to consciously avoid the medium or the extent to which it is virtually inevitable. The less one can avoid it, the better.
- *Target group control/exhaustion* refers to the targeting of the medium at a delimited target group. The better the targeting and the wider the coverage, the better the medium can be assessed.
- *Flexibility in usage* refers to the availability of the medium for promotional usage. The more degrees of freedom the application design allows, the better it is considered.
- *Demonstration possibilities* aim at the ability of a medium to make a product or its advantages "understandable" in the sense of hands-on experience. The more directly this is possible, the better.
- *Topicality/reactivity* refers to the ability of a medium to react to current developments. This mainly depends on the lead times of the application; the shorter these are, the better.
- *Pre-sales fitness* refers not to the end users of an offer, but to any intermediaries in the sales channel. It should be checked to what extent a medium is specifically capable of addressing these intermediaries or not.

If one starts from these criteria in the following, one can try to assess the previously mentioned non-classical media with regard to each of these criteria. Naturally, this assessment depends on the concrete circumstances of the individual case, such as product type, lifecycle status, competition, etc., so no generalizing statement can be made.

7. Integrated marketing communications

If an advertiser uses even some of these media in parallel, the demand for integrated communication arises. The goal of integrated communication is to create a consistent image of the sender for the target group from differentiated communication sources. This is urgently recommended in order to counteract the danger of diffusion and instead achieve a desired profile.

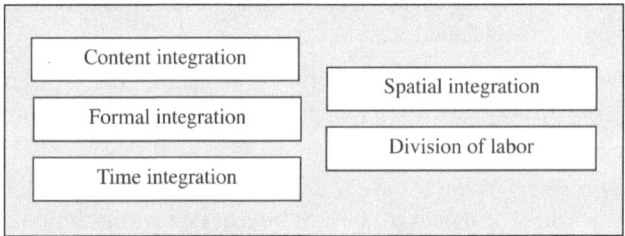

Fig. 45: Requirements for integrated communication

7.1 Integration substance

For the purpose of integration substance, five areas of measures can be used (*see figure 45: Requirements for integrated communication*).

The advertising messages should follow a *central message* which is retained unchanged across all media. It is conceivable to add individual sub-messages and to repeat the content in whole or in part.

In order to achieve a creative bracket for all measures in the various media, the common use of *formal elements* is indicated. This includes all corporate design elements as style constants. The form can be adapted in each case medium-adequately or constantly maintained.

The measures should also be coordinated in terms of *time*. According to the intensity, different approaches can be taken. The mix of media used can remain constant or be varied over time.

The areas of application of the measures must also be *spatially* coordinated. They can be subdivided according to local, regional, national, international or global use. In addition, a spatial compression of the application can be made.

The aim is an effective and efficient *division of labor* between the media for the optimal achievement of the communication goals. The media weighting, i.e. the relative share of the media in the overall mix, the number of media, i.e. the variety of media used, and the summary by media, by target groups or even combined are also important.

In order to achieve a consistent implementation of the positioning within the framework of integrated communication, the philosophy of brand communications is used. This means the *integrative coordination of all communication instruments which are capable to differentiate brands/companies in relation to the competition and to profile them in relation to customer target groups.*

This definition contains of the following parts:

- "Integrative coordination" indicates that the goal is communication which is harmonized in terms of content, form and space/time; "of all communication instruments" indicates that the use of channels of communication which go beyond classical media advertising is considered necessary on a regular basis.
- "Which are capable ..." implies strategic goal planning and the determination of the most suitable means/media for this purpose.
- "Brands/companies" indicates that predominantly offers are in question which are capable of brand building, i.e. which meet certain requirements which are considered necessary for the constitution of a brand; this also applies to companies.
- "To differentiate in relation to the competition and to profile them in relation to the customer target groups" refers to the general contents of communication with competitive discrimination and benefit-related claims and serves as a rounding off.

Integrated communication thus encompasses the areas of content/statement, form/design and time/space of messages. The aim is to achieve sender identity, equality of a product/company with itself from its own perspective as self-image and the perspective of third parties as public image. Every offer has identity factors attributed to it due to its presence and can acquire or take over further identity factors through communicative measures.

With all this, it is highly recommended to maintain a uniform conception. This has to be well thought out and appropriately planned in order to keep it unchanged in the long term. And if changes are necessary or deemed necessary, they should only be made in small, cautious steps.

7.2 Corporate identity

Corporate identity (CI) is in theory as well as practice an extraordinarily dazzling term. It means the *entity and conformity of presence, words and actions of an enterprise with its formulated self-concept*, thus the uniform presentation of an enterprise and its parts in the face of third parties.

CI is to be distinguished from the:

- Corporate philosophy, which expresses the fundamental economic, socio-political and social values, objectives and competences of a company in relation to itself and its position in its environment,

- corporate culture, which encompasses all the norms and values, attitudes and beliefs which underlie the behavior and decisions of the people in the company,

- corporate image as the public's idea of an object, which may only partially correspond to reality. This is the emotionally colored expression of identity within an opinion space.

The corporate identity knows two kinds of the enterprise view. The self-image, which largely derives from the subjective ideas and goals of the company, and the public image, which reflects the view of the market partners. It is now a matter of defining the self-image more closely and adapting the external image to the self-image. The basis for this is to define the corporate mission. This expresses the fundamental economic, political and social values, goals and competencies in relation to oneself as business mission and one's position in society as value mission. This is usually defined in the form of guiding corporate principles, which must be strictly observed as the practical implementation of the mission statement.

Corporate mission is the meaningful vision of the company, which defines its contribution to society beyond the mere provision of goods and services. It states what an organization, institution or company essentially stands for, what its vision is and where it derives its market authorization from ("What is our business? What are our customers? What is of value to our customers? What will our business be in the future? What should our business be?"). The initiators of large, successful communities at that time had clear basic assumptions and a consistent vision of their intended position in society. However, with increasing expansion and a time lag from the founding stage, this vision is in danger of being lost today. It is quite natural that purely operational concerns such as profitability, productivity, liquidity, etc. come to the fore. This was not a problem as long as the environmental conditions were favorable, i.e. manageable and expansive, but these times are probably finally gone. Today's environment is complex and restrictive, and resources are strained. And the question of the social legitimacy of private and also public communities active in the economy naturally arises. And for this, the intention to make a profit and secure the future are not enough on their own. Rather, this is only the goal of the company; society makes quite different demands on its existence. The question therefore arises as to how to communicate the precisely defined, strategic orientation to an increasingly critical and information overloaded public. Because deficits in social role play have a particularly negative effect on the marketing of ideas, products and services. Therefore, the original vision of the organization must be uncovered and examined to see to what extent it still fits or does not fit into the future environment. Above all, however, it must again be lived out internally and externally. So that society perceives its meaningful content (modern: purpose or attitude) and rewards it through acceptance. And so that the employees become aware of the meaningfulness of their actions again and are motivated to work responsibly.

Appropriate qualitative marketing research surveys provide extensive information about the *public image*. Very important are also employee opinions in the workforce, among store stewards, works councils, upper and middle managers, customer contact employees, informal groups, both among key persons who bundle the opinions of many and influence them, and finally also problem groups. The public image thus gained is contrasted with the self-image.

With regard to *self-image*, the company should refer back to characteristics and character traits which distinguish it. It is a good idea to view the company as a living organism, similar to a human being, as it is in the modern view of business science. Just as familiar people are stamped by their characteristics and traits, a company can also be described in a true-to-life way by its features. To be aware of these, to manage and stabilize them responsibly is the very first prerequisite for the clear profile of every provider. Because without clarity about oneself, all activity remains random.

Each community can be described with regard to these or other criteria in how it sees itself or wants to be seen by others and how others see it or how it actually presents itself.

If the defined self-image is completely or largely congruent with the public image, only a low level of activity is required to maintain this congruence or to correct any remaining deviations. However, this is a rather rare stroke of luck. On a regular basis, it will rather be the case that self-perception and the perception of others more or less strongly diverge. Then three options arise. The image of the others can be accepted and the self-image can be adjusted accordingly. This is equivalent to a denial of the company's personality. However, if one can live well with the characteristics and character traits of the image in the target group, one can at least save a lot of correction effort. Or one can aim at adapting the image in the target group to the image of oneself, because only then can the own values be adequately conveyed to the public, and thus to the target groups. This is then primarily a task of marketing communication. Finally, and this is by far the most common case, an adjustment in both dimensions may become necessary, i.e. a change in the desired self-image compared to the status quo and a change in the image of the outside world in the direction of this new self-image.

7.3 Public perception of the advertiser

The public perception of a vendor is also of crucial importance because it can often explain market successes which cannot be determined by objective factors in any other way. It serves people as orientation in an increasingly complex reality on the basis of inner images. These move on a meta-level, possibly detached from the real level.

After all, marketing does not only consist of the "naked" product itself, but of a conglomerate of the objective product and its subjective perception. In the case of objective performance, it is becoming increasingly difficult to offer the market anything extraordinary, because the performance dimensions have already been largely exhausted, and what one provider offers more here, the other offers more there. Therefore, the hope of achieving a better market position through objective performance alone is often in vain. On the other hand, the conditions are much more favorable when it comes to the subjective perception of the offer. Preferences can be built up which give more weight to the performance on the part of the demanders and thus also cause a greater willingness to buy.

It takes a comparatively long time until shortcomings in the external perception of the company are reflected in operating results, but once this has happened, the decline of the company is almost unstoppable, because it takes at least as long to get the public presentation up and running again, and this period of time overtaxes the survivability of many vendors.

The enterprise advertisement aims at communicating the self image outwardly correctly. Three interpretative directions can be distinguished *(see figure 46: Corporate identity elements)*.

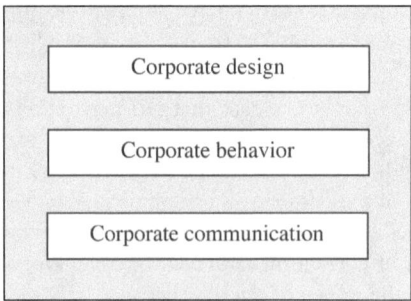

Fig. 46: Corporate identity elements

The design-oriented approach in *corporate design* focuses on the formal appearance of the sender. They are the visible counterpart of culture as the visual design of the artifacts with which a company presents itself to the public in order to enable accurate identification and recognition. As a means of determining the appearance, they include the

- object design as embodiment of performance or design of ideas,
- architectural design, i.e. primarily buildings, furnishings and equipment,
- graphic design, i.e. central image elements (see above),
- language design, i.e. the tonality of the address as corporate wording.

Corporate design thus defines the appearance characteristics of the organization in its environment, which are design constants in all measures. These must be examined to see whether they adequately reflect the values and norms of the message sender.

The leadership-oriented approach in *corporate behavior* understands this task primarily as a process of internal decision-making and implementation in order to achieve a uniform awareness and identification of employees, but also externally, for the goal-oriented focus of the organization in behavior. It represents the guideline for acting in the market, i.e. towards suppliers, customers, current and potential competitors and various other interest groups as stakeholders.

The image-oriented approach in *corporate communication* is based on the coordination of appearance and behavior, of internal and external activities under a uniform concept. Communication programs thus serve to identify and influence the attitudes of target groups. Differentiated advertising messages are used as a means to achieve this. These concern both classical and non-classical media.

In total, this results in sympathy and competence, acceptance and trust in the sender as corporate goodwill. Sympathy and competence are the cornerstones of acceptance. A vendor which is only competent is respected but not necessarily loved. And a vendor which is only sympathetic is liked, but does not radiate security. Only both sizes together are able to generate public trust.

Within the framework of the CI, corporate behavior is increasingly coming to the fore. The reason for this is the behavior of companies and their managers, which is rather justified from a microeconomic point of view, but which is not understood by society as a whole. These include the victory sign of Deutsche Bank CEO Josef Ackermann in the Mannesmann trial in which he was indicted, or the collection of high contractual severance payments, as in the case of Ron Sommer when he left his position as CEO of Deutsche Telekom. In addition, there are reactions such as the rise in share prices on the occasion of the announcement of mass dismissals, as at Siemens, or the threat of mass dismissals in the case of an unpleasant collective bargaining agreement, as at PIN parcel shipping. The result is a growing public pressure of opinion, driven by incomprehension and envy, fired by the media and politicians who are not sufficiently opposed by those affected. In order to avoid sanctions, companies submit to voluntary commitments as part of their corporate social responsibility. These state that not everything which is possible and legally permissible must be done. In addition, corporate compliance regulations are intended to ensure better self-regulation and put a stop to such perceived excesses. However, these are purely reactive approaches. On the other hand, it would make sense to have a qualitatively value-oriented corporate management in which the company sees itself and acts as a good citizen of the whole community as corporate citizenship.

Example Deutsche Bank:

Deutsche Bank's miscommunication has a principle. Here are a few examples from the leading German bank institute: in 1994 "Peanuts" was chosen as the misnomer of the year, it originated from the press conference of the then CEO Kopper in the Holzmann insolvency and refers to 30 million DM (about € 15 million) outstanding craftsman invoices. In 1999, non-private banking customers were spun off into Bank 24, which was then reintegrated in 2002 following protests. 2002 Breuer, then chairman of the board of directors, announced on television that he no longer considers the Kirch Group to be creditworthy, which later led to their bankruptcy. Deutsche Bank announced the merger with Dresdner Bank, but this failed in the detailed negotiations (Dresdner Bank was then taken over by the Allianz Group). Deutsche Bank announced the merger with Postbank, but the detailed negotiations also failed for the time being. In 2004, a record profit of € 2.55 billion was reported, and at the same time the dismissal of 6,400 employees was announced after 22,000 jobs have already been cut since 1999. The remuneration of the Chairman of the board Ackermann was reported at 10 million DM p. a. (about € 5 million) The slogans changed from "Trust is the beginning of everything" (1995) to "The Bank for Europe" (1999) to "Leading to results" and "Passion for performance" (2013), after which a slogan was dropped at all.

In recent times the term *"purpose"* is popular as viewpoint advertising on socially relevant content. But indeed a company does not have to take a stand on every thinkable issue, but only on those which are relevant to its core business. Target groups also do not expect any statement on issues which are not part of it. Moreover with every such statement, members of interested parties and potential buyers may be irritated, so that statements on widely accepted topics, such as diversity, gender equality, etc., are also not useful. So in many cases, keeping quiet would obviously be the better choice.

7.4 International marketing communications

International marketing communications face additional challenges compared to national advertising. These result from several factors, including

- Higher uncertainty about market conditions abroad, resulting in additional risk, increased coordination effort in the management of advertising, deviations in the media structure, which make media advertising more difficult, different advertising restrictions which require adjustments, sometimes different brand names for identical products, different interpretations of brand names, nationally different advertising target groups resp. consumer behavior.

The culture or cultural differences are used as an explanation. Culture is generally man-made, i.e. the product of social interaction and thinking of individual people. It is supra-individual and a social phenomenon which outlives the individual. It is learned and transmitted through symbols. Through norms, rules and instructions, it controls behaviour. *Culture is thus the totality of the basic assumptions, values, norms, attitudes and beliefs of a social entity which has developed in a multitude of behaviors over time.* Because culture strives for inner consistency and integration, there are various approaches to explaining it, especially in an international context.

7.4.1 Hypotheses of global advertising

Global advertising is based on three general economic hypotheses (based on Levitt):

- Cost degression is associated with high production requirements, low costs also mean high competitiveness.

- However, this effect only occurs if the product range is transnationally highly standardized.

- Standardization in turn requires a centralization of operational functions, especially management.

In addition, the theses can be traced back to two further areas with regard to communication as follows.

Cross-border communication *can no longer be prevented at all* by modern transmission technologies, especially satellites. In the past, national borders constituted effective barriers to the flow of information between markets. To this extent, communication was also nationally oriented. This is no longer the case. Since extraterrestrial broadcasting stations have been in operation, since cabling has been progressively extended with a significantly wider range of programs offered by foreign radio and television stations, the flow of information across national borders as media overspill has also been favored. As a result, cultures which have developed in part autonomously are coming into closer informational contact with each other and, consequently, different advertising concepts which were developed autonomously. It is easy to understand the disadvantage that the buyer of a brand in one country is now confronted with the more or less different message of the same brand, which is actually intended for another country. This can lead to irritation and uncertainty of the buyer about the brand image he/she is familiar with. This may even lead to abstinence from buying or brand switch through cognitive dissonance, provided there is sufficient penetration and sustainability. A scenario which must be alarming for every branded company. In fact, cross-border communication still has some limitations, mainly due to the technically not yet satisfactorily solved voice transmission problem, the limited transmission capacities of the satellites, the equally limited reception possibilities, but above all due to the limited potential of globally marketable offers, e. g. through deviating brand names.

In addition, *convergent social structures* provide increasingly favorable conditions for cross-border communication. After World War II, the modern industrial societies of the Western world experienced an enormous upswing almost in parallel. This has been accompanied by an essentially similar development of national social structures. Today, young people, managers, housewives, etc. in different countries are supposed to be more similar in attitude and behavior than within a single country. This enables companies internationally addressing a target group which can be narrowed down to a certain extent, being regularly the case, to use the same forms of address and content within different countries. This has the advantage of a favorable relationship between development and production costs on the one hand and the associated switching volume on the other. Because for a brand no longer necessarily country-specific advertising concepts and associated conversions must be compiled and paid. Instead once is thought and finished, that however all the more thoroughly and from the outset generalizing, comprehensive and uniformly. This improves the ratio of initial costs to placement costs. Even complex implementations pay off, because their costs are spread over a larger number of countries.

However, the previously practiced *domestic advertising* also offers tangible advantages. Because despite the possible convergence of international cultural structures, which remains controversial in detail as for example with multi options society (based on Naisbitt), there are still enough significant differences depending on the market environment, which require different approaches in terms of content and form. These market specifics are all the more usable for the vendor, the more apt, striking, pointed concept and implementation can profile and differentiate a brand in advertising. Or vice versa, any unavoidable or intended generalizations in communication almost inevitably lead to losses in effectiveness, which can only be optimally used and influenced under given national marketing conditions by advertising measures specifically adapted to the respective situation. This means that the efficiency advantages of global advertising are at least counterbalanced by disadvantages in effectiveness, which is all the more serious as this is the core requirement for every communication service. In principle, the discussion ultimately revolves around the fact that the advocates of a global, standardized sales concept put the potential advantages of positioning consistency and implementation cost savings before the possible disadvantages of rarely contestable efficiency losses, while the opponents believe exactly the opposite, a valuation which depends on the circumstances of the individual case. Compromises such as "think global, act local" or "glocal" only mask these problems.

7.4.2 Focusing alternative

In terms of marketing implementation, there is the option of focusing on localization benefits with corresponding differentiation of advertising or generalization to globalization benefits with corresponding standardization of advertising. The following reasons are given for focusing.

A lack of consideration of country-specific characteristics, which can have a negative impact on sales success, cannot otherwise be ruled out. There are considerable differences in the media landscape in terms of structure and usage, e.g. in terms of print or TV media dominance. Deviating product use conditions cannot be corrected if they are only explained by the cultural and mental context of the country. There may be different phases in the market life cycle which require different marketing because different groups of people are to be addressed in the diffusion process. In the end, central control and coordination is not practicable, since this would have demotivating effects and unacceptable delays in decision-making. The not invented here ("NIH") syndrome, which is based on understandable national egoisms, hinders the adoption of external preparatory services. Different sales methods, forms, channels, and systems of distribution require different approaches. On closer inspection, generalizing cost savings turn out to be lower than often assumed, so that they are easily overcompensated by disadvantages in effectiveness. A different price structure according to demand, competition, costs requires a different price positioning of the respective products and services.

On the other hand, there is the opinion that the cultural dimensions and marketing conditions not only do not converge, but even diverge evolutionarily. Therefore, on the contrary, an individualization of the advertising must be striven for. Thus, the concepts of global generalization and global focus are in conflict with each other.

7.4.3 Generalising alternative

As reasons for a generalization, however, the following are mentioned above all. It is possible to reduce research and development costs to a version of the product range which can be marketed across all sales areas. A uniform product/company image can be created in all the markets served by the same positioning. Efficient planning is facilitated by uniform objectives, which do not require the consideration of diverging interests. Similarities in the target groups and their increasing mobility lead anyway to a convergence of marketing conditions. Coordination and control is simplified by better clarity and reduction of the number of strategies. The exploitation of know-how transfer through similar implementations on tactical and operational level is successful. A centralization of the management leads to more efficient control of the company by the bodies entrusted with it. In reality, an internationalization of the competition arises, whereby no longer single markets but market contexts become relevant for decision-making. Media overlapping or unstoppable cross-border communication as a result of satellite broadcasting or foreign print titles can be exploited.

This mainly concerns markets for raw materials, high-tech and high-touch products. It is therefore possible for internationally active companies to standardize their advertising, apply the same sales concepts everywhere and guarantee performance standards. As a result, it is still possible to realize cost savings. In this respect, the conflict of objectives between quality and price should be overcome. This is why globally operating companies are ostensibly more successful.

However, it is undisputed that despite the unmistakable convergence of international social structures and the internationalization of competition, there are still enough significant differences depending on the supply environment, which require a marketing communication which differs in form and content from country to country. Such market specifics are the better usable for a supplier the more apt, striking, pointed his positioning is. Or vice versa: Unavoidable generalizations of the sales concept almost inevitably lead to losses in effectiveness, since the specific marketing conditions in each case are more usable by individually coordinated activities than by global ones.

Example Gillette:

Gillette, the American body care company, was one of the pioneers of global advertising. In the mid-1980s, the group approached its lead agency BBDO, New York, and commissioned it to develop a globally applicable campaign for Gillette wet razors. The BBDO headquarters passed the order on to selected national affiliates which appeared to be particularly creative, with the express reference to develop a campaign which could be used globally. The intention was to collect the various campaign suggestions and present the best of them to the client Gillette for a decision. After some time, feedback came from the national offices, and it was anything but encouraging. Each agency branch reported that it could very well create an interesting campaign for its own cultural area, but that it was so different from the rest of the world that it was not viable as a campaign to go beyond that, because the campaign would then necessarily have to be too profane. In the headquarters they were ready to capitulate until then CCO Phil Rosenshine took on the task. His basic idea was to examine which motivations unite all men on this earth. If these attitudes and behaviors could be determined, a global campaign which appeals to all men equally could be built upon them. His considerations led him to the classic motives of self-realization of every man: to be successful in one's job, to be a good family father, to accept and master challenges, to achieve something one can be proud of, to hold comradeship among men, to be a loving spouse, etc.

BBDO was convinced that these motives apply across cultural areas, so the Gillette campaign was based on image sequences in the basic advertising medium of TV, which showed precisely this self-realization and suggested that it would be easier to achieve through a smooth, clean shave. Thus BBDO London was also commissioned with the implementation for the Central European market. In the context of pattern campaigns, this is limited to an adaptation in the sound range and a translation of the wording and the text super (slogan). Image material was supplied for this purpose, from which particularly suitable sequences could be selected. But even with this footage there were unexpected problems, as sequences showed blond haired men, because they are considered to be particularly youthful. In Northern Europe these models were also accepted, because they looked like the way Northern Europeans are commonly imagined. Southern Europeans, however, could not identify with these models, and thus not with the brand they promoted, because in Southern Europe black hair color is dominant. Consequently, only black-haired men were accepted as models. However, it was found that Northern Europeans also identify with black-haired men, as they remind them of the lifestyle and atmosphere of their last vacation in the South. In this respect, the central European campaign implementation preferably used black-haired models, whose image sequences had to be re-shot to this extent.

Especially in Germany another problem was added. The slogan in the global Gillette campaign was "Gillette. The best a man can get." The translation into German, however, led to unique selling propositions which were prohibited at that time for reasons of competition law. Therefore, a new slogan had to be invented for Germany, which formulated the same content in a legally permitted form. However, this was not so easy because the slogan was not spoken but sung. So the lyrics had to be not only legally sound, but also fit the pulse of the music. So the German BBDO branch got down to work. Now it is highly recommended to always have slogans approved by a lawyer before they are used in the field. But all slogan suggestions of the advertisers were shot down by the lawyers during this preliminary examination because of considerable reservations. Lawyers have the habit of adhering strictly to the text submitted for review and either approving or rejecting it. However, they are usually in no way creative themselves by making their own constructive suggestions. In their desperation, however, the agency approached the in-house lawyer not only to always explain what is not permitted, but instead to explain what would be permitted. For fun, the lawyer replied: "Gillette. For the best in a man", would be possible. Because this is a subjective superlative which is always allowed, similar to "the whitest white of my life" or "this coffee tastes best to me". Glad to have finally found a slogan formulation which was legally proper and also sounds well, this slogan was chosen. The trick was only that one syllable was missing in the text for the beat of the underlying music. So it became: "Gillette. For the be-e-est in a man". Finally this global advertising spot went on air for years.

7.5 Advertising agency integration

Advertising measures do not belong to the core competence of a company. Therefore, it is generally recommended not to take them on yourself, but to outsource them. In this respect, advertising always raises the question of make or buy. In the case of "make", the organizational structure decides who takes over this work such as shared service center, specialist department, marketing function, sales function, etc. In the case of "buy", communication agencies are called in whose core competence these tasks correspond to. In the following the elements of servicer types, selection criteria, contact framework evaluation, briefing and workflow are enlighted (*see figure 47: Advertising agency integration*).

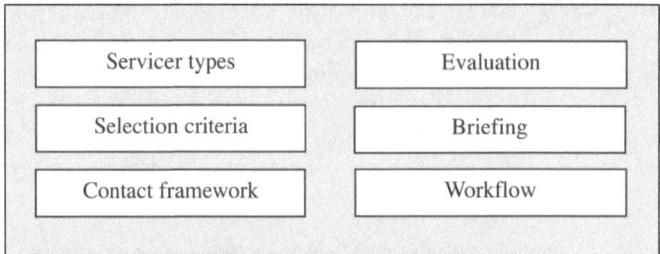

Fig. 47: Advertising agency integration

7.5.1 Servicer types

Different criteria are relevant for the selection of the individually most suitable advertising agency. First of all it has to be decided which type of agency is the right one for the given situation. Beside advertising agencies also market-oriented management consultancies offer advertising, and hotshops/freelancers supply punctual creative services.

Management consultancies have a strong affinity for marketing aspects. Whether, on the other hand, the creative performance is exemplary, remains questionable. Furthermore, advertising measures are not part of the core business of consultants, but are offered primarily for reasons of customer loyalty and to extend the value chain. Hotshops and freelancers are available on the market in large numbers. Many of them are specialized on individual communication instruments, as access to classic campaigns is made more difficult because they are often tied up in the alignment of international agency chains and these no longer shy away from supporting complex campaigns. In addition, the quality of these suppliers is often arguable and their market stock is not permanent.

Traditional advertising agencies take over advertising in the package as full service, because that is important for their clients and they expect this in such a way. Many of them have set up or bought in specialized units to cover the entire range of communication services, such as sales promotion, direct advertising, public relations, life advertising or online advertising. However, the uniformity of appearance between classic and non-classic advertising may suffer as a result. Nevertheless, at least one contact person is provided, so that further interfaces are not necessary.

7.5.2 Selection criteria

For the outsourcing ("buy") the selection criteria are now important, which are put on for an assignment. The following are examples of such criteria:

- *Internationality* raises the question of whether an international network integration is really necessary. If so, an examination of the network in terms of coverage according to countries and exclusion of competitors according to budgets is necessary. Sometimes a mere network association is sufficient. However, an examination of the intensity of the exchange is then advisable, as these are often only "patchworks" without an essential exchange of work and experience.
- Referred to *agency size*, as in all industries, a polarization on the market can be observed, i.e. a thinning of the middle class with increasing distance from both large and small advertising agencies ("hourglass shape"). In this respect, the alternative is essentially a small, owner-managed agency or a large network branch.
- To what extent proximity or distance of the *agency location* from the client's location is actually a selection criterion depends on the work organization. The more organized the client's work is, the less the spatial proximity plays a role in view of information and communication media. Nevertheless, especially in day-to-day business, there is, despite videoconferencing and home office, a lot to be said for spatial proximity.
- *Industry experience* is doubtfull because opinions differ here. Because industry experience can mean greater efficiency through faster familiarization or blinkers through unnecessary "scissors in the head". It is certainly true that markets, as diverse as they may appear at first glance, all function according to similar mechanisms. In addition, the exclusion of competitors has a limiting effect here.
- *Agency age* too is doubtfull. There are many arguments in favor of young, "hungry" agencies which think unconventionally, but are they really reliable? Moreover, the vast majority of new agencies are flops. An experienced, proven

agency, on the other hand, is established, but is it still imaginative? Not infrequently, there are indeed burn-out appearances.

- Adherence to *delivery dates* is a criterion widely regarded as central. Punctuality, speed and reliability are the most important practical requirement criteria. A functional project management with traffic and internal organization by progress chasers offers sufficient guarantee for this ex ante.

- *Cost consciousness* is for sure of enormous importance. It is mainly about the adherence to cost estimates (no work without cost approval), but also about a favorable price-performance ratio. The objectification of the underlying services in comparison, especially ex ante, is problematic.

- *Employee qualification* is less about formal qualifications, which alone are not very meaningful, but rather about the standing of the employees in the industry, which is documented by career development, work experience and product expertise.

- *Agency philosophy* means. that the agency credo must actually be lived and must not just be lip service. The proof of implementation must be in work, whereby the old discussion flares up again and again whether advertising is art or craft, clearly the latter.

- *Creation* is undoubtedly the core product of any agency work by primacy of creation. The success can be judged by the agency's awards, creative rankings, industry standing, etc. However, creation is always also "people business", so it depends on who in the agency is actually working on a campaign/project.

- *Media experience* means, qualitatively, a question of whether the advertising agency is familiar with the relevant classical and non-classical media genres. And quantitatively it is about whether the agency disposes of a network of relationships and, if applicable, whether it has buying power vis-à-vis publishers and broadcasters as to conditions.

- *Requirement profile* means, that a creative agency which provides conceptual services in the context of a campaign or an implementation agency which acts according to a given concept can be required. The latter concerns above all activities in the course of non-classical advertising.

7.5.3 Contact initiation

In order to initialize a contact, the framework for selection, the evaluation of potential servicers, the briefing of the preferred agency partner and the actual workflow in day to day-outsourcing are relevant.

7.5.3.1 Framework

By applying/evaluating these and other criteria, the circle of potential advertising agencies can be narrowed down to a shortlist, and the question of the appropriate approach arises. Typically, contact is established by means of an agency presentation, an exemplary presentation of the work or the naming of references from the client base. In the process, both sides must critically examine whether an intensive and long-term cooperation appears possible and worthwhile.

If several agencies are included on the shortlist, a direct comparison of potential contractors can be made by means of a competitive presentation as preferably paid pitch based on a uniform briefing. The presentation can only refer to the verbalized concept or more or less already concretely implemented advertising material. For comparison purposes, a list of criteria should be drawn up in advance, which then leads to a scoring to select the preferred agency. In order to achieve a higher degree of security, it is also conceivable to initially place a trial order only, in order to test the fit between client and contractor in practical cooperation and to stabilise it if it stands the test or to terminate it without major losses if it does not.

Furthermore, it must be clarified whether one or more agencies should be employed. The fact that coordinated measures, i.e. from one source and one house, can be expected speaks in favor of only one contractor. In addition, there is a clear control system and a clear interface with one contact person. On the other hand, there is probably a lack of core competency in the individual communication disciplines and the dependence on one partner in the case of questionable, because rarely exploitable, synergy potentials. A better expected quality of the work results with presumably higher efficiency and effectiveness speaks for several specialized agency partners. On the other hand, the difficult integration of the media has to be done by the client himself, which requires a complex control.

Before the *selection* of an advertising agency can be tackled, however, the following questions must be clarified:

- Can the initial problem really be solved by communication? Many problems are rather structural in nature and therefore not tangible through advertising measures. Marketing communications will not help those which offer an outdated range of products and services, which do not offer competitive prices, which are financially not capable to make themselves sufficiently known and familiar to the target group and which cannot develop sufficient sales pressure to prevail against opponents.

- If it is a one-time project, which is to have a selective strengthening effect, or a continuous campaign with branding and CRM. It is rare to find both of these investments combined in one supplier of high quality. Mostly it is more about how both talents can be combined.

- Who coordinates the activities during this process? Collaboration with external parties always requires coherent interface management. At these gates, there is always a considerable loss of information, which leads to a loss of time and money and thus reduces the effectiveness of specialists through inefficiencies which have to be accepted.

- What funds are available and how are they distributed? Without a clear budget allocation, all efforts are fruitless. This raises the question of which budget is appropriate. This is difficult to answer and can at best be based on experience from past activities, activities of other business units in the company, other companies in the same industry, etc. Corresponding figures can also be researched from secondary sources such as advertising statistics.

- What form of remuneration should be chosen? There are several options which have to be weighed up against each other in their pros and cons. Competitive models also play an important role. Furthermore, the relation of preliminary costs to market-effective costs must be clarified. This is often unfavorable, especially for smaller budgets, because economies of scale are missing.

- Which decision makers are to be involved? The rule is to involve as few as possible, as much as necessary. However, this proves to be difficult, especially in large organizations with a high degree of division of labor. Oversized decision-making bodies are often created with correspondingly problematic finding processes, time delays and lazy compromises.

- What exactly are the goals of agency selection? First and foremost, it is a matter of determining the division between the work to be done internally and the work to be done externally. In addition, a variety of qualitative requirements must be taken into account. In order to objectify the decision, it makes sense to set these goals in written form.

7.5.3.2 Evaluation

Detailed information can be obtained by utilizing individual questionnaires for "supplier evaluation". These generally refer to the following contents.

The *agency name/slogan* is not only a purely administrative information as entry in the commercial register, but one must assume that the company and slogan have a programmatic claim, i. e. are meaningful in terms of internationality, significance of creativity, focus of work, owner management, etc.

The information on the *date of incorporation/capital resources* is subject to interpretation. Thus, an early date of foundation and thus a long company history can indicate a lot of experience and a high storm resistance. But it can also indicate tradition and a lack of flexibility. This would not be a reference, especially in the creative business. The capitalization means the financial backing of the business and is therefore an important indicator of stability and crisis resistance. This is particularly important if longer-term customer-supplier relationships are to be established.

The naming of *executive managers* obeys the principle of freelance service, where in the end it is always people with competence and sympathy who are decisive for a sensitive and complex cooperation as in advertising. Above all, it must be ensured that this profile is applied in direct consulting, as it cannot be delegated to other employees. After all, communication consulting as a professional service cannot be delegated, or only to a very limited extent.

The *professional experience* of the managing directors by their last three employments is at least informative about the strengths of a service provider seen in this way and the quality of the advice to be expected. However, established consultants are often already beyond the zenith of their work or are no longer involved in day-to-day business, but rather ambitious, up-and-coming young professionals have greater potential. This must be weighed up.

Also relevant is the *number of permanent employees* differentiated by work areas or gross income as status and development of the last three years. Here the statement is ambivalent. For example, a large agency organization can show a finely divided structure staffed by specialists. However, it remains questionable whether this structure benefits all customers, including small and medium-sized ones, or whether it is reserved for key accounts, which makes perfect business sense. Small agencies, on the other hand, are usually much closer to their customers, although their expertise is usually less developed or has to be purchased externally, which can lead to further interface friction. After all, if the small agencies were as good as the big ones, they would not be small, and excuses à la "small but fine" can not help this.

With regard to *industry experience* differentiated by market sectors, there are two points of view. The first is that an agency without industry or product experience cannot provide effective consulting services because it must first laboriously familiarize itself with a new field of activity. The other says that it is precisely this experience which leads to "company blindness" and "scissors in the head", which restrict creativity. It is a fact that when hiring a "new" agency, one has to pay their expensive apprenticeship fee, which is only acceptable if a long-term cooperation is planned. But it is also a fact that practically all industries and products have to face the same basic challenges and function according to similar principles, so that a transfer is reliably possible.

Activity regions are of particular interest to international clients who want to use advertising measures in the same or a similar way across national borders. In this case, the local presence of the agency with central control in the respective regions is helpful. However, this aspect is hardly relevant for nationally active companies or those which adhere to ethno-centralist principles.

The *customer list* with referenceable addresses is a very important criterion, since it can be assumed that these clients have already checked the suitability of the service provider and decided positively. Moreover, one feels more and more at home in an adequate environment. However, the decision of other companies cannot be transferred to one's own company without further adjustment, since different market, industry and demand conditions exist there. And companies where this is not the case usually face the competitive exclusion clause.

With regard to the number of employees in the *creation department* differentiated according to work areas, the creative output is the central component of the consulting service. This is not a matter of "free spinning", but always of practice-oriented creativity, i.e. finding and implementing innovative solutions within conditions imposed by restrictive environmental factors. Free creativity usually leads to confusion and stress. On the other hand, innovation which takes into account relevant framework conditions creates acceptance and a unique position.

To substantiate the claim of practice-oriented creativity, it is helpful to check the professional experience of the *creative directors* by their last three employments. This is done on the basis of expertise and work examples of the creative directors, which can show whether the creation of activities corresponds to the style and expectations of a potential client. For it can be assumed that their handwriting will also be found in the later self-assigned work.

The presentation of a *representative task* for potential clients in the same industry, if available, serves to illustrate the claimed performance. It is important, however, not only to apply "colorful pictures" but to obtain a complete advertising case, i.e. with explanation of the problem, initial situation, objectives, conceptual planning, goal-oriented solution and success of the campaign. The fact that their positive exaggeration takes place in the process is to be accepted in doubt as typical for the industry and can be relativized by own experience. Company and business secrets are to be observed sensitively.

The presentation of representative tasks for customers *from other industries* also serves as an illustration. In fact, the flexibility of a potential advertising agency can be inferred from this if it does not have any concrete experience in the industry. Those who can prove that they are able to familiarize themselves quickly and effectively with new industries can be expected to do the same in their own industry. Furthermore, it can be left aside whether standardized solutions predominate or individual ones.

Examples of *cooperation* with processing servicers are important, because success is only achieved when an idea is properly executed, i.e. it is flawless in terms of time, space, target group and form presentation. The joy about a creative idea quickly fades when annoying quarrels arise during the implementation. In the case of subcontracting, it is important to have a well-rehearsed team to ensure that the process activities are carried out properly. But it is also conceivable that the execution part is taken over by an internal company department.

The agencies pre-selected on the basis of the above or similar criteria are then subjected to a closer examination. There are two possible approaches to this. The agency presentation takes place through personal or media self-presentation via agency brochure, extranet/CUG, Skype/teleconferencing or similar, whereby the personal form is always recommended. This can take place at the potential client or on site, but if possible in the agency premises. The agency should definitely name the actual prospective supervisors and have them "presented". One should not accept "presenters", because the "chemistry" of the partners is crucial for the later cooperation.

A credentials presentation will take place on the basis of work examples, preferably several and according to one's own selection. In order to achieve a high level of significance, the following elements should be included:

- Initial situation for the communication with the problem definition which had to be solved,
- considerations of the agency in order to develop a goal-oriented solution,
- solution path of the implementation for the creative realization of measures,
- reproducible results/success of the measures.

Before deciding on a new agency, it is definitely worth giving the existing agency another chance. It has a considerable know-how advantage, its weaknesses are known and others "also put on their trousers one leg at a time". However, if there is a fundamental dissatisfaction or wear and tear which no longer allows for any element of surprise, a change is probably inevitable. And the selected, no more than four, agencies should be briefed.

7.5.3.3 Briefing

Briefing is generally understood to be a precise delivery of information, here specifically about the communication task to be supervised. All briefing contents must always be thoroughly thought through and approved in advance by all decision-makers. The briefing must always refer only to the problem definition, not to solution specifications, i.e. no own creative ideas, not even as suggestions. The briefing is always documented in writing. It is always concise (so-called single sheet), because if it does not fit on one page, it has not been properly thought through. Briefings should always be explained in a personal conversation and should not be sent anonymously, nor should they be held in parallel in group briefings, but should always be carried out in a uniform manner. A re-briefing should be written by the agency in its own words to enable a comparison of understanding. The briefing contents as plan are at the same time a binding assessment standard for the evaluation of work results presented later in review.

The briefing generally refers to the following contents:

Presentation of the market environment

- What is the market in which the company operates. e.g. size, segments, development, etc.?

- *Which competitors does the company face there and how can they be characterized?*
- *How do the communication activities in the market under consideration present themselves?*
- *Who are the company's intermediate and end customers and how can they be characterized as to buying and decision-making behavior?*
- *What does the company's offer provide in detail and make it superior?*
- *Are there special boundary conditions which need to be considered, e.g. political, self-imposed?*
- *What are the advertising objectives*
  - *quantitatively, e.g. market share, sales/turnover, growth rate,*
  - *qualitative, e.g. awareness, image, reputation, sympathy?*

Where is the purchasing power from which the offer wants to exist, i.e. the source of potential demand?

- *Who are the target persons who should buy the offer*
  - *description under demographic and actiographic aspects, e.g. age, gender, profession, income, place of residence,*
  - *description under socio-psychological aspects, e.g. motivation, attitude, behavior, opinion leadership, family status.*

How does the offer differentiate itself from the competition and how does it profile itself against the demand?
  - *What can credibly be suggested to be better than with anything else (claim)?*
  - *How can this claim be substantiated objectively (reason why)?*

In individual cases certain pieces of information can be omitted, for example in case of a long-standing collaboration, or more can be added, for example in case of special projects such as sales promotions, events or web design.

7.5.3.4 Workflow

The *presentation* of results after a briefing can be done in several steps. In the concept presentation only the communication strategy is presented, there is no implementation. Although this is cost-saving, all in all it is very problematic, because often the imaginative ability of the decision makers is not sufficient to imagine how even a pale concept can become an impressive campaign. Nevertheless, this form is often chosen for financial reasons.

7.5 Advertising agency integration

In the copy platform presentation, the communication strategy, combined with a rough conceptual implementation in the form of headlines/slogans together with stock photos are presented. Whether this is functional depends on the level of experience of the decision makers. Again, there must be a capacity for imagination, which can be assumed to be non-existent for deciders not familiar with advertising. Again, cost reasons are decisive for this form.

During the creative presentation, communication strategy, copy platform and prototypical, close-to-finish implementations are presented. Here, the conceptual idea is already concretized in advertising material, which at least indicates the direction of an expected implementation. It is advisable to arrange at least this stage of the presentation. Many agencies choose this, even if only a concept or copy platform presentation is honored, for security reasons or to gain a pretended competitive advantage.

Finally, the campaign presentation presents a closed communication strategy, copy platform, finished implementations and media planning. This results in a assured impression of the campaign, which at the same time serves as a quorate basis. Since this stage is considered necessary anyway, the preliminary stages do not save time.

In any case, it is important to hold all presentations in a timely manner and to shield the different agencies from each other. There should be no less than six and no more than eight weeks between briefing and presentation. In fact, the deadlines are usually shorter because so much time has already been wasted in the run-up to the event that this time is not available for the preparation of the presentation. This is regrettable and detrimental to quality. With regard to the scope of the presentation, it is common for agencies to present only one single recommendation as well as alternatives, although experience shows that inexperienced clients have the disastrous gift of choosing the inferior one. Alternatives are nevertheless presented in order to increase the likelihood of winning the contract, but then it is advisable to present them with a clear recommendation.

The *results* should be assessed on the basis of objective criteria, not just on the basis of good feeling. Conceivable criteria which can be scaled and, if necessary, weighted are as follows:

- Analytical considerations as knowledgeable information processing, own contribution to the provision of information, correct situation analysis, market/industry knowledge, differentiated media selection, adequate selection of sales sources, adequate target group determination, clarification of positioning,

- conceptual solution as pinpoint creativity on central customer benefit, attention-grabbing design, e. g. uniqueness, aesthetics, etc., message which arouses interest by originality, etc., convincing argumentation, e. g. competence, credibility, etc., suitability to influence buying behavior through encouraging character, etc., chain up customers to buy again, strengthening the brand sender/corporate identity,

- creative implementation as adherence to schedules/quickness, cost-performance ratio, cost transparency/traceable billing system, media planning quality, competence for all media types (B-t-l), offer of external/internal services, e.g. film/radio/television, artbuying, consultants in day-to-day business known and accepted, success controls provided,
- "soft factors" as enthusiasm/identification of the agency team, power/perseverance of the agency, contact ability of the agency employees, sympathy and competence of the agency employees, flexibility of the agency/criticism, manageability and professionalism of the agency, organizational background.

Furthermore, the follow-up of an agency selection is of great importance. This includes the personal communication to winners and losers, and at the same time also the return of presentation materials to the eliminated participants, unless the rights to them are purchased separately. An explanation of the results as feedback for the rejected agencies (so-called de-briefing) should also be a matter of course. Any press releases must only be made after the contract has been signed.

A recommendable way is, if possible, to place a trial order to get to know the real "cooperation". For this purpose, a temporary project contract will be concluded or a contract for the time being only for one product as an entry or only for one market area or customer group. The outcome of this trial period will then determine the further, fixed cooperation. It is also conceivable to hold a joint workshop outside of the operative work in order to understand each other, how the partners' chemistry works, which development perspective they offer and what can be expected from an actual cooperation.

In the course of the cooperation, a conscious process interlocking with the advertising agency should be aimed at by coordinating the work processes of re-briefing, de-briefing, feedback talks, etc. This also includes "rules of the game" for the collaboration. Regular reviews to stabilize results by audits through ongoing agency evaluation are helpful for this.

The procedure described above also applies in principle to the screening and identification of agencies specializing in individual communication instruments in the below-the-line sector. Although specific aspects are added and general aspects are omitted, the basic approach remains the same. The decision has to be made whether to commission several specialized communication service providers, which leads to considerable complexity in day-to-day business, or to contract only one agency, which is likely to affect the quality in the specialized disciplines. An acceptable compromise is offered by network agencies which offer generalist and specialized companies under one roof.

As an alternative to commissioning external service providers, it is also possible to use the *internal advertising department*, also as a spun-off marketing service center. This can relate only to the conceptual area, i.e. management of external service providers, or only to processing, e.g. to the sales team, or to both. The following reasons, among others, endorse an internal assignment:

- Ongoing quality control is possible, already existing capacities in staff and equipment can be utilized to capacity, the level of knowledge in the discipline remains up to date, servicer profits can be retained, there is autonomy in decision-making, secrecy is guaranteed, less coordination effort involved, fast/flexible reaction to market, competition and demand, high identification with the company goals.

However, the following main reasons speak against this:

- No use of specialist know-how, fixed costs and capital commitment, no cost-efficient solution through tendering, no complaints in the event of quality problems, no concentration on core competence, no call-off as required in the event of capacity bottlenecks, distribution conflicts over scarce operational resources are common, high demands are placed on the qualification and motivation of employees, specialization/scaling advantages cannot be used appropriately.

7.6 Ethics in advertising

Marketing communication activities are increasingly subject to public criticism. Indeed, in addition to important advantages, considerable problem areas of advertising must be accepted. In the following, some of the most important ones are listed.

Advertising generally promotes market transparency by improving the information level of demand and, above all, by enabling comparison between different offers. This directly benefits the protection of a high competitive intensity. However the increasing information overload has in the effect a veiling of the market transparency as consequence. The interest-steered information delivery of the offerers in the advertisement can lead therefore to the subjective wrong information and cause a restriction of the individual level of information with the danger of the exploitation of the associated unawareness. This ultimately reduces the intensity of competition. First of all, too high market transparency is not desirable in any case.

The competitive model usually assumes a medium degree of market imperfection in the context of wide oligopolies, because the classic model of perfect competition leads to "sleepyhead competition" and does not seem realistic in other respects either. A medium degree of intransparency is desirable inasmuch as too little market perfection hampers pronounced competitive relationships by forming preferences and too much market perfection hinders dynamic competitive processes of advance and pursuit. Advertising is therefore only conducive to competition insofar as it does not leave the area of medium transparency. It is generally believed, however, that high market transparency benefits above all new providers, who can only make themselves known to potential customers. In reality, however, the high advertising expenses tend to exclude new providers, unless they can take advantage of high internal subsidies. Then, if at all, advertisement in the effect increases the market transparency tendency in favor of existing offerers.

But very few providers are interested in achieving market transparency in the sense of better comparability of offers. Because an offer has the greater chance of acceptance on the market, the more it is taken out of the direct comparability to competition. In times of me-too-offers only the generation of preferences is suitable to increase own sales chances. Thus, originally more or less identical offers are subsequently profiled by means of communication. As a result, the offer overview is reduced. Finally, the information message of certain low-involvement products is quite modest. But even with product groups which require explanation, advertising is increasingly limited to emotion. The reasons for this lie in the short, unfocused viewing time of advertising media and the impossibility of adequately conveying product explanations below this limitation. However, this presupposes that advertising actually contains relevant information. In many industries, especially with intensively advertised offers, advertising is based predominantly or exclusively on non-thematic, affective moods as pure emotionality. This has little news value because it is not very meaningful about the profile of the offer itself. This is particularly true for homogeneous goods such as cigarettes, low interest products such as razors and problem-free goods such as tissue papers. Their high advertising expenditure does not seem to be justified from this point of view. Moreover, every advertiser naturally only mentions the advantages of his offer, but not its disadvantages, which is absolutely legitimate. As a result, no objective information is available at all. Because this requires the honest naming of all, also the disadvantageous aspects, in order to then be able to weigh qualified as a target person among those. But understandably no advertiser finances this. In this respect, only a limited level of information results from advertising. This function is therefore only fulfilled with little reliability. The interest-controlled information delivery of the providers in advertising can lead to subjective misinformation and cause a restriction of the individual level of information with the danger of exploiting the associated ignorance. This ultimately reduces the intensity of competition.

The chance of the advertising announcement of different offers leads to the increase of the selection possibilities at the market due to communicative differentiation and offers thereby concretely a piece of quality of life. However the serious danger of irrational program proliferation arises, which may result in a reduction of the subjective selection possibilities by confusion of the information situation due to objectively hardly comprehensible differences in offers. In the absence of factual unique selling propositions/USPs, communicative unique advertising propositions/UAPs (also UCP for unique communication proposition) are established, but this does not change the fact that offers are increasingly interchangeable. However, this argument can only be valid for the rare to impossible case that firstly all providers on the market advertise and secondly this with the same intensity. But this is in reality by no means the case. Only comparatively few providers of a branch use advertising at all, and this to a very different extent. Even the difficult solution of the problems can be left open, whether the advertising is done in proportion to the market shares or egalitarian and how its effectiveness should then be evaluated. Therefore the market variety is represented only distorted, certain players dominate, others do not appear at all. The impression from the advertisement does not correspond thus to the market reality. The selection possibilities are hardly increased thereby in any case.

A crucial simplification of the purchase by uncertainty reduction and time saving with the selection is made possible only by the assurance of defined, generally well-known offer characteristics as quasi quality warranty from the advertisement. Under circumstances this leads to the increase of uncertainty by artificial complication of the purchase with introduction of social and psychological additional services, which are to be weighed beyond the pro and cons of the pure product achievement. The subjectively felt risk of a purchase rises with its by advertisement alleged external and internal effect.

Only advertising enables the realization of price reductions through mass media addressing with the broadest possible publicity by means of higher quantities from mass production, procurement and sales. However, there is the danger of price remanence and the inclusion of advertising costs in the price through apportionment. If there is no compulsion to pass on any cost reductions, e.g. in the case of procedural monopolies, coordinated oligopolies, etc., such prices can also be enforced on the market. Thus, advertising-intensive industries may promote inefficiencies by retaining non-performance margins. Incidentally, by building up monopolies of opinion on preferences, advertising generally leads to a reduction in primary price competition and to a decrease in price responsiveness. The tacit prerequisite for this assertion is also that advertising per se is capable of creating more sales. However, this very effect remains controversial. It is hardly possible to conclusively prove what share which advertising measures have in the market success of an offer, or not. An impressive argument, which is often used recklessly by the advertising industry, is that tobacco sales in countries with a ban on tobacco advertising after its introduction will remain constant or even increase. These results suggest that a rather loose causality between advertising and market-wide sales success can be assumed. Even if a direct positive correlation is assumed, this argument only applies to competitive markets, i.e. those in which strong competition forces cost savings to be passed on in the price. However, the reality of highly concentrated markets speaks against this. For example, cost savings may just as well be fully or partially retained by the manufacturer as an increase in profit.

Intermediary advertising in particular serves to open up new sources of supply for consumers. This leads to an expansion of alternative uses in the existing market and promotes the entry of new suppliers, e.g. by implementing the innovator's pension resulting from technical progress. However, high advertising expenses also act as market barriers for new suppliers who are not yet able to cope with these initial expenses. At best, integrated groups are able to do this by internal cross-subsidization of their divisions. As a result, there is a tendency to cement market conditions and possibly inhibit the progressive impact of functioning markets. This can lead to distortion of competition and misallocation of scarce resources.

Advertising which stimulates consumption expands markets and thus has a positive impact on the economic cycle. As a result, overall economic growth and the individual and consequently general impression of prosperity are promoted. However, advertising also tempts consumers to spend their money unnecessarily by creating a social climate which stimulates a steady quantitative and qualitative increase in the level of consumption as overbuying. This may lead to social dissatisfaction in those parts of the population which cannot keep up with these expectations. The extent to which such behavior is still justifiable in the face of dwindling resources remains doubtful.

Tailored fulfillment of needs as a result of fine market segmentation increases buyer satisfaction by giving them the chance to choose exactly those offers which best fit their preferred lifestyle. However, there is a tendency towards hypersegmentation with the resulting lower market transparency and purchase security. In particular, there is the danger of manipulating the buyers by means of sophisticated social engineering, from which one can no longer escape, whether one wants to or not, and which therefore has an obsessive effect as an externally guided consumer and runs opposite to the liberal element of the market economy. Only a subjectively felt benefit serves as an equivalent for the money spent in connection with the purchase decision. The fact is that advertising often generates such expectations of benefit in the first place. To differentiate the offers, for example, unnecessary additional services which make the goods more expensive are presented as indispensable, social or psychological mechanisms are used to build up a subjectively perceived compulsion to buy, or products which are subject to artificial obsolescence are suggested for new purchase. This means that benefit expectations are not concretized, but created in order to create sales potential for the own offer.

The stabilization of demand through preference formation for the brand and monopolization on the market as to price stability is a prerequisite for companies to plan market activities. This in turn is essential due to the increasing fixed cost burden of production. Advertising is the only effective instrument for this. However, advertising expenses build up an additional fixed cost burden, especially procyclically, and thus further increase the supplier risk. Furthermore, this market power-oriented attitude tempts companies to establish offers on the market via pure penetration and the generation of artificially created demand in order to save at least parts of inflexible investments.

Advertising measures lead to an increase in the quality of the market offer through the announcement and dominance of the most advantageous offers in terms of performance, price or price-performance ratio. However, low share of advertising reduces the market opportunities for high-performance offers, which do not bear the high advertising costs, especially at the beginning of their market existence and especially with new providers. This means that advertising primarily has a structure-preserving effect as long as not all providers can afford the same advertising pressure. In this respect, it is conceivable that, contrary to the philosophy of political order, the dominance of performance-based offers may occur, especially if their false qualities are not obvious or verifiable. At first glance, the important regulatory function for promoting the providers' performance awareness seems obvious. In fact, however, advertising expenditure probably serves for the most part rather to neutralize unproductive competition and thus has a restrictive effect on market entry. Ultimately, only the balance of advertising investment can have an acquisition effect; the masses represent a macroeconomic waste of funds and effectively exclude new providers from attractive markets, unless they take advantage of internal subsidy benefits from diversification and can accept more or less long phases of initial losses. Ultimately, advertising may even lead to poorer market results in so far as their costs are passed on by the providers in the price according to the viability principle.

Advertising facilitates the diffusion of new products in the market by means of offer announcement, differentiation and profiling. It thus reduces the risk of introduction and promotes innovation as an opportunity for a faster return on investment on the part of companies. However, the danger of product hectic on the market due to extremely short life cycles as a result of physiological and/or psychological obsolescence cannot be ignored. Likewise, the compulsive product differentiation of similar products promotes an artificial heating of the demand influence.

The control of the use of advertising according to time, space, personnel and material dimensions allows the smooth adjustment of the sales conditions to the supply conditions of goods and services. However, it is precisely the demand which is adapted to the supply and not, as is desirable for an emancipated market economy, vice versa, the supplier potential is used to satisfy shortages based on consumer wishes. Whereby it is to be noted that demand from itself is not creative, but can react always only to the market-present offer.

Through advertising, hundreds of thousands of specialized and thus highly value-added jobs are created in the advertising industry. And not only there, but also in the service supplementing industries of suppliers. However, advertising represents a waste of social resources, at least in the context of neutralization expenditures, which nowadays make up by far their largest share, which can overcompensate positive employment effects through their unproductive use and thus, from a macroeconomic point of view, rather lead to a reduction in prosperity. The fact that advertising, even if only a comparatively limited number, creates highly specialized and thus objectively immobile jobs cannot be cited as an ethical justification for this. The same applies to the armaments or nuclear power plant industries, for example, without it being possible to deduce a value claim for these or other industries. This means that a positive contribution to employment cannot be regarded as a sufficient argument in favor of advertising.

The advertising effort promotes media diversity through its cost-covering contribution to support the editorial program. By means of affordable prices, media are thus made accessible to broader sections of the population in the first place. However, the danger of the financial dependence of the editorships on the interests of large advertisers due to attempts to influence also the non-advertising contents of the advertising media, which cannot be excluded, is connected with it inseparably. Such dependence has political dimensions. In this respect, this assertion is indeed true. Many spectacular media offerings can only be financed by the overt or covert sale of advertising space. In view of the increasingly penetrating publishing and broadcasting programs, however, the question arises as to whether the price of this expanded and more interesting media offering will not soon be hypertrophied and a meaningful limit reached. Only readers and viewers who accept the inseparable advertising pressure based on archetypal influencing mechanisms can really enjoy these attractive contents.

Market research studies repeatedly reveal that consumers largely welcome advertising as informative and entertaining. Obviously, there is an audience-desired function of advertising, and it is not seen as mere hard selling, although the research design should be examined. However, advertising statements do not necessarily offer objectivity, naturally withhold certain information or exploit consumer ignorance. Here, the impression of manipulation arises again and again. This is the case if someone exerts influence for his own benefit while omitting the benefit of the recipient, provided that techniques are used which are difficult for him/her to understand and give the impression that he/she is free to decide on actions. First characteristic is thereby that the sender exercises his influence consciously and for the sake of the own advantage. This is undoubtedly the case with advertising. It is used in a planned manner and is intended to achieve certain economic and/or non-economic goals in advance, which increase the performance and competitiveness of the advertiser. Secondly, the influencer exerts this influence without regard to the advantage of the influenced. Even if the value proposition of advertising repeatedly suggests that the perception of an offer ultimately only serves the best of the people being advertised, the advantage effect remains relative. Thus advertisement is not at all able to recommend the objectively best problem solution to consumers, but naturally only the own offer, even if inferior to competition, is expenditure-praised. That the competition conditions of the market economy implicitly lead to best possible overall results in the satisfaction of the demanders is obvious. But this high level of performance is the result of a mixture of more or less good offers, especially when their objective quality is usually difficult or can only be determined afterwards. Thirdly, the influencing party consciously chooses techniques which are not or only with difficulty transparent to the influenced party. Here the unconscious advertising is in the focus. The controversy about subliminal perception is the main difference. In the meantime, it has been sufficiently proven that mechanistic forms of subliminal influence remain fiction. However, there is no doubt that even perceived advertising exerts a more or less intense unconscious influence which has an associative effect and thus in turn initiates mental processes which are largely beyond cognitive control. The majority of advertising messages are virtually designed to do this by making use of non-thematic content. Ultimately, the influenced person must retain the feeling of having freely decided on his or her judgment and action. This is also typical for advertising which is conditioned and aims at learning outcomes which result in successful actions with subjective autonomy of the target persons. Examples are the use of the herd instinct, the law of scarcity or the emphasis on commonalities. Thus advertising is undoubtedly manipulation. However, it is important to remember that manipulation also means seduction. And that is something quite positive. Because, who does not like to be seduced? And advertising seduces, for example, to buy a beautiful car, with which one can reach a destination more comfortably and safely, to buy a new hi-fi system, which elicits finesse from one's favorite songs for the first time, to buy a pack of cigarettes, whose smoke has a pleasurable relaxing and stimulating effect, to buy a wristwatch, which turns time into a completely new experience and so on.

It does not correspond to the reality that as a consumer you feel tricked by advertising after each purchase decision. The rule is that buying experiences are stimulating because of advertising impulses. And who does not use also in private life seduction arts, in order to reach egoistic goals, without this being equal reprehensible.

Consumers can finally think and are in the market-economy system by force of demand free sovereign, so that manipulation by no way is opened door and gate. However, consumers are traditionally poorly organized and atomistic, so there is no denying the problem of abuse of power by a lifestyle dictatorship which makes consumption the central, self-value-determining form of life. Particularly since the lack of rationality in their behavior makes it even more difficult. Thus, extensive basic rights for consumers are claimed, such as the formation of consumer organizations and consultations, the training of consumer behavior, the implementation of neutral product tests, a say in economic policy and legislation, and abuse control over companies and their liability. Other rights relate to the right to safety, protection against harmful products, objective product information, free choice between several substitutive products, and consultation in product design and marketing. However, this is far from being the case, and advertising is not a substitute for it, nor does it particularly help to support the rights being demanded. It seems unrealistic to want to reduce the wheel of communication development. But in view of the not inconsiderable reservations about the side effects and mechanisms of advertising, the desire to prevent its uncontrolled proliferation remains. At present, however, it is already subject to numerous controls. A look at the U.S. and the experience that American conditions generally spill over to Europe with time lag shows that extreme commercialization of the expression of opinion quickly has a penetrating effect. However, there is little hope of avoiding these conditions. For state sanctions are at best to be regarded as the last resort in solving this problem. And appeals to the advertising industry (manufacturers/service providers), to advertising intermediaries (agencies) and advertising media (publishers/broadcasters/tenants) must remain largely ineffective in view of the given manifest economic interests.

Ethics in advertising is therefore a particularly sensitive aspect. For this reason, the advertising industry has prescribed guidelines for the self-control of advertising in an act of anticipatory obedience. In contrast to legal regulations, violations of self-control guidelines do not entail legal sanctions. However, the rules do have an indirect legal effect, since the courts can use them as a basis for assessing the fairness of advertising measures.

The German advertising council is not as important as comparable institutions in other countries, which is partly due to the already tightly woven, differentiated German advertising law. However, the conflict-regulating effect of this ethical authority is of great importance. Public criticism of individual advertising measures finds access to those responsible through the German advertising council. In the case of justified criticism, the committee attempts to eliminate the nuisance; but it also protects the advertising industry if the criticism is unjustified. Even without a judge or injunction, disruptive advertising activities can be eliminated. The concrete activity refers to individual complaints, rules of conduct and information.

In the case of illegal, unwanted, or dubious advertising, the German advertising council acts on its own initiative or following suggestions and complaints from outsiders. According to the Council's rules of procedure, anyone is entitled to submit complaints, individual consumers, politicians, journalists or competitors; however, anonymous complaints will not be processed. An important task is the processing of statements and representations in advance of the statutory bodies. In the case of clear violations of the law, the matter will be forwarded to the Centre for protection against unfair competition, and in the case of a violation of the provisions of the law on the advertising of medicinal products, to the association for fair advertising of medicinal products. If the German advertising council feels the need to intervene, it may demand that the advertising measure be discontinued or modified. If there is no reaction, a public reprimand can be issued as the ultimate measure.

The development of guidelines is another important field of work. While the processing of complaints serves to correct mistakes and developments, the German advertising council tries to prevent them. At the same time, it promotes consumer-oriented advertising. These voluntary codes of conduct are monitored by the committee and the media with regard to compliance. Guidelines relate, among other things, to advertising with and in front of children in advertising radio and television, advertising with accident-prone images, advertising for alcoholic beverages, the depiction of women in advertising, etc.

It is also attempted to reduce the number of cases to be dealt with preventively by raising awareness of self-discipline through the communication of facts and information on developments and trends. To this end, all groups in the advertising industry, politicians, the media and other public sectors are kept constantly informed about the views, demands and developments in consumer policy, the work of the German advertising council and the legal decisions relevant to advertisers. This is intended to avoid state regulations in advance and to strengthen confidence in the liberal constitutional state and the willingness of its citizens to assume responsibility.

In addition, there are voluntary self-restrictions of the advertising industry. This is because the market is not a morally neutral zone. Therefore, the advertising industry in particular cannot escape the obligation of ethical behavior. The publicity of advertising causes the emergence of public criticism. The duty to act ethically is not limited to confronting this criticism, but also to promoting self-critical reflection and questioning one's own actions; it also means disciplining oneself without coercion. Individual industries accomplish this task through the voluntary establishment of rules of conduct.

In addition, there are arbitration boards for consumers at the Chambers of industry and commerce (IHK), which also mediate in advertising disputes. This service is not legally anchored, but has come about through private initiative. On an international level, the rules of conduct for advertising practice of the International chamber of commerce (ICC), which are constantly updated, are worth mentioning. There are special rules of conduct for direct mailings and advertising with environmental labels and arguments as well as the application and enforcement of the rules of conduct in marketing.

The public image of advertisers nevertheless is indeed tarnished. According to Forsa market research institute, employees in advertising agencies still rank behind politicians, union officials, tax inspectors and journalists and only just ahead of Telekom employees and insurance representatives. There is nothing more to say.

8. Marketing communications controlling

Marketing communications controlling refers to the degree of goal attainment, cost-efficiency and performance-effectiveness of advertising. The better the sender's message reaches the recipients, the higher the performance.

Efficiency means to do things right, whereas effectiveness means to do the right things. The relation between input and output is decisive for the assessment of whether one „does things correctly". For the evaluation, whether one does „the accurate things", however, the relation of input and target is to be questioned. The measurement of *efficiency* is therefore primarily quantitative and starts with the profitability of advertising. The measurement of *effectiveness*, on the other hand, is of a more qualitative nature and starts with the medium suitability of the advertising measures to achieve the target.

8.1 Measurement of advertising performance

Measurement is generally understood to be the assignment of numbers or symbols to objects, here: advertising measures. Measurement in the context of communication is considered particularly difficult because there are no clear criteria for such an unambiguous assignment. First of all, it is important to divide the generic term efficiency into two measurement areas, efficacy in the sense of efficiency and effectiveness. Both terms are often used synonymously, but this regularly leads to irritations about what exactly is to be measured.

It is important to separate efficacy and effectiveness when assessing advertising performance. For example, a measurement result which is achieved with the economic use of resources can be checked off as "adequate", but it can also be questioned whether a better result would not have been possible with a more appropriate design. If, on the other hand, a measurement result which does not meet economic efficiency requirements is claimed to be insufficient, it must still be examined to see whether internal or external resistances have prevented measures from having the desired effect.

The measurement of advertising efficacy can refer to two contents:

- The *advertising impact measurement* examines the achievement of qualitative advertising objectives, usually referred to as cognition, affection and conation.

- The *advertising success measurement* examines the achievement of quantitative advertising objectives. The elementary significance of this distinction is due to the fact that both target values are not equivalent, but are arranged rather in an end to end relationship, i.e. the advertising impact is a necessary, but not sufficient prerequisite for advertising success.

Another dimension of advertising performance is the differentiation according to the time of measurement. This can be done before the advertising is used (ex ante) or thereafter (ex post). It remains unsatisfactory to obtain clues about the presumed efficacy of activities only afterwards, i.e. after the advertising has taken place. Because then the advertising budget is already spent and can only be "saved" for the following periods.

The pre-measurement of advertising performance concerns the efficacy prognosis, the measurement afterwards the efficacy check.

		Content of measurement	
		Advertising impact	Advertising success
Time of measurement	Prognosis	Advertising impact prognosis	Advertising success prognosis
	Check	Advertising impact check	Advertising success check

Fig. 48: Types of marketing communications controlling

The two dimensions of controlling described so far, content and timing, are combined to form four fields of investigation (*for context see figure 48: Types of marketing communications controlling*):

- *Advertising success check* concerns the verification of the achievement of objectives in the form of purchase acts, often wrongly used as an umbrella term for the entire efficacy measurement (8.5).
- *Advertising impact check* concerns the verification of the achievement of objectives in the form of images, etc. (8.4).
- The *advertising success prognosis* concerns the prediction of the achievement of objectives in the form of purchase acts as behavior (8.3).
- And the *advertising impact prognosis* concerns the forecast of the target achievement in the form of images, etc. (8.2).

8.2 Advertising impact prognosis

Within the advertising impact prognosis, i.e. the prediction of the achievement of psychographic target values in advertising, various methods can be used (*see figure 49: Methods of advertising impact prognosis*).

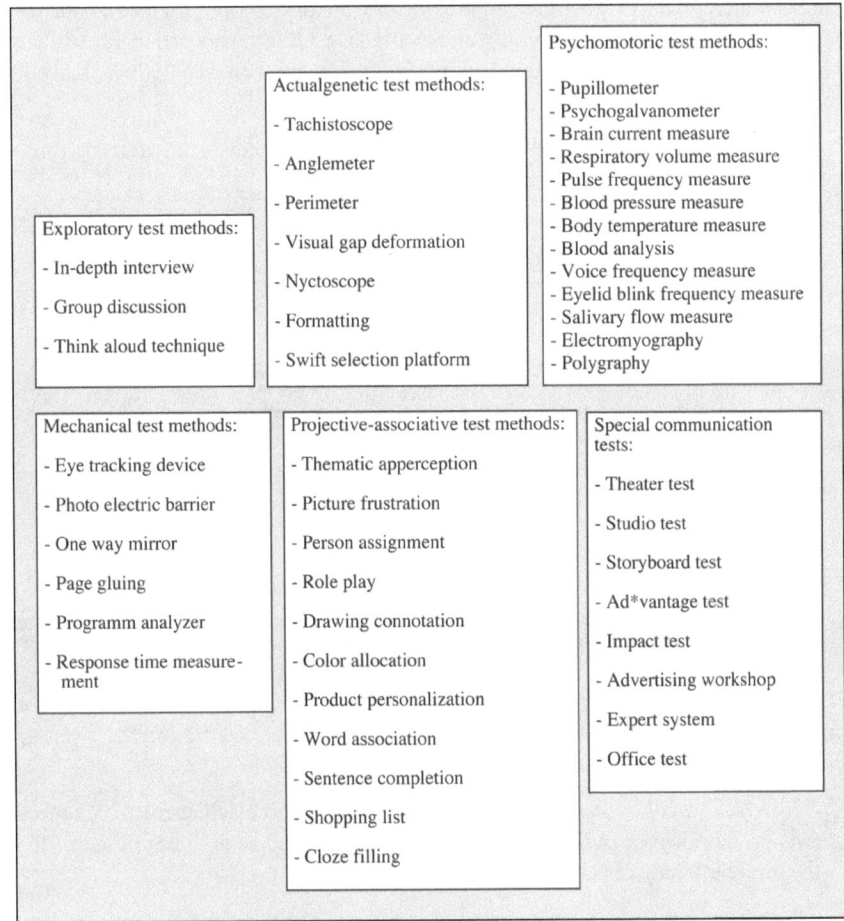

Fig. 49: Methods of advertising impact prognosis

8.2.1 Exploratory test methods

Exploratory test methods make use of surveys and group discussions as a means of forecasting advertising impact. The mostly oral *inquiry* is conducted as an in-depth interview by a psychologically trained interviewer. This intends to adapt the interview to the individuality of the respondent in order to establish a relationship of trust with increased willingness to provide personal information. The interview is based on a discussion guideline, the minutes are recorded on tape or by taking notes. However, there is considerable scope for interpretation. A test person is asked to deal intensively with an advertising medium intended for realization. Afterwards, the impression of the advertised product/environment is discussed. This is done successively in order to reach deeper and deeper layers of consciousness, where the causal factors for impressions are predisposed. However, for reasons of time and cost, this form of survey can practically always only take place in a small "headcount", so it makes no claim to represent the findings.

A very practicable form, however just as without any requirement on representation, is the *group discussion*. For this purpose, target persons, buyers, laymen, experts, etc. are invited to a round table discussion. Recruitment of the discussion partners is done from existing address files or by "digging" from the street. The discussion is led by an experienced psychologist, the duration is about one hour, the group size is 8–12 persons. The participants, who do not know each other, exchange views on attitudes, behavior, motives, etc. regarding a product specified by an advertising medium. There is also the possibility of unnoticed or undetected covered participation. Group dynamic effects lead to a dialog. Women are generally more communicative than men. However, there is a risk that opinion leaders in the group will try to control the course of the discussion and dominate the opinions of others. Group discussions, however, otherwise provide good insights into the unbiased view of the target persons. They are also inexpensive and can be conducted quickly.

In *"think aloud"*, a test person gives an oral record of the thoughts which occupy him or her when selecting, evaluating and deciding on advertising messages for products. These are recorded on paper/sound file and thus allow an evaluation of the voting behavior, the pros and cons of a purchase decision. Purchase decision protocols can be created across several test subjects, revealing the system of information, conclusions, prerequisites, etc. and the role of advertising messages in this process. This knowledge is important for the further procedure, because exactly those contents should be transported which turn out to be decisive in the protocol.

However, all of these procedures suffer from the lack of consciousness-controlled statements. If one assumes that advertising effects are essentially emotional in nature, the filter of the mind lies between the actual advertising effect and its measurement. This means that statements are distorted and do not reflect the causal factors, but only the mind-distorted form of these factors. Therefore, attempts are made to arrive at measured variables in a different way.

8.2.2 Actualgenetic test methods

Actualgenetic test methods work with means of perceptual difficulty. Advertising which has a special consistency of shape is more successful than others. There are many different procedures for this, here only the most important ones.

In the case of the *tachistoscope*, the quick-release fastener of a beamer lens makes it possible to present advertising motifs for an extremely short period of time, well below 1/20 second, where the human eye can still perceive images, but no longer consciously recognize them. The presentation time is continuously extended. An advertising template is considered the "better" the shorter the time span for its correct identification. The main problem is the artificial test situation, which may lead to the test subject's attention being drawn too much in order to "score" particularly well in the test. It is also unclear which conclusions can be drawn from the fact that an advertising object is only "seen" as a tree, witch, mountain or similar for an extremely short span of time. Therefore, perception theory today is based on different principles than those of holistic psychology.

The *anglemeter* displays advertising material in a distorted perspective as side, top and bottom views, as is often the case in reality. With the *perimeter*, an advertising object is displayed at the edge of the eye's field of vision, which is also a practically frequent perception situation, for example when passing through billboards. With the *visual gap deformation*, only a small section is recognizable as a keyhole effect of the overall motif, it is questionable whether this is already correctly identified from this, which would be positive. With the *nyctoscope*, the ambient brightness is continuously increased, starting with total obscuration. The sooner an advertising medium can be recognized, the better. During *formatting*, the advertising medium is reduced or enlarged to simulate viewing distances. In each case, the "best" advertising media are those which are still correctly identified under the most unfavorable conditions. However, all these methods only measure pure perception, which is at best a prerequisite for advertising impact. The actual effect, on the other hand, is only achieved when the advertising medium is dealt with more closely/for longer/more frequently.

The *swift-selection platform* is a stage-like apparatus, which releases several advertising media, e.g. advertisement proofs, for a short time, of which the test person has to choose one spontaneously before the curtain closes again a short time later. This allows, above all, to test the assertiveness in direct comparison of several advertising media. This is certainly relevant in view of the explicit competitive orientation of most markets and the gigantic information overflow there.

8.2.3 Psychomotoric test methods

Psychomotoric test methods rely on involuntary bodily reactions that cannot be influenced by humans, since it is assumed that verbal statements of the test subjects are always mentally distorted. Again, there are many different procedures, here the most important ones.

The *pupillometer* measures the change in the pupil size of the test person between "normal state" and the presentation of an advertising medium. A change in size means psychological activation, i.e. emotional involvement with the advertising message, which is interpreted as a good sign. Problematic here is the uncertainty about the quality of the activation, i.e. enthusiasm or frightening. This in turn can only be determined by questioning.

A *psychogalvanometer* measures the skin resistance, which increases in comparison to the "normal state" in the tonic level during activation by perception of an advertising message as a result of sweat secretion on the skin surface in the phasic level. For this purpose, a low-voltage current is passed through electrodes on the underside of the hand or foot and the resistance of the skin is measured. High loss of current means high resistance and low perspiration therewith low activation. The main problem is the unfavorable relation between the high basic resistance of the skin and the extremely low potential change. In addition, changes in the resistance value can be caused by many other factors besides activation.

Via *electroencephalography* (EEG) measuring sensors on the scalp are used to infer mental activation when an advertising medium is presented. Beta waves with high frequency and low amplitude indicate here that a conscious confrontation is taking place.

The *respiratory volume measurement* also indicates activation, because a higher activation requires more oxygen, i.e. higher respiratory volume. The same applies to measurements of *pulse frequency, blood pressure* or *body temperature.*

Blood analysis can be used to determine the hormone release as an activation indicator before, during and after the presentation of an advertising medium. The *voice frequency* is influenced by respiratory rate, muscle tension and tremor, the measurement of which very reliably indicates activation. In addition, it does not require any disturbing equipment or the presence of third parties. Furthermore, an increased *eyelid frequency* indicates activation for better fluid distribution on the retina and thus for better vision.

In advertisements for food products, the *salivary flow* with test persons indicates the "appetite appeal". This can be measured with a probe similar to the saliva aspiration at the dentist. Muscle changes in the face are measured by *electromyography* and compared with normalized muscle constellations in a "facial atlas" for which the respective psychological interpretation is known. Finally, *polygraphy* works analogously to the lie detector by parallel measurement of breathing, peripheral blood circulation, pulse rate and skin resistance.

The major problem with this and similar procedures is that only body reactions are measured and a reliable connection to the advertising impact is claimed for them. This connection is however very questionable, assured only is that the bare body reactions are measured, thus pupil size, skin resistance, brain waves, etc. Which conclusions one can draw from it, remains then extremely speculative.

8.2.4 Mechanical test methods

Mechanical test methods make use of non-participatory observation to avoid interference. There are a variety of methods for this purpose, again following the most important ones.

The *eye mark recorder* uses a device similar to ski goggles to record the course of the pupils' gaze over an advertising medium and displays it on a monitor. This makes it possible to recognize which elements of an original are really perceived, these are fixations, and which are indeed ignored, these are saccades. The sequence, repetition and total duration of the viewing can also be displayed. The main problem is the test situation which is far from reality because of forced exposure. Other methods, such as Compagnon, make an unconscious video recording of the perception through a plate mirrored on one side. This macro effect, however, only makes it possible to identify which pages of a submitted test booklet are opened for how long, but not what the viewing pattern of adverts in it is like. Again, interpretation is problematic, because a long/repeated viewing can, for example, also be based quite simply on incomprehensibility of the statement instead of special interest.

The *light barrier* is used to measure the passing frequency or the viewing distance of test persons to an advertising medium. The infrared measurement serves the same purpose. *One-way mirrors* through a thin silver layer on a glass pane and darkened observation space behind them allow above all the evaluation of body language through gestures, facial expressions, etc. of test persons when confronted with an advertising medium. This can be photographed or video recorded. The easy *gluing of advertisement pages* in a test booklet provides information about which pages have been opened and which have not, even without the presence of observers.

The *program analyzer* consists of two joysticks, one each for favors and dislikes, which are to be operated during a commercial presentation. The test person should trigger the signal generator which corresponds to his current perception quality. A time comparison can be used to identify which elements in commercials cause exactly positive or negative reactions.

The *response time measurement* is computer-aided and evaluates how much time passes between the appearance of a question about the advertising medium on the monitor and the answer input via the keyboard. This is seen as an indication of the degree of conviction. The imperative is the shorter, the better.

The goal of avoiding observation effects is thus bought here by numerous imponderables, which affect the meaningfulness of the results in terms of advertising impact.

8.2.5 Projective-associative test methods

Projective test methods work with the third person technique as a survey experiment. This is based on the assumption that opinions which are valid for one's own person but are not expressed for social reasons such as taboo, desirability, etc. are instead projected into fictional third persons. Welcome help is offered for this. Through associative test procedures, spontaneous, undirected connections between advertising messages and memory or emotional content in the experiential environment are provoked. Again, there are various procedures for both approaches.

In *thematic apperception test*, test persons are presented with a series of more or less blurred photos showing typical purchase and consumption situations with the advertised product. A story is told to show how the product to be advertised is included. In the *picture frustration test*, product-related conflicts between two people are presented as caricatures with speech bubbles. A speech bubble remains open and is to be filled in by the test person. Again, it is interesting in which form the product to be advertised is included. In the *person assignment test*, a series of portrait photos, but also animal symbols, quotations, car brands, etc., are to be assigned to different advertised products as typical for them. From this, their point of view is inferred.

The same applies to *role-playing*, in which the advertised product is to be assigned a role in a social relationship, or to *drawing tests*, in which test persons are asked to draw the product to be advertised as a symbol such as a tree or a house. From this, the test person's point of view is deduced. In the *assignment of colors*, typical colors should be related to advertised products. The assignment is interpreted according to the findings of color psychology. In *product personification*, characteristics such as strengths, weaknesses, greatest achievements, career, etc. of products to be advertised are asked for.

In the *word association test* (WAT), test persons are asked to name terms which come to their mind spontaneously, i.e. under time pressure, for emotive words related to the product to be advertised. With the *sentence completion test* (SCT) sentence beginnings are given with the product to be advertised, which are to be completed by test persons after personal evaluation.

The *shopping list test* (Dichter) gives two shopping lists, which are otherwise identical up to the product of interest, e. g. instant coffee, in one list resp. a substitutive product, e. g. coffee beans, in the other. Test persons are asked to characterize the householder behind these lists according to given criteria. Differences between the results then can only be attributed to the product to be advertised.

The *cloze text* provides product-related sentences with gaps left open, which usually have to be filled in by adjectives or attributes completed by test persons. In each case, the product's point of view can be inferred from these associations.

8.2.6 Special communication tests

Communication tests include procedures which have been specially developed for advertising impact prognosis. In the *theater test*, test persons are first asked to select from a list of competing products, which they would like to receive as a prize later on, before a film screening (so-called pre-choice) begins. The same request is made after the screening (so-called post-choice), under the pretext of an unsuccessful first entry. Changes in preferences are then attributed to the advertising which has been shown in the meantime.

The *Ad*vantage test* (GfK) is a consultancy product as combination of these methods. It determines both the recall of commercials within a 1.5-hour TV program with commercial breaks as well as opinions and preferences before and after their presentation with regard to the advertised product. For advertisements, test persons are asked to leaf through a folder containing the advertising material to be tested while distracting questions are asked. Again, opinions and preferences are measured. The impact test measures the recall of the advert and individual advert elements in a similar way. The studio test measures the recall of individual advertising spots after a block of about ten spots with competing motifs have been presented.

In the *storyboard test*, the essential scenes of an advert are illustrated by draft, animated or cut as "stealomatic" and are assessed according to their impression on the target persons of the advert. In *advertising workshops* a group of target persons from the focus group is confronted with advertising material drafts and invited to an informal exchange of ideas.

These and other constructions, no matter how elaborate they may be, can always only ascertain the advertising impact as a prerequisite, but do not make any statements about the market success of the advertisement. Even computer-supported procedures as expert systems, which not only evaluate advertising motifs by machine on the basis of given knowledge modules, but also constructively create suggestions for better implementation on the basis of this knowledge, change little about this.

A widespread form is also the *office test*. For this purpose, apparently uninvolved persons in the environment, in practice often cleaning staff, are arbitrarily asked about their subjective assessment of the presumed effect of the use of planned advertising media ("this appeals me"). This is undoubtedly by far the worst of all the variants listed. Nevertheless, astonishingly enough, far-reaching decisions are still made dependent on it.

8.3 Advertising success prognosis

Within the advertising success prognosis, i. e. the prediction of the achievement of economic targets, various methods can be used (*see figure 50: Methods of advertising success prognosis*).

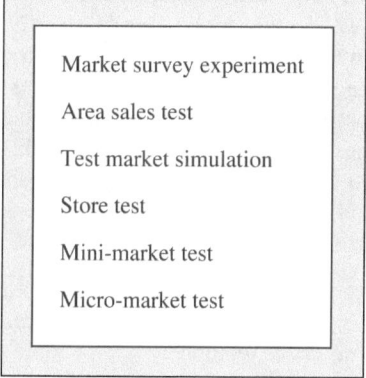

Fig. 50: Methods of advertising success prognosis

The *market survey experiment* is based on a test market in which two groups of target persons are surveyed with regard to their market-relevant behavior, one group, the experimental group, which is exposed to the advertising to be measured in its success, and a second, the control group, which is not exposed to this advertising. If all other relevant characteristics are identical in both groups, differences in behavior, i.e. purchase or non-purchase or purchase intensity/frequency, can only be attributed to the influence of advertising. Several experimental designs can be used for this purpose, the most common being the EBA – CBA design. The experimental group (E) as well as the control group (C) are measured at the beginning of the test (B), i.e. before the application in the experimental group, and after the application (A) with regard to their respective purchasing behavior. This means that deviations in the initial situation as group effects and due to temporal over-radiation as carry-over effects as well as external factors as spill-over effects and unavoidable learning results as development effects cannot be avoided, but are nevertheless arithmetically recognizable. This results in the prospective advertising success. However, these disruptive factors not only influence the output variables, but also lead to distortions as interaction effects which cast doubt on the meaningfulness of the result. Only formal experimental designs can provide a remedy, but these are difficult to implement in practice due to their unrealistic premises.

The *area sales test* concerns the trial use of the planned advertising in a well-defined market area, or alternatively in the other market area if advertising is omitted, with measurement of the respective sales results. If a product has already been distributed and advertised, but is to be tested with regard to a change in advertising, only one market area is sufficient. The prerequisite is the isomorphic condition, i.e. the similarity of demand, i.e. sociodemography, purchasing power, etc., trade, i.e. structure, assortment, etc., competition, i.e. type, size, etc., and media with regard to availability, use, etc., both between the test area and to the intended overall market. Then, but only then, can conclusions be drawn about sales/prices which result from the use of certain advertising media in comparison to a situation without advertising or in the case of a changed or increased use of advertising in comparison to the existing advertising known in its success. In practice especially the isomorphic condition is hardly to be fulfilled. In addition, the size of many test markets causes considerable costs for product stock, spreading budget, etc., and secrecy towards the competition is no longer guaranteed. There is also the danger of over-testing and a lack of stabilization of the repurchase rate with longer purchase intervals.

Therefore, test market replacement methods are increasingly used. They dispense with the high demands of area sales tests, which cannot be met anyway, and instead look for more practicable methods.

The *test market simulation* is the realistic reproduction of the market reality in model form, e.g. by means of shopping situations simulated in a studio, and its simulation in a realistic way, e.g. with shopping vouchers for test persons. After recruiting the test persons, an initial interview is conducted on product-related attitudes and behavior. Afterwards, the test subjects are confronted with the advertising media to be tested, usually in a realistic environment like video advertising block, advertising folder, etc. This is followed by the actual purchase simulation in a competitive environment. The products purchased must be paid for with own money at real prices, taking the vouchers into account. In the post-purchase interview, reasons for buying or not buying are ascertained. Non-buyers receive the advertised product free of charge. The test persons are then supposed to use the products in their private environment. In the final interview, product evaluation and advertising influence are queried.

The *store test* involves the evaluation of the trial use of new/changed advertising under largely controlled sales conditions, but in 30–50 real stores which are specifically recruited and distributed for this purpose. The procedure includes stocking the stores with the test product, using the advertising in the catchment area of these stores and determining the volume of purchases there. Frequently, a design from two test areas with retail panels is used with stores which are otherwise comparable, and covered in two periods alternating with existing advertising and new advertising.

In a *mini-market test*, not only the sales side but also the reaction of the customers is realistically recorded by including household panels. To this end, regular buyers in the test stores identify themselves with an identification card assigned to them when they make their purchases, so that the sales made can be allocated to individual customers according to their cause. The other elements, such as stockpiling, advertising influence, etc., remain unchanged. This approach offers the great advantage of being able to draw from a single source, i. e. the traders included in the panel sell exactly those goods which are used in households also included in the panel. Thus, one does not only experience global values, but also specific statements. However, only on the output side, i. e. the advertising input is not sufficiently controllable. Likewise, there is no way to prevent households from making relevant purchases in stores other than the test stores or from selling them by test stores to households other than the panel households. Therefore, the desire for further influence on the test design has arisen.

The *micro-market test* is a combination of household panel for recording consumer behavior, retail panel with scanner cash register for in-store sales recording via GTIN/global trade item number barcode and household identification card, locally controlled TV and print advertising as well as supporting sample and leaflet distribution in a selected location (Haßloch/BehaviorScan/MarketLab). The results are presented in a management report.

It is important to note that the underlying data are not test results, but rather real purchasing behavior to meet household needs. Thus, in Haßloch in Rhineland Palatinate, a targeted approach of each individual wired household with TV advertising is possible, also separated into experimental and control groups. Furthermore, the market area is well defined, can be operated economically and is sufficiently representative according to population structure and purchasing power. The involvement of the retail is contractually secured. This is again a single-source approach and, thanks to the high-tech facility, the most elaborate method for forecasting advertising success. However, the costs amount to approximately € 100,000, which is however a good investment in view of the imminent losses for larger companies when using suboptimal advertising. However, only bulk goods of daily use (so-called fast moving consumer goods/FMCGs) with a short repurchase rate in food retail can be tested. For niche products, the absolute number of target persons is too low. Regional peculiarities cannot be reproduced, nor can the listing acceptance of retail. In addition, there is a risk of over-testing the area, not least through advertising overspending. Also, no qualitative statements, e. g. likes/dislikes, are made about the advertising, i. e. no indications of improvement in the case of unsatisfactory success are given.

8.4 Advertising impact check

Within an advertising impact check, i.e. monitoring the achievement of psychographic targets, various methods can be used (*see figure 51: Methods of advertising impact check*).

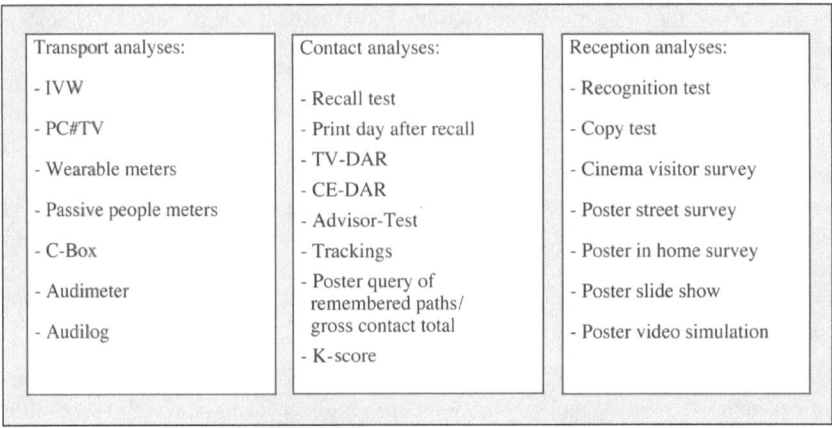

Fig. 51: Methods of advertising impact check

8.4.1 Transport analyses

A contact analysis determines whether the communication could potentially come into contact with target persons. In the print sector, the circulation and thus the technical reach is checked by external auditors (*IVW*/Information association for the determination of the distribution of advertising media). Advertisers who comply with the IVW statutes, which require, among other things, a precisely itemized reporting of the circulation and the approval of random checks on site, may use the IVW logo, which is a seal of quality in the industry, in their advertising media. This is particularly important in the context of professional advertising, where the structure of the readership is also evaluated. This ensures at least the circulation of the advertising medium.

In the case of electronic media, the technical reach is decisive. Here, contact can be established in three ways: Firstly, terrestrially, i.e. via antenna, secondly, via cable connection, and thirdly, orbitally, i.e. via satellite. In this order, the range decreases while the number of channels increases. This means that the highest chances of contact are given to programs received via antenna, because they have the greatest technical range and the least competition from other programs. However, the technical range says nothing about the usage.

For TV, usage is therefore surveyed by *PC#TV* television research (GfK). For this purpose, an additional device (TC Score) is inserted between the antenna socket and the TV set in 5,640 representative households with about 14,800 persons. The TC Score records when TV sets are switched on and off and which programs are called up by viewers in between. The date, time, duration and demographic data of the viewers are displayed. Likewise, it can also identify teletext, online/PC or DVD operations. The results are transferred by remote data transmission at night to a central computer, from where they can be called up the next morning ready for evaluation. Special analyses record, among other things, visual usage, program structure, vision migration/station bond/overlapping. These data are the basis for the ratings given in the media as people ostensibly present in front of devices which are switched-on on a station at airtime and for the evaluation of the placement of switched-on or possible future commercials. However, there have been some irregularities in the evaluation in the past which give cause for concern.

For the recording, each person in the household has to log in and out individually as a viewer. Up to seven people plus one guest are recorded. Provided that the selected households are representative, that their television usage does not change under the influence of the recording, that each person always logs on and off properly and watches television attentively during the registration period, the data obtained do indeed provide information on media performance.

However, doubts are justified, especially whether these numerous requirements are met. Therefore other methods are used. *Wearable meters* are worn on the body of the test person, e.g. as a wristband, and respond to audio signals within range of the TV or radio set, allowing the identification of which stations are switched on at any given time. *Passive people meters* measure whether a person is within range of the TV or radio based on the body's own heat radiation. Both can at least ensure the physical presence of test persons at the time of the advertising broadcast. In the *C-Box*, a camera lens is built into the measuring device, which records the audience in front of the TV set and thus provides further information on whether or not the test person is attentive when receiving the advertising.

For radio, similar procedures as for TV spots are used, the recording is done by means of an audimeter between the antenna socket and the radio or by writing it down as an audio log. An additional problem is the much smaller number of cases due to the fractionation of the audience to different broadcasting stations.

Especially problematic is the control of advertising effectiveness in outdoor advertising. For lack of a better basis, practical experience (API formula) is assumed as the basis for determining the performance values.

8.4.2 Contact analyses

Ad hoc surveys, which are conducted on a case-by-case basis, include a variety of procedures. The *recall test* examines a target person's recall of advertising media. A distinction is made between the aided recall under specification of the advertiser to be surveyed and unaided recall without such support, the latter being the much harder value. Spontaneous recall and, in addition, individual communication contents are collected.

The *print-day after recall* (P-DAR) surveys people who receive a magazine for review through follow-up interviews regarding their recollection of individual adverts by going through the magazine page by page with them and asking for recollection. *TV-DAR* measures the recall of commercials broadcast the day before by people who claim to have watched television. The problem is the very low percentage of viewers who remember any commercials at all, and if they do, then unfortunately often incorrectly. For this reason, the same day recall (SDR) asks for reminders by telephone on the same day the commercials are broadcast.

In *controlled exposure-day after recall* (CE-DAR), people are first shown a block of commercials in the studio, while distracting questions are asked. The next day, these people are then asked about their advertising recollection. Although this is much more economical to survey, it is also more unrealistic. In the *ADVISOR* test, the test persons are also pre-recruited, motivated to watch TV in a targeted manner and then asked about their recollection of the particular spot for the tested product.

In *tracking studies*, changing, but representative persons, in contrast to the panel, of the target group are questioned at regular intervals about their advertising recall. In this respect, it is a matter of continuous monitoring of the advertising impactt in terms of assertiveness as recall and impression value as impact. From this, changes in the competitive environment and changes in advertising expenditure can be concluded. Practically all major market research institutes offer such wave surveys as standard information services.

In the outdoor advertising sector, there is the poster survey based on *remembered paths* (GfK) and the *gross contact total* (Nielsen). This shows the performance of an outdoor advertising medium on a working day for an average daytime hour between 7:00 a.m. and 7:00 p.m. as well as for an average attention-grabbing poster and for all groups of passers-by, i.e. pedestrians, car drivers, public transport passengers, in each traffic flow, i.e. main flow and counterflow. GPS measurements and telephone interviews with 40,000 representatively selected people serve as a basis. The sum of the values results in the *K-score*, calculated with 10.5 days per decade. Weighted criteria for the site condition are the duration of the contact chance, the minimum lateral distance to the traffic flow, the possible concealment of the poster site, the poster sites in the vicinity, the angle of the poster site to the roadway, the environment complexity, and the possible lighting.

8.4.3 Reception analyses

A recipient analysis determines whether communication has actually conveyed the desired message to target persons. In the print sector, this is traditionally done through *recognition tests*. The global value is broken down to its elements by going through templates in advertising media one by one and breaking them down into whether test persons have noticed the advertising medium in question ("noted"), whether they correctly state the advertised product or advertiser as brand ("seen"/"associated") and whether they have actually used this advertising medium predominantly ("read most"). In the controlled recognition test, fake adverts are also included in the template in order to quantify misstatements which are actually very common.

Publishing houses also use these methods intensively to optimize their editorial content in *copy tests*. They offer advertisers, who are represented with adverts in the corresponding magazine copy, to join in free of charge with a limited number of individual additional questions.

With regard to movie theater advertising, they use on-site *cinema visitor surveys* are common or, after asking visitors for their telephone number, call them by phone and one day later.

For outdoor advertising, the recipient analysis is very difficult. One possibility is *street surveys* of passers-by behind a billboard after recognition of a motif. With the *in-home survey*, photos of poster motifs are queried after recognition. In the *poster slide show*, these motifs are presented tachistoscopically integrated in the real environment. In the *poster video simulation*, a journey through the streets of the city is carried out with a query of the poster motifs recognized in the process.

8.5 Advertising success check

Within the advertising success check, i.e. the monitoring of the achievement of economic targets, again various methods can be used (*see figure 52: Methods of advertising success check*).

Panel surveys are generally understood to be procedures which are carried out repeatedly at regular intervals for a specific, constant group of survey units, i.e. persons, households, trade outlets, companies, etc., on the same subject of investigation as a longitudinal analysis.

The *consumer panel* collects needs and attitudes individually and aggregated for consumable goods and durable goods representatively from end consumers resp. users, namely individuals or households. Purchases are recorded by writing them down as household accounts or by reading the GTIN codes on packages

8. Marketing communications controlling

> Consumer panel
>
> STAS-Potenzial
>
> Ordering with reference to advertising
>
> Direct survey
>
> Advertising elasticity
>
> Return on advertising invest

Fig. 52: Methods of advertising success check

using hand scanners or smartphones. The evaluation is carried out at short notice. All households and individuals must live and buy in the area of distribution of the advertisement. The market success of new or modified advertising can then be read from the panel figures. *Results* refer, among others, to the following:

- Purchases in quantity/value of the individual/household per check period,
- purchase quantity in % of parent product category,
- price per quantity as average purchase price,
- number of purchase acts at least once within the check period,
- buyer penetration as share of buyers of the product in all buyers of the product category,
- buyer penetration as share of buyers of the product in all panel members,
- number of repeat buyers having bought at least twice within the check period,
- number of repeat buyers in % as share of repeat buyers in all buyers of the product,
- demand coverage rate as share of the product in all purchases of the individual/household,
- purchase quantity/value per buyer on average.

However, there are numerous problems. Panel mortality is caused by the departure of participants due to fluctuation, contribution fatigue, death, marriage, relocation, etc. and can be as high as 50% p. a. This loss is continuously compensated by participants held in reserve, although the definition criterion of the same group of people therewith is increasingly being lost. In addition, panel routine occurs, i. e. the regular follow-up of purchases is missed. This inevitably leads to distorted results.

The panel effect causes a change in behavior under the impression of the purchase registration. Overreporting refers to purchases indicated by end customers which are actually not made, e. g. for reasons of prestige. Underreporting refers to purchases which are actually made but not indicated, e. g. taboo products. One tries to counter these problems by rotating the participants, giving small rewards for participation and a "learning phase" without data evaluation.

In connection with TV advertising, the *STAS potential* (short-term advertising strength) is cited. It measures the difference between the purchases of a particular brand by households which have not seen advertising for the brand in question in the seven days preceding the purchase and those households which have seen it in the seven days preceding the purchase. The starting point here is the ability of commercials to assert themselves in a competitive advertising environment. However, doubts about the validity of these findings are warranted.

The possibility for *order with explicit reference to advertising* is classically given with order coupons in the context of direct advertising in media. The identification of the occupied advertising medium, e. g. by means of a code printed in adverts or the final digit of the telephone number mentioned in a TV spot, superficially allows an easy efficiency comparison. However, this is only really the case if an offer has not been advertised via any other channel apart from this medium. In reality, this is rarely the case due to the media mix used in most cases. In fact, it is possible to measure the success of teleshopping offers which are only offered once.

In the *direct survey*, target persons are asked about the influence of advertising on their purchase decision. This requires on the one hand the identification of the persons actually reached by advertising, and on the other hand their opinion survey. However, both are questionable in practice. For example, experience shows that people who claim to know an offer from advertising may in fact just as well have come into contact with it via other communication channels. In addition, it is hardly possible, even from a purely subjective point of view, to trace the causation of certain advertising for the purchase. In this respect, however, the success of advertising cannot be sufficiently isolated and monitored.

Advertising elasticity is the quotient of advertising-related changes in sales as a consequence in the enumerator and variations in advertising expenditure as a cause in the denominator. It lies between 0 and ∞. A value of 1 indicates a proportional change in advertising budget and sales, a value < 1 indicates that the change in sales is less than the change in advertising budget which causes it, i. e. sales increase/decrease less than the change in advertising expenditure. Advertising elasticity is then rigid, whereas a value > 1 indicates that it is greater, i. e. sales increase/decrease more than advertising expenditure, and advertising elasticity is then flexible. In direct comparison with competitors, the cross advertising elasticity can be used to calculate the relationship between competing advertising budgets and product sales.

Although this is theoretically well feasible, in practice this approach to advertising effectiveness control fails because the change in turnover caused by a change in the advertising budget must remain unknown, because changes in turnover can be caused by many factors other than changes in advertising expenditure. However, this means that the values for the coefficient and the overall elasticity are missing.

RoAI (return on advertising invest) is based on the investment theoretical net present value method. The minimum required return on advertising invest plays a central role in the assessment. In essence, it this the relationship between the expected return on an advertising activity and its actual commercial result. The result is thus linked to the individually required return. For evaluation purposes, all activities must therefore be viewed in a uniform time period or standardized by discounting on end value/finish date or present value/start date. According to this, an advertising activity cannot alone be classified as successful because it at least recovers its costs, but only when it generates a return above the required minimum return on the budget used. This minimum return is in turn dependent on the income from the allocation of possible alternative activities. At the very least, a return is to be achieved with a largely risk-free, systemic investment of the amount on the capital market. However, this is usually not sufficient, as the endowment of advertising activities also entails the risk of the loss of the involved amout, which means that a risk premium must be included. This is to be determined on a company-specific basis depending on the individual risk aversion, then higher, or risk greed, then lower. So only when the return on capital employed is above the systemic and individual return requirements advertising success can be determined. Of two or more advertising activities, the one with the highest return on investment is comparatively the best.

8.6 Problems of advertising test methods

Because of the qualitative nature of the advertising test matter, there are significant problems, which arise and are discussed in the following.

8.6.1 Potential problems with pre-tests

Some relevant problems arise in the application and evaluation of the advertising test procedures. For reasons of time and cost, often *only one motif of an advertising campaign* is included in a pretest. In this way it can happen that a powerful campaign idea is tilted because of a weaker motif. For reasons of time and cost, a subject is usually judged after only one contact with the advertising material. This, however, conceals learning successes which almost inevitably occur over time and can be considered to have an influence on purchases. Test templates are

8.6 Problems of advertising test methods

usually presented in isolation and *not realistically integrated in a multi-channel advertising environment*. However, it is precisely through multimedia stimuli and the coordination of the media within an integrated concept based on the division of labor that the full advertising impact can unfold.

The *case numbers used for the study are generally too small to be reliable*. This inevitably leads to distortions when deriving statements from the sample examined with regard to the population of interest. The structure of the sample is often not representative for the composition of the population. In addition to the quantitative lack there often is the qualitative lack of wrong quotation comes. This is oriented rather at pragmatic availability criteria than at the psychographic consistency with the strategic target group. Each test result is *individual*, therefore a meaningful basis for comparison is often missing as an evaluation yardstick, which could objectively indicate whether a test was successfully completed or not. But this is precisely what is crucial.

Standard surveys are often too coarsely screened and produce distorted results, as they do not address the individuality of each campaign with sufficient detail and fairness. Therefore, the standardization of test conditions is not a solution. Coupling with other test objects leads to improper influencing of the results. Positive or negative impressions on related topics, such as quality assessment, willingness to pay, etc., which are usually included for pragmatic reasons of time and cost savings, irradiate on the advertising statements and thus affect the test results. Diverse, *subjective evaluations of the market researchers* are included as interpretations. Thus the management summary, which is usually only used for simplification reasons, often deviates not insignificantly from the data part of the report volume, whose study one saves oneself gladly.

Social phenomena cannot be anticipated and remain therefore out of consideration. Straight therein lies however often the strength of the advertisement as social engineering, especially in social media. In the laboratory, however, the interdependencies resulting from market events in the course of evolution cannot be simulated. The often *artificial laboratory situation* leads to altered reactions in the test persons. They feel called upon to be more critical, more involved and more thoughtful than usual. Since the test persons know about their function, their expression of opinion usually deviates considerably from the unconditioned consumption situation in the field. *Apparative survey methods* for the alleged exclusion of distortions cause this all the more. In addition, this results in test refusers who are not included in the results with their reaction, even though they belong to the target group. This leads to a considerable survey bias.

Psychomotoric test procedures only measure physiological dimensions, but not indications of market success. They lack the ability to distinguish cause and reason, or more precisely, the indispensable stringency between the observed, measured reflex and its condition. Therefore the results are ambivalent. Spontaneous rejection for the unfamiliar can change during the assimilation process of the real market environment to agreement. To simplify matters, people tend to categorize their environment and reject everything which does not immediately fit into this pattern of thinking. But in the laboratory this does not happen at all. *Heuristic valuations cause inadmissible revaluations of the result.* The objectivity, which is the reason why tests are conducted at all, is gone. Every interpretation and revaluation implies personal value judgements and thus distortions of the results.

This is probably why advertising tests have already thwarted the publication of many good campaign approaches. The reason for their continued popularity is their ability to support and justify managers' decisions.

8.6.2 Potential problems with post-tests

Advertising is only *insufficiently delimitable within the marketing mix*. Thus it is not known, due to which marketing parameters an offer success came off exactly and which *portion has the advertisement to it*. The same goes for the temporal advertising impact which is only insufficiently delimitable. Thus it is unknown when exactly the initiation for an advertising success took place, which manifests itself sometime in a purchase. Such carry-over effects distort the measurement of advertising efficiency. The *spatial* advertising effect can only be delimited insufficiently. Thus, it is not known where exactly the communication which is causal for an attitude or behavioral success has taken place. Such spill-over effects also distort the measurement of efficiency.

Advertising is only *insufficiently delimitable within the communication mix.* An image or purchasing effect can be created by both classical and non-classical advertising media, and within these, in turn, by a variety of individual media, so that attributions are ultimately not possible. There is a lack of isolation from *informal communication*. This is because a result does not even have to have come about as a result of formal corporate activities, but can also result from informal contacts, e. g. word-of-mouth. There is a *lack of isolation from the predispositions of customers*. Even effective advertising cannot always compensate for historically caused negative predispositions because of image remanence, i. e., in the end, it can remain unsuccessful even though it works well.

There is a lack of differentiation from *autonomous competitive activities*. The success of advertising is always influenced by successful or unsuccessful activities of competitors. A campaign which works in itself can therefore still be doomed to failure. There is a *lack of differentiation of endogenous changes in buyer behavior*. An offer can be successful not only due to good advertisement, but alone already, because a strong social trend in the clientele works on it. Conversely, a product can also be socially "outlawed". The central criterion *attention* is only one, but necessary, prerequisite for market success, but not to be regarded as sufficient. For attention alone does not create success in the markets.

There are also *distortions of statements* regarding changes in the market environment between the period of use and the evaluation period. A positive or negative result cannot be primarily caused by the tested campaign. Above all, a campaign which works well can perform badly if the general conditions are disadvantageous for it in retrospect, but a campaign which works badly can also perform well by pure chance.

References

Further readings German literature

Baumgarth, Carsten: Markenpolitik, 4th ed., Wiesbaden 2014

Bruhn, Manfred: Kommunikationspolitik, 9th ed., München 2018

- Sponsoring, 6th ed., Frankfurt/M. 2017
- Unternehmens- und Marketingkommunikation, 3rd ed., München 2014
- Integrierte Unternehmenskommunikation, 6th ed., Stuttgart 2014

Bruhn, Manfred/*Esch*, Franz-Rudolf/*Langner*, Tobias (Editors): Strategische Kommunikation, 2nd ed., Wiesbaden 2016

Bruhn, Manfred/*Esch*, Franz-Rudolf/*Langner*, Tobias (Editors): Instrumente der Kommunikation, 2nd ed., Wiesbaden 2016

Esch, Franz-Rudolf: Strategie und Technik der Markenführung, 9th ed., München 2017

Esch, Franz-Rudolf: Strategie und Technik der Werbung, 7th ed., Stuttgart et al 2011

Esch, Franz Rudolf (Editor): Moderne Markenführung, 4th ed., Wiesbaden 2013

Esch, Franz-Rudolf/*Langner*, Tobias/*Bruhn*, Manfred (Editors): Handbuch Controlling der Kommunikation, 2nd ed., Wiesbaden 2016

Felser, Georg: Werbe- und Konsumentenpsychologie, 4th ed., Berlin/Heidelberg 2015

Fuchs, Wolfgang/*Unger*, Fritz: Management der Marketing-Kommunikation, 5th ed., Heidelberg 2014

Hartleben, Ralph E./*von Rhein*, Wolfram: Werbekonzeption und Briefing, 3rd ed., Erlangen 2014

Häusel, Hans-Georg: Neuromarketing, 4th ed., Freiburg 2019

Hettler, Uwe: Social Media Marketing, München 2010

Heun, Thomas: Werbung, Wiesbaden 2017

Holland, Heinrich: Direktmarketing, 4th ed., München 2016

Kloss, Ingomar: Werbung, 5th ed., München 2012

Kroeber-Riel, Werner/*Gröppel-Klein*, Andrea: Konsumentenverhalten, 11th ed., München 2019

Lammenett, Erwin: Praxiswissen Online-Marketing, 6th ed., Wiesbaden 2017

Langner, Tobias/*Esch*, Franz-Rudolf/*Bruhn*, Manfred (Editors): Techniken der Kommunikation, 2nd ed., Wiesbaden 2016

Mast, Claudia: Unternehmenskommunikation, 7th ed., München 2018

Pepels, Werner: Erfolgreiche Produkteinführung, 2nd ed., Berlin 2020
- Käuferverhalten, 3rd ed., Berlin 2017
- Handbuch des Marketing, 7th ed., Berlin 2016
- Moderne Marketingpraxis, 3rd ed., Berlin 2016
- Kommunikationsmanagement, 5th ed., Stuttgart 2014

Ruisinger, Dominik/*Jorzik*, Oliver: Public Relations, 2nd ed., Stuttgart 2013

Scheier, Christian/*Held*, Dirk: Wie Werbung wirkt, 3rd ed., Freiburg 2018

Schimansky, Alexander: Der Neue Wert der Marke, 2nd ed., München 2019

Schnettler, Josef/*Wendt*, Gero: Werbung und Kommunikation planen, 5th ed., Berlin 2015

Schweiger, Günter/*Schrattenecker*, Gertraud: Werbung, 10th ed., Konstanz 2021

Trommsdorff, Volker/*Teichert*, Thorsten: Konsumentenverhalten, 9th ed., Stuttgart et al 2019

Tropp, Jörg: Moderne Marketing-Kommunikation, 3rd ed., Wiesbaden 2019

Unger, Fritz/*Fuchs*, Wolfgang/*Michel*, Burkhard: Mediaplanung, 6th ed., Heidelberg 2012

Wirtz, Bernd W.: Medien- und Internetmanagement, 10th ed., Wiesbaden 2019

Zurstiege, Guido: Werbeforschung, Konstanz 2007

Further readings international literature

Blakeman, Robyn: Integrated Marketing Communication, 3rd ed., Lanham et al 2018 (Rowman & Littlefield)

Blythe, Jim: Essentials of Marketing, 6th ed., Harlow 2016 (Pearson Education)

Cateora, Philip R./*Gilly*, Mary C./*Graham*, John L./*Farah*, Maya F.: International Marketing, 17th ed. London 2014 (McGraw-Hill)

Chernev, Alexander: Strategic Marketing Management, 10th ed., Chicago 2019 (Cerebellum Press)

Eagle, Lynne/*Czarnecka*, Barbara/*Dahl*, Stephan/*Lloyd*, Jenny: Marketing Communications, 2nd ed., Abington 2021 (Taylor & Francis)

Egan, John: Marketing Communications, 7th ed., Los Angeles et al. 2020 (Sage)

Felton, George: Advertising: Concept and Copy, 3rd ed., New York 2013 (Norton & Comp.)

Fill, Chris: Essentials of Marketing Communications, Harlow, Essex 2011 (Pearson)

Fill, Chris/*Turnbull*, Sarah: Marketing Communications, 8th ed., Harlow 2019 (Pearson)

Hall, Simon: B2B Digital Marketing Strategy, London 2020 (Koganpage)

Hollensen, Svend/*Kotler*, Philip/*Opresnik*, Marc Oliver: Social Media Marketing, Independently published 2020 (Opresnik Management)

Homburg, Christian/*Kuester*, Sabine/*Krohmer*, Harley: Marketing Management, 2nd ed., London 2012 (McGraw-Hill)

Hooley, Graham/*Nicoulaud*, Brigitte/*Rudd*, John M./*Lee*, Nick: Marketing Strategy and Competitive Positioning, 7th ed., Harlow 2020 (Pearson)

Iacobucci, Dawn/*Churchill* Jr., Gilbert A.: Marketing Research, 12th ed., Nashville 2018 (CreateSpace)

Jobber, David/*Ellis-Chadwick*, Fiona: Principles and Practice of Marketing, 9th ed., London 2020 (McGraw-Hill)

Katz, Helen: The Media Handbook, 7th ed., New York 2019 (Routledge)

Keller, Kevin Lane/*Swaminathan*, Vanitha: Strategic Brand Management, 5th ed., Harlow 2020 (Pearson)

Kotler, Philip T./*Armstrong*, Gary: Principles of Marketing, 17th ed., Harlow 2017 (Pearson)

Mansell, Robin/*Raboy*, Marc (Eds.): The Handbook of Global Media and Communication Policy, Chicester 2011 (John Wiley & Sons)

McDowell Marinchak, Christiana L./*Persuit*, Jeanne M.: Integrated Marketing Communication, N. N. 2018 (Lexington Books)

Mooij, Marieke de: Global Marketing and Advertising, 5th ed., London 2010 (Sage Publications)

Mullins, John F./*Walker* Jr., Orville C.: Marketing Management, 8th ed., London 2012 (McGraw-Hill)

Pelsmaker, Patrick de/*Geuens*, Maggie/*Bergh*, Joeri van den: Marketing Communications, 6th ed., Harlow, Essex 2017 (Pearson)

Percy, Larry/*Rosenbaum-Elliott*, Richard: Strategic Advertising Management, 5th ed., Oxford 2016 (Oxford University Press)

PR Smith/Ze Zook: Marketing Communications, 7th ed., London 2020 (Koganpage)

Pricken, Mario: Creative Advertising, N. N. 2008 (Thames & Hudson)

Rossiter, John R./*Percy*, Larry/*Bergkvist*, Lars: Marketing Communications, Los Angeles et al. 2018 (Sage)

Sissors, Jack Z./*Baron*, Roger B.: Advertising Media Planning, 7th ed., London 2010 (McGraw-Hill)

Taylor, Heidi: B2B Marketing Strategy, London 2018 (Koganpage)

Wirtz, Bernd: Media Management, 2nd ed., Cham 2020 (Springer Nature)

Young, Antony: Brand Media Strategy, 2nd ed., New York 2014 (Palgrave MacMillan)

Zimmerman, Jan/*Ng*, Deborah: Social Media Marketing, Hoboken 2017 (Wiley & Sons)

Central internet sources

acta-online (Allensbach computer and telecommunications analysis)

adm.de (Working group of German market and social research institutes)

agf.de (Television research consortium)

agma-mmc.de (Working group for media analysis)

agof.de (Working group for online research)

ard-werbung (1st German television advertising sales & services)

awa-online.de (Allensbacher market and advertising media analysis)

bauermedia.com (Bauer publishing group)

bdvw.org (Federal association of the digital economy)

burda-community-network.de (Burda publishing group)

bvda.de (Federal association of German advertising papers)

bvm.org (Professional association of German market and social researchers)

bdzv.de (Federal association of German newspaper publishers)

crossvertise.com (various media analyses)

faw-ev.de (trade association for outdoor advertising)

gfk.com (typology)

gik.media (typology)

gujmedia.de (Gruner & Jahr publishing group)

gwa.de (German association of communication agencies)

horizont.net (trade magazine)

ip-deutschland.de (Private television station RTL media group)

ivw.de (Information association for the determination of the distribution of advertising media)

media-perspektiven.de (1st German television trade journal)

media-spectrum.de (Media data trade journal)

medialine.de (Focus magazine)

mediapilot.de (Springer publishing group)

nielsen-netragings.com (Nielsen market research)

owm.de (Organization of advertisers in the brand association)

planung-analyse.de (trade journal)

pz-online.de (consumer magazines)

rms.de (Radio marketing service)

sevenonemedia.de (Seven one mediagroup)

sinus-institut.de (typology)

spiegel.de (Spiegel publishing group)

tdwi.com (typology of desires)

vdz.de (Association of German magazine publishers)

vprt.de (Association of private broadcasting and telemedia)

vuma.de (Consumer and media analysis)

wuv.de (Advertising and sales trade journal)

zaw.de (Central association of the German advertising industry)

zdf-werbefernsehen.de (2nd German television)

zmg.de (Newspaper marketing society)

Index

Adress handling 235
Advert, optional extras 99
Advert, special format 98
Advertising, basic principles 85
Advertising, goals 31
Advertising, non-classical 201
Advertising agency, briefing 277
Advertising agency, contact initiation 272
Advertising agency, framework 273
Advertising agency, evaluation 274
Advertising agency, integration 270
Advertising agency, selection criteria 271
Advertising agency, servicer types 270
Advertising agency, workflow 278
Advertising area 53
Advertising budget 37
Advertising budget, experience-based 38
Advertising budget, model-based 42
Advertising campaign, formatting 63
Advertising coverage 54
Advertising density 56
Advertising flexibility 152
Advertising impact, actualgenetic test 294
Advertising impact, check 302
Advertising impact, contact analyses 303
Advertising impact, exploratory test 293
Advertising impact, mechanical test 296
Advertising impact, prognosis 292
Advertising impact, projective-associative test 297
Advertising impact, psychomotoric test 295
Advertising impact, reception analyses 305
Advertising impact, transport analyses 302
Advertising intensity 53
Advertising inventory 151
Advertising material adverts 92
Advertising material insert 98
Advertising material posters 114
Advertising material spots 100
Advertising material, pre-sales 245

Advertising objectives, psychographic 33
Advertising objects 35
Advertising performance measurement 290
Advertising period 50
Advertising placement 151
Advertising success check 305
Advertising success prognosis 299
Advertising timing 50
Advertising types 26
Advertising test methods, problems post-tests 310
Advertising test methods, problems pre-tests 308
AIDA formula (modified) 21
Affinity score 139
Allocation of budget 49
Ambient media 117
Ambush marketing 216

Banner ad, integrated 181
Banner ad, layer 183
Banner ad, new window 182
Banner advertising 181
Benefit promise 79
Brand characteristics 58
Brand content 57
Brand licensing 251
Brand name development 60
Brandpark presentation 230
Brochure 242
Budgeting techniques 38, 40, 42, 45
Business advertising 147
Business target group 63
Buyer classes, development 32
Buying center 66

Catalog 244
Cause-related marketing 218
City magazines 97
Citylight poster 116

Index

Classical advertising media 92
Classical advertising, intermediary comparison 125
Classical media profiles 118
Collective advertising, forms 29
Communication, chain 18
Communication, definition 25
Communication, direction 22
Communication, disturbance sources 20
Communication, phases 20
Communication, principles 15
Communication, semiotic elements 19
Communication basics 15
Communication channels, design 23
Communication process 18
Communication scope, alternatives 24
Communication terms 22
Community 189
Composite advertising 30
Concerted advertising 30
Consumer target group 70
Contact intensity 139
Corporate behavior 263
Corporate communication 263
Corporate design 263
Corporate identity, elements 262
Corporate publications 97
Corporate website presence, advertising 175
Corporate website presence, concept 168
Corporate website presence, usability 173
Cost-efficiency (media) 140
Creative design (DM) 239
Cultural sponsorship 214
Customer club 219

Demarcations, actiographic 73
Demarcations, demographic 71
Demarcations, psychographic 75
Demarcations, sociographic 77
Direct advertising, documentation 242
Direct advertising, electronic offline, radio 233
Direct advertising, electronic offline, television 232
Direct mailing 235
Direct-response advert 235
Direct-response radio 233
Direct-response television 232

Directory entries 97
Disturbance sourcing 20
Domain name 169
Duplex channel 23

Ecological sponsorship 215
Electronic advertising, characteristics 100
Electronic mail, design 163
Electronic mail, newsletter 164
Electronic media 112
Endbenefits 79
Ethics in advertising 281
Event 229
Exhibition 224

Free sheets 96

General interest titles 94
Global advertising, focusing 267
Global advertising, generalising 267
Good advertising practice 85
Gross rating points 143
Group advertising 30
Guerilla marketing 216

Individual communication 24
Infomercial (TV) 108
Innovator types 69
Integrated marketing communications 258
Integration substance 258
Intermedia comparison classical advertising 125
Intermedia comparison, non-classical advertising 255
International advertising, coverage 54
International advertising, market penetration 55

Joint advertising 29
Journals, categories 94

Live advertising 223

Magazines 93
Market-media analyses 128
Market actors (B-t-b) 64
Market characteristics (B-t-b) 63
Market penetration, international 56

Index

Marketing, cause-related 218
Marketing communications, controlling 290
Marketing communications, cornerstones 26
Marketing communications, integrated 258
Marketing communications, international 265
Marketing objectives, economic 31
Mass communication 23
Media conditions, calculation 156
Media distribution map 160
Media documents 159
Media implementation 150
Media performance, identifiers 138
Media performance, optimization 145
Media plan 159
Media planning 134
Media prepayment overview 160
Media processes 159
Media production schedule 161
Media purchasing, worktools 154
Media ranking 137
Media selection, classical advertising 127
Media selection, qualitative 126
Media selection, quantitative 123
Media studies, individual 130
Media studies, typology 131
Media tariff 155
Media validation 135
Mediaplan combination 140
Mediasharing 192
Microblog 192
Mobile advertising, applications 199
Mobile advertising, modes 197
Mobile advertising, multimedia 195
Movie theater, advertising forms 114
Movie theater, categories 113
Movie theater display 113

Newsletter management 164
Newspapers 92
Non-addressed mailings 241
Non-classical advertising 201

Offer sheets 96
Olfactoric impact 219
Online advertising 162
Online advertising, non-web applications 163

Online media 162
Organizational buying behavior 65
Outdoor advertising, mobile 116
Outdoor advertising, special forms 116
Outdoor advertising, stationary 115

Perception, levels 28
Perception, subliminal 28
Perception, unconscious 28
Performance profile magazine 119
Performance profile movie theater 122
Performance profile newspaper 119
Performance profile outdoor poster 120
Performance profile radio 121
Performance profile television 121
Personal communication 252
Placement, admissibility 211
Placement, types 209
POS presence 229
Poster advertising 115
PR, internal 208
PR, market actor 203
PR, opinion leader 205
Print advertising, special forms 98
Product features 250
Program sponsorship 107
Public relations, modern forms 209
Public relations, traditional forms 203
Purchase decision process 21

Radio advertising 109
Radio advertising, special forms 110
Radio formates 111
Ranking (Classical media) 137
Reach value 138
Reading circle folders 96
Role understanding (Opponent) 68
Role understanding (Promoter) 67

Sales literature 242
Sales promotion 246
Search engine advertising 180
Search engine marketing 179
Search engine optimization 179
Search engine types 177
Shopping center poster 117
Simplex channel 22
SoA – SoM 43

Social bookmarking 193
Social network 188
Social sponsorship 215
Special interest titles 94
Special segment titles 94
Sponsoring 212
Sports sponsorship 213
Style components (creative) 83

Target group, determination 63
Targeting (Online) 185
Telephone advertising, active 233
Telephone advertising, passive 234
Television broadcasting 121
Teleshopping 109
TV advertising, special forms 105
TV broadcaster, private commercial 101
TV broadcaster, public service 101
TV channel graduation 104
TV cross-spot advertising 108
TV station, specific advertising formats 108
TV stations, landscape 101

Usability (Webpages) 173
User navigation (Website) 172

Validation (Classical media) 135
Viral marketing 217

Web advertising, special forms 184
Web advertising, success measurement 186
Website (Advertising medium) 175
Website contents 169
Website graphics 170
Web 1.0 applications 168
Web 2.0 applications 187
Weblog 189
Wiki 193

About the author

Werner Pepels had been working for nine years as a marketing communications consultant in international advertising agencies. He advised branded companies primarily with very large, in addition, also middle budgets, from the industrial and service sector. Three further years he was active as managing partner of two advertising agencies, specialized on sales promotions for international branded companies in the B-t-c sector as well as small sizes specialists.

Afterwards he was appointed professor for business administration, especially advertising and marketing, a position he held for 27 years. He is currently active as a foundation principal and economics scientist author. His textbooks are among the best-selling in their field in the German speaking region, with over 180,000 copies sold let alone in print.

The following of his titles are also published at Duncker & Humblot, Berlin (all in German language):

- Handbook of Marketing, 3 volumes, 7th edition
- Product Management, 7th edition
- Professional Marketing, 2nd edition
- Modern Market Research, 3rd edition
- Communication Management, 5th edition
- Service Marketing
- Successful Product Launch, 2nd edition
- Handbook Services
- Handbook Communication Management in Marketing

Werner Pepels

Professionelles Marketing
In zwölf Schritten zum Vermarktungserfolg

»Professionelles Marketing« erscheint in der zweiten Auflage mit dem unveränderten Ziel der kompakten Darstellung der relevanten Tools im Marketing. Im Vordergrund steht die Umsetzung, jedoch auf Basis analytischer Fundierung. Damit unterscheidet sich dieser Band von anderen Praxistiteln, denen es oft an einer hinreichenden Systematik der Inhalte mangelt, und auch von einigen Theoriewerken, denen zuweilen die Anwendbarkeit des dargestellten Wissens fehlt.

»Professionelles Marketing« ist die geeignete Einstiegslektüre in die Marketingmaterie, dient aber auch zum Brush up des Marketingwissens bei schon länger zurückliegender Ausbildung. Sie unterstützt Quereinsteiger, die komplexe Struktur dieses Sektors zu erfassen, und rüstet Aufsteiger mit State of the art-Fachwissen aus. Vor allem hilft sie Studierenden der BWL und verwandter Fächer bei der Prüfungsvorbereitung. Das Buch ist stringent untergliedert, arbeitet mit Hervorhebungen, zahlreichen Praxisbeispielen und Schaubildern.

2., erweiterte und überarbeitete Auflage
Zahlr. Abb., 359 Seiten, 2020
ISBN 978-3-428-15949-9, € 49,90
Titel auch als E-Book erhältlich.

www.duncker-humblot.de